Social and Cultural Anthropology for the 21st Century

Social and Cultural Anthropology for the 21st Century: Connected Worlds is a lively, accessible, and wide-ranging introduction to socio-cultural anthropology for undergraduate students. It draws on a wealth of ethnographic examples to showcase how anthropological fieldwork and analysis can help us understand the contemporary world in all its diversity and complexity.

The book is addressed to a twenty-first-century readership of students who are encountering social and cultural anthropology for the first time. It provides an overview of the key debates and methods that have historically defined the discipline and of the approaches and questions that shape it today. In addition to classic research areas such as kinship, exchange, and religion, topics that are pressing concerns for our times are covered, such as climate change, economic crisis, social media, refugees, sexuality, and race. Foregrounding ethnographic stories from all over the world to illustrate global connections and their effects on local lives, the book combines a focus on history with urgent present-day social issues. It will equip students with the analytical tools that they need to negotiate a world characterized by unprecedented cross-cultural contact, ever-changing communicative technologies, and new forms of uncertainty.

The book is an essential resource for introductory courses in social and cultural anthropology and as a refresher for more advanced students.

Marzia Balzani is research professor of anthropology, New York University Abu Dhabi. She has published on the anthropology of South Asia, political ritual, diasporic Islam, and gendered and religious persecution. In 2003–08, she was chief examiner for social and cultural anthropology for the International Baccalaureate, and in 2010–12, she was chief examiner for Anthropology for the A level (AQA).

Niko Besnier is professor of cultural anthropology at the University of Amsterdam and honorary research fellow at La Trobe University. He has published widely on globalization, sport, sexuality and gender, economic relations, and language. In 1998–2003, he was chief examiner for social and cultural anthropology for the International Baccalaureate, and in 2015–19, he edited the journal *American Ethnologist*.

"Marzia Balzani and Niko Besnier have embarked in a most challenging journey: that of writing an introduction to sociocultural anthropology. A discipline that constantly interrogates the fields of power that surround the production of knowledge is difficult to introduce, yet the task needs to be done. Balzani and Besnier speak to the reader in simple terms that explain complexities: they engage with classical themes such as kinship in new ways; they underline process, relations, and mobilities; they address scale from the immediate intimacies of the body to global transnational power, and they do it brilliantly. They tell the story in a clear language, beautifully interlaced with ethnographic cases and historical grounding, without forgetting to present some important theoretical and methodological debates. *Social and Cultural Anthropology for the 21st Century* is a masterful feat that underscores how anthropology is about exploring the connections that make life possible."

Susana Narotzky, University of Barcelona

"Anthropology textbooks have all too often relied on discussions primarily of traditional societies for an audience mainly of Anglo-American readers. *Social and Cultural Anthropology for the 21st Century: Connected Worlds* is expressly designed to avoid both of these pitfalls, and does so admirably, in its discussions of the present and future as much as of the past, and in its vast array of examples from societies across the globe. It is also really interesting and fun to read: I will certainly use it in my own introductory anthropology class."

Gordon Mathews, Chinese University of Hong Kong

"Over the decades that I've been teaching anthropology at university, students at all levels have asked for an introductory text that clearly explains the discipline, its perspectives, practices, and insights. This is the book, leading the pack by a mile. It is authoritative, up to date, engagingly written and strikingly illustrated.

The book's chapters focus on topics long central to the social sciences, among them, kinship, marriage, sex and gender, exchange and gift-giving, nation and state, and rank, caste and class. The book couches an understanding of the history of ideas in contemporary examples that bring these topics to life, making them thinkable and discussable. The book's style is sure to get readers reflecting and debating, as they convey the combination of observation, contextualization and critical interpretation that is central to anthropology.

Written by two anthropologists with extensive research experience in the Pacific, Asia and Western societies, this book will richly reward its readers with an understanding of the discipline."

Francesca Merlan, Australian National University

"This book is a much-needed and timely introduction to social and cultural anthropology for a new and media-savvy generation of learners. It is accessible and visually attractive, but also suitably and refreshingly challenging. By making global connections and marrying classic themes with contemporary concerns, the authors have brought the subject bang up to date and have provided a compelling introductory textbook for our time."

Jeanette Edwards, University of Manchester

Social and Cultural Anthropology for the 21st Century

Connected Worlds

Marzia Balzani and Niko Besnier

Routledge
Taylor & Francis Group
LONDON AND NEW YORK

Cover image: Photograph: © Heidi Härkönen. Young Cuban women in the middle of the photo shoot that constitute the most important part of their quinceañera, a ritual celebration of their fifteenth birthday and coming of age.

First published 2022
by Routledge
2 Park Square, Milton Park, Abingdon, Oxon OX14 4RN

and by Routledge
605 Third Avenue, New York, NY 10158

Routledge is an imprint of the Taylor & Francis Group, an informa business

© 2022 Marzia Balzani and Niko Besnier

British Library Cataloguing-in-Publication Data
A catalogue record for this book is available from the British Library

Library of Congress Cataloging-in-Publication Data
Names: Balzani, Marzia, author. | Besnier, Niko, author.
Title: Social and cultural anthropology for the 21st century : connected worlds / Marzia Balzani and Niko Besnier.
Description: Abingdon, Oxon ; New York, NY : Routledge, 2022. | Includes bibliographical references and index. |
Identifiers: LCCN 2021028832 (print) | LCCN 2021028833 (ebook) | ISBN 9781138829091 (hardback) | ISBN 9781138829121 (paperback) | ISBN 9781315737805 (ebook) | ISBN 9781315737805 (mobi) | ISBN 9781317571780 (epub) | ISBN 9781317571797 (adobe pdf)
Subjects: LCSH: Anthropology. | Anthropology--Fieldwork. | Globalization--Social aspects.
Classification: LCC GN25 .B35 2022 (print) | LCC GN25 (ebook) | DDC 306--dc23
LC record available at https://lccn.loc.gov/2021028832
LC ebook record available at https://lccn.loc.gov/2021028833

ISBN: 978-1-138-82909-1 (hbk)
ISBN: 978-1-138-82912-1 (pbk)
ISBN: 978-1-315-73780-5 (ebk)

DOI: 10.4324/9781315737805

Typeset in Bembo
by SPi Technologies India Pvt Ltd (Straive)

Contents

Figures

Acknowledgements

We have worked on this book over many years and in the process have accumulated debts to many individuals who have helped us conceptualize and write it. The idea of writing the textbook emerged a long time ago in the context of our work with the social and cultural anthropology programme of the International Baccalaureate, for which we served as successive chief examiners. We then worked with editors at Routledge, Lesley Riddle, who originally suggested the project, Katherine Ong, Alexandra McGregor, and editorial assistant Eleanor Simmons, whose patience and support we are grateful for. We are also indebted to two scholars, Serena Nanda and Matt Tomlinson, who took the time to read and comment on all the chapters. A number of other colleagues offered advice on one or more chapters: Kalissa Alexeyeff, Susan Brownell, Elina Hartikainen, Daniel Kelly, Helen Lee, Raymond Madden, Francesca Merlan, Makiko Nishitani, Alan Rumsey, Stephen Sawyer, John Taylor, and Linda Woodhead, as well as anonymous reviewers for the press. Numerous others, too many to name, read specific sections.

For their invaluable assistance with many aspects of this project, we thank Nour El-Mesary, Yoojin Lee, Jana Pocuchova, Keira Simmons, Hafsa Ahmed, and Trey Wang, students at New York University Abu Dhabi; Maha Khan, student at the London School of Economics; Nadia Balzani Zamir, student at Bryn Mawr College; and Gabrielle Fradin, MA student at the University of Amsterdam. We also thank the scholars and photographers who allowed us to publish their images.

Marzia Balzani worked on this book while teaching social and cultural anthropology at New York University Abu Dhabi and continuing in her role as a senior examiner for the International Baccalaureate. Niko Besnier worked on this book primarily while visiting professor at La Trobe University in Melbourne and on fellowships at the Center for Advanced Study in the Behavioral Sciences at Stanford University and at the Helsinki Collegium for Advanced Studies. Many ideas he contributed to this book were inspired by the work of many scholars who submitted article manuscripts to *American Ethnologist* while he was editor of the journal.

Preface

We have written this book for an international readership of undergraduate students and advanced secondary school students who have no prior knowledge of social and cultural anthropology. We became aware of the need for such a book while teaching introductory courses in anthropology at various universities in the United Kingdom, Europe, the United States, the Middle East, and New Zealand. In addition, our work as chief examiners for social and cultural anthropology for the International Baccalaureate gave us the opportunity to work closely with one another for many years and with teachers of anthropology in secondary schools around the world, designing curricula, running teacher workshops, setting and marking examination papers, and marking numerous student essays. These experiences have taught us a great deal about how to present anthropology to young inquisitive minds in international contexts.

We have aimed to present a picture of social and cultural anthropology as it is practised today by scholars working in academia as well as by practitioners of anthropology working in government, NGOs, cultural institutions, industries, and other contexts. We have covered the topics that have been foundational to the discipline, such as kinship, marriage, and exchange, but have highlighted the relevance of these topics for the contemporary world. For example, we explain traditional kinship categories, such as patriliny, milk kinship, and bilateral descent, since they continue to be relevant to the lives of many people around the world, but we also explore emergent forms of kinship relations, such as those enabled by assisted reproductive technologies and elective kinship relations. We present the materials in accessible language and in a way that stresses the relevance of anthropological knowledge to contemporary lives.

Throughout the book, we showcase globalization as the context of contemporary dynamics in society and culture, which is why the book is subtitled *Connected Worlds*. Thus, rather than relegating globalization to a separate chapter at the end of the book, as many other textbooks do, we have explained how global flows, colonialism, capitalism, and neoliberalism colour much of what happens in people's lives today. For example, the discussion of caste in India emphasizes that the caste system is as much the creation of British colonialism as it is rooted in ancient history, demonstrates how caste has been affected by labour migrations, and shows that the caste system today is intersected by concerns about social class, global mobility, and the labour market. Whenever possible, we have specified the historical context of the ethnographic information we present and discussed how this historical context informs our account.

While this book aims to illustrate the breadth of anthropology as a discipline, we recognize that we cannot do justice to the entire scope of this dynamic discipline. Thus we address some topics, such as those that traditionally fall under the purview of political anthropology or medical anthropology, across several chapters rather than in a single chapter. Users of the book are encouraged to read the relevant sections together to make the book 'work' for their interests. We hope that instructors will supplement the book with materials that explore issues that we can only treat cursorily. This is not a book about the history of anthropology or a book designed to explore anthropological theory in depth, although we invoke both history and theory as it becomes relevant to the materials we present. We have showcased ethnographic examples from a broad range of world contexts to illustrate general points, as we recognize that ethnographic richness is what attracts many students to anthropology. We aim to convey to students a sense of excitement about anthropology and about what anthropology can tell us about ourselves and others.

The first two chapters of the book present the key concepts of the discipline. Chapters 3 to 7 focus on the person in relation to such categories as kinship, marriage, and the body. Chapters 8 to 15 scale up the discussion to matters such as social class, the nation, and the environment. While each chapter can be read as a stand-alone self-contained text, students who are new to the discipline will benefit from reading Chapters 1 and 2 first to familiarize themselves with the concepts and methods of the discipline and the distinctive insights on the social world one can gain from a socio-cultural anthropological approach. Most chapters begin with an ethnographic vignette that provides a hook for the topic of the chapter. At the end of the book, users will find a glossary, a cumulative list of references, and an index. In the text, terms that are defined in the glossary are in bold when they first occur in each chapter. We have tried to keep quotations and citations to a minimum, knowing that most students are more interested in ideas than in the source of these ideas. Only when identifying an author or a work is directly relevant to an understanding of the ideas do we foreground these in the text. We generally provide the in-text citation to a work on which we base an explanation at the end of the first sentence of each relevant passage.

We have made a number of decisions in referring to certain concepts that are the object of terminological debate. As we explain in a boxed text in Chapter 2, we use the term 'research participants' to refer to the people whose lifeways anthropologists try to make sense of. The terms 'Global North' and 'Global South' are labels we use to contrast the contemporary indus-trial world, where capitalism originated and dominates, with areas of the globe that were until the mid-twentieth century under the colonial domination upon which capitalism was built. We are aware that these terms are imprecise and possibly contentious, since not all capitalist societies are located in the northern hemisphere and since some societies, such as China and Brazil, do not easily fit either label, but the vagueness of the terms is what makes them useful in arriving at generalizations. In our view, these terms are preferable to older or more prob-lematic contrasts such as 'Western' vs. 'non-Western', 'developed' vs. 'developing', 'First World' vs. 'Third World', or 'centre' and 'periphery'. However, when writing about historical contexts other than the contemporary moment, we sometimes use other terms if they are more tem-porally appropriate.

In choosing images, we have prioritized whenever possible images supplied by scholars whose work we showcase in the text and whose context we can explain. A few images were kindly provided by professional photographers. The source of all images is acknowledged at the end of each caption. The cover image depicts young Cuban women in the middle of the photo shoot that constitutes the most important part of their *quinceañera*, a ritual celebration of their 15th birthday and coming of age, held in different forms throughout the Spanish-speaking Americas. The image was taken in 2003 by anthropologist Heidi Härkönen of the University of Helsinki in the early stages of her ethnographic fieldwork on changing practices of kinship, gender, and life cycle in Cuba, during which she took part in numerous *quinceañeras*. We feature her work on the subject in Chapter 8.

Chapter 1

Society and culture in the 21st century

In a medium-sized city in Morocco, young female university students worry about finding the right man to marry. As devout Muslims, the young women believe that God has already chosen a husband for them, but they also think that they need to work hard to make this predestined fate happen. Anthropologist Alice Elliot (2016) befriended these young women during her 17-month fieldwork. The city where they live is a migrant hub, which means that local men regularly return from overseas, primarily Europe, where they have acquired wealth and sophistication that the young women find attractive. Every evening, the young women would spend hours together preparing themselves, applying makeup, drinking tea, and joking, before going out in groups in the old city, which was teeming with potential husbands. But when they were out in public, they behaved with the irreproachable modesty that their religious faith demanded, averting their eyes and walking at a measured pace. While Muslims are often represented as firm believers in predestination, namely the fact that the future is already determined by God, these young women assert that destiny is equally the product of work and effort on their part.

In Dar es Salaam, Tanzania's largest city, electricity blackouts are frequent, the power level often unreliable, and household energy bills keep going up every year as people acquire more mobile phones, sewing machines, refrigerators, and other electricity-dependent appliances. Anthropologist Michael Degani (2017) spent 18 months in the city in the early 2010s researching how inhabitants develop new ways of coping with this situation: they connect to the grid illegally; they rely on self-appointed specialists to repair the deteriorating infrastructure; and they try to negotiate overdue bills with power company employees. However, there are clear limits to this underground trade: for example, while one can steal wires and poles, one should not steal electricity meters. The bootstrapping practices with which urban Tanzanians try to cope with the unreliable and expensive power supply are thus governed by an unspoken code that dictates how far they can go to bend the system without compromising morality. Dar es Salaam residents regularly break the law but do so in a principled way.

Argentinians' passion for football is well known all over the world. But for a small minority of Argentinians, it is not football but rugby that is the object of their passion. The wealthiest families in Buenos Aires belong to exclusive clubs where younger male family members play rugby. But, as anthropologists Daniel Guinness and Sebastián Fuentes (2018) document, the clubs, while ostensibly focused on sport, play a much broader role in the lives of the members. Boys begin to play rugby at a tender age, forming tight-knit age cohorts that stick together all the way to adulthood: they attend the same schools, go to university together, and spend all their leisure time in each other's company. When they reach adulthood, the young men are likely to marry each other's sisters. They generally come to occupy prominent professional positions as lawyers, politicians, doctors, and corporate executives, relying on each other's services and

DOI: 10.4324/9781315737805-1

assistance. The exclusive clubs in Buenos Aires are thus spaces in which elite families maintain their privileged positions from one generation to the next, and sport functions as a vehicle for the transmission of this privilege.

These three vignettes illustrate that anthropologists are primarily concerned with connections. The nature of these connections can be very diverse. People are connected to one another through bonds of friendship and sameness that exclude others, as in the case of the upper-class members of Argentinian sport clubs. People can try to establish new connections with others, as in the case with young Moroccan female students searching for suitable husbands, while nurturing their connections to God. And people are connected to corporations, the state, and infrastructures, sometimes in uneasy ways, as urban Tanzanians demonstrate in their dealings with the companies in charge of the power supply.

What anthropologists do is to discover how these connections work, how they make daily life possible, and how they are entangled with other kinds of connections. How are aspects of our lives that at first glance seem to occupy very different spheres of life, such as morality, the economy, politics, religion, actions, people, and objects, connected to one another, and why does it matter? This question can be rephrased abstractly as how do society and culture work?

Society

Society is made up of structured **social relations**, namely human behaviours that have as their object other human beings, as well as, in some contexts, non-human animals, material things, or supernatural entities. In their daily lives, people in all societies interact with many others. But they draw important distinctions between them: young Moroccan women interact with one another very differently from how they interact with men in the street; urban Tanzanians have to deal with employees of the power company and with the self-appointed street experts, but in different ways; and within the tight-knit groups that young privileged rugby-playing Argentinians form, the social relations are characterized by a closeness that excludes interactions with others. Everywhere, people interact with their parents differently from how they relate to their boss, friends, relatives, co-workers, neighbours, and housemates. In other words, all social relations are structured, that is, governed by patterns that predict how people will think and act when they are interacting with other people or with other entities that matter. The study of society concerns what makes these relationships similar to or different from one another. To understand these similarities and differences, anthropologists consider factors that come into play in people's relations with one another, such as kinship, age, wealth, power, education, and personal affinity (Figure 1.1).

Social relations are characterized by **rights** and **duties**. In all societies, children have the right to expect that their parents will feed and shelter them until they are considered able to take care of themselves; in turn, children have the duty to treat their parents with some form of deference and respect. On a general level, these are universal expectations, but the details differ significantly across societies. For example, among some social groups, children are expected to be independent early in life and contribute to the welfare of the **household** by taking care of younger siblings or helping with food production. Such is the case of poor families in the Global North, in which young people are expected to support their parents as soon as they have reached the minimum education level required by law. Among the middle classes of the Global North, in contrast, parents frequently support their children well into their 20s, affording them the possibility of pursuing educational goals or life passions that will give them a social and economic advantage over children of lesser privilege. Some types of social relations are not governed by rights and duties to the same extent as others, and thus are not as central to the

Figure 1.1 Friendship is a social relation that is governed by particular rights and duties, as well as norms of conduct that may change over time; when this photo was taken in 1986, both young and elderly people held hands with members of the same gender in public and wore suits sewn from rationed cloth, but by the 1990s younger Chinese found both to be a remnant of an outdated social order. (Courtesy of Susan Brownell)

constitution of society. For example, one's network of 'friends' on social media is made up of social relations, but they are rarely if ever associated with specific rights and duties; if a Facebook 'friend' tries to make demands or offer help that one has not asked for, one would not hesitate to 'unfriend' her or him.

People go about their lives and interact with one another with little conscious awareness of the rights and duties that characterize their social relations, unless these are violated. For example, if parents neglect their children by underfeeding them or keeping them in unhygienic conditions, they will be seen by others as practising poor parenting and the state may intervene. It is in such situations that we become conscious of what constitutes social relations and that we act to redress what we see as a violation. The rights and duties that characterize social relations can be enshrined in the laws of the state, although they often are not, as the case of urban Tanzanians trying to deal with the electric infrastructure illustrates vividly: even when Dar es Salaam residents break the law, they are constrained by rules that limit how far and in what ways they can break the law.

Society as a concept is an organized system of the rights and duties that define social relations among people. Each instance of such a system is *a* society. When viewed in this light, a society refers to a group of people who share at least a certain degree of consensus over how to conduct social relations. It is here that considerable ambiguity emerges, for a number of reasons. One is that the human groups that constitute a society can be very diverse in size, composition, or definition. For example, a city neighbourhood can sometimes be considered to be a society; so can a group of people scattered over a territory that share some sort of commonality; and so can an entire country.

Relative size is not the only way in which societies differ from one another. Differences can arise from the fact that the social relations that constitute society always take place in a political and economic context. The political context determines who has power over whom, who is able to dictate what is right, and how things should be conducted. The economic context is a matter of some people and groups having more than others. Both contexts mean that rights and duties are the basis of **inequality**, that is, differential access to power and resources such as money, education, political influence, and social status. For example, even in the most gender-equal societies, women continue to make less money, suffer more if they divorce, and are much less likely to reach senior positions in politics and the corporate world than men. So we cannot understand society, whether small or large scale, without considering the economic disparities and political inequalities that are integral aspects of its makeup.

The boundaries of societies are always porous. Even in small-scale, relatively isolated societies, newcomers have always been incorporated, new technologies have enriched people's lives, and ideas from elsewhere have been adopted. This is particularly obvious in today's world, in which societies are more complex and diverse than ever, as large numbers of people move during their lives for different reasons. It is true that large-scale movements of people have taken place in the course of history: for example, in the late nineteenth and early twentieth centuries, millions of people migrated in search of a better life, such as Europeans to North America, South America, South Africa, Australia, and New Zealand, and Chinese people to Southeast Asia, North and South America, Australia, and Europe. Yet many observers agree that people today are moving at an unprecedented rate and on a scale never seen before in history.

Technological advances since the middle of the twentieth century have made travel increasingly convenient and affordable. Today's migratory patterns are also qualitatively different from those of previous eras: British or Italian people who migrated to Australia in the 1950s typically returned for a visit to the 'home country' once in their lifetime, while today people may move to a new place for a few months or years and then move on to a different location, or move back and forth between their original home and their adoptive country. Between visits, they maintain regular contact with their relatives, neighbours, and friends back home through phone calls, social media, and **remittances** (money or goods sent to relatives and friends they support). **Globalization**, namely the increasingly interconnected nature of the world, has enabled a much greater density and complexity of social relations than ever before, often over distances that in the past constituted insurmountable obstacles.

These complexities raise questions about the makeup of society in the contemporary world. If we think of society as being constituted by social relations and if social relations can be maintained across large distances, then we can expand the concept of society as traditionally defined so that it is no longer confined to a group of people who occupy a contiguous territory. A society thus can be made up of groups of people who live in different countries and nurture social relations with one another by acting upon the rights and duties expected of these social relations. One instance of such a society is a **diaspora**, defined as a people who have dispersed to different locations but maintain over the generations a common identity and a sense of belonging to an original homeland. For example, Armenians have moved from their original homeland to many other places, particularly since the end of World War I, a time when they experienced oppression in their homeland, including a genocide in which over one million were killed. Diasporic Armenians have forged lives in North and South America, Western Europe, Russia, and the Middle East, but many continue to identify as ethnically Armenian and to see Armenia, in the Caucasus, as a place from which their families originated.

New patterns of inequality are, for our understanding of society, another consequence of globalization. For example, some countries export their workforce to other countries: workers from the Philippines seek employment in the Middle East and North America, people from North Africa have migrated to Europe in search of a better life, and Eastern Europeans move to Western Europe to find work. These patterns of mobility result from the fact that some societies supply labour while others make use of this labour, although the latter retain the power to control migratory movements from the labour-supplying societies. Many things other than people circulate across national boundaries, including objects, ideas, money, technologies, and images, each moving around the world in patterns of circulation that operate independently of one another (Appadurai 1996). In many cases, these patterns tend to confirm and accentuate global inequalities between countries of the Global North and countries of the Global South (Figure 1.2).

The internal diversity and porous boundaries of many contemporary societies make us rethink whether society was ever as homogeneous in the past as many people think, a point to which we will return in this book. For example, while French society today incorporates many people of different races, religions, and cultural backgrounds, it has always been diverse, as in the past people spoke different languages such as Breton and Provençal, followed different laws, and conducted their lives in different ways. It was only during the French Revolution that efforts to erase internal diversity created the illusion of a homogeneous nation, by suppressing local languages for example. The longing for a time when the society was more homogeneous than it is now, which populist politicians use to their political advantage, results from a nostalgic longing for a situation that never existed. Other societies that present themselves as homogeneous do so by ignoring exceptions. Most Japanese people, for example, think of themselves as all alike, but this is true only if one overlooks the social differences that divide the society, as well as minority groups like ethnic Koreans and Chinese, descendants of historically marginalized castes (*buraku-min*), Okinawans, the indigenous Ainu, and recent migrants from many different countries.

Culture

Equally important to our understanding of the organization of human life is the concept of **culture**. Culture can be described as a system of symbols, if we think of a symbol as anything that stands for something else, such as an object, a belief, a representation, an explanation, a moral judgement, or any other way in which human beings represent the world around and beyond them. Thus young Moroccan women's conviction that God has already worked out

Figure 1.2 Clothing discarded by inhabitants of countries of the Global North find their way to markets in cities of the Global South such as this one in Mtumba, Tanzania, where people often meticulously mend them to give them a new life. (Courtesy of Nasirumbi/Wikimedia, licensed under a Creative Commons Attribution-Share Alike 4.0 International license.)

their future and Dar es Salaam residents' moral code about the limits of law breaking are both aspects of culture. An idiosyncratic idea that only one person believes in is not cultural. Many people must recognize the existence of an idea for it to be cultural, but they do not need to agree about its validity or worthiness.

While society is made up of human beings and their social relations, culture is made up of symbols and of how humans use them to act and manage social relations. Culture is the basis of what we think of as common sense, which tells us what to eat or not eat, who to marry or partner with, how to raise children, and how to conduct ourselves on a day-to-day basis with people (and other entities) with whom we sustain social relations. It is anything that humans learn, primarily during childhood but also later in life. Culture contrasts with what we carry in

Box 1.1   How do humans differ from other animals?

Humans are an animal species, members of the primate order. Their closest genetic relatives are chimpanzees, which live in tropical Africa north of the Congo River, and bonobos, whose habitat is in the Democratic Republic of Congo, south of the Congo River.
(The two species are very similar but because they cannot swim they have evolved separately on each side of the enormous river.) *Homo sapiens*, who appeared about 200,000
years ago, has undergone dramatic changes compared to other animals. What is it that
makes us uniquely human?

The answer to this question has changed considerably over the decades as we have
learned more about other animals, and it continues to change. For example, human language, the system that enables its users to construct sentences and communicate complex
and abstract ideas, is a uniquely human trait that probably evolved between 200,000 and
300,000 years before the present time. As far as we know, no other species has ever had
the cognitive capacity required for language, and humans have evolved so that their throat
and mouth enables them to control the flow of air to produce the range of different
sounds that make language possible. Yet other primates appear to utilize sophisticated systems of communication in which vocalizations can carry specific meanings, and species
like whales and dolphins communicate with one another using complex sound systems.
So while it may be true that humans are the only creatures that use language, systems of
communication used by other animals share some of the qualities of human language.
However, the world's languages are structurally very diverse, much more so than the range
of communicative strategies that particular animal species use (Evans and Levinson 2009).

In the 1960s and 1970s, scientists conducted experiments with primates to find out
whether they could be taught human language. Because primates are physiologically
unable to produce the sounds of language, they were taught sign language, which is
just like any spoken language in its complexity and capability. One of the most serious
experiments was with Washoe, a chimpanzee who was taught American Sign Language
at the University of Nevada at Reno by psychologists Beatrix and Allen Gardner. Washoe
learned several hundred signs and would use them creatively, combining them to form
simple sentences. But these experiments were very expensive and ultimately proved
inconclusive. Scientists today have turned away from them in favour of trying to understand how non-human animals communicate with one another in their natural habitats,
rather than with humans in captivity.

Because they are able to handle symbols, humans can communicate abstract thoughts.
In contrast, animals are by and large unable to handle abstract representations and thus
their communication is confined to what is immediately available. Thus a dog may be able
to communicate relatively complex messages to its master, such as running towards the
front door wagging its tail to indicate that it is excited at the prospect of going for a walk,
but it relies on the fact that the ideas it communicates are immediately relevant to the
situation. But here again, some primates, such as orangutans, have been shown in the wild
to plan for the future, which involves thinking about situations other than the immediate
context, although this is commonly limited to a near future. In addition, humans reflect
on the fact that they have beliefs and other forms of representation, and they evaluate
each other's and their own behaviours thanks to this ability for self-reflection. Non-
human animals pay considerable attention and react to each other's behaviour, but they
do not reflect on what motivates behaviour.

The sophisticated systems of social relations we define as society and complex systems of symbols that constitute culture are other aspects of human life that seem to distinguish it from animal existence. But other animals, particularly primates, also organize their lives in complex ways. They are capable of cooperating with one another, they use tools to accomplish tasks, they think about what others know, they distinguish between truth and deception, and they can teach skills to one another.

The scientific consensus today is that non-human animals have many of the capabilities that make us human, but in less-developed versions. Human language, society, culture, and theory of mind are extremely sophisticated compared to what non-human animals have access to. This is also what makes us humans so dangerous: we have destroyed other species, our habitat, and each other at a rate that no other animal has achieved, and life on earth is gravely endangered because of human intelligence – or lack thereof.

our biological makeup, including our digestive, cardiovascular, and nervous systems, which operate more or less independently of what we learn in life. Since culture is learnt, it is also the product of communication as well as what enables us to communicate. An important component of culture is the faculty that humans have to reflect on who they are, what they do, and why they do what they do, which we refer to as **reflexivity**.

Society and culture always work together, in that everything that people do is informed by culture, and culture emerges out of social relations. For example, marriage is at once a way of organizing social, economic, and political relations and a matter of emotions, beliefs, and values. One can of course study marriage as either a social institution or a cultural phenomenon, but to understand marriage in all its complexity, one needs to think holistically and take into consideration both its social and cultural dimensions. Every aspect of life is embedded in systems of social relations, which constitute society, but is also the object of representations and beliefs, which is what culture consists of.

Language plays an important role in communicating culture; a parent telling a child off for texting during the family meal is an example of how language is used to shape proper behaviour. But language is not the only medium through which culture is communicated: body posture and movement, for example, can communicate cultural norms of behaviour to children as they grow up. In Samoa, in the western Pacific, babies are frequently coddled by many different caregivers (e.g., parents, relatives, friends) and passed around, and caregivers hold them so that they face other people. Along with many others, these practices socialize babies to pay attention to others and discourage them from forming exclusive attachments to mothers (E. Ochs 1988). In contrast, in most middle-class Western contexts, the baby's primary caregiver, who may be the mother or a hired worker, tend to hold the baby so that they face each other, developing a relationship that will remain primary throughout the child's preadult years.

We commonly use the term 'culture' in everyday conversation. Its everyday meaning is related to its anthropological meaning, but is not the same. Often, people use it to refer to the objects and activities that society finds aesthetically pleasing, technologically important, or intellectually significant, such as the art displayed in galleries or music performed in concert halls, great literature, the rituals of the state, history, and philosophy, as well as the food, clothing, objects, and rituals that many consider to constitute a people's heritage. A term that is often applied to this version of culture is 'highbrow culture'. 'Culture' is also used to refer to objects and activities that have mass appeal, such as popular music, graffiti, memes, films, reality television, body modification, dance parties, and street fashion. These forms are generally referred to as 'popular' or 'lowbrow culture'. Highbrow and lowbrow cultures often oppose each other, in that people who consider that high culture is what defines taste bemoan popular culture, which in their view simply reflects what people find easy to enjoy and understand. In return, people who place value on popular culture decry highbrow culture as boring, intellectual, retrograde, politically conservative, and appealing only to fuddy-duddies.

The two are actually much more closely related than consumers of either generally think. While a few people have wide-ranging tastes and listen to both opera and hip-hop, it is more common for someone who is passionate about hip-hop to be conscious of the fact that it is very different from opera. The two musical genres are different aesthetically, but they also appeal to different kinds of people, who are likely to occupy different political, social, and economic positions. This kind of opposition transforms what is at first glance a matter of personal preference into the expression of the diversity and tensions inherent to any social group.

Another manifestation of the close relationship of different forms of culture is the fact that what is lowbrow at one moment in history can become highbrow at another, and vice versa. For example, Shakespearean drama, which today is highbrow culture, was hugely popular entertainment in nineteenth-century North America (L. Levine 1984). Theatre tickets were cheap enough that even manual workers could afford them, and everyone flocked to theatres to watch productions of Shakespeare's plays, which emphasized the storms, the ghosts, the murders, and the battles to appeal to everyone. Audiences sometimes rowdily expressed their delight or discontent. It was only in the late nineteenth century that theatre-going became increasingly confined to the middle and upper-middle classes: tickets became expensive, audience behaviour became staid, and the performances no longer showcased dramatic spectacles but rather foregrounded the intellectual content of the plays. A cultural form that had been considered popular had been transformed into an elite cultural form.

For anthropologists, both highbrow and lowbrow culture are integral elements of culture, and so are the dynamics that locate cultural forms in one category or the other. But culture for anthropologists encompasses considerably more than the tangible and intangible forms that constitute culture in its everyday sense. Some uses of the term 'culture' in public discourse come close to what anthropologists consider to be culture, including expressions like 'culture wars', 'corporate culture', 'culture of fear', and 'cancel culture'. To quote a definition from nineteenth-century anthropologist E. B. Tylor, which remains difficult to match to this day (save for the gendered language), 'culture, … taken in its broad, ethnographic sense, is that complex whole which includes knowledge, belief, art, morals, law, custom, and any other capabilities and habits acquired by man as a member of society' (1871, 1). In this sense, which was inspired by German Romantic philosophers, culture is made up of all the taken-for-granted, self-evident beliefs and views that enable us to organize our everyday lives.

Where twenty-first-century anthropologists part company with Tylor is in recognizing that culture is always embroiled with politics and economics. The history of Shakespearean drama is a clear example: different social classes held different views on how the plays should be performed and how much theatre tickets should cost, with the middle-class view eventually winning over the working-class view. The tension between highbrow and lowbrow cultural forms (e.g., opera vs. hip-hop) maps onto social differences between contrasting categories of people defined by social class, race, and age. When cultural ideas have potential political implications, they are referred to as **ideology**. For example, different people in a society may hold different ideas about how women and men should comport themselves, and present these ideas as matters of morality and decency, yet they have political consequences for women's and men's economic and social positions.

Culture is evident in just about everything that humans do, but some aspects of culture are of greater interest to anthropologists than others. For example, in Europe, the Americas, and the Middle East, friends and relatives kiss each other on the cheek when they meet, a practice that does not exist in East Asia. In North America, the norm is one kiss, in most parts of France two, and in the Netherlands three. Men kiss other men in the Middle East, Latin America, and parts of Europe, but generally not in Britain and North America. Old-fashioned elite European and Latin American men kiss ladies' hands. We can definitely describe these different practices as cultural, but the conclusions we can draw from them are limited. In contrast, how people organize funerals, how they bring up their children, and how they classify their relatives are aspects of culture that have important implications for many other aspects of life, and thus these aspects of culture are of much greater interest to anthropologists.

Politics is embroiled in many aspects of life that anthropologists consider cultural. For example, in many countries of the Global North, in the decades that followed World War II, cigarette smoking became a sign of middle-class affluence. Cigarette advertisements often depicted glamorous women and virile men with cigarettes on their lips. Today, decades of public-health education have demonstrated that smoking is dangerous for everyone's health, and relatively few middle class people now smoke. However, smoking remains common among poorer people, along with the health problems that it causes. In societies like China, tobacco production and consumption are booming and cigarette manufacturers adorn cigarette packages with **nationalist** images, such as panda bears and Beijing's Forbidden City, which identify smoking with pride in being Chinese (Kohrman 2018). Particularly among men, declining to smoke with others is interpreted as anti-social and an individualistic refusal to belong to the group. The decision to smoke or not, which appears on the surface to be a personal choice, is in fact a decision based on cultural, social, political, and economic factors.

Culture changes constantly, and as such it appears to differ from what is commonly called **tradition**. In its everyday usage, tradition refers to practices that are thought to be anchored in the past and embody a fundamental essence of society. Christmas celebrations in Britain, Europe, and North America are generally thought of as traditions. However, prior to the mid-nineteenth century, people celebrated the end of the year rather than Christmas (Carrier 1995, 181–7). People organised feasts and gave presents, but these were given by high-ranking people to their social inferiors, such as servants and merchants, rather than to family members. It was only in the middle of the century that celebrations shifted to 25 December, and the publication of Charles Dickens's *A Christmas Carol* (1843) exerted a major influence on this change. Decorated Christmas trees, which originated in Germany, were soon adopted in the English-speaking world and elsewhere. Family members only began exchanging presents when the family became a nuclear unit in urban settings, but the tradition of buying the presents, rather than making them, did not begin until the 1880s, when department stores, a new concept at the time, began setting up Christmas displays.

Christmas is an illustration of what two British historians whose ideas have exerted considerable influence on the social sciences, Eric Hobsbawn and Terence Ranger (1983), have called an **invented tradition**, capturing the fact that traditions are the product of people's actions at a particular moment in time. It is important not to confuse the term 'invented' with 'fake' or 'deceptive'. Ultimately, all traditions are invented, and the addition of the adjective simply reminds us that what appears to be timeless and strictly cultural is in fact grounded in particular historical, political, and economic dynamics. Anthropologists are interested in how certain cultural practices become elevated to the status of tradition at particular times; as the example of

Christmas demonstrates, the dynamics involved may be social, such as the nuclearization of the family and the growing importance of city life; economic, such as the emergence of department stores; and cultural, such as the popularity of a novella like Dickens's and its moral and political messages.

Comparison, diversity, and relativism

The anthropological study of society and culture has a number of specific qualities. Fundamental to anthropological research is a focus on **comparison**, the purpose of which is to evaluate similarities and differences. Anthropological comparison can take different forms. One is the comparison that is naturally embedded in the situation in which anthropologists conduct research among people who are not their own. This inevitably leads researchers to compare what they observe with their own society and culture (Gingrich 2012). For example, an anthropologist from Western Europe investigating the respect with which old people are treated in an African society cannot help but contrast this respect with the unkind way old people are often treated in Europe.

Comparison can take other forms. Anthropologists can compare, say, how meals are consumed in a particular society with the data that another anthropologist has gathered on meals in a different society, and interesting results can derive from the comparison. For example, lengthy midday meals in France contrast with the individualistic wolfing down of food at work desks in the United States, and the comparison suggests significant differences in people's understanding of food, work, and leisure in the two societies. It is also possible that members of the same society have different ways of eating (e.g., many urban French people today with precarious jobs do not have lingering lunches but instead gulp down fast food at lunchtime), and this also invites comparison and explanation. Not all comparisons lead to useful generalizations, and what one compares must be judiciously chosen to ensure that the comparison yields useful insights.

Yet another way in which anthropologists have placed comparison at the centre of their research is by conducting collaborative research that involves several researchers working on different themes in the same location or similar themes in different locations. For example, between 1957 and 1992, U.S. anthropologist Evon Z. Vogt directed a large project focusing on the Mayan people of Chiapas in southern Mexico (Vogt 1994). It supported numerous postgraduate students who each wrote a doctoral thesis focusing on one aspect of Mayan life, including subsistence, exchange, ritual, cosmology, language, and so on. Because all projects focused on contiguous villages, they benefited from each other's insights and together amounted to a vast documentation of life in the area. This kind of project, however, is a thing of the past, from a time when anthropological research could count on generous financing and no one worried much about the potential colonial implications of numerous researchers from the Global North descending on a handful of poor villages in Mexico.

Closely related to comparison is the discipline's aim to understand and explain **diversity**. Anthropologists focus on how people around the world construct society and culture in different ways. This is what originally led early anthropologists to conduct research on what were at the time considered to be exotic peoples. They sought to demonstrate that their practices, which may appear irrational and strange to the uninformed observer, had their own logic. Today, however, anthropologists no longer think of their discipline as the study of the exotic and many focus on people who live in industrial, urban, and capitalist societies.

Anthropologists are also concerned with diversity within societies, whether it is based on social class, religion, ethnicity, race, gender, sexuality, or other factors. These categories have had different meanings at different times and have different meanings in different locations. For example, while race is paramount in public discourse in the United States, many Europeans find it difficult to talk about race, even though racism is alive and well throughout the continent. Furthermore, human beings have a strong tendency to transform diversity into structures of inequality. Even inconsequential ways in which some people can differ from the majority, such as the language they speak or the shape of their body, can be the basis for treating them inequitably.

Diversity often gives rise to conflict. For example, some people with conservative religious convictions object to treating lesbians and gays like everyone else, arguing (rightly or wrongly) that religious texts raise objections to sexual desires that do not conform to heterosexuality. In contrast, some people who think of themselves as secular protest when certain religious groups erect buildings and make their presence known in their neighbourhood, as is the case when mosques are built in European cities. These are the manifestations of human diversity that anthropologists find particularly important to try to understand and, one hopes, help find a solution to, so that people of diverse identities can coexist in relative peace while respecting each other's differences.

Anthropologists do not stop at simply documenting interesting facts about how human beings in different societies organize their lives. Rather, they try to arrive at generalizations and develop theories to explain human diversity. The patterns in tobacco consumption that we analyzed in the previous section are an example of what these generalizations look like, and we will see many others in the course of this book. People who think of themselves as individuals who make decisions of their own accord may find the idea of a generalization disturbing, but in fact individual decisions (such as whether to smoke or not) always fall into patterns, which generalizations are designed to identify and explain. Generalizations seek to demonstrate how different aspects of people's lives, such as their economic practices, their kinship structure, their religious beliefs, and their political organization, interact with one another. Explanations in anthropology are **holistic**, in that they focus on how different areas of life are integrated with one another.

At the foundation of anthropologists' interest in comparison and diversity is a concept that has been fundamental since the early twentieth century, namely **cultural relativism**. The idea has a long history, but it was elaborated in the early twentieth century by Franz Boas, the founder of North American anthropology (even though he never used the term). Cultural relativism is the recognition that each society and culture is unique and that it is the product of its own history and context. It has an immediate methodological implication: in order to understand social and cultural practices, one must make sense of them not against the values and practices of another society (as nineteenth-century scholars were prone to do), but in terms of the logic that organizes the society in which they occur. This means that practices that appear to make little sense to an outsider always have a logic within the context in which they occur.

A classic example is offered by an analysis of the **potlatch**, a ritual performed by Native Americans of the Northwest Coast, such as the Kwakwaka'wakw (formerly referred to as the Kwakiutl), among whom Boas conducted research in the 1880s. The term 'potlatch' derives from the Chinook word for 'to give away' or 'consume'. It refers to a spectacular ceremony held at funerals, weddings, and other important events, during which a village chief gathered large quantities of valuable material goods, including food, shields made of copper, blankets, and furs, and redistributed them to the people who took part in the event. Chiefs of villages who had been invited to a potlatch were under the obligation to organize another one at a later date, and the reciprocating potlatch had to match or exceed in lavishness the previous one. If not, the organizers of the return potlatch would be shamed, or worse, could be enslaved by the organizer

Figure 1.3 During a ceremony an elderly man of the Kispiox First Nation feeds dollar notes to a participant dressed as a killer whale at a modern potlatch, Kispiox Skeena Valley, British Columbia, Canada, 1971. (Courtesy of David A. Barnes/Alamy)

of the previous potlatch. At the centre of the practice was fierce competition in generosity among high-ranking men. As the nineteenth century progressed, potlatches became so extravagant that the organizers set piles of goods on fire to demonstrate how wealthy they were (Figure 1.3).

To outside observers, the potlatch defies an economic logic that dictates that one should not be wasteful. Indeed, this logic is exactly what motivated the Canadian federal government to ban potlatches in 1885. From the perspective of Kwakwaka'wakw people, the potlatch made perfect sense, as Boas demonstrated: power and prestige in their society were acquired by giving away resources rather than by accumulating them, and potlatches were ways in which chiefs and villages competed with one another for power. Furthermore, when a chief died, several people could potentially inherit his title, which meant that the person who did succeed him was under pressure to demonstrate that he was a worthy chief, and one way to do so was to stage an extravagant display of generosity and power. Furthermore, the alternative to competitive giving was war, so the potlatch was an infinitely preferable way of dealing with the political tensions inherent in Kwakwaka'wakw culture. This is the kind of explanation that cultural relativism advocates.

But Boas witnessed the potlatch at a specific moment in history, when two events had taken place (Wolf 1982, 184–94). One, Northwest Coast Native Americans had become wealthy by selling animal furs to white traders for the European market. And two, the Europeans had introduced diseases, such as syphilis and smallpox, that killed many Kwakwaka'wakw people. As a result, there was considerable wealth circulating in a greatly diminished population, which encouraged extravagant displays. For later anthropologists who, like Eric Wolf, see culture as always changing and economics as a major force in these changes, relativism explains what people do in terms of not only the internal workings of a culture but also in the context produced by colonialism and economics.

Sometimes relativism is mistaken for an extreme position whereby one is not entitled to evaluate morally what people do in other societies because 'that's their culture'. For example, Sally Engle Merry, a U.S. legal anthropologist who has written extensively about gender and human rights, recounts a time when a radio journalist interviewed her about a young woman in Pakistan who had been gang-raped with the approval of the local tribal council as an alleged customary punishment for the transgression of a male member of her family (2003, 55). The journalist was pressing her to agree that we must respect the local culture no matter what, a position that the anthropologist was absolutely not willing to take. Some governments have also been known to rely on this version of relativism to argue that the values of the society over which they rule have nothing to do with the values that underlie universal notions of human rights, and therefore they should be left in peace to oppress their citizens. Sri Lankan anthropologist Gananath Obeyesekere (1966) called this position 'philosophical relativism' (other writers have used the adjective 'moral'), which he contrasted with the 'methodological relativism' that anthropologists have inherited from Boas and others.

In addition, who decides what 'local culture' is, and whose perspectives are left out of this definition? To recall, culture is neither uniform nor unchanging. In this case, the gang rape is very likely to be an example of an expediently invented tradition seeking to justify violence in an oppressively patriarchal context. Furthermore, philosophical relativism assumes that cultures are discrete entities that are both internally homogeneous and clearly differentiated from other cultures, which the example of Wolf's reanalysis of the potlatch demonstrates is untenable. Thus, while we should strive to understand the logic underlying the thoughts and actions of racist neo-Nazis, murderous narcotraffickers, slumlords who take advantage of poor people, and populist politicians feeding on citizens' sense of disenfranchisement, this certainly does not prevent us from being critical of these thoughts and actions as counter to basic principles of social justice.

When trying to make sense of culture, anthropologists need to arrive at what Clifford Geertz, following Bronislaw Malinowski, memorably described as the 'native's point of view', where the term 'native' is used in tongue-in-cheek fashion (1974). But they must recognize that there is never a single point of view; instead, there are always multiple perspectives on any aspect of society or culture, and anthropologists must discover what these different points of view are and how they relate to one another. For example, they must investigate why the poor young woman was gang-raped on that fateful day in Pakistan and why the local tribal council authorized it, but also who disagreed with the decision and what were the consequences of the rape, in addition to the terrible harm it obviously inflicted on its victim.

A very brief history of anthropology

Human beings have always been interested in why people living in other societies differed from themselves, and early authors who grappled with these issues were often great travellers or lived in areas where people of different origins mingled. For example, the Greek scholar Herodotus (c484–c425 BCE), who lived in Halicarnassus, a busy trading centre where people of all kinds interacted, described at great length in his work *The Histories* the exotic customs and practices of Barbarians, namely anyone who was not Greek (Figure 1.4). His ultimate purpose, however, was to show why Greeks were superior to everyone else in the then-known world, confirming an orthodoxy that was part of the ancient Greeks' project to establish themselves as the only true

Figure 1.4 A statue of Herodotus in the centre of his home town, Bodrum (formerly Halicarnassus), in present-day Turkey; as the first author to write about peoples and their history, he is often called the 'father of history', but his casual relationship with facts has also earned him the nickname 'father of lies', 2020. (Courtesy of Niko Besnier)

civilization. Another memorable figure who lived much later, Zheng He (c1371–c1433), born into a Muslim peasant family in Yunnan and taken captive in the service of the future emperor of China, rose to command seven maritime expeditions to Southeast Asia, India, the Persian Gulf, and East Africa. He opened a world of exotic goods, practices, animals, and people to Ming Dynasty China, but here again Chinese superiority was never in doubt.

Other thinkers at other times in history proved more open minded. Among them was French philosopher Michel de Montaigne (1533–92), who mused in an essay titled 'Of Cannibals' (c1580) that Amazonian Indians were just as human as Europeans despite the fact that they ate the flesh of their slain enemies; had he been born among them, he conjectured, he would have done the same. This idea, which was radical at the time, was an early form of cultural relativism.

These early thinkers, however, were not anthropologists. As an intellectual endeavour, anthropology did not emerge until the middle of the nineteenth century. It rested on a number of developments in the history of ideas. One was the Enlightenment that emerged in eighteenth-century Europe, whose advocates maintained that scientific research should be based on first-hand empirical observations, in contrast to, say, Montaigne, whose method consisted in sitting in his study and reflecting. Also emerging during the Enlightenment was the notion that, despite human beings' different looks and practices, humanity was one, a notion that would eventually lead to the abolition of slavery, nominally at least, in the nineteenth century. Another idea was that human life could be subjected to the same kind of systematic description as aspects of nature like fauna and flora, liquids and gases, and the planets. From these emerged the social sciences, which in the late nineteenth century split up into different disciplines, including sociology, demography, political science, and economics, as well as anthropology.

Yet another factor that played an important role in the development of anthropology was Europe's colonial conquest of the rest of the world. Colonialism arguably began when Columbus landed in the New World in 1492 and it expanded in the nineteenth century, to the point that at the beginning of the twentieth century most of the world was under the political control or influence of a European or North American power. Colonialism, with which anthropology has had a complicated and uneasy relationship, placed observers of European descent in close contact with what came to be referred to with the necessarily vague term 'the Other', namely people other than middle-class Europeans or people of European origin. At the same time as Westerners were coming into contact with people living in exotic places, they were beginning to take an interest in the 'local' Others, namely peasants, working-class people, domestic servants, and all others whose lives had been ignored by those in power. From this interest emerged a kindred discipline, namely folklore.

This is why anthropology was at first defined as the study of exotic peoples, an image from which the discipline today has long distanced itself. In the mid-nineteenth century, writers like E. B. Tylor, whose definition of culture we quoted earlier, Herbert Spencer in England, and Lewis Henry Morgan in the United States developed the theory of **cultural evolutionism**, which maintained that all of the world's societies were ordered along an evolutionary continuum, with 'primitive' cultures at one end and 'civilized' cultures at the other. According to this now thoroughly discredited theory, the primitives were stuck in an earlier form of humanity characterized by little technology, social simplicity, and relative lack of intelligence, while civilized peoples, of which Westerners were the apogee, were technologically sophisticated, socially complex, and intellectually superior.

The end of the nineteenth century witnessed a reaction against these misguided ideas. The work of Haitian anthropologist and politician Anténor Firmin (2002) stands out as an early effort to debunk racist evolutionary theory, particularly widespread in France at the time, that alleged differences in intelligence were grounded in the physiology of race. Evolutionists tried to make sense of what went on in other societies by relying on the accounts of observers other than themselves, including missionaries, traders, and explorers, and they thus had no first-hand understanding of the societies they were writing about. For example, they maintained that societies that did not practise agriculture were inferior to those that did, but in fact agriculture is only useful under some conditions (e.g., sedentary living, availability of plants that can be domesticated). This is why nineteenth-century anthropology is often referred to, somewhat disparagingly, as 'armchair anthropology'.

At the end of the century, rather than trying to come up with a theory of cultural evolution, social scientists became preoccupied by the differences between the small-scale **communities**

Box 1.2 Anthropology and sociology: kindred disciplines

As they are practised today, anthropology and sociology share a common theoretical origin that recognizes the works of nineteenth- and early-twentieth-century thinkers such as Marx, Durkheim, and Weber as foundational. At the beginning of the twentieth century, a division of labour emerged, whereby sociologists focused on the industrial societies of what we call today the Global North, while anthropologists studied small-scale communities in the Global South, which at the time largely fell under the colonial rule of Western powers. The two disciplines developed divergent methods: in anthropology, ethnography (which we explore in Chapter 2) became the dominant methodology, while sociologists relied on surveys, questionnaires, and interviews to obtain their data, and many analyzed these with quantitative methods, which play only a minor role in anthropology. While both disciplines take 'connections' as their subject of inquiry, they approach them differently.

The questions that early sociologists and anthropologists asked also differed because the people they studied had different priorities. For example, kinship, the focus of Chapter 3, became a central concern in anthropology because it played such an important role in the lives of people in small-scale societies, in contrast to the inhabitants of industrial societies, whose lives were organized in terms of labour, social stratification, and the state. Similarly, the study of culture occupies a central role in many anthropological traditions, while sociologists consider society as their primary topic of research. These differences, however, were also the result of what sociologists and anthropologists chose to concentrate on or ignore.

This disciplinary division of labour lasted many decades, although already in the 1920s and 1930s the Chicago School of Sociology was advocating ethnographic methods for the study of urban life. In the 1960s and 1970s, the gap between sociology and anthropology began to narrow. Anthropologists no longer confined their attention to societies of the Global South, and realized that the societies that they had traditionally studied were dealing with problems that they shared with industrial societies, such as inequality and migration. During the same period, many anthropologists shifted their focus to industrial and urban contexts, while some sociologists worked in the Global South. Today, there is considerable overlap between the two disciplines, even though some differences remain, such as the importance that many sociologists attach to quantitative analysis. Lastly, although they are often lumped together in a single department at smaller universities, sociology and anthropology remain largely separate disciplines for institutional reasons, with separate journals, conferences, and scholarly associations.

---

they were encountering in the non-Western world, much of which had fallen under the colonial rule of the West, and large-scale societies, such as those of Western colonial powers. For them, the typical preliterate community had a subsistence economy focused on the production of the food they needed and a social life that was largely determined by customs and traditions. In contrast, in a typical society, the economy was based on industry, literacy was profoundly engrained in all activities, and social life was governed by impersonal laws and contracts. Scholars proposed different versions of this contrast, like German social scientist Ferdinand Tönnies, from whom the English language has borrowed the German terms *Gemeinschaft* 'community' and *Gesellschaft* 'society', as well as his compatriots Karl Marx and Max Weber, whose influence on anthropology we discuss later in the book.

These ideas already had a long history, even though modern European scholars ignored much of it. For example, in the fourteenth century, North African scholar Ibn-Khaldūn had proposed, in his great work titled *Kitāb al-'Ibar (Book of Lessons)*, that tribal nomads of the North African desert were socially cohesive because they placed considerable value on *aṣabiyyah*, or solidarity. In contrast, when the group expanded and became urban and more 'civilized', solidarity waned and society became fragmented. Nineteenth-century French social scientist Émile Durkheim developed a comparable model that exerted considerable influence. He maintained that society could only function properly if their members felt **solidarity** with one another, that is, the conviction that they must cooperate to ensure that society does not fall apart. He distinguished between **mechanical solidarity** based on felt similarities between people, who feel solidarity simply because they are roughly the same and do similar kinds of work, and **organic solidarity** based on the mutual dependence between people, such as the cobbler needing bread from the baker who needs shoes from the cobbler. The term 'organic' is a metaphor of organs in the body of living creatures (e.g., heart, liver, lungs) that depend on each other's functions to make the entire body work.

For Durkheim, the contrast between mechanical and organic forms of solidarity was closely related to population size and how labour is divided: in small-scale communities, everyone has similar skills and holds similar beliefs about the world. When a community becomes a society, life becomes more complex and skills specialized, meaning that people have to depend on one another for their survival. Nineteenth-century social scientists disagreed on minor aspects of the contrast between community and society, but they all agreed that it was fundamental, and it became the basis upon which anthropology and sociology diverged into two different disciplines: one specialized in the study of communities and the other in the study of societies.

In the English-speaking world, anthropology in the early twentieth century developed with two different orientations in Britain (as well as Australia, New Zealand, and South Africa) and the United States. In Britain, Bronislaw Malinowski, an anthropologist of Polish origin, laid out the methodological foundation of the discipline, which we explain in the next chapter, and became one of the founders of the discipline. Another founder of British anthropology, A. R. Radcliffe-Brown, developed Durkheim's ideas on social cohesion. He proposed that the institutions that make up society, such as kinship, the economy, and religious life, were all designed to contribute to the maintenance of society. This perspective came to be known as **structural functionalism**: 'structural' in the sense that society is systematically organized, 'functionalism' in the sense that the function of institutions is to maintain this structure in good working order.

Structural functionalists made two important assumptions that anthropologists would later demonstrate were flawed: one is that each society is internally coherent, with every member more or less agreeing on its values and principles; the other is that society is a bounded, closed, and stable system, insulated from other societies and unchanging over time. For example, E. E. Evans-Pritchard, another British anthropologist, conducted fieldwork in the 1930s among the Nuer, who live in what is today South Sudan, a proud, warlike, and **egalitarian** people whose lives revolved around the cattle they kept. Even though they had just experienced a violent campaign of pacification by the British colonial administration and conflicts continued to erupt among themselves, Evans-Pritchard downplayed the effects of colonialism and analyzed their conflicts as if they were purely internal events.

Structural functionalists assumed that everything in society was designed to reinforce the stability of social structures. As a result, they were ill-equipped to understand that society could in fact be internally diverse and that it was constantly changing. In the second part of the twentieth century, scholars trained in this approach began questioning some of its assumptions. The best known is Max Gluckman, who conducted fieldwork in urban centres and mining towns of southern Africa, in which many ethnicities lived side-by-side and society was always diverse and in flux. He founded the Marxist-inspired Manchester School of anthropology, which was interested in social change and conflict, and was critical of colonialism.

On the other side of the Atlantic, the figure of Franz Boas, a German immigrant to the United States, loomed large in the development of the discipline at the beginning of the twentieth century. Boas was particularly critical of the assumptions of cultural evolutionism and of the racist policies of the U.S. government, and he considered that anthropology's mission was to document all aspects of the lives of a people. According to him, anthropologists should work in four broad areas: how society and culture are organized, the topic of social and cultural anthropology; language and its relationship to society and culture, the topic of linguistic anthropology; human evolution through the study of people's physiologies, the topic of biological or physical anthropology; and prehistory and history based on material remains, the topic of archaeology. This approach came to be known as **four-field anthropology**, which is distinctly North American. Elsewhere in the world, biological anthropology is typically considered to be a branch of biology and archaeology is a separate discipline often associated with the study of classics. In this book, we use the term 'anthropology' as a shorthand for social, cultural, and linguistic anthropology.

Four-field anthropology developed in the context in which Boas and many of his students conducted research, namely among Native North Americans, who were widely believed at the time to be on the verge of extinction under pressure from white settlers' expansion. Boas considered that anthropology had the urgent duty to record all aspects of the lives of these people before they disappeared. This is sometimes referred to as **salvage anthropology**. Today, anthropologists are critical of this approach for several reasons. One is the assumption that lifeways can simply vanish, which says more about the Western nostalgic construction of the Other than about the peoples in question. Another is the sense of entitlement with which some salvage anthropologists approached the task of collecting information about people, whether they consented to it or not. Yet another is the fact that Boas and his students seemed to be more interested in documenting lifeways than in critiquing the colonial conquests and forms of oppression that were endangering the lives of the people they studied. Anthropologists of the time noted the destitution, marginalization, and exclusion that colonialism had foisted upon Indigenous peoples, but they were unable or unwilling to confront these problems.

Franz Boas had numerous students and trained an entire generation of anthropologists. Among them were Ruth Benedict and Margaret Mead, who became two of the most celebrated figures in the history of anthropology. Their work was largely concerned with understanding the organization of culture and its relationship to the psychological makeup of individuals. This endeavour was known as the **culture and personality** school of anthropology. Margaret Mead became prominent in the United States not so much for her academic work but for her role as a **public anthropologist**. In the 1960s, she attained celebrity status for her popular writings and public appearances that questioned received assumptions about such matters as child rearing, gender roles, sexuality, and family life.

Elsewhere, different traditions of anthropology emerged in the course of the twentieth century. In France, anthropologists developed ideas inspired by Durkheim and his students, particularly his nephew Marcel Mauss, which we examine in Chapter 9. The best-known French anthropologist in the mid-twentieth century was Claude Lévi-Strauss, who revolutionized the discipline by developing **structuralism**, a theory inspired by developments in linguistics and computing taking place at the time, which maintained that all aspects of human existence can be explained in terms of systems of binary oppositions (e.g., hot vs. cold, left vs. right, male vs. female) that reflect the organization of human cognition. Another French scholar, Frantz Fanon (2008), born in the Caribbean and trained as a psychiatrist, stands out as one of the first to write about the traumatic effects of the racist foundation of colonialism on the colonized, using his own experience of racism and bringing to anthropology a critique of its own blindness to colonial relations. In the 1970s and 1980s, Pierre Bourdieu, whose early work was based on fieldwork in colonial Algeria, developed **practice theory**, which focused on the combined effect of social and cultural dynamics in structuring inequality. This work had a strong influence on French sociology and North American anthropology.

In Germany and Eastern Europe, anthropology, which went under the name 'ethnology', was long concerned with the folkways of peasant society. After World War II, strongly influenced by Marxism, South American anthropologists conducted politically engaged research on peasantry, social inequality, and economic development. Anthropology also developed as a discipline in countries such as Japan, India, and the Soviet Union. Unfortunately, the influence of these other national traditions has been limited by the political dominance of the English language on world anthropology, which has marginalized works written in other languages.

After World War II, various theoretical approaches competed with one another in North American anthropology, sometimes acrimoniously. Some scholars advocated a return to evolutionism, but without the racial overtones of its nineteenth-century version, focusing in particular on the effects of the ecological context in which people lived on their social and cultural organization. In contrast, **symbolic anthropology**, spearheaded in particular by Clifford Geertz, maintained that the goal of the discipline was to understand how human experience was shaped by the symbols through which people made sense of the world.

In the 1970s, many anthropologists in North America, Britain, and Continental Europe turned to Marx, whom scholars had neglected because it was politically dangerous to invoke Marxism in the West during the Cold War. They developed a brand of anthropology that was historically focused, politically engaged, and critical of inequality and colonialism. Eric Wolf's work, discussed earlier, figured prominently in these developments. In the 1980s, some anthropologists became critical of the assumptions that earlier anthropologists had made in their work, particularly that anthropology is a scientific endeavour in which the anthropologist could authoritatively describe a society. They maintained that anthropological knowledge was produced in the context of a dialogue between the observer and the people being observed. This recognition led the proponents of the **reflexive anthropology** movement to rethink the power relations inherent in anthropological research, influenced by the **postmodernist** suspicion of the faith in science inherited from the Enlightenment and insistence on the fact that knowledge is always contingent on the context in which it is produced. Particularly influential was the work of Palestinian-American literary scholar Edward Said (1978) on **orientalism**, namely the European and North American tradition of representing 'the Orient' in various forms, including literature, art, and scholarship, that reified this ill-defined notion and fed into Western colonial designs. Since the late twentieth century, scholars have emerged in the societies that white anthropologists traditionally studied, such as postcolonial and Indigenous societies, developing a critique of the intellectual colonialism that European and North American anthropology had exerted to date.

Power relations in anthropological research also became the concerns of **feminist anthropology**, which was emerging at the same time. Its original impetus was to correct the overwhelming male biases that had characterized anthropology. Early works were often written by the wife in a husband-wife team of anthropologists, who documented women's lives in the societies where they conducted fieldwork together. Later, feminist anthropologists demonstrated that the lens of gender, and later sexuality, provided a radically different perspective on traditional anthropological topics, such as kinship, exchange, and ritual. For example, Eleanor Leacock (1981) revived Marx's collaborator Friedrich Engels's work on the origin of gender oppression in the rise of private property and the nuclear family, and evaluated it against her fieldwork materials from southern Africa. However, as Marilyn Strathern (1987), a towering figure of contemporary anthropology, argued, feminist politics and anthropology have an uneasy relationship in that the former seeks to abolish **patriarchal** oppression while the latter is critical of it but remains open to the complexities of different perspectives on any social process, including patriarchy.

Different traditions of anthropology had divergent ideas about the main object of anthropological research (G. Ribeiro 2014). For many decades, North American anthropologists were more concerned with understanding culture than social structure. Boas and his students were the first to use the term 'cultures' in the plural to refer to human groups in terms of their belief systems, and they commonly referred to the subdiscipline as 'cultural anthropology'. Even though Boas's four-field model encompassed all aspects of people's lives, from material objects to mythology and religious beliefs, his students concentrated on making sense of myths, values, beliefs, and other kinds of representations in people's lives, in other words, the **ideational** aspects of human existence. In contrast, British and European anthropologists, dominated until the middle of the twentieth century by structural functionalism, were primarily preoccupied with developing scientific models of how society was structured through kinship, political institutions, and economic activities, which constitute the **material** aspects of human existence. They did not think that culture could be studied scientifically and characterized the discipline as 'social anthropology', focused on the social. These very broad contrasts only capture tendencies; for example, Lévi-Strauss's work in France was equally concerned with kinship, a social institution, as it was with myth, an aspect of culture, and E. E. Evans-Pritchard wrote about culture and religion. Today, no anthropologist would maintain that any aspect of human existence can be approached solely as material or ideational. Thus social anthropology and cultural anthropology are no longer seen as different endeavours, but as complementary and overlapping ones, a perspective that is often referred to as socio-cultural anthropology.

The study of society and culture in the twenty-first century

From Herodotus's efforts in ancient Greece to demonstrate that the Greeks were, after all, the most perfect manifestation of humankind, Zheng He's voyages that opened a world of new things to Ming dynasty China, Ibn Khaldūn's theory of social cohesion, to Montaigne's musings about cannibals, the questions of what constitutes human diversity and commonality have long preoccupied thinkers. But the social sciences only emerged as disciplines in the nineteenth century, as part of a large-scale project, which began in the Enlightenment, of developing a systematic way of investigating the world. They also benefited from the massive expansion of education, extraordinary scientific and technological developments during the Industrial Revolution, and a nineteenth century that was a period of relative security and political stability in the Global North, as well as the colonial subjugation of the rest of the world by European and North American powers. In the course of its history, anthropology has witnessed a series of schools of thought that all made society and culture their object of study in various ways, and the concerns of the ancients with making sense of human diversity and human commonality still matter today.

At the same time, the discipline of anthropology in the twenty-first century is radically different from the musings of the philosophers of the past. Contemporary anthropologists recognize that all societies of the world today are intricately connected to one another, yet that local concerns continue to matter. They realize that all representations, including the anthropologists', are grounded in particular social, cultural, political, and historical contexts. Anthropologists understand that all aspects of life, such as social relations, economic activities, politics, and the realm of ideas, are interconnected, and that explanations in anthropology must engage with the resulting complexity. And, in contrast to earlier anthropologists, they study the Global North just as often as they study societies of the Global South.

For all the attention that anthropologists pay to human diversity, the movers and shakers in the history of anthropology have been remarkably predictable: with a few exceptions, they were white men living in wealthy countries, many based at elite universities. The few women who left their mark on the discipline were often professionally marginalized. For example, despite their important contributions to anthropology in their times, Margaret Mead never held a permanent university position and Ruth Benedict only received institutional recognition at the very end of her life. Zora Neale Hurston, an African American woman who studied with Boas, was marginalized in graduate school and instead forged a career as a novelist and journalist writing about race and sexuality in the American South. Her interviews with Cudjo Lewis, a slave who was transported to the United States on the last slaving ship, could not find a publisher; they finally appeared almost 60 years after her death (Hurston 2018). Another woman who studied with Boas, Cora DuBois, became the first female tenured professor at Harvard University in 1953, but she was paid less than her male colleagues and excluded from departmental meetings (Seymour 2015). Until recently, there were very few non-white anthropologists, and scholars from the Global South who have made important contributions to the discipline have invariably been from privileged backgrounds who have pursued careers in elite institutions in the Global North. In recent years, some anthropologists have mobilized to **decolonize anthropology**, that is, to recognize the inequalities in the development of the discipline and rethink the power dimensions of anthropological practices. In this book, we do our best to follow this lead.

Key thinkers mentioned in this chapter:

Ruth Benedict; Franz Boas; Pierre Bourdieu; Cora DuBois; Émile Durkheim; E. E. Evans-Pritchard; Clifford Geertz; Max Gluckman; Zora Neale Hurston; Eleanor Leacock; Claude Lévi-Strauss; Bronislaw Malinowski; Karl Marx; Marcel Mauss; Margaret Mead; A. R. Radcliffe-Brown; Marilyn Strathern; Ferdinand Tönnies; E. B. Tylor; Max Weber; Eric Wolf

Key terms mentioned in this chapter (see Glossary):

Community; Comparison; Cultural relativism; Culture; Decolonize anthropology; Holistic; Inequality; Invented tradition; Reflexivity; Society; Social relations

Questions for discussion/review:

1   How do anthropologists distinguish society and culture?
2   Describe the different forms anthropological comparison may take.
3   What does it mean to say that anthropological explanations are holistic?
4   How does methodological cultural relativism differ from philosophical cultural relativism?
5   Why did anthropology emerge during colonial times and how has the discipline changed since colonialism ended?

Chapter 2

Anthropologists at work

Anthropologists take an interest in anything and everything, from second-hand clothes markets in Zambia to the New York stock exchange, and conduct work on questions of many different scales, from individual life histories to global phenomena. They conduct research in villages, urban neighbourhoods, social institutions, corporations, and **cyberspace**, or several of these locations at once. What distinguishes anthropologists from researchers working in related disciplines such as sociology and psychology is not only this breadth but also how they gather their data, as well as what they consider to be data. In this chapter, we explore what is distinct about the methods of anthropology and the data that anthropologists collect.

The method that is widely considered to be fundamental to anthropology is **ethnographic fieldwork**. Fieldwork involves spending time with the people whose lives the anthropologist seeks to understand and doing so in their natural context, documenting their activities, thoughts, and relationships. This is research in the field, by which we mean wherever people live and work, in contrast to a laboratory. Anthropologists typically conduct fieldwork for extended periods of time. In many cases, they remain in close contact with their research participants over many years, sometimes during their entire lifetime, often developing relationships with them that resemble bonds of kinship. They analyze the data they gathered in the form of an **ethnography**, a detailed study of a particular location, group, or phenomenon that forms the basis for general theoretical debates and discussions in the discipline.

Ethnographers employ many different techniques to gather data. The most important is **participant observation**, which consists in observing people's lives while simultaneously participating in their activities to understand the experience of the activities as fully as possible. While conducting participant observation, ethnographers must negotiate between being part of the action and remaining at the same time on the margin of it. There are obvious limitations to participation: for example, when ethnography concerns people who engage in a highly specialized activity that requires training or abilities that ethnographers do not have (e.g., medicine, art, fishing), they must adapt their expectations of the level of participation that is feasible. Participant observation presumes at least minimal competence in a relevant language or languages, and language learning is a central aspect of fieldwork. Anthropologists generally contract the help of one or more local research assistants, who play a crucial role in helping them gain access to people, locations, and events, and help the anthropologists understand and interpret what they observe, a fact that anthropologists in the old days often failed to acknowledge. Some anthropologists today share the authorship of their publications with their research assistants, and all have a duty to express their debt to them in writing (Middleton and Cons 2014).

Typically, the ethnographer records observations in **fieldnotes** that constitute the data on which the anthropologist will later base the analysis. Fieldnotes are records of everything and

DOI: 10.4324/9781315737805-2

Box 2.1 The 1898 Cambridge Anthropological Expedition to Torres Straits, the precursor to modern fieldwork

Alfred Cort Haddon, a professor of zoology with an interest in marine biology, travelled to the Torres Straits Islands, between Australia and New Guinea, in the 1880s to study coral reefs, and while there he developed an interest in the people who inhabit the islands. He thought that recording information about their lives while their traditional ways of life were still accessible to science was a priority. In 1898, he organized an expedition to the islands with a group of scientists that included W. H. R. Rivers, a physician and psychiatrist who was a pioneer in the study of kinship; C. G. Seligman, a physician and anthropologist; and Sidney Ray, a linguist. This was arguably the first time that social scientists had systematically collected ethnographic data directly from Indigenous people. They were equipped with the best technology of the day, including still cameras, film cameras, and wax-cylinder recording phonographs.

The group gathered a vast quantity of data on customs, music, language, folklore, material culture, genealogy, and psychology. They documented intensively one group of islanders for a short period of time and then repeated this process with another group, an approach that came to be known as **survey work**. It was a significant improvement on earlier data gathering methods that divided anthropological work between those who gathered data in the field, such as missionaries, traders, and administrators, and those who analyzed the data without ever visiting the peoples they wrote about. Yet it very soon became apparent that even this survey data was not sufficient to provide a real under-standing of the society and culture of Indigenous people. By 1913, Rivers was advocating instead for 'intensive work', which would require fieldworkers to gather their own data and to do this by remaining at a field site for a year or more, working in the language of the people and noting down every feature of their customs and practices. This is what Malinowski went on to do a few years later and memorably advocated in his writings.

anything the ethnographer observes that can potentially be of use when the anthropologist goes on to develop ethnographic generalizations. These may be bits of conversation, plans of homes and other spaces, maps, diagrams of relationships, and a multitude of other titbits that could eventually prove useful. In the past, anthropologists carried notebooks everywhere they went to jot down notes, which they organized at the end of the day, on a typewriter in the past or on a computer today. Many anthropologists use electronic devices such as tablets, although these come with limitations (e.g., they are not very useful in a tropical downpour and they attract attention) and some anthropologists continue using old-fashioned tools. Fieldnotes are gener-ally extensive. They can be messy because they are taken on the run and are often intelligible only to the fieldworkers. They can also be a liability, for example, in situations where people have reasons to be suspicious of someone taking notes about what they are doing or saying.

Ethnographers use a variety of techniques besides participant observation. They often con-duct **interviews**, which complement participant observation by eliciting research participants' own views and explanations of what they do. Most anthropologists, however, consider inter-views to be secondary to participant observation because they represent one perspective on reality and inevitably neglect others, and there are many aspects of people's lives that are difficult to articulate. Interviews constitute a specific kind of interaction with which middle-class people in the Global North are intimately familiar; in contrast, people in other societies are not necessarily comfortable with them. They also have their own structure of power, with the interviewer asking the questions and thus directing the conversation, and the interviewee replying. Other data that anthropologists may gather during fieldwork include censuses, questionnaires, inventories, catalogues, texts, photographs, and audio or video recordings of events such as gatherings, rituals, and conversations. Like historians, anthropologists read documents in archives, when these are available, to help them place their fieldwork materials in a historical context.

Like all methodologies, ethnographic fieldwork has advantages and disadvantages. Among its advantages are the contextual richness of the materials it gives access to; its emphasis on a multiplicity of perspectives; the diversity of what constitutes 'data', which enables the researcher to arrive at an analysis from different angles; its ability to generate materials that are not accessible with other methods; and a focus on the complex relationship between people's actions and people's explanations for their actions. Among the disadvantages of ethnography is its time-consuming nature. Fieldwork can also be an emotionally draining activity for the researcher, who may be living alone and in an unfamiliar society.

Ethnography has been criticized for being subjective, although anthropologists turn this problem into an asset by focusing on as many subjective perspectives on a problem as possible. If they conduct fieldwork in a culture that is not their own, ethnographers gradually develop a sensibility of the social world they study. This sensibility requires them to reflect on the prior knowledge and assumptions they bring with them from their own culture as they enter the new culture. This **reflexive** understanding of the **situated knowledge** with which ethnographers enter the field is important as ethnographers have to unlearn during fieldwork how they do things at home and what seems natural there. This makes it possible to incorporate the knowledge and acquire the **habitus,** or socially internalized ways of being, to live successfully in their fieldwork locations. In short, ethnographers have to work to recognize their own culture-based assumptions and social biases. These are the commonly accepted and usually unquestioned ways of doing things taken for granted in our everyday lives at home but which, if we are not careful, may prevent us from grasping other ways of living. These assumptions and biases are defined as **ethnocentrism,** namely falling back on one's customary ways of doing and thinking as the 'normal', 'common-sense', or 'obvious' way things should be done without questioning how one's own culture shapes these ways of thinking.

Another distinctive feature of ethnographic research is that, while ethnographers set out to do fieldwork with a plan to study topics and issues they are interested in, they cannot be certain about what they might encounter in the field. Unlike other social scientists, such as economists or psychologists, anthropologists often do not start with a precisely worked-out hypothesis. Rather, the theory comes from a combination of a general theoretical framework that ethnographers begin with and their empirical observations and experiences. This is a form of inductive reasoning, in which observed patterns and regularities in behaviour slowly lead to generalizations and from there to theories. Such an approach allows for the unexpected and the serendipitous to play an important role in the development of ideas, and hence allows for creativity and imagination to play its part in data collection and analysis. As fieldwork progresses, researchers continually review ideas, fieldnotes, and experiences to see what new insights they might yield. Charting how different, better ideas over the course of fieldwork replace the ideas one started with is an inescapable characteristic of good ethnographic research.

Box 2.2 Bronislaw Malinowski (1884–1942)

A scholar of Polish origin who spent much of his adult life in Britain, Bronislaw Malinowski is considered one of the founders of modern anthropology. Originally trained in mathematics and physics, he gravitated towards anthropology while reading nineteenth-century anthropological writings. In 1914, he was in Australian-controlled New Guinea when World War I broke out. He was traveling on an Austrian passport because Krakow, where he was born, was then part of the Austro-Hungarian Empire, which made him an enemy of the British Commonwealth and he was thus unable to return to England. The Australian government offered him the opportunity to conduct ethnographic fieldwork in New Guinea and he chose Mailu Island on the southern coast of New Guinea to begin his work. Malinowski visited the villagers on Mailu everyday, witnessed ceremonies, and conducted interviews through interpreters. But he soon found that he was not getting the depth of data he was seeking, as he could not communicate directly with the people and was not spending enough time in the village. He decided to abandon this work and start again in another location, this time not repeating the mistakes of his first fieldwork attempt.

Malinowski then moved to the Trobriand Islands, in the eastern part of what is today the Milne Bay Province of Papua New Guinea, and pitched his tent in the centre of the village so that he would not miss any activities that took place. He set about learning the language so that he did not have to depend on interpreters. This also allowed him to record the words of the Trobrianders in their own language, Kilivila. Malinowski was able to gain a deeper understanding of the ways of life in a traditional society than any anthropologist ever had before.

His first ethnography based on his fieldwork in the Trobriands, *Argonauts of the Western Pacific*, was published in 1922, the same year that James Joyce's *Ulysses* came out and a time of considerable optimism for humanity, following the carnage of World War I. It was immediately recognized as a landmark text, changing how anthropologists would henceforth gather data. Even though others, such as W. H. R. Rivers, had already advocated for 'intensive work', Malinowski was the first anthropologist to spell out systematically how this work should be conducted. In the introductory chapter of *Argonauts*, using the gender-biased language of the time, he defined ethnography as a project designed 'to grasp the native's point of view, his relation to life, to realize *his* vision of *his* world' (1922, ix). Later in the book, he articulated the importance of empathy in anthropological research, though he did not use the term: 'the Science of Man in its most refined and deepest version should lead us to such knowledge and to tolerance and generosity, based on the understanding of other men's point of view' (1922, 518).

At the same time, Malinowski's relationship with Trobriand Islanders was undoubtedly complicated. His personal diaries betrayed the impatience, loneliness, and anger that he sometimes felt during his research, and are peppered with racist remarks. When after his death his widow published the diaries (Malinowski 1967), even though Malinowski never meant them to be read by others, they caused widespread consternation because they revealed a radically different picture from the empathetic relationship he advocated in his published writings. Today, anthropologists recognize that ethnographic fieldwork is just as complicated as any other social situation, in which multiple and contradictory feelings may coexist (Figure 2.1).

Figure 2.1 Bronislaw Malinowski watching children at play, Teyava village, Kiriwina, Trobriand Islands, May 1918. (Courtesy of the Library of the London School of Economics, Malinowski Papers reference 4.18.10)

Ethnographic fieldwork is predicated on the availability of two resources, money and time. Fieldworkers need money to travel, subsist, purchase equipment, hire a research assistant, and compensate research participants in one way or another. To obtain funds for fieldwork, researchers apply to public institutions in charge of distributing research funds, such as the Economic and Social Research Council in Britain, the European Research Council, the Australian Research Council, the National Research Council of Canada, and the National Science Foundation in the United States. These institutions review applications in a highly competitive selection process and only fund a small percentage of the applications they receive. Some private foundations also provide funding for social science research. A notable one is the Wenner Gren Foundation for Anthropological Research, which was established in 1941 with an endowment from the Swedish inventor of the vacuum cleaner, who was an amateur archaeologist.

The other resource needed for fieldwork is time. In the past, anthropologists would typically spend one or two years studying a community and were able to make return visits throughout their lives. Today, this is increasingly difficult. Training programmes in anthropology typically allow postgraduate students to spend one year conducting fieldwork, but universities and education ministries around the world put pressure on programmes to encourage students to finish their doctorates quickly. Anthropologists who teach at privileged universities are granted periodic research leaves, but most must juggle fieldwork with teaching and administrative duties, in addition to personal life. Anthropologists outside of academia generally find it very difficult to secure time for fieldwork, unless it is part of their employment duties.

The goal of fieldwork is to explain people's lifeways to audiences that may not have experienced these lifeways and who are interested in understanding them, bearing in mind that these explanations are always partial, selective, and context dependent. From ethnographies of particular places at particular times, anthropologists develop comparisons and extend generalizations about human lifeways across diverse social groups and historical periods. This is why comparison is a fundamental aspect of anthropology, as we discussed in Chapter 1.

Box 2.3   What do anthropologists call the people whose lives they study?

In the early days of the discipline, anthropologists referred to the people whose lives they were interested in understanding as 'informants' – the implication was that they 'informed' the anthropologist about their lives, whether directly through their explanations or indirectly through their actions. In the late twentieth century, anthropologists began to feel uncomfortable with the utilitarian, power-laden, and somewhat derogatory connotations of the term. One alternative, 'respondent', is less problematic although it still conjures an image of the anthropologist asking questions and local people being expected to answer. Other terms used in contemporary ethnographies include 'collaborator', 'consultant', 'interlocutor', and 'friend', but each comes with its own problems; for example, 'collaborator' has the undesirable connotation of someone siding with the enemy in times of war, while 'consultant' evokes highly paid entrepreneurs who sell their services in a business-like transaction, both of which are far removed from the relationship that most anthropologists and the people whose lives they work to understand seek to cultivate. Recognizing that ethnographic information is not constructed solely by the ethnographer but is the product of an interaction in which everyone plays a role, the term 'research participant' is often favoured and it is the term that we use in this book.

Social relations in ethnographic fieldwork

To understand the logic of people's thoughts and actions, anthropologists strive to develop **empathy** with the people whose lives they try to understand. Empathy is an emotional connection that people develop with one another that enables them to imagine what the world looks like from the perspective of others. It is different from sympathy, which is an emotional alignment whereby a person feels concern for another person but does not attempt to see the world in the same way as the person they sympathize with. All societies have a concept of empathy because it is so fundamental to social relations, although its details and what it encourages people to do may vary.

Empathy in fieldwork is always affected by other feelings, as it is in all social situations in which human beings interact with one another. In many circumstances, anthropologists may empathize with some people much more than with others or they may empathize with some aspects of their lives while finding other aspects unpleasant. Anthropological fieldwork, after all, is a human situation like any other. Needless to say, people among whom anthropologists conduct fieldwork may have similarly complex feelings about the anthropologist as a person and what she or he writes. While early anthropologists conducted their research in the confident belief that their work was safely removed from the people whose lives they documented, anthropologists in the twenty-first century can no longer rest on this assumption. Today, literacy is widespread throughout the world, the internet and other technologies carry information across vast distances, and the remotest locations are now connected to the world's centres.

People read what is written about them and react to it in a variety of ways. In some cases, people treasure what anthropologists have written about them and use these writings to their advantage. This is the case of the books that Raymond Firth wrote about Tikopia, a small and

isolated island in the Pacific politically incorporated in the Solomon Islands, where he conducted research in 1928–29. Tikopians today refer to Firth's work as an authority on their
society and history and are proud of the fact that it made them famous throughout the world
(Macdonald 2000). They see the scholarly interest that Firth took in their society as proof of
their own importance, particularly in contrast to other groups in the country.

In other cases, people have other kinds of reactions to the ethnographic works of which they
are the subject (Brettell 1993). Most often, people find anthropological writings about them of
little relevance to their lives. Others have reacted negatively to anthropological works, particularly when it is entangled in a historical and political context over which the anthropologist has
little control. Indigenous groups such as Australian Aboriginal people, Māori people in New
Zealand, American Indians in the United States, and First Nations people in Canada see the
work that anthropologists have conducted about them since the nineteenth century as yet
another form of **colonial** appropriation of their knowledge and lifeways, and no longer welcome researchers. This has led some to argue that work conducted by an 'insider' or a 'native'
anthropologist is inherently more 'authentic' than work produced by an 'outsider'. However,
this position quickly runs into difficulties because identity is always the product of multiple factors such as age, social class, education, and gender, all of which can create social distance just as
easily as they can emphasize insiderness (Narayan 1993). In addition, the very act of conducting
research creates a divide between the researcher and the research participants.

There have been cases of ethnographic work causing major discontent because they have
exposed aspects of social life that contradict the narratives that people want to tell others and
themselves about their society. For example, in the 1990s, Anastasia Karakasidou conducted
fieldwork among Greek Macedonians, a minority group living in Greece, and argued that they
felt greater affinity with Slavic Macedonians to the north than with the Greek majority. This
somewhat unsurprising finding contradicted the Greek national ideology of unity, and the
author and the publishers that had agreed to publish her book received death threats from
Greek nationalists. The prestigious publishing house reversed its decision to publish the book,
prompting the condemnation of many anthropologists. The book was eventually published by
another, equally prestigious press (Karakasidou 1997).

What these various examples demonstrate is that, because anthropologists study people in the
context of their culture and society, all anthropological knowledge is situated, meaning that it is
always coloured by the context in which it is produced, particularly by the structures of power
that are inherent in any kind of research that involves other people. This is a recognition that
anthropology has inherited from **postmodernism**, which is suspicious of the faith in the power
of science and insists that there are always multiple perspectives on every aspect of human life.

Ethics in ethnographic fieldwork

Respect, care, and sensitivity are concerns of utmost importance when conducting ethnographic fieldwork. Anthropologists' actions have consequences, and they do not embark on
ethnographic projects that are likely to result in foreseeable harm to the research participants, to
the anthropologist her- or himself, or to the discipline of anthropology (e.g., by preventing
other anthropologists from conducting research in the same location in the future). Unlike
some anthropologists in the past, today's researchers cannot coerce research participants to divulge
information with which they are not willing to part, and the welfare of research participants
always overrides the interests of science. Anthropologists also have to obtain permissions from the
authorities governing the location of the fieldwork, in the form of a research visa for example.

Box 2.4   Margaret Mead's fieldwork in Samoa

Margaret Mead (1901–78), one of the best-known anthropologists of the twentieth century, was a student of Franz Boas at Columbia University in the 1920s. Boas suggested that
she conduct fieldwork about adolescence on a small island of American Samoa, where
she spent about six months in 1925–26. By today's anthropological standards, her fieldwork was brief, but for a young woman at that time to set off for a far-away place for an
extended period of time was exceptionally daring, particularly as Mead was frail and sickly.

In 1928, she published a book for a popular readership titled (in the vocabulary of the
time) *Coming of Age in Samoa: A Psychological Study of Primitive Youth for Western Civilization*.
It was designed to demonstrate that the understanding of adolescence as a period of turmoil that was then thought to be universal to humanity was in fact specific to Western
societies. The book described Samoan society as carefree about sexuality, echoing representations of Polynesian societies that had circulated in the West since early European
contacts in the late eighteenth century. She framed the book as a 'lesson' for an American
readership that was designed, in the spirit of cultural relativism, to shatter conventional
and conservative ideas about sexuality. This lesson contributed to the book's sensational
reception at the time. It is widely thought to have been a major inspiration for the sexual
revolution of the 1960s, and Mead remained a figure of considerable public visibility until
her death.

A few years after she died, Derek Freeman, a New Zealander teaching at the Australian
National University who had also conducted fieldwork in Samoa but published very little
about it, authored a book titled *Margaret Mead and Samoa: The Making and Unmaking of an
Anthropological Myth* (1983). He argued that Mead had been deceived by the Samoan young
women with whom she had spent time and that in fact Samoan society was repressive,
puritanical, and conservative, just like much of the rest of the world. Freeman garnered considerable media attention, in which the debate was frequently over-simplified, and claimed
that his critique questioned the credibility of anthropology as a discipline in its entirety.

Freeman brought to his analysis his own deeply conservative assumptions about
humanity, in stark contrast to the liberal and relativistic stance taken by Mead, who was
anxious to demonstrate that societies can be vastly different from one another. Before
Freeman, many anthropologists had already taken Mead's book and the message it was
designed to convey with a grain of salt; it was a work of its time. Mead and Freeman were
writing about different aspects of Samoan society which, while seemingly contradictory,
in fact operate simultaneously. Neither is completely right or wrong, despite Freeman's
insistence that Mead had been 'hoaxed' by Samoans. As for educated Samoans who have
followed the controversy, they maintain that what Westerners write about them is of little
relevance to their lives and that neither Mead nor Freeman really understood their society. If anything, Samoans have reacted negatively to the over-exoticized picture of their
society that Mead had painted.

What the controversy highlights is that there is never a unique understanding of how
society and culture work. Rather, society and culture are always subject to multiple interpretations, depending on whose perspective one takes and the assumptions one has. The
task of anthropology is to understand how particular perspectives, whether those of the
anthropologist or those of research participants, shape the views that emerge from one's
research (Shankman 2009, Tcherkézoff 2000).

After fieldwork, anthropologists ensure that they store their data securely to prevent them from being accessed by parties who may cause harm to research participants, and they do not publish information that may have the same effect. When disseminating the result of their analysis, they exert care to ensure that the identity of research participants remains confidential, unless the latter have specifically agreed to be identified. When publishing photographs or releasing video footage, anthropologists ensure that the people depicted have consented explicitly to being photographed if they are identifiable. If possible, anthropologists maximize the possibility that their research will improve the lives of research participants, and they ensure that research participants have access to their publications or other forms of dissemination if they so desire. Altogether, these concerns constitute the **ethics** of fieldwork. In many respects, fieldwork is no different from any other social situation in which people interact with one another: they must respect one another and be attentive to each other's priorities and needs.

Anthropologists ensure that the people whose lives they seek to understand are participating in the research willingly and that they understand the purpose of the research as much as possible. This precept is referred to as **informed consent**. Psychologists, sociologists, medical researchers, and many others are also required to obtain informed consent from the people involved in their research. In these disciplines, researchers are required to hand out a form to research participants explaining the purpose of the research and the participants' rights, and to ask participants to sign the form.

While these ethical principles may seem uncontroversial, they hide considerable complexities. For example, respecting the interests of some research participants may have the unintended effect of harming other research participants. It is sometimes difficult to predict how the results of ethnographic research will be used by third parties, particularly when the fieldwork takes place in situations where there is considerable power imbalance. Situations in which an ethnographer witnesses illegal or immoral activities (e.g., drug dealing, human trafficking, predatory lending, domestic violence) pose particularly thorny questions, and may bring the anthropologist's materials to the attention of authorities. Written informed consent forms are often problematic in fieldwork for a number of reasons: research participants are not necessarily literate; they may see written documents as a form of institutional surveillance that they would rather avoid; they may undermine the trust they have established with the ethnographer; and they may question how being asked to sign a form articulates with the promise of anonymity (Wynn and Israel 2018). Anthropologists must navigate these complexities as tactfully as they can. For example, they may establish research participants' informed consent orally rather than in writing and ensure that it covers interactions over a long period of time.

Because of these complexities and because fieldwork is often unpredictable, ethical principles for anthropological fieldwork take the form of general guidelines rather than precise rules. Fieldworkers encounter many situations in which they have to make decisions based on their best judgement. To help anthropologists think through the ethical implications of their research, professional associations of anthropologists in different countries have produced documents that spell out ethical guidelines. These guidelines first appeared in response to moments of crisis in the discipline in the 1960s, such as accusations that U.S. anthropologists had conducted covert research abroad during the Cold War. The need for ethical guidelines in research across disciplines also emerged as a result of scandalous events in medicine, when it transpired that medical researchers had conducted research on vulnerable people (indigents, prisoners, racial minorities) that involved withholding treatment for illnesses or administering drugs known to have harmful effects. Guidelines for ethics in anthropology thus emerged in a context of acute sensitivity about the ethics of research in general.

Box 2.5   Ethical guidelines

National anthropological associations have devised ethical guidelines that reflect local priorities, values, concerns, and contexts as well as subscribe to generally accepted norms and standards of conduct for anthropologists. These guidelines are periodically revised to deal with new situations and issues.

The American Anthropological Association adopted a Statement of Principles of Professional Responsibility in 1971 following allegations that anthropologists had conducted secret intelligence-related or counterinsurgency work. A new code of ethics was proposed in 1984 and a revised code was adopted in 1990. The British Association of Social Anthropologists' (ASA) first Ethics Guideline was adopted in 1987 and revised in 1999. Its most recent Ethics Guidelines were drafted by the ASA Executive Committee in 2010–11 and approved in October 2011. The Australian Anthropological Society adopted its first Code of Ethics in 1985. This was revised in 2003 and further revisions were adopted in 2012. The Association of Social Anthropologists of Aotearoa New Zealand Incorporated Code of Ethics was adopted in 1987 and amended in 1990 and 1992.

The principles laid out in ethics guidelines are broad and require anthropologists to interpret them in the context of their research. They can be fruitfully supplemented by case studies that consider specific situations in which anthropologists were faced with ethical issues and describe how they managed the situations (Cassell and Jacobs n.d.). With the passage of time and as professional priorities change, ethics codes are revised and updated, and this in itself makes clear that there can be no one ethical code that will do for all anthropologists working in all contexts and for all time. It also follows that the work of anthropologists from earlier periods cannot always be judged by contemporary standards. For example, early ethics guidelines did not refer to informed consent, while recent guidelines do.

On a pragmatic level, professional anthropologists, including postgraduate students, must seek the approval of an institutional review board or ethics committee of a university prior to undertaking fieldwork. An application typically presents the research in broad strokes and describes how ethnographers will ensure that they comply with ethics principles. Because review boards are frequently made up of scholars working in other disciplines, anthropologists sometimes find it difficult to explain the specific characteristics of ethnography, which are very different, for example, from psychological experiments conducted with participants that the psychologist will never see again. The complexities of informed consent often generate bottlenecks in these processes.

Ethics review boards form part of the increasingly time-consuming and authoritarian **audit culture** in which we find ourselves, namely an environment in which bureaucratic procedure has become more important than what the procedures are supposed to achieve (M. Strathern 2000). Viewed cynically, institutional review boards are more concerned with protecting universities and institutions from legal action if something goes wrong with the research than with ensuring that research is conducted ethically.

Do no harm: a complicated agenda

If ethics in fieldwork can be summarized in one brief sentence, it is the following: 'do no harm'. But the simplicity of this admonition is deceptive, as David Mosse, an anthropologist of development, discovered. After working for several years as a development consultant in rural India on a British aid project focused on poverty, Mosse was asked by the U.K. Department for International Development to write an ethnography of the project. He described this task as 'a chance to reflect on what had been a rich, challenging and frustrating experience, through which I learned much about bilateral aid, participation, project management and the livelihoods of very poor "tribal" communities in a politically and administratively marginal region of India' (2005, viii). Following contemporary conventions, Mosse sent drafts of his ethnography to people who had worked on the project to ask them for comments. Throughout the research Mosse had been their co-worker, studying while also working as an **applied** or **practising anthropologist**. As a consultant, his job was to produce evaluations and recommendations, but as an anthropologist his task was to question the assumptions on which the project was based, such as the usefulness and efficacy of international aid. While many of the people who read Mosse's work before it was published approved of it, some, particularly those in management positions, objected to his account, disagreed with his conclusions, and opined that much of the book manuscript should be rewritten. Mosse offered to add a postscript outlining the objections, but he was not prepared to rewrite the manuscript. There followed a series of written complaints to Mosse's academic managers, his publisher, his university's institutional review board, and to the chair of the United Kingdom's Association of Social Anthropologists. In an attempt to resolve matters, a daylong meeting was arranged between the different parties involved. In the end, Mosse was able to publish the book, but with some added alternative points of view. However, the process had strained friendships and undermined trust. It is also likely that some development organizations will think twice in future before allowing an anthropologist to conduct fieldwork in their midst.

The ethical issues in this case had nothing to do with informed consent, which Mosse had obtained. Rather, they concerned possible harm, as those who complained found the ethnography too critical of the project it analyzed. Predicting the possible consequences of a book is never straightforward, and negotiating between what one group considers negative and what another reads as honest poses challenges. Ethnographies are not simply accounts of events; rather, they present multiple perspectives, which may differ from the 'authorized interpretations' of events, in this case those of the managers. In addition, the ethnographer recognizes that the ethnography is itself a part of the social world it seeks to represent. In short, fieldwork is always political because it involves dealing with competing perspectives, power relations, and messy social encounters, and it is itself value laden.

Ethnographic ethics in wartime

Even though ethics guidelines were formalized only in the last few decades of the twentieth century, ethical issues were just as relevant to earlier generations of anthropologists as they are today. Throughout the history of the discipline, anthropologists have periodically voiced their ethical position on current events, sometimes at their own peril. A well-known case is that of Franz Boas publicly objecting, at the end of World War I, to anthropologists working as war spies, for which he was roundly criticized by the American Anthropological Association (AAA) on account of the fact that the objection shed a negative light on the profession. Since then, he has been applauded for the stand he took.

During World War II, many American, British, and other anthropologists supported the war effort against the Axis powers by working with the military and other government organizations. For example, the U.S. Far East Office of War Information (OWI) employed a dozen anthropologists to learn about Japanese society and culture and used this knowledge to evaluate the likely success of particular military strategies, including the production of propaganda leaflets to persuade Japanese soldiers to surrender. However, while anthropologists had some success in changing the attitudes of the military and bringing about what they hoped would be a speedy conclusion to the war, some were dismayed when their employers did not take their work seriously in developing policies (Price 2002). In the spring of 1945, the director of the OWI told the U.S. president that his office predicted that Japan was ready to surrender, but the United States nonetheless went ahead with plans to drop two atomic bombs on Japanese cities, with incalculable loss of civilian lives.

Anthropologists did not take a unified stand during World War II. Some were concerned that their knowledge would be used against the people they studied. Others sought to use their skills to help bring an end to a terrible war as quickly as possible and considered it their duty to fight against fascism, totalitarianism, and genocidal regimes. Some who had contributed to the war effort, including Margaret Mead, resolved never again to produce materials that would be kept from the people they were written about. On the German side, anthropologists also had to make choices, in some cases to leave Germany rather than remain in a fascist state, and in others to produce research that supported the racist ideology of the Nazi regime. In 1964–65, at the height of the Cold War, the U.S. military funded Project Camelot, a secret project that contracted anthropologists and other social scientists with expertise in Latin America to determine the factors that would predict social unrest and thus political opposition to right-wing regimes. When it was exposed, it became a major impetus for the professional organisations to establish codes of ethics.

These issues today are not simply of historical interest, as militaries continue to employ the services of anthropologists. Between 2007 and 2014, the Human Terrain System (HTS) of the U.S. military employed anthropologists to gather information in Iraq and Afghanistan. The U.S. government presented HTS as a means to win the 'hearts and minds' of the occupied populations, potentially reducing the number of military confrontations. But gathering ethnographic information about people on the other side of a conflict is not only extremely difficult, it is also against basic ethical principles since this information is for the benefit of an invading power and can potentially be used to select individuals as targets of violence. Furthermore, the situation would prevent anthropologists from obtaining anything that resembled informed consent (González 2008). In October 2007, the AAA issued a statement condemning the HTS initiative for violating its code of ethics (American Anthropological Association 2007).

Ethnography: multidisciplinary, practising, and engaged

Because anthropologists conduct research on a very broad range of topics, it is common to identify areas of specialization within the discipline in terms of topical areas, such as environmental anthropology, medical anthropology, economic anthropology, legal anthropology, the anthropology of religion, or the anthropology of education. These areas of specialization are not mutually exclusive; for example, an anthropologist who studies the environment can also focus on legal, economic, and political aspects of environmental degradation or grassroot environmental activism. Because anthropologists cast such a wide net over their object of study, many of the questions they address overlap with those of other disciplines, such as, in this example, environmental science, law, economics, public health, and political science. Anthropologists often see these overlaps as an opportunity to understand human problems from a multidisciplinary perspective that benefits from different approaches to the same problems. As a result, anthropology is perhaps the most multidisciplinary of all social sciences. At the same time, anthropologists' focus on people's lived experience, a diversity of perspectives, the interaction between local and global dynamics, and holistic explanations has a great deal to offer to sister disciplines.

While the gravitational centre of the discipline continues to be the academic institutions that host anthropology programmes, an ever-increasing number of anthropologists practise their skills in other professional contexts, such as government, business, international bodies, philanthropic foundations, and non-academic research organizations. Some use their anthropological expertise to advise corporations on matters such as consumer behaviour or the organization of workplaces. Others work in areas of social welfare; for example, senior managers in global cities with diverse populations require professionally trained experts to provide information on the needs of diverse constituencies that make use of hospitals, schools, and transportation. One prominent Korean American anthropologist and physician, Jim Yong Kim, was director of the HIV/AIDS programme of the World Health Organization in 2004–06 and president of the World Bank in 2012–19. Such anthropologists are known as applied or practising anthropologists.

Until the mid-twentieth century, anthropology was mostly focused on small-scale communities embedded in colonial empires, what Michel-Rolph Trouillot (1991) called the discipline's 'savage slot'. Indeed, early anthropologists were able to do their work thanks to colonialism, in that it gave them access to the colonized societies they documented. Since the 1980s, however, the colonial roots of anthropology have become the subject of considerable self-criticism and criticism by others, notably educated members of the societies in question. This has led to calls to **decolonize** the foundations and practices of the discipline (Alonso Bejarano, López Juárez, Mijangos García, and Goldstein 2019). Another consequence is that today anthropologists research a much broader range of topics and locations in both the Global South and the Global North, and are doing so with a considerably greater political edge than before. Thus, in contrast to the past when anthropologists would conduct fieldwork in the colonial world without needing to mention colonial oppression, there is today a strong tendency among anthropologists to focus on marginalized, oppressed, and disenfranchised groups. Joel Robbins (2013) termed this focus the discipline's 'suffering subject', which has replaced the 'savage slot' of yesteryears. It has led anthropologists to be critical of the structural factors that place research participants in vulnerable positions and to champion their cause in various ways. For example, anthropologists have provided evidence to help research participants' legal claims, documented the impacts of environmental degradation on villages and neighbourhoods, and campaigned against resource-extraction projects that disrupt lives and endanger people's health. They have worked with communities to reverse the loss of Indigenous languages. They have denounced in the media injustices perpetrated by governments on minority populations. They have worked with development agencies and communities to ensure that development projects are sensitive to social and cultural contexts rather than imposing unquestioningly a capitalist vision of progress on local groups. This is **engaged** or **activist anthropology** (Kirsch 2018).

Paul Farmer, a medical anthropologist and physician, is one anthropologist who has committed to a lifetime of work to raise awareness of the social conditions that have an impact on health and well-being. Along with Jim Yong Kim, the former president of the World Bank mentioned earlier, and others, Farmer founded in 1987 Partners in Health, an NGO dedicated to improving healthcare among the poor in various countries of the world. A key focus of his work has been to understand **structural violence,** namely the recognition that the lack of access to basic resources (e.g., food, water, healthcare, education, stability) increases the likelihood that people will suffer from poor health. For example, poverty leads some young women to seek economic survival in sex work or enter into relationships that offer the promise of a better life, and thus increases the risk of sexually transmitted infections like HIV to themselves and their children (Farmer 2001). Structural violence differs from physical violence. It is the outcome of a complex set of intersecting factors that together make the lives of the poor, marginalized, and powerless shorter, less healthy, and more difficult than those of the privileged.

Global dynamics are often implicated in structural violence. The many countries of the Global South that have experienced economic crises since the 1980s have turned to the International Monetary Fund, the World Bank, and wealthy countries for loans, but these loans have come with strings attached. Donor organizations and countries expect countries that receive aid to implement **structural adjustment programmes**, which have cut budgets for health and education. Economic development projects designed to boost national economies (e.g., mines, dams, agriculture, forestry projects) often drive the poor from their lands and render them unable to support themselves. Yet poverty is not inevitable; it is invariably the result of policies pursued by powerbrokers, politicians, and corporations. Engaged anthropologists are uniquely positioned to shed light on large- and small-scale factors that together create poverty, ill health, and suffering.

Working on behalf of marginalized people is a matter of not only good intentions but also understanding situations that are often more complex than meets the eye. For example, Nayanika Mookherjee (2010) conducted fieldwork in Bangladesh among *birangona*s or 'war heroines', women who had been raped by the Pakistani military during the brutal Bangladesh war of independence in 1971. These women have since lived with the consequences of sexual violence, compounded by poverty and marginalization. Their gender, social-class position, and poverty mean that their voices are not heard, yet more powerful middle-class activists, who themselves are former victims, call on them when they can be of strategic use to advance whatever cause they may be promoting. Activists from privileged backgrounds incorporated the *birangona*s' stories into their own narratives of the 1971 war, but rather than giving voice to them, they silenced them by refashioning their experiences to fit the story the activists wanted to present. Even though they were motivated by good intentions, powerful women nevertheless exploited the trauma of powerless women to come to terms with their own past experiences of violence. At the same time, Mookherjee recognizes the danger that she too could become a part of what she critiques. Engaged anthropology thus recognizes the multilayered complexity of activism on behalf of the oppressed that goes beyond simply the desire to do good.

An emphasis on holism (the recognition that human existence is always informed by many different dynamics) enables anthropologists to make sense of complex problems. For instance, when Gillian Tett (2010) resolved to understand how different parts of the financial sector in the Global North worked, or rather how they ultimately did not work, she set out in painstaking detail how each part of the sector intersected with all the others. Two years before the financial crash of 2008, Tett had realized that financial institutions moved debts around the financial system in ways that were not sustainable, yet when she publicly predicted the crash, she was either ignored or denounced. Tett had originally conducted fieldwork in Tajikistan, where she studied diverse topics such as marriage rituals and goat herding, to understand how all aspects of Tajik life fitted together, and her anthropological training led her to analyze how all parts of a system were connected to one another, rather than just focusing one sector of finance.

Engaged anthropologists need both professional skills and social networks to make their fieldwork possible. Two anthropologists, Marianne Maeckelbergh and Karen Ho, the former as an activist with anarchist anti-globalization groups and the latter as an investment bank employee on Wall Street, worked for the organizations or groups they write on and are part of the cultures they analyze (Maeckelbergh 2009, Ho 2009). They both recognize that their work as anthropologists would not have been possible had it not been for their prior activism and employment, respectively. But they also had to consider carefully the ethical issues that arose when their roles changed from activist and employee to researcher. They were ethically unable to use information about specific individuals and situations that they were privileged to prior to their research (Figure 2.2).

Figure 2.2 Occupy Bank of America, 15 March 2012. Activists 'moved in' to a branch by setting up a sidewalk living room reasoning that 'the bank took our homes so we're moving in with them'. A half-dozen people were arrested. (Courtesy of Mike Fleshman)

The ethnographies by these two anthropologists deserve comparison for several reasons. Both dealt with global issues and both were based on fieldwork in 'home' spaces. But in both cases, the physical location of the fieldwork was often hard to pinpoint in the **deterritorialized** and virtual spaces in which global finance and alter-globalization protest movements take place. Both anthropologists focused on the global inequalities that have become increasingly more pronounced, albeit from different starting points.

The Wall Street investment bankers among whom Ho conducted fieldwork prior to the 2008 crash were hard-working high achievers from privileged backgrounds, typically graduates of Ivy League universities. In the banks, they had the best-paid and most prestigious front-office jobs. The economic models they used were carefully selected to legitimize the status quo. They naturalized assumptions about markets and wealth, leading them to believe that these assumptions reflected the only possible way in which economies could prosper. So tenacious were these beliefs that bankers held on to them even in the face of their repeated failure to produce long-term growth and prosperity. Yet the ideas they worked with were the consequence of the elimination by the government of banking regulations that had been put in place in the United States after the Great Depression of 1929 to prevent the shortsighted profit-oriented speculations of bankers from causing future crises. The 2008 financial crisis thus happened because of the cultural assumptions of professional and political elites and their lack of historical knowledge of how they came to have these assumptions. Ho was only able to access this world because of her 'institutional kinship', which is to say her affinity to the culture she studied.

Maeckelbergh's ethnography concerned alter-globalization activists who protest against global corporations that seek profit at the cost of human and environmental well-being. As the

Box 2.6 Fieldwork in time of pandemic

Medical anthropologists have always worked in places where contagious diseases such as Ebola, bubonic plague, and SARS have caused fear, sickness, and death. They study ongoing global pandemics such as HIV/AIDS, tracking different cultural responses, the discourses surrounding them and unequal access to care (Benton 2015). Some anthropologists help develop culturally informed education campaigns to raise awareness of viral or bacterial transmission of disease (Sams et al. 2017). The rapid worldwide spread of the novel coronavirus Covid-19 beginning in December 2019 is the latest such disease. This time all anthropologists, rather than just those who specialize in medical issues, find that they need to take disease into account in their work because most ethnographic fieldwork assumes that ethnographers and research participants are able to interact with one another in face-to-face contexts, which places everyone in danger of infection.

With many countries in lockdown in 2020 and 2021, many ethnographers had to leave their fieldwork sites and traditional participant observation was abruptly halted. Some anthropologists directly experienced the precarity they often study, with futures suspended and jobs at risk. Others managed to maintain everyday forms of sociality with their interlocutors through social media. For example, no longer able to take part in live music performances, ethnomusicologists explored musical gatherings on balconies in Italy, showing how such shared rituals boost morale, reduce isolation, and foster social solidarity (Jacobsen 2020). Others considered how illness can become a pretext for stigmatization and victim blaming, often targeting groups that are already at risk of infection and death because of poverty, racism, and other forms of structural violence. But anthropologists also recorded how communities come together to help each other where states fail to provide adequate support. In New Orleans in the United States, carnival krewes built on pre-existing cultural practices to purchase and deliver food to health workers, keeping local restaurants in business and employing out-of-work musicians to deliver the food (Radice 2020).

In times of global pandemic, anthropologists can help shed light on not only individual and shared trauma but also the resilience and cooperation that sustain human groupings.

socially just world that the activists aim to bring about does not yet exist, Maeckelbergh wrote an ethnography of how activists understand and organize their activism. For them, means and goals are not distinguished, as they describe it: 'the processes we use to achieve our immediate goals [are] an embodiment of our ultimate goals, so that there is no distinction between how we fight and what we fight for, at least not where the ultimate goal of a radically different society is concerned' (2009, 66). Unlike Wall Street bankers who accept and reinforce the status quo, alter-globalization activists work to find alternative solutions to the world's problems. They see decision making not as the imposition of a majority position on a dissenting minority but as the outcome of consensus. It is not without conflict, but it is based on inclusive and participatory principles that recognize the needs of all members of society.

Both Ho and Maeckelbergh seek to understand the everyday practices and assumptions of the cultures they study. They were simultaneously insiders and outsiders in these cultures and both tackled, from very different perspectives, what is perhaps the most pressing social issue of our global world today, social inequality.

Anthropologists' works and lives

Modern anthropology is based on ethnographic fieldwork. The requirement to spend significant periods of time living among research participants, learning their language, viewpoints, concerns, and lifeways has remained constant for over a hundred years. Ethnography continues to be a fundamentally embodied empirical exercise that requires ethnographers to use themselves as a primary methodological tool through which they gather data and then organize, interpret, and analyze the information that they have collected.

In other respects, the aims and methods of anthropology have undergone considerable changes, as ethnographers have turned to novel ways of conducting fieldwork and interacting with research participants. The dividing lines between anthropologists and research participants have blurred. This is particularly so when anthropologists study their own ethnic, religious, or professional groups and have to deal with the methodological and ethical complications this situation poses for their work.

Ethical issues have long mattered to anthropologists. Over time, anthropologists have become increasingly concerned about ethics and have developed ethics guidelines to negotiate the difficulties they encounter during and after fieldwork. This is also a reflection of the recognition that the people anthropologists write about have access to what is written about them and the result of concerns about situations in which the work of anthropologists may be used against the very people with whom the anthropologist works.

The questions anthropologists ask, the issues they seek to understand, and the scope of their work have changed as the world has changed. However, the desire to understand each other in spite of difference or disagreement remains unchanged.

Key thinkers mentioned in this chapter:

Franz Boas; Paul Farmer; Bronislaw Malinowski; Margaret Mead

Key terms mentioned in this chapter (see Glossary):

Applied or practising anthropologist; Engaged or activist anthropology; Ethnographic fieldwork; Ethics; Ethnocentrism; Ethnography; Habitus; Informed consent; Participant observation; Situated knowledge; Structural violence

Questions for discussion/review:

1   Outline the distinctive features of ethnographic fieldwork.
2   How do anthropologists work to tackle ethnocentrism during fieldwork?
3   What do you understand by informed consent and why is it often complicated to obtain?
4   Why are ethical issues of such importance for anthropologists?
5   Describe the differences and similarities between applied anthropology and activist anthropology.

Chapter 3

Kinship

A typical exercise when teaching introduction to anthropology is to ask students to draw a kinship chart of their family. Over the years, we have seen many such charts and each one adds to our knowledge of both the predictability and diversity in how students understand the people they refer to as relatives. While some of the ideas that emerge are not surprising, for example, the fact that students from some parts of the world refer to their 'uncles' with different terms depending on whether they are a mother's brother or a father's brother, others are less predictable. For example, the accommodations some families are willing to make or refuse to make for unions between individuals of different ethnic or religious backgrounds reflect societal norms, the social and economic capital of the individuals involved, and the political and cultural contexts in which families make decisions.

Some students' gaps in knowledge about their own family are sometimes poignant. In one situation, a student's family chart consisted of just three people: his mother, his brother, and himself. His mother was the only daughter of Jewish parents who had arrived separately in Britain as children before World War II and so survived the Holocaust. The parents' names had been changed to English ones while they were children and they had died without ever telling their only daughter their birth names. The student's mother did not know precisely where in Europe her parents had come from. This student's chart was a stark visual reminder that the consequences of events like war and displacement can last for generations.

By contrast, some of our Scandinavian students have produced charts of great historical depth. Sometimes they bring to class privately published books with extensive genealogies going back several hundred years, reproductions of relatives' portraits, maps of family farms, and photographs of large family reunions. This extensive historical knowledge produces a clear sense of identity over long periods of time focused on the family farm, which is passed down over the generations, usually in the male line, even when family members have moved far away. Typically, it is a senior member of the family who takes it upon her- or himself, as guardian of the family heritage, to keep the family genealogy up to date by recording births, marriages, and deaths.

However, kinship is not just about recording who is connected to whom by **descent** and marriage, but it is also about the emotional bonds we have with others and the shared identities that shape us as persons and make these bonds possible. In one class, a young woman described how she and her twin sister were close. In this family, the mother was white and the father black. One twin looked like their mother and the other like their father. Both sides of the family treated the women equally well and yet one twin felt more comfortable with the father's side of the family and the other with the mother's side. Wider social attitudes and differences in the ways people are treated because of skin colour resulted in each twin feeling closer to the side of the family that shared her skin colour. Belonging may be shaped by forces in wider society beyond the family.

DOI: 10.4324/9781315737805-3

Another student's attempt to construct a kinship chart caused some bemusement and much discussion when presented in class. The student made the case for excluding from his family chart a sibling he did not get on with and including instead the pet dog he adored. No one in the class was surprised by the sibling conflict. The sticking point was not even whether to include the dog in the chart but where to place it. Should it be considered a quasi-sibling or perhaps a non-human child? Each available option would have resulted in a different configuration of the chart.

Complex intersections of historical and personal memory, place, love, conflict, identity, and the social and economic institutions that shape them are all entwined in the study of **kinship**, namely how people are related to one another and thus consider themselves **kin**. Perhaps more than any other aspect of our lives, kinship straddles and intermingles the public and the private, the biological and the social. It questions the very nature of these distinctions. This is why kinship has been a central focus of anthropology since its early days and continues to be, although in ways that have changed considerably over time.

Kinship old and new

Early anthropological works on kinship were both pioneering and imaginative. In the nineteenth century, as anthropology was forming as a distinct discipline, kinship came to occupy centre stage and marked out a field of study in which anthropologists could claim expertise. They documented the enormous complexity of the kinship systems of the peoples that inhabited the colonized world, demonstrating that, after all, they were not stuck in the 'primitive' state that colonial administrators, missionaries, and others often considered them to be. In the societies that nineteenth-century anthropologists studied, kinship was often a key social institution through which the political, economic, and religious life of the group was organized.

In the mid-nineteenth century, Lewis Henry Morgan, a lawyer from a well-to-do family with an interest in Native Americans, spent time in upper New York State among the Iroquois, who had developed a complex political confederacy. Based on his studies of how they organized kinship, he divided all known kinship systems into **classificatory kinship systems** and **descriptive kinship systems**. Classificatory kinship systems group together sets of kin, such as siblings and cousins, using a single term for both, while in descriptive kinship systems sets of kin are described using different terms, for example, calling siblings and cousins with different terms. In many classificatory systems, one word describes both a father and father's brother, while in a descriptive system, a father and a father's brother are described by different terms, such as 'father' and 'uncle'.

Collecting kinship terminologies required systematic and methodologically sophisticated work, such as the **genealogical method** of collecting social and vital statistics that W. H. R. Rivers, who participated in the 1898 Expedition to the Torres Straits described in Chapter 2, developed in the late nineteenth century. It consisted of asking people questions, such as 'what do you call So-and-so (when you need her attention)?' and 'how do you refer to So-and-so (when you talk about him to others)?', in order to elicit kinship terms, which were then mapped onto categories of biological relatedness. This method led to the production of kinship charts of the type still in use today, although the ways in which we now use and understand such diagrams is different.

Anthropologists used the kinship material gathered during the nineteenth and early twentieth century in order to support the prevailing evolutionary ideas of the time. They ranked different kinship systems according to the supposed evolutionary stage of development of the societies in order to show that the simpler systems had evolved into those considered more advanced, from less to more civilized forms of social organization. For these anthropologists, less advanced societies were not likely to survive when they came into contact with more advanced societies. And many nineteenth-century social theorists considered societies that trace descent through women and those with classificatory terminologies as less advanced. For example, in 1861, Johann Bachofen, a Swiss anthropologist, set out a theory that early societies had been 'matriarchal', by which he meant that they were dominated by women, but that as they evolved they became 'patriarchal' societies, in other words dominated by men. For him, contemporary societies in which descent is traced through women were lingering remnants of earlier forms of matriarchal social organization and evidence to support his evolutionary theory. Today, we know that matriarchy, which is unlikely to have ever existed as Bachofen imagined it, is a fundamentally different concept from matrilineal descent.

In a similar vein, some anthropologists thought that in the past there had been group marriage. As evidence, they described classificatory kinship systems in which only one term referred to the father and father's brother and perhaps all men of the father's generation, so that children would call 'father' any man who could potentially have been their biological fathers. John McLennan, a Scottish lawyer, imagined an earlier social state in which marriage did not exist and people lived promiscuously, which eventually turned into **polyandry**, a system in which one woman is married simultaneously to two or more husbands, and ultimately into **monogamy**, a system in which one woman and one man are married to each other (Stocking 1987). Today, these conjectural models are considered historically interesting but deeply flawed because there is no evidence to support them and they betray the **ethnocentrism** that underlies them.

Over time, the hypothetical reconstructions of the Victorian anthropologists gave way to studies of how kinship systems actually worked, rather than how they might have worked in an imagined past. In the nineteenth century, social scientists considered Australian Aboriginal people to be the prototypical representatives of an evolutionarily inferior form of humanity, which justified the land confiscations and other forms of violence that colonial settlers perpetrated against them. When anthropologists began documenting their descent and marriage rules, they encountered enormously complex and varied systems that became important for the development of anthropology. In the twentieth century, both British anthropologist A. R. Radcliffe-Brown and French anthropologist Claude Lévi-Strauss showed in different ways that underlying the extreme diversity of kinship systems were a few basic principles that enabled them to classify these systems into a finite number of categories. The tension between diversity and systematicity was central to all anthropological work on kinship for many decades.

The systematic collection and analysis of kinship systems were groundbreaking achievements, generating new theories and considerable interest in the kinship systems of distant and diverse societies. Over time, however, they became arcane and somewhat mechanical studies of rules and regulations which sometimes gave the impression that the members of the societies in question followed kinship rules unquestioningly because that is what tradition and the elders in the society expected. By the mid-twentieth century, for many students of anthropology, kinship studies had become an esoteric, quasi-mathematical, and somewhat dull field (Figures 3.1 and 3.2).

Kinship was revived and reinvigorated as a subject of study by moving away from legalistic rules and considering how individuals and groups strategically used their knowledge of kinship systems to achieve their own aims. Anthropologists had to understand how kinship rules worked and then try to understand how people talked about, manipulated, bent, and sometimes even broke them.

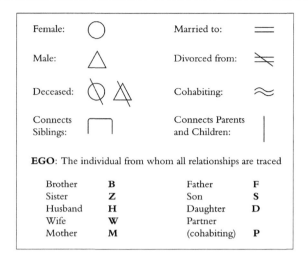

Figure 3.1 Symbols used in kinship diagrams.

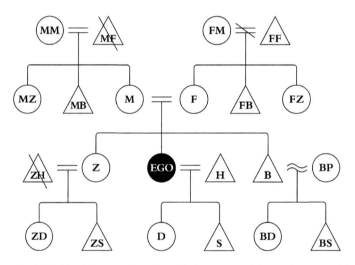

Figure 3.2 Standard kinship diagram showing relations traced from the central individual Ego.

In this respect, French sociologist Pierre Bourdieu's work in Algeria was groundbreaking. During fieldwork in a Berber (Amazigh) village in the 1950s, he recorded what people said about their kinship system and also what people actually did in practice (Bourdieu 1977). What people said they did and what they did overlapped but were not the same. Furthermore, whenever people in that society said anything, other people would interpret their statements in terms of who the person and his relatives were. For example, a man might claim that he had arranged a good marriage for his son to enhance his own social standing. In this society, marrying cousins who are related through men is more prestigious than if they are related through women. The man might present the marriage as one contracted between his son and his father's father's

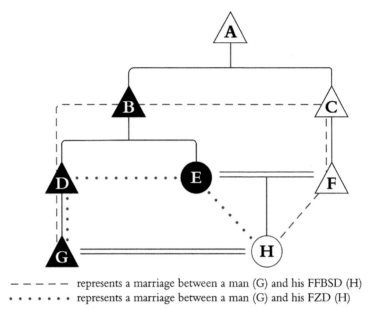

− − − − − represents a marriage between a man (G) and his FFBSD (H)
• • • • • • • represents a marriage between a man (G) and his FZD (H)

Figure 3.3 Kinship diagram showing marriage of G to H, who are cousins but also share the same great-grandfather. (Adapted from Bourdieu 1977, 42).

brother's son's daughter while in fact, more simply, it was between the young man and his father's sister's daughter. Both are possible as people are related as cousins in more ways than one. Those within the family would know if the marriage had in fact been arranged through the women in the family, rather than through men. In public, they may support the man's version in order to enable him to save face, but in private they may describe the simpler, but less prestigious account of how the marriage was arranged (Figure 3.3).

On the basis of these observations, Bourdieu showed that the kinship diagrams anthropologists had been producing until then were not the objective records of facts that they thought they were. People could describe kinship links in ways that served their purposes and anthropologists needed to take these factors into account. Today, the strategic maneuverings and the official accounts of how marriages are arranged are part of the data that anthropologists use to understand the complexities of actual kinship relations in practice, in the same way that people on the ground pay a great deal of attention to these different perspectives in their everyday lives.

Systems of descent

The **family** is a social institution found, in one form or another, in every society. A seemingly simple and straightforward definition of the family is a unit of people who are related by marriage and descent. However, what counts as a family and how the family is structured vary widely across and within societies. For example, in sixteenth- and seventeenth-century England, the term 'family' referred to not only the spouses and their children but also anyone who lived under the same roof, including servants and other non-relatives (Saller 1984). Even further back in time, among the ancient Romans, from whom the English language has inherited the word 'family', a *familia* included **agnates**, that is people related by blood through males. Children belonged to the same family as their fathers' brothers, the latter's children, and their father's sisters, but crucially not to the same family as the children of their father's sister or the children of their mother's siblings. What constitutes a family is thus a question laden with both social and cultural meaning. When children are born, they are part of a **lineage**, which is made up of older generations and ancestors who are also part of the same descent group. Lineages may control the right to work on land and transmit property and status to their members. They give individuals an identity and a group they belong to, and they offer protection against rival lineages.

In many societies, descent is **unilineal**, meaning that a person belongs to either the mother's or the father's lineage, but not both. All members of society belong to a single clearly defined lineage. People in such societies still recognize as kin individuals who are genetically related to them but belong to a different lineage; rather, they inherit property, positions, names, and other attributes that define the lineage only through one of their parents, and at events where kinship is important, such as weddings and funerals, they will act as members of the lineage of only one of their parents. In **patrilineal descent systems** (from Latin *pater* 'father'), children born to a man belong to his lineage. But all his daughters' children belong to the **patriline** of their own father. In these systems, children inherit wealth and status from their fathers. Because women are born into one lineage and marry into another, they help men form alliances between different lineages, although they can also undermine these alliances. In patrilineal systems, one key relationship is that between a man and his mother's brother, who is expected to be indulgent and generous towards his sister's son. By contrast, fathers may discipline sons in order to raise them as worthy members of the lineage. A boy may seek refuge from a stern father in the home of his mother's brother, who belongs to a different lineage. These roles are normative and each man will be both a strict father to his sons and an indulgent mother's brother to his sister's sons. Patrilineal descent groups are common around the world (Figure 3.4).

Patrilineal descent systems contrast with **matrilineal descent systems** (from Latin *mater* 'mother'). In such systems, children belong to their mother's **matriline**, rather than to their father's lineage. While descent is through the mother, children generally inherit wealth and status from their mothers' brothers, and thus it is still men who hold power. While the status of

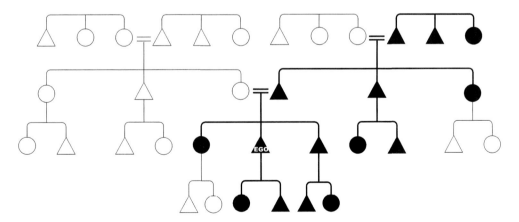

Figure 3.4 Patrilineal descent: the symbols shaded in black are members of the same patriline.

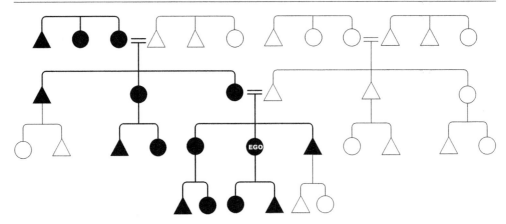

Figure 3.5 Matrilineal descent: the symbols shaded in black are members of the same matriline.

women varies across matrilineal societies, they tend to have more autonomy, power, and prestige than in patrilineal societies. As in patrilineal systems, the relationship between a man and his mother's brother is very important, but it has a different quality, as the mother's brother is the disciplinarian of his sister's son, while the father, who belongs to a different lineage from his son, is the indulgent relative, thus mirroring what happens in patrilineal systems. Matrilineal systems are less common than patrilineal systems, but they are found in widely different regions of the world, such as West Africa, South Asia, Melanesia, and in some Native American societies and among some minority groups in China. Some matrilineal groups have become patrilineal in recent history under pressure from state authorities or as an adaptive response to changes in social and economic conditions (Figure 3.5).

In contrast to unilineal descent systems, **bilateral descent systems** classify children as belonging to both their mother's and their father's descent line. This means that, unlike unilineal systems of descent, bilateral descent systems can never be exclusive and unique groups, as one person's set of kin differs from another's, with the exception of the unmarried children of a couple, who share the same kin. People in bilateral descent systems may inherit from both descent lines, though what they inherit from each side may vary from one society to another. While bilateral descent systems include all kin on both sides of the family, many societies have a patrilineal bias. This is evident in European societies and societies derived from Europe, where children traditionally inherit their father's last name.

Joining together two families through marriage is usually expected to result in the birth of children for the lineage to which the children belong. The children are kin to relatives on both sides of the family, that of the mother and that of the father, even though only in bilateral systems do they belong to both descent groups. In many cases, each parent is considered to contribute something particular and distinct to the child. While modern scientific understanding informs us that a child has an equal share of genetic material from her or his mother and father, in some societies people consider that children are made of the flesh of the mother and the bones of the father, or that the paternal seed outweighs the maternal blood that together make a child. In yet other cases, fathers are thought to have no role in the conception of children, although their input may be necessary for the development of the foetus and later the child's growth.

Such ideas have a profound effect on how individuals view themselves and their place in the family and in wider society. It may also have implications for what happens to people when they die. For example, in some Chinese societies, a deceased person undergoes a period of transition from living to dead to eventually become an ancestor with a place in the family tomb (Watson 1982). This transition requires that the flesh that came from outside the lineage through the mother, who married into the lineage, be removed so that only the bones that came from the father, and hence from the patriline, are placed in the tomb of the lineage. In this way, the deceased remain part of the family and may offer protection to the living members of the lineage. Storing the bones of the ancestors is a powerful symbol for the continuity of the family and ideas of shared substance.

In the late 1960s, the anthropologist David Schneider analyzed kinship as a symbolic system and North American kinship as based on symbols such as blood. Relatives by descent (blood) and relatives by marriage (law) may be equally kin, but people do not always consider them to be the same kind of kin. People have different expectations of both kinds of relatives and consider relatives by descent to be closer and more dependable than relatives by marriage. However, blood connections are not by themselves sufficient to keep a kin relationship active. For this, social interaction is required. Without it, blood kin will cease to consider each other as kin. Such is the case of brothers and sisters who are not in touch for long periods of time for many different reasons, including geographical distance, ideological, political, and social-class differences, and the fragmentation of kinship through divorce and remarriage. Blood may be a powerful symbol of kin connection, but on its own it is not enough.

The term kin may include more than just those who are born or married into families. People can become kin in a variety of ways, for example by adoption, by co-residence or through the consumption of shared substances such as breast milk. Modern reproductive technologies today make it possible for some individuals to have babies who are genetically related to them when natural conception is impossible. Who can access these reproductive technologies and which techniques are permitted or forbidden, even if medically viable, is legislated by state institutions and pronounced on by religious authorities. The recognition of a person as kin is a social phenomenon and the criteria on which this recognition is based varies across societies and over time.

The household

One concept that partly overlaps with the family but is not equivalent to it is the **household**. A household is a residential and economic unit (Yanagisako 2015). A household comprises people who live in a common home, which is also referred to as 'household', although what constitutes a home varies widely, even within the same society (e.g., house, flat, compound, camp, caravan, etc.). People who live in the same household contribute to the welfare of the unit by supplying food and other essentials, pooling wages, maintaining the physical environment (e.g., cleaning, organizing, repairing), and caring for members of the unit who need extra attention (e.g., children, the old, the ill). All of these tasks require domestic labour, both of a **material** kind, such as ensuring everyone has enough to eat, and of an **ideational** kind, such as meeting the emotional needs of others. The two elements of the definition of household are necessary because not all units of residence in which people live together are considered a household. For example, army barracks, elderly care facilities, and university residence halls are not households because their residents do not perform the kind of labour that is expected of members of a household. At times, a household can include people who are living somewhere else, for work for example, but still consider it as their home.

Members of a household sometimes belong to the same family, as in the traditional and somewhat idealized image of the nuclear family in the Global North, in which the mother, the

Box 3.1   Matrifocal households in a changing socialist society

In Cuba, the 1959 revolution led to a reconfiguration of families and residential arrangements (Härkönen 2014). Many low-income Cubans do not place much value on marriage and there is little difference between legalized and other types of conjugal relationships. A woman may call a man her 'husband' (*marido*) after a single date. Marriage is not seen as necessary to have children and there is no stigma attached to children who are born out of wedlock – all children are cherished equally. The ability to reproduce is valued above the marital bond, and children, rather than marriage, are the path to social adulthood. The bond between women and children is especially strong. While men are often described as irresponsible 'missing' fathers, fatherhood is nevertheless important for a man's social position and many men feel a strong emotional bond to their children, even when they may have lost contact with them for many years.

As a result, many households in Cuba are organized around a matriarch, who organizes the lives of other household members, particularly the children. This kind of residential organization is called a **matrifocal** household. Men with whom the matriarch has relationships may live in the household at different times, but the main responsibility for the economic and social life of the household rests on the woman. Matrifocal households are common throughout the Caribbean, particularly among poor people, who are predominantly descendants of African slaves. Middle-class white people in Caribbean societies have traditionally attributed matrifocal households to the moral deficiency of poor black people, blaming them on their members' inability to form nuclear families. However, matrifocal households are heir to the memory of women and men during centuries of slavery living under the constant threat of being separated and sold to a different slave owner. Today, they are an adaptive response to poverty and the precarity of work.

When the Soviet Union came to an end in 1991, the economic aid that Cuba had received from it ceased, salaries fell, and prices rose, making life hard for many people. Women became increasingly dependent on men's material contributions for survival. When they consider a man's suitability as a partner and a father for her children, women evaluate critically the extent to which he is capable of providing for their needs. This situation places men who struggle to make a living at a particular disadvantage and at risk of remaining childless. If they have failed to establish relationships with women in their youth or have lost contact with their children because of poverty or lack of interest, ageing men often suffer from loneliness. Regretting his earlier conduct, a man may seek to re-establish contact with his children, sometimes after decades of absence. Conversely, a woman may become the respected 'queen' (*reina*) of the family during old age. The more children and grandchildren she can gather around her, the more her status increases.

father, and their unmarried children all live together under one roof. But the reality is often much more complicated. Households everywhere include other people (e.g., a grandparent, a child from a previous marriage), who may or may not be related. In the Global North, particularly where housing costs make living by oneself or as a young couple prohibitively expensive, young people often share a household with one another as housemates (or 'roommates' in

North American English). They may share meals, help each other in times of need, and be close to one another, but they are not literally related to one another through kinship: for example, they do not inherit each other's wealth and do not pass on each other's family names to their respective children.

Lodgers were and still are a common feature of many households, particularly among the working classes, and they can be considered to be part of the household if they participate in its operations. In many societies of the Global South, urban households include younger relatives from the countryside who have come to town for their schooling, to see the bright lights, and to help urban relatives who are employed and cannot manage the household by themselves, particularly if the household is extensive. In some societies that practise **polygyny**, households sometimes consist of large compounds with several buildings around a yard, each designed to house a co-wife and her children; if they coordinate their economic activities by pooling or cooperating, then they can be considered to form a household.

The typical composition of households often changes over time. For example, a middle-class European household in the nineteenth century included one or more servants, which was no longer the case by the middle of the twentieth century because most households could no longer feed, house, and pay servants, and technology took over many tasks that servants were formerly responsible for.

Households adapt to changing circumstances, both material and otherwise. In countries like Spain and Italy, the collapse of the economy that followed the 2008 financial crash forced many younger adults with precarious jobs or no jobs, and sometimes their own children, to move back in with their ageing parents more or less temporarily, surviving as well as they could on the latter's pensions and savings (Narotzky and Pusceddu 2020). In the best of circumstances, members of the household live in relative harmony with one another, although adult children's dependence on their parents is often a source of shame. But the situation can become tense when adult children and their ageing parents do not share political and social values.

The household plays a central role in everyone's life in all societies, even though they are inherently unstable units of social organization, and tensions can easily arise between kinship organization and household composition.

Making kin: adoption

Adoption is a widespread way of creating new kin. In Polynesian societies, children frequently acquire new parents for a variety of reasons. Biological parents can 'give' a child to relatives who do not have children or to a grandmother who wants the company of a child, on whom she often dotes. Adopted children do not sever their relationship with their biological parents but simply add a new set of kin, which can come in handy when the children find that their biological parents are too disciplinarian or when there is not enough food in their biological home. Polynesians, who describe the adopted relationship as 'feeding', view the biological parents' action as a commendable act of love and compassion for the adoptive relatives and the adoption is always acknowledged by everyone. In these societies, adoption is a process of adding relatives rather than substituting them, as is the case in the Global North. Adoptive parents may record the relationship with the state, in which case the child can inherit property from the adoptive parents, or they may leave it as an informal and sometimes temporary arrangement, referred to as **fostering**.

Among Hindus in India, people traditionally adopted only if the social origin of the child was known. Having a son is important and couples without one may adopt the younger son of a close paternal relative, preferably the husband's brother's. Social considerations are satisfied since the adopted child was born into the same caste, lineage, and religion as the adoptive parents. In addition, a younger son who would have been under the authority of his older sibling gains in status by becoming an only son, who will eventually inherit his adoptive parents' estate.

In contrast, in the contemporary Global North, adoption often takes place across national boundaries and legally joins parents and children of different backgrounds. In recent decades, transnational adoptions have increased as fertility rates in the Global North have declined and the number of children locally available for adoption has fallen. Transnationally adopted children are placed in the care of couples from wealthy countries, often desperate to feel complete as a family by integrating a child into their extended families (Howell 2006). This is an active process: newly adopted children are made into kin through the clothes they are given, the food they are encouraged to enjoy, and the shared tastes they develop in their new family. Adopted children become kin through everyday shared experiences on special occasions such as birthdays and national holidays that are recorded in family photographs and videos. The state is concerned with the legal aspects of adoption, formally registering the children as citizens, changing their names, issuing new birth certificates, and recognizing the adoptive parents as their legal guardians. Transnational adoption entails both repeated symbolic acts and formal institutional documentation.

However, as the transnationally adopted children grow up, they often realize that while they may, for example, speak perfect Norwegian, like Norwegian food, and identify with Norwegian culture, they will always look Korean or Chinese. Yet they cannot speak Korean or Chinese nor feel at ease in a Korean or Chinese cultural context. Adoption agencies may facilitate 'homeland tours' for transnationally adopted children, along with their parents, to visit the country where they were born. Such tours include visits to the hospitals or orphanages where the adoptees may have spent time but they never include meetings with the birth parents or other biological kin. These tours do not help the adoptees engage with the culture and society of their birth, but instead reinforce their awareness that they are strangers in their country of birth and that they only belong in the country and culture into which they were adopted, however conditionally.

Making kin: assisted reproductive technologies

For those who feel that they cannot be a 'real' family without children but who cannot or do not wish to adopt, modern technology has made possible what was once impossible. **Assisted reproductive technologies** (ARTs), such as **in-vitro fertilization** (IVF) and **surrogacy**, enable individuals and couples to have their own children with a biological connection to at least one parent. However, as with all innovations, what is possible scientifically may not be culturally acceptable or legal, and countries have legislated ARTs in different ways. In some countries, single women, same-sex couples, women over the age of 50, and even the deceased may conceive children using ARTs. In other countries, ARTs are restricted to young married heterosexual couples and only the eggs from the wife and the sperm from the husband may be used to produce an embryo, which must be gestated in the womb of the wife. In these countries, often for religious reasons, no reproductive material from anyone other than the married couple is permitted to enter into the family and take the place of a 'legitimate' descendant.

A comparison between what is permitted in Israel and in some other countries in the Middle East helps show just how much access to the medical science of ARTs is mediated by states with different national and religious agendas. For a person to be considered Jewish, she or he must have a Jewish mother. In Israel, which has defined itself as a Jewish state, rabbis make religiously informed decisions about who counts as Jewish and they have permitted some third-party sperm donations from non-Jewish donors in fertility treatments (Kahn 2004). Non-Jewish sperm donation avoids any future unwitting genetic incest between the children resulting from the anonymous donation of sperm. Surrogacy is also permitted and single Jewish women are the preferred choice for a surrogate. This ensures that the child is Jewish through the gestating mother and the marital status of the woman means that there is no question of adultery, as might otherwise be implied if the woman were married. Lastly, because the state of Israel encourages Jewish citizens to have children, treatment in IVF clinics is subsidized by the state for Jewish patients, including both single women and lesbian couples.

The situation regarding IVF treatment in countries like Egypt and Lebanon could not be more different (Inhorn 2006). Third-party donations of any kind (sperm, eggs, embryos, uteruses) are not considered acceptable. Once again, science, technology, and religion intersect in the decision to make some treatments morally, religiously, and in some cases legally permissible, but others not. The situation in the Muslim world is further complicated by the fact that Muslims are divided into two main religious groups, Sunni and Shiʻa. Sunni and Shiʻa Muslims have different understandings of what is permitted in IVF treatments, and these are articulated in religious pronouncements, or *fatwas*, issued by the respective religious authorities. *Fatwas* are non-binding religious pronouncements but, as most Muslims seeking IVF treatment wish to conceive in religiously approved ways, they are taken seriously. For both Sunni and Shiʻa Muslims, IVF treatment is only offered to married couples, as conception should only take place within marriage. For Sunni Muslims, third-party donation is considered to be the equivalent of adultery and a child resulting from such IVF treatment will be considered illegitimate because such donation leads to a confusion of genealogy. In such cases, the child will not be able to inherit from the wife's husband.

For Shiʻa Muslims, the situation is more complex. In the late 1990s, an influential *fatwa* allowed married couples to seek IVF treatment using donor reproductive material. There are, however, religiously mandated consequences. For example, if a woman donates an egg to an infertile woman, the donor remains the mother of the child and the child will inherit from her, while the infertile mother who received the egg is considered as an adoptive mother. The same applies theoretically to a child born from third-party sperm donation. In this case, the child carries the name of the sperm donor and will inherit from him, while the man who raises the child, the social father, is considered his adoptive father. However, not all *fatwas* are accepted by all members of a sect and some Shiʻa religious authorities forbid sperm donation. In Iran, which is predominantly Shiʻa, it is illegal to use sperm from a man who is not a woman's husband in fertility treatment, as this would be considered akin to adultery. By contrast, because Shiʻa Islam allows for both polygyny and temporary marriage, a man can enter into a temporary marriage with an egg donor, who must be either single or widowed, as no married woman can have two husbands at the same time. In this situation, all those involved in the IVF treatment, the wife, the husband, and the temporarily married egg-donor wife are in a religiously, morally, and legally permissible situation, and a child born from this arrangement is legitimate. What appear to be at first glance neutral scientific technologies are made available globally, but they are redefined in local contexts where cultural, religious, and moral norms lead to the rejection of some technologically possible treatments and the creative incorporation of others.

Box 3.2   Posthumous conception: when the dead become parents

ARTs have made it possible for the dead to conceive biogenetically, as reproductive materials may be removed for preservation from a person before or after death. The first posthumous conception occurred in 1977 and the first child born from posthumous sperm retrieval in Britain took place in 1998. The right to reproduce is increasingly viewed as one that requires safeguarding and those who risk their lives, for example, by going to war, may sign 'biological wills' that specify what should be done with their genetic material should they die (Sabatello 2014). In Israel, such wills can be deposited in a biological will bank; in the United Kingdom, the Ministry of Defense offers pre-deployment fertility services for military personnel and recognizes the rights of deceased soldiers to conceive posthumously. Yet the possibility that the dead may become parents, sometimes several years after their death, raises complex religious, cultural, legal, and ethical questions about such matters as consent, inheritance, and legitimacy.

For example, in Britain in 1995, 30-year-old Stephen Blood fell gravely ill, and while he was in a coma, his wife Diane persuaded doctors to extract some of his sperm (B. Simpson 2001). Because he died without giving his consent to the procedure, the courts ruled that the sperm had been obtained illegally and refused the widow's request for it to be used in IVF treatment. She was eventually allowed to seek treatment abroad and conceived a son, Liam. However, as Liam was born more than two years after his bio-genetic father had died, the law did not allow Mrs. Blood to have the father's name on the child's birth certificate. It was only in 2008 that the law was changed in the United Kingdom to allow the name of a father to appear on the birth certificate of a posthumously conceived child in cases where the father had consented in writing for his sperm to be used by a specified woman after his death (Sabatello 2014).

Those who oppose posthumous conception argue that a child born this way ends up being treated as a 'substitute' for, or as a living memorial to, the deceased parent, which can cause psychological harm. They also question whether the parents of a deceased child have the right to use her eggs or his sperm to become grandparents when it is clear that children born this way will never have the opportunity to know their biological mother or father. This raises the question of the rights of parents to become grandparents even when their daughters and sons have died before producing heirs. People have always maintained relations with the dead through remembrance and ritual, and in some societies by transforming the dead into ancestors who can bless the living. Posthumous conception is perhaps no more than a modern way to deal with death and to turn a loss into something positive, namely a new life.

Since the end of the twentieth century, requests for posthumous conception that makes it possible for the dead to reproduce have increased significantly. In polls conducted in the United States and Japan, most people are in favour of allowing posthumous conception. What such requests make clear is that, for many people, the desire for children remains strong and is increasingly considered a right, even for the dead. For those who support posthumous conception, it is the biogenetic connection that makes 'real' kin.

ARTs make it possible to share genetic material within families and across generations. In some countries, for example, a fertile woman can donate eggs to her infertile sister. The biological mother of the child from the egg donation, the **genetrix**, becomes the social aunt of the child rather than its mother, while the gestating mother, who is the biological aunt, becomes the child's social mother, the **mater**. In this case the donation of an egg by one sister to another may be viewed as an act of substitution, the gift of a fertile egg to replace infertile ones. However, not all reproductive material donation between siblings is viewed as acceptable. The donation of sperm by a man to his sister so that she can conceive via ARTs would be viewed by most people as a problematic mixing of shared substance, as 'incest in a petri dish', even when no sexual intercourse is involved (Edwards 2000, 234).

In countries such as the United States, where ARTs are subject to fewer regulations, profit-driven private clinics can offer ARTs that are not permitted elsewhere. In some cases, such clinics offer services that enable individuals to make families to meet their understanding of marriage and family. In one case, a woman in her 50s referred to as Flora wanted to have a child with her much younger second husband (Thompson 2006). Because she was past menopause, natural conception was unlikely, so she asked one of her adult daughters from a previous marriage to donate eggs. The daughter's egg was fertilized with the sperm of Flora's current husband, with the understanding that the baby would be raised as the sister, rather than the child, of Flora's daughter. From one perspective, Flora was giving birth to her own grandchild, but from a social perspective she was establishing a heteronormative family with her new husband using her daughter's egg, genetic material from her own body at a generation's remove. The baby was also genetically related to Flora's first husband. The possible connotations of **incest** and adultery in this case were kept at bay by the technology offered by the clinic, with the daughter and her stepfather providing the genetic materials for the child to be gestated and raised by the mother and wife, Flora.

Where same-sex couples are legally entitled to use ARTs, decisions about how to plan a family often fall back on ideas of shared biogenetic substance to reinforce the connections between parents and children. In a lesbian couple, for example, one woman may choose to provide the egg and the other to gestate the embryo in her womb. In this way, both women are biologically connected to the child they have together, although they assume different roles (Machin 2014). If an anonymous sperm donor is selected, he is the biological father, the **genitor**, with no social or legal responsibilities to the child and the child has two mothers but no social father, or **pater**. The choice of sperm donor may become complicated when the lesbian couple is of mixed race (Newman 2019). In such a situation, if both women decide to conceive using their own egg, they face a choice: either to prioritize shared biogenetic relations between the children they will gestate by using the same sperm donor so that the children will be biological half-siblings, or to select egg donors who share the racial identification of each woman.

The global spread of ARTs demonstrates not only how important families continue to be but also how much time, effort, and money many people are willing to expend to have a family. In some cases, this has been transformed into the notion that one has the 'right' to be a parent, based on the ideology that modern individuals can choose when and how to have a child. This right of course assumes that the individual has the resources to make the choice to be a parent in the first place. Economic factors thus play a pivotal role in how people make their families.

Making kin: milk kin

In Arab countries, South Asia, and southeast Europe, it was, and sometimes still is, possible for two children who are not biogenetically related to one another to become kin when both are breastfed by the same woman (Clarke 2007). Such children are termed milk siblings.

Opposite-sex milk siblings are not permitted to marry. In Muslim households, girls are not required to cover their head after puberty in the presence of their opposite-sex milk siblings. Milk kinship is thus one way in which people ease social relations within households while adhering to religious and cultural norms about the separation of genders. In a society where first cousins are preferred marriage partners, a father may choose to prevent such a marriage if he sees it as politically or economically undesirable by making his child's first cousin a milk sibling.

Milk mothers, however, need to be carefully chosen for their moral qualities and character, sometimes even their looks, which are thought to be transmitted to the children they breastfeed. Women may refuse to breastfeed the child of another woman in certain circumstances, as happened in one case in Syria, where a couple had adopted a baby girl. The adoptive father tried to persuade his brother's wife to breastfeed the baby so that she would become the milk sister of his brother's child. The child would then have become the milk niece to her adoptive father and as such would not need to veil before him after she reached puberty. This was important, as in Islam the full adoption of a child is not permitted and the adopted daughter would remain bound by rules of segregation unless she became the milk niece of her adoptive father. The brother's wife, however, was not prepared to do this, possibly because babies available for adoption are suspected to be the result of illicit sexual relations and are thus stigmatized.

In the more distant past, milk kinship was not only an inter-familial matter but also one that served political designs (Parkes 2004). In societies made up of related lineages that joined together to further the goals of the collective group, powerful lineages required women from less powerful lineages to breastfeed their sons so that members of the less powerful lineage would support the powerful lineage in case of need. Milk kinship reinforced political alliances between lineages of different status, turning a matter of kinship into a matter of politics. Such systems were in place in southeast Europe and the Caucasus, where they were recorded in dynastic documents from the fifth to the fifteenth century, as well as northern and western India.

In recent decades, the rate of milk kinship has declined in the Arab world. Where it continues, women who become milk mothers to each other's babies often do so to turn a close friendship into an enduring kin connection through their children. Such relationships may be incorporated into state bureaucracy, as in the United Arab Emirates, where milk sibling relationships have to be registered. This is presumably to ensure that no marriages take place between milk siblings.

State-level metaphors of kinship

Kinship terms are often used as metaphors for a people's relationship to the nation, the state, or its leader. Many rulers in the history of the world have been called 'father', such as Mohandas Gandhi in India, Ho Chi Minh in Vietnam, Atatürk in Turkey, and Alexander the Great in ancient Greece. In India, it is common to refer to the nation as 'Mother India'. The scaling up of kinship to the level of the state is sometimes dramatized through rituals. For example, among the Merina of Madagascar before they were colonized by France in 1896, the king ritually blessed his subjects at the turn of the lunar year (Bloch 1987). This blessing replicated the ritual blessing that took place in every Merina household when the ancestors blessed the living family members through the intermediary of a family elder. Blessing was hierarchical: ancestors blessed their descendants just as the king blessed his subjects and incorporated them into the kingdom. Prior to the blessing ritual, both elders and the king visited the tombs of their respective ancestors to emphasize the continuity and togetherness of the lineage in one case and the society in the other.

Within families, blessing was emotionally charged and showcased fertility, prosperity, and the power of the ancestors to care for their descendants. The king's blessing of his people drew on the emotional charge of the family blessing, but it was a political ritual that legitimized the king's rule. The difference between the two rituals was that junior kin who received the ancestors' blessing would eventually become ancestors after death, whereas the king's subjects who received the king's blessing would never become sovereigns.

Kinship plays a central role in people's lives in all societies of the world. This is why it can serve as a powerful metaphor to strengthen the cohesion of society and emphasize the legitimacy of rulers. This is an example of what Émile Durkheim termed solidarity, the glue that holds society together. At the same time, we can shed a critical light on these dynamics and, from a Marxist perspective, analyze metaphors that rest on institutions that people think of as fundamental to life as a way of making them accept the social inequalities that keep them in positions of subservience.

Making kin: unclear families, voluntary kin, and commodified kin relations

People create kinship relations in many other ways. In the Global North, people believe that a typical family is a 'nuclear' entity consisting of a mother, a father, and their biological children, all living in one household, and that this arrangement takes its roots in ancient history. As many historians have demonstrated, at no point in the history of Europe and other industrial societies has the nuclear family been the majority family form, and its idealization is a nostalgic longing for a time that has never existed (Coontz 2016). Prior to the twentieth century, many women died in childbirth and their widowers remarried and had more children, many of whom also died young. Families also frequently included elderly kin, who had no one else to take care of them, and adult children commonly lived with their parents well after they married and had children in some parts of Europe, such as central Italy.

The nuclear family is as much a myth today as it has ever been and reflects a period in the life cycle of a family rather than a permanent condition, insofar as a couple may remain childless for several years before starting a family and are a nuclear family only so long as they remain together and their children are living in the same household. When children leave home, the nuclear family ceases and the parents return to being just a couple. In contemporary Europe and the Americas, the high divorce rate has replaced death in childbirth as the reason why many families today are complex combinations of kin, some related to each other by blood, others by marriage, others by not much, and the idea of the nuclear family has given way to that of the 'unclear' family (B. Simpson 1994). In families with step-parents, step-siblings, and an assortment of aunts, uncles, and grandparents, family members have to negotiate how to relate to the complex range of possible kin. Yet another consequence of divorce is the financial reckoning that follows when family courts order ex-spouses, usually ex-husbands, to provide child support to their ex-spouses. In Britain, over half of all fathers lose contact with their children within a few years of divorce, one reason being the emotional difficulty men experience in translating their love and responsibilities for their children into cash terms (B. Simpson 1997).

Alternatively, people may form strong bonds with other people who are not kin but replace their blood relatives and are often closer than the latter. These **voluntary** or **fictive** kin, who may form **chosen families**, often replicate local ideals of what a kin relation should be, provide emotional and material support, and can endure over time (Weston 1997). The term 'fictive', from the Latin *fictio* 'making, forming, or fashioning', implies a creative act rather than a sense of being somehow 'false'. Such bonds are common among people who do not fit into

heteronormative models of family, such as lesbian, gay, and transgender people, who may have been rejected or ignored by their blood relatives, and are often grounded in intimate relations that have given way to other kinds of intimacy, as well as commitments to children who may have various genetic and emotional relationships to the adults in the group. During the AIDS crisis of the 1980s and 1990s, when the illness in the Global North primarily affected gay men and the governments in Britain and the United States failed to act, chosen families became a crucial source of care for the ill and dying. Because they are not normative, such families must explicitly negotiate how to make a family in sometimes creative ways that are nonetheless based on a culturally contextualized understanding of what a normative family is.

When kin relations are established between people who are socially unequal, as in the case of women employed to care for the children of a working couple, they are often commodified by a contract of employment and payment for the services rendered. In the past, particularly among the wealthy in Western societies, nannies and servants took care of children and carried out the household labour. Even though the domestic labourers were paid for their services, they often formed voluntary kin relations with the children they cared for that were sometimes more significant than the children's relationship with their own parents. This is still the case today in many parts of the world.

A key difference between the past and the present is that, in the past, the domestic labourers were generally members of the same society as the employer but belonged to a different social class, whereas today they often are migrant labourers of a different national, ethnic, and religious background from their employers. Domestic labourers who care for wealthy people's children often leave their own children in the care of their own relatives, such as their sisters or mothers, as they migrate to work in a foreign country. This situation, called a **care chain**, constitutes a feminized and globalized transnational labour force raising the children of strangers in order to earn enough to support children at home, who sometimes hardly ever see their own mothers as they grow up. This is one form of the modern family and if the transnational element were removed it would not be so different from the family form of the wealthy classes in the past.

Domestic labour in the past was a manifestation of social inequalities based on social class and gender that operated within society. Today's transnational domestic labour and care chains are illustrations of the fact that social inequalities are still gender- and class-based, but now on a global scale. But they both produce similar voluntary kin relations, which in both cases are characterized by affection but also perpetuate inequalities.

Kinship as a fundamental way of organizing life

For many people in the world, kinship is the most fundamental institution through which they organize their social relations, their intimate life and their place in society. The family can be an institution that one can rely on for emotional and material support; when it is not available, we create alternative forms of kin relations. Families are made and unmade, reconstituted, reordered, and reshaped in complex ways that require both biological and customary or legal frameworks to organize people into groups that are culturally recognized as a family. Memory, technology, and ritual all play their part in making families. Sharing substance, caring for each other and reproducing relations as well as people are all part and parcel of family life.

Key thinkers mentioned in this chapter:

Johann Bachofen; Pierre Bourdieu; A. R. Radcliffe-Brown; Claude Lévi-Strauss; John McLennan; Lewis Henry Morgan; W. H. R. Rivers; David Schneider

Key terms mentioned in this chapter (see Glossary):

Adoption; Agnates; Assisted reproductive technologies; Bilateral descent systems; Care chain; Chosen families; Classificatory kinship systems; Descent; Descriptive kinship systems; Family; Fostering; Genealogical method; Genitor; Genetrix; Incest; Kin; Kinship; Lineage; Mater; Matrifocal; Matriline; Matrilineal descent systems; Monogamy; Pater; Patrilineal descent systems; Patriline; Polyandry; Unilineal descent; Voluntary kin

Questions for discussion/review:

1   What is the difference between a descriptive and a classificatory kinship system?
2   What difference do you think it makes to a kin relationship in a classificatory system when you call a cousin 'brother'?
3   In what respects are kinship diagrams not as objective as they might at first appear to be?
4   Is the family a human universal? Explain your answer.
5   What are some of the ways people make kin and why is it important for them to do so?

Chapter 4

Marriage

Some of the fiercest political battles waged in many countries since the turn of the millennium have been about marriage. One country after another has changed the legal definition of marriage so as to allow same-sex couples to marry. In many cases, however, this change has created intense conflict pitching conservative groups, which argue that marriage can solely be the union of a man and a woman, against progressive forces, which maintain that limiting marriage to heterosexuals is discriminatory. In France, the months leading up to the legalization of same-sex marriage in 2013 witnessed large demonstrations on both sides, one of which counted 1.4 million supporters of the reform. The Roman Catholic Church unexpectedly emerged into the limelight in this largely secular country as a formidable force mobilizing detractors of the law. In India, a Muslim man can be married to several women at once under Muslim personal law but the practice was challenged in 2018 before the Supreme Court. Child marriage is strongly opposed by many national and international organizations, but it continues to take place in many parts of the world, even where it has been outlawed. Clearly, marriage is a topic that can bring up intense emotion, and anthropologists, who have paid considerable attention to marriage practices around the world, have a lot to say about it (Figure 4.1).

What marriage is

Marriage is one of the most fundamental social and cultural institutions through which humans organize their social relations. While descent, on which the previous chapter focused, creates kinship relations by producing or acquiring children, marriage is the creation of kinship through **affiliation**, namely the coming together of persons to form a social unit. Relatives through marriage (i.e., spouses, in-laws, cousins by marriage, some step-relatives) are called **affines**. Marriage operates closely with descent in that one of the cornerstones of marriage as it is understood in many societies is to ensure the **social reproduction** of the kinship unit through biological reproduction, that is the production of children, and by extension to ensure the social reproduction of the entire society.

That said, it would be a mistake to see the institution of marriage as solely designed to produce children. Not only do many marriages not result in procreation, but marriage has many purposes other than biological reproduction, any of which can be given priority in particular contexts. For example, it may be seen as the culmination of the love between two people, and thus a deeply personal 'commitment' (the term often cited in weddings). In other contexts, marriage can be a way in which families settle conflicts or cement alliances, a way to recruit labour into the kinship unit, an arrangement that enables the circulation of wealth, or the opposite,

DOI: 10.4324/9781315737805-4

Figure 4.1 Thousands of supporters of the anti–same-sex-marriage movement 'La Manif Pour Tous' (demonstration for all) waved flags as they gathered near the Invalides in Paris on 26 May 2013. (Courtesy of Emeric Fohlen)

namely a way to ensure that family wealth is not dissipated. Anthropologists recognize that marriage takes many forms, has different but often concurrent goals, and can mean different things to different people. This diversity explains why marriage is so difficult to define and why it can become such a battleground.

Kinship relations that are formed through marriage often have an uneasy and contingent quality. In some societies, marriage takes place in the context of tense relations between groups and aims to defuse the possibility of violence: 'they are our enemies, we marry them' is a proverb that Max Gluckman reports many groups in southern Africa were in the habit of quoting (1956, 18). In the Global North, off-colour jokes about mothers-in-law are symptoms of the uneasy relationship between in-laws. In contrast to kinship through descent, affinal kinship is fragile: one cannot easily get rid of one's parents, siblings, or children, but in many societies one can divorce one's spouse without too much effort, although divorce may have painful consequences. These examples also demonstrate that, contrary to widely held beliefs in many societies of the Global North, marriage is never solely the union of two individuals; rather, it always involves many people.

While almost all societies of the world have an institution that one can recognize as marriage, there are important variations across societies about what constitutes marriage and how it relates to other social practices. The different forms that marriage takes are associated with different moralities, living arrangements, ways of thinking about the person's individual desires in relation to the priorities of the group, as well as economic, social, and cultural contexts. Yet only a finite number of variations are found across the world's societies.

Who one marries

All societies have norms that determine who one may or may not marry, but these vary between and even within societies. A basic contrast exists between the rule that one should choose one's marriage partner outside of one's group and the rule that states that one must marry members of one's group. Marriage within the group is called **endogamy** and marriage outside the group **exogamy**. What societies interpret as the 'group' can be the extended family, the clan, the village, the caste, or the entire society. The two concepts are relative: a society can practise exogamy in that it prescribes that people marry outside the clan but also practise endogamy if it specifies that people should not seek marriage partners outside the society.

Viewed from a **materialist** perspective, exogamy and endogamy are ways of dealing with two contradictory dictates. Exogamy enables groups to incorporate outsiders, expand the group's political and economic alliances, and encourage the circulation of wealth, as in the case of the in-marrying spouse bringing resources into the family or the in-laws becoming new exchange partners. Endogamy, in contrast, keeps wealth within the family and thus strengthens the economic and political bonds between people who are already related through descent.

In an essay that since then has become famous, French anthropologist Claude Lévi-Strauss (1963) compared marriage practices in Native North American societies, which are organized in **clans**, each symbolized by a **totem**, and Hindu Indian society, which is organized by **caste**, traditionally defined by the labour that members of each caste perform. The clan-based societies of Native North America do not have a clear **division of labour**, and members of different clans contribute similar goods and services to society. In contrast, in a caste system, members of one caste may be cobblers or barbers, members of another take care of the religious welfare of the society, and members of yet another are in charge of military defence. Because everyone needs shoes, military protection, and the benevolence of the gods, but only members of particular castes are able to provide these different goods and services, castes are dependent on one another. In clan-based societies, people must marry outside the clan, that is, find marriage partners among clans with a different totem; in caste-based societies, people must marry within the caste. Lévi-Strauss argued that in societies where goods and services circulate from one subgroup to the other, spouses do not; and in societies where goods and services do not circulate from one subgroup to the other, spouses are required to do so. In other words, seemingly very different systems of endogamy and exogamy are governed by the same logic: if goods are exchanged, people are not; if goods are not exchanged, people are.

While Lévi-Strauss's argument displays all the elegance and explanatory power of the theory of **structuralism** that he adapted to anthropology, it also assumes that societies are historically fixed and bounded, an assumption that contemporary anthropologists no longer find acceptable. We know, for example, that many people in India today are more concerned about social class and migration overseas than about caste and endogamy, and that many Native American groups are more worried about the abject poverty of reservation life than about totems and exogamy.

When a woman 'marries up', that is marries someone who is wealthier, of higher rank, or more privileged in some fashion, she practises **hypergamy**, but when she 'marries down' the social hierarchy, the phenomenon is called **hypogamy**. The terms hypergamy and hypogamy were devised to translate Sanskrit words found in Indian law manuals to describe socially approved marriages, which were hypergamous, and their opposite which were not considered acceptable, that is, hypogamous unions. Yet such distinctions are not limited to India: the stereotypical image in the Global North of a young and beautiful woman marrying a rich old man is an example of hypergamy, as are the marriages in many European folktales, like 'Cinderella' and 'Beauty and the Beast'. In many nineteenth-century novels, by an author like Honoré de Balzac,

Box 4.1   Matrimonial advertisements in India: finding an ideal spouse in under 50 words

In India, there is a long-standing tradition of advertising in newspapers to find a spouse. Matrimonial advertisements are considered an effective way to find a spouse, to which no stigma is attached. They are modern extensions of the networks of family members, priests, and matchmakers who in the past were responsible for finding spouses for young people.

Because newspaper advertisements are limited to 50 words, a lot of information about caste, education, height, income, occupation, family status, and skin tone has to be condensed in a short text. In addition, Hindus generally also include the astrological constellation at the time of the person's birth (*nakshatra*), so that no one wastes time responding to an advert if they are astrologically incompatible (Ramakrishnan 2012). Families continue to play a critical role in arranging marriages in twenty-first–century India, and over half of the advertisements are written by a parent or sibling of the person seeking a spouse. This is particularly true for women, which reflects gender ideology: women should be modest and thus not initiate such inquiries.

Age, height, and skin tone feature prominently in matrimonial advertisements. Women should ideally be a few years younger and a little shorter than their husbands, with light skin tone. Individuals often describe their skin tone on a continuum from very fair, to 'wheatish', and dark. Most women describe themselves as fair or wheatish, even in advertisements that state complexion does not matter in a future spouse, and virtually no advertisement describes the person as having dark skin.

Caste remains important for both Hindus and Indian Muslims. Increasingly, however, members of the urban Hindu middle classes write 'caste no bar' in their advertisements because they are more concerned about the prospective spouse's social class. Advertisements also increasingly state an interest in the future spouse's individual traits, an indication that younger people are becoming less concerned with caste in their choice of spouse. One interesting exception is among diasporic Indians, who are less accepting of inter-caste unions because they are concerned with maintaining an essentialized cultural identity while living overseas (Rajadesingan, Mahalingam, and Jurgens 2019).

In English-language matrimonial advertisements, education is very important, and most people who advertise in this medium have university degrees. While many educated women state that they are 'homely', which in Indian English means that they are happy to be a housewife, nowadays, as dual incomes are needed, professionals increasingly seek to marry other working professionals. Education, profession, and income, all forms of achieved status, are prominently featured in advertisements, alongside other non-acquired traits such as caste as markers of material and symbolic capital.

In the age of the Internet, matrimonial online agencies have sprung up offering their services to people looking for their 'special someone', as the shaadi.com (literally marriage.com) website states, both within India and in the South Asian diaspora. One new feature of these agencies is that happy couples can post albums and video stories of finding love, including wedding photos, photos of children, and other endorsements of the matrimonial agency, serving to commodify visual images of marital bliss. Obviously, couples who meet through online agencies but do not live happily ever after do not feature on the websites.

Indian matrimonial advertising may seem calculated, rational ways of commodifying people, evaluating them on the basis of caste, earnings, and skin tones. Yet Indians view compatibility of family, expectations, professions, and incomes as necessary for a successful marriage. Couples expect to find love, but only after ensuring social compatibility and family approval.

a typical scenario involves marriage negotiations between a gentleman of aristocratic and impoverished background and the daughter of a wealthy but middle-class family, which enables the aristocratic family to become wealthy again and the middle-class family to acquire a title for its descendants. In contrast, a woman who marries beneath her status is said to marry hypogamously. In India, this happens when a woman marries a man from a lower caste than herself. While it is legal, it may still lead to family discord and in some cases the couple may be disowned or harmed by the woman's family. In the Global North, women often marry men who are as well educated as themselves, but they continue to earn less than their husbands, and in this restricted sense many contemporary marriages are hypergamous.

Sexual or marital relations between people who are too closely related through descent according to locally specific rules are called **incest**. One form of incest, namely the marriage between a sister and a brother is today illegal everywhere, although it took place in the past under specific circumstances, such as the Inca god-kings and the high chiefs of Hawai'i, whose divine statuses were maintained through such unions. In ancient Egypt, over a period of several centuries, brother-sister marriage may have been a common form of marriage among ordinary people and was not considered incestuous (Hopkins 1980).

It is a well-known medical fact that people who are married to close relatives, if they carry particular recessive genes, are more likely to pass on health problems that have a genetic basis to their offspring than those who are not closely related. However, this does not mean that children of parents who are biologically related will always exhibit health problems. What is interesting is that in many societies people associate prohibited sexual relations with illness, but often it affects the people who engaged in such relations rather than any offspring who may result from them. In the Trobriand Islands, when people who belong to the same matrilineal clan have sexual relations, both individuals risk coming down with an illness called *sovasova*, which manifests itself as serious stomachaches, boils, and a general malaise (Lepani 2012, 137). But *sovasova* only affects people who repeatedly breach the rules or who actually marry against the rules of exogamy. Trobrianders do not worry about the effects of a one-off tryst and some apply a 'morning after' remedy to prevent harm resulting from the encounter.

In some societies, the definition of incest appears to mirror biological relatedness. In Tuvalu, Central Pacific, any sexual relation between pairs of first, second, and sometimes third cousins on both father's and mother's side is considered incestuous, and marriage between them is strictly prohibited. On a day-to-day basis, cousins of the opposite sex are expected to avoid one another physically. If co-presence cannot be prevented on these small islands where avoiding people is sometimes difficult, they must not address one another directly and people around them must refrain from cracking jokes or referring to anything that could evoke thoughts of sexuality. Women in particular explain that being in the vicinity of their male cousins makes their skin crawl. They explain these **avoidance** practices as mutual respect, called *fakammalu*, and of a certain kind of love, termed *alofa*, which manifests itself as empathy and the urge to ensure that the object of the feeling is well fed and well taken care of, but not necessarily to interact with the person face-to-face. This kind of love is antithetical to sexual desire.

Even in Tuvalu, biology is in fact not what determines the definition of incest because the prohibition to interact applies equally to adoptive **cross-cousins**, who are not necessarily biologically related to one another. Furthermore, rules of avoidance apply more strictly to cousins of the opposite sex than to sisters and brothers of the same parents, even though the latter are more closely related to one another than cousins. So incest is a social concept rather than a biological one. In other societies, the social nature of incest is even more obvious. For example, the Yąnomamö people living on the Venezuela-Brazil border make a distinction between the kinds of cousins one may marry. They prefer marriage between **cross-cousins**, namely people

Box 4.2   Consanguineous marriage and genetic disease in the United Arab Emirates

Until the late 1950s, the region of the Arabian Gulf that became the United Arab Emirates (UAE) in 1971 consisted of desert sheikdoms that engaged in limited agriculture and the precarious businesses of fishing and pearling. In the late 1950s, oil was discovered and within a generation, the country went from the dire poverty that today's elderly people still remember to a high-income oil-based economy complete with all the trappings of a materialist, developed urban nation.

Emiratis, who are Arab Muslims, recognize their tribal affiliation and shared common descent in one of the 70 tribes of the UAE. As is typical of Islamic societies of the Middle East, kinship is patrilineal and the preferential form of marriage is endogamous, ideally to a paternal parallel cousin. The potential downside of cousin marriages is that it increases the chance of children inheriting genetic diseases from parents who share the same ancestors. In 2002, a Ministry of Health Annual Report listed birth defects as the fourth cause of death in the UAE, and another report in 2006 ranked the UAE 6th of 193 countries for the rate of birth defects (Al-Gazali and Ali 2010). There are over 270 genetic diseases reported in the country with approximately 60% resulting from children inheriting two copies of an abnormal gene, one from each parent, a phenomenon known as autosomal recessive disorder. Because of endogamous marriages over a long period of time, some genetic disorders are limited to specific families, villages, and tribal groups, which differ widely in the extent to which they suffer a high burden of the disorders.

With the increasingly widespread knowledge of genetic disorders and the reality of everyday life caring for children with disabilities, the rate of cousin marriage is declining but it still remains common. A study in the 1990s found that 26% of marriages were with first cousins and 17% of these with paternal first cousins. As wealth from oil led to improved living conditions and the availability of modern medicine, the life expectancy of Emiratis has increased. Having invested in the health and well-being of the population, the government has turned its attention to tackling the high rate of genetic disorders and has instituted mandatory premarital genetic screening.

Since 2009, before a marriage can take place, prospective couples have to be screened and issued a medical certificate valid for three months. If both parties are found to be at risk of transmitting genetic disease to their future offspring, the couple (or the man and a representative of the woman) are offered genetic counselling, during which the risks of having children with genetic disease is explained, and the couple receives a certificate of incompatibility, but they are still allowed to marry. In 2016, in one of the poorer Emirates, Ras Al Khaimah, all couples who were told they were at risk of having disabled children nonetheless went ahead with their marriages (Salama and Saleh 2016). For now at least, the social and familial benefits of **consanguineal** marriages appear to continue to outweigh the risks involved.

born of opposite-sex siblings, but forbid marriage between **parallel cousins**, namely people born of same-sex siblings (Figure 4.2).

Other societies practice parallel-cousin marriage by encouraging marriages between cousins within the same **patriline**. In many parts of the Islamic world, families prefer patrilateral parallel-cousin marriage, that is, marriage between a woman and a man who are cousins on

Marriage

Yąnomamö cross cousin marriage (male ego)

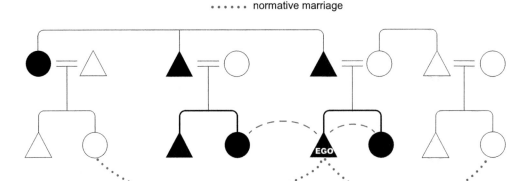

Figure 4.2 Marriage prescription and proscription among the Yąnomamö: The male ego is permitted to marry his cross-cousins but not his parallel cousins. Marriage with a parallel cousin is considered incestuous.

their respective fathers' side. For a woman, it means that her parents-in-law are also her aunt and uncle, and thus she is at lesser risk of exploitation and domestic abuse in the patrilocal marital home where she is simultaneously both a blood and affinal relative. Such women also benefit from family support from close kin on both sides of the family to ensure that the marriage succeeds. For men, the marriage helps ensure that money and property remain within the patriline, and so it makes good economic sense. These marriages ensure that family status, honour, prestige, and wealth are all preserved.

Some groups have complex marriage practices that articulate with descent groups. In traditional Aboriginal Australia, societies were typically divided into two descent groups, called **moieties** (a term derived from Anglo-French *moitè* 'half'), and marriages must take place across, not within, moieties. While these practices have been disrupted as many Australian Aboriginal people have been displaced from their land and have lost connections to their group, many continue to be able to reckon kinship on the basis of the system that was in place before the British colonized Australia, and base their everyday relations on this recognition.

Some marriage rules are strictly applied, while others more loosely so. **Preferential marriage rules** state a social and cultural preference but allow for deviations. In contrast, both **prescriptive marriage rules**, which set out who one should marry, and **proscriptive marriage rules**, which dictate who one is prohibited from marrying, must be followed and do not tolerate deviations. For example, the Islamic rule of patrilateral parallel cousin marriage described above is preferential, because people are free to marry people other than the preferred relative, such as their parallel cousin on one's mother's side, their cross-cousin, or someone who is not related. In some parts of the Islamic world, cousin and non-cousin marriages are distributed along social-class lines; today, wealthier and better-educated people are less likely to follow what they view as 'tradition' and more likely to be concerned about the potential health implications of family endogamy than less well-off or less well educated people. A clear and almost universal example of a proscriptive marriages rule is the prohibition against two siblings marrying.

Box 4.3   How to speak to your brother-in-law in Aboriginal Australia

Relationships between in-laws around the world are often tense, or at least distant and careful. Among speakers of languages that make a distinction between polite and familiar forms of the pronoun *you* (e.g., French *vous* vs. *tu*), a son-in-law often addresses his wife's parents with the polite form. Among the Guugu Yimithirr, an Australian Aboriginal people that lives on the Cape York Peninsula in northern Australia, a son-in-law does everything to avoid being in the presence of his mother-in-law; if co-presence is unavoidable, a son-in-law is supposed to sit silently and stare at the ground. Brothers-in-law also maintain a respectful distance, but they can talk to one another as long as they do so in quiet tones, avoiding facing one another and addressing each other directly.

In the olden days, the Guugu Yimithirr language had a special vocabulary of respect called *guugu dhabul* that people had to use when addressing in-laws. *Guugu dhabul* was not a different language, but rather consisted of a small specialized set of terms that were considered to be particularly polite and appropriate to the respectful relationship that in-laws are expected to maintain with one another.

When anthropologist John Haviland (1979) conducted fieldwork among the Guugu Yimithirr in the late 1970s, the vocabulary was no longer in active use, but older men remembered some of it and everyone thought of *guugu dhabul* as 'deep' and important. Some words were simply unique to *guugu dhabul*; for example, the word *balil*, which does not exist in the ordinary vocabulary, is used between in-laws to refer to any kind of motion, including 'go', 'walk', and 'paddle'. Some terms that are used in ordinary talk are absent in *guugu dhabul*, including all terms that refer to or could be interpreted as referring to sexual organs or sexual activity; talk about such topics would be completely inappropriate to the relationship between in-laws.

Few people today speak Guugu Yimithirr on a regular basis and the language is in danger of disappearing as people speak a mixture of English and Guugu Yimithirr or just English to converse with one another. Yet men who are related to one another through marriage or who could become in-laws because of the rules of marriage continue to maintain a respectful distance, speaking to one another in quiet tones even in English and avoiding talk about topics that may be considered crude.

In comparing preferential, prescriptive, and proscriptive rules, complications arise because laws, customary practices, and actual practices may conflict. Thus people may tell outsiders, including anthropologists, that a particular form of marriage is absolutely forbidden, while in fact practice contradicts the rule. In some societies, if a non-conforming marriage takes place, after people have come to terms with the violation, the rules remain in place but the kinship system is reconfigured to redefine the marriage as conforming to the rules. These situations have led anthropologists to question whether the distinction between preference on the one hand and prescription and proscription on the other is tenable (Leach 1961).

Where one lives

An important question at marriage is where a newly married couple is expected to live, and here again societies follow different rules. In cases where newlyweds must live in or near either the husband's father's **household** or the wife's mother's household, the arrangement is called

patrilocal and **matrilocal residence**, respectively. If the newlyweds are expected to form a new household, the practice is called **neolocal residence** (from Greek *néos* 'new'), which is relatively rare across the world's societies but is becoming more widespread.

Residence rules are independent of descent rules. This matters little in matrilineal societies that practise matrilocal residence, in patrilineal societies that practise patrilocal residence, and in bilateral societies. But some combinations required what early anthropologists thought were delicate negotiations. For example, among the Ndembu in what is now Zambia, on whose lives Victor Turner based his ethnographic work between the 1950s and the 1970s, descent was matrilineal while residence was patrilocal, which meant that a man lived in a different household from his sisters' children, who would inherit his wealth after he died (Turner 1979).

A man thus had conflicting obligations to his wife and their children on the one hand, who lived with him but were not part of the same lineage, and his sisters and her children on the other, who were part of the same lineage but did not live with him. A woman, likewise, was potentially torn between her husband and her brothers, as well as their respective children. The situation resulted in people changing households more frequently and in a higher rate of divorce than in most other societies. But later generations of anthropologists, particularly those informed by feminism, criticized earlier anthropologists for not understanding that in matrilineal societies the bond between a woman and her brother takes priority over the bonds of marriage, and that this system is not more problematic than one in which the bonds of marriage overrule other kinds of relationships.

How many spouses

Most nation-states of the world today only recognize marriage between two people. This pattern is called **monogamy**, an exclusive alliance that unites two people in marriage. But some societies allow and sometimes encourage **polygamy**, in which one spouse is married to several other people simultaneously, although such marriages are usually sanctioned by religion or tradition and not by law. When one man is married to several women, the practice is called **polygyny**; when one woman is married to several men, it is **polyandry**. Polygyny is often depicted negatively by NGOs, international organizations, and politicians as a system that is demeaning to women and a symptom of a pre- or anti-modern way of thinking. Yet monogamous marriage is by definition no less oppressive of women than polygynous marriage, and when women are oppressed in polygynous societies, it is frequently for reasons other than polygyny.

Until recently, the Bakgalagadi of Botswana practised polygyny (Solway 1990). The economy was largely based on agriculture, which was the responsibility of women and young men. The more a man who was rich in land could mobilize women's and young men's labour, the more he could expect his land to increase his wealth and prestige. As a result, only wealthy men, who could afford to pay **bridewealth** and support large families, had more than one wife. Polygyny enabled them to put spouses and offspring to work and to forge alliances with other families, thus extending their political and economic networks. Polygyny was a matter of male power and wealth.

This was not all there was to Bakgalagadi polygyny. Women held various perspectives on polygyny. Some saw in it a way to develop friendships and share the agricultural and household labour with other women. Older co-wives often treated younger ones in motherly ways. Polygyny could also alleviate the pressure on women to bear children, which could free them to pursue other activities. But other women emphasized the tensions that could arise between co-wives who competed for the same resources, such as food and attention for their children. It is not surprising that in Sotho, the language that the Bakgalagadi speak, the term for 'polygyny' is *lefufa*, literally 'jealousy', and a co-wife is called *bagadikano*, literally meaning 'rival'.

In the late twentieth century, the Bakgalagadi largely abandoned polygyny because the circumstances that made it viable in the past had changed. Many people no longer depend on agriculture for their livelihood, and thus multiplying the number of able hands is no longer a priority. While a few people have become wealthy, the majority remain impoverished and maintaining a large household is now a liability. The small minority of wealthy people find ways other than kinship and marriage to forge political and economic alliances and women have claimed greater independence. Finally, the growing importance of Christianity, which considers polygyny immoral, has contributed to the erosion of the practice.

Considerably rarer than polygyny, polyandry is practised primarily in societies of South and Central Asia. In these societies, co-husbands are often brothers, a system called **fraternal polyandry**, because it results in more stable and less conflict-prone marriages than marriages in which the co-husbands are unrelated. The Nyinba, an agriculturalist Tibetan people in Nepal, practised fraternal polyandry because it encouraged brothers to share the labour on undivided family land and to cooperate rather than compete with one another (N. Levine 1988). Men had to leave for extended periods of time to trade, thus co-husbands were frequently away from the household, so in practice they took turns at being the man of the house. Conflicts sometimes arose, for example, when junior co-husbands resented the authority of the first-born brother. Fraternal polyandry, which was patrilocal (the wife moved in with her husbands), was particularly common in aristocratic patrilineal families that owned land, and the practice helped these families retain their wealth and privilege. Other forms of marriage, such as monogamous matrilocal marriages, existed in the Nyinba valley, although they were less prestigious because they were historically associated with slave households, which did not own land that required labour. The difference between patrilocal polyandry and matrilocal monogamy reflected class and status positions as well as everyday matters such as where spouses lived after marriage and where children grew up.

The last logical possibility, **complex marriage**, in which many men are married to many women, is rare. One example is the utopian intentional Oneida community in the northeast United States that formed around religious leader John Humphrey Noyes between 1848 and 1881, which explicitly aimed to resist dominant marriage practices. Men and women had consensual sexual and romantic relationships with different partners and raised all children communally. Among the matrilineal Nayar in South India, marriages were traditionally both polygynous and polyandrous (Gough 1959). Brothers and sisters lived in the same household throughout their lives, and 'visiting husbands' would go to their wives after dinner and leave before breakfast. These marriages were strictly regulated to avoid incest and a woman's husbands could only be men of a suitable status. Under pressure from the British colonial administration, these practices ended in the early twentieth century.

Different marriage practices result in distinct family forms and produce diverse relationships among kin joined by both marriage and descent, shaped in each case by what is possible as well as what is considered normative for each kind of marriage. Marriage is thus embedded at once in material conditions, social structures, and cultural values.

What changes hands

Marriage is frequently the occasion for the circulation of goods and services. At modern weddings in many societies, relatives and friends are expected to provide gifts to the newlyweds, a practice that in the Global North is often formalized as wedding lists entrusted to a department store and that requires the newlyweds to send thank-you cards after the wedding, a task that usually falls on the bride. In traditional Europe, a family would hand over a **dowry** when the bride joined her husband's family, wealth that could range from a simple chest of clothing to valuable items such as jewellery. The dowry was compensation from the bride's family to the husband for taking charge of the bride's welfare. It may also be viewed as the woman's premortem inheritance from her natal family and as her material contribution to the marital home, although this view is subject to contestation. When the dowry was substantial, it became the object of protracted negotiations and legal arrangements.

In other societies, the wealth flows in the other direction, from the groom and his family to the bride's family. **Bridewealth** (sometimes called bride price) is made up of gifts that circulate from the husband and his family to his wife's family, while **bride service** is the labour that the husband is expected to provide to his wife's family, often over a protracted period of time and sometimes for his entire life. Bridewealth can be any resource that is culturally significant. Because the practice is associated in particular with pastoralists and agriculturalists, it often consists of cows or pigs. In many societies of southern Africa, for example, where women are responsible for agriculture and men for animal husbandry, bridewealth in the form of cattle from the groom's herd is viewed as compensating the bride's family for loss of her labour in the family's fields. Such transfers of cattle also mean that rights in children born to the woman belong to her husband's family. In some societies, bridewealth can be very onerous and subject to inflation over time, and younger men have difficulties mobilizing the wealth necessary to get married, a situation that can lead to their resentment of older men who may also be practising polygyny and thus viewed by younger men as 'hoarding' women. In the Papua New Guinea Highlands, some women resent being exchanged for pigs and valuables and are infuriated by their husbands' obsession with exchange and political alliances (Wardlow 2006). They express their frustrations by engaging in transactional sex with other men, thus turning their sexual favours, which for their husbands is their most valuable asset, into disposable commodities (Figure 4.3).

People in the Global North tend to be anxious when matters of love and affection, those that marriage is supposed to be predicated on, become too obviously embroiled with material concerns. So they can become suspicious of the 'real' intentions of a younger woman marrying an older wealthy man or, more rarely and more scandalously, a younger man marrying an older wealthy woman, accusing the younger party of being a 'gold digger'. They may react to the material concerns surrounding marriage in most of the world with amusement, surprise, or horror. Yet marriage in the Global North has always had a material underbelly, which comes to the surface when people sign prenuptial agreements or sue each other for divorce, as we discuss in the next section. So the idealization of marriage as being primarily about romance and love is always only one part of the story.

Why one marries

Marriage always involves complex decisions. In some groups, such as the urban middle classes in the Global North, the decision about who to take as husband or wife is largely seen as the responsibility of the individuals involved, often after a period of living together and sometimes after having children together. This marriage arrangement, referred to as an **elective** or **companionate marriage**, has only progressively emerged in the course of the twentieth century. It is also predicated on a level of material privilege that allows individuals to survive independently in small households. It is grounded in an ideology of individualism, the belief that a

Figure 4.3 During a ceremony in Goroka (Eastern Highlands, Papua New Guinea) conducted at the house of anthropologist Angela Kelly-Hanku's neighbour in November 2011, the groom, originally from the country's capital Port Moresby, displays a written list of bridewealth items and their respective values to members of his bride's family and his own. (Courtesy of Angela Kelly-Hanku)

person is responsible for making her or his own life decisions. But this ideology masks the important role that considerations of social class, race, religion, and other factors continue to play in selecting a spouse.

In many other societies, these arrangements make little sense. Marriage is far too important to be left to two young people with limited life experience and should instead be arranged by the families, often with the support of other people such as religious figures and marriage brokers, who search for an appropriate spouse and negotiate the terms of the union. In India, families weigh up such matters as social status, economic standing, and moral reputation of the prospective spouses and their families, as well as the prospective spouses' education and looks, in their efforts to find suitable spouses for a young person (Nanda 2000). The two young people often do not know each other and their opinion is only one of many aspects that families take into consideration (Figure 4.4).

From an outsider's perspective, **arranged marriages** may appear to disregard the role of romance and love. But love as many people understand it in societies of the Global North is a relatively new phenomenon, although most people around the world are exposed to idealized portrayals of romantic love in Hollywood, Bollywood, or Nollywood movies and in romantic fiction. Of course, the idea of romantic love did exist in the past, as we know from poetry from the Medieval Islamic world and the European chivalric romance tradition that it inspired. What

Figure 4.4 While arranged marriages are frequent in India, upper-middle-class professionals, such as Prathmesh Kapoor and Pallav Ganatca, are increasingly opting to choose their own spouses; weddings are lavish events that incorporate traditional and religious rituals, as depicted here. (Courtesy of Serena Nanda)

differs across time and space are the expectations of where and when love is appropriate and what role it plays in marriage, as well as how it is defined. Historical poetry was in fact more often about unrequited love than about love that led to marriage. In arranged marriages, people expect that love will follow marriage as the married couple gets to know and appreciate one another. To critics who depict arranged marriage as a violation of an individual's right, members of societies that practise it point to the high rate of divorce in the Global North, which demonstrates that elective marriage is not such a great success after all. And indeed, the conjugal bond that arises out of an arranged marriage is often nurtured by entire structures of kinship, exchange, and morality, in addition to individual feelings, thus making it stronger than marriage that merely rests on the feelings of two people.

Where the obligation to marry for the good of the family is a duty that cannot be circumvented, love and related feelings are often found not in the marital bond but elsewhere, such as in relations outside marriage, in children, or among relatives. In Tuvalu, for example, married people develop affective bonds that are comparable to romantic love as people in the Global North understand it, but they are expected to keep them private. The North American, and increasingly global, habit of repeating 'I love you' within families (could it be a sign of anxiety that love may not be there tomorrow?) would be met with utter consternation. The social relations that matter for day-to-day life are between men and between women, a pattern called **homosociality**. In public, relations between a wife and a husband are aloof, and a married couple who spend too much time together are derided as *solopuu*, a term that also describes a child who 'clings to her or his mother's skirt'. People attribute this behaviour not to love but to jealousy and possessiveness.

The distinction between elective and arranged marriages becomes blurred when we observe them in actual practice. In societies where arranged marriages are the norm, marriages are publicly presented as arranged to maintain appearances, but nowadays they are frequently the result of the bride and the groom's personal choice. Conversely, families have considerable say on who children marry. The 'properly brought up' young woman who brings home to her middle-class parents her biker fiancé, clad in a leather vest that allows others to admire the tattoos dripping down his arms and chest, will quickly realize the importance of social-class compatibility in marriage.

While one would expect the preference for arranged marriages to decline as societies become more 'modern' and cosmopolitan, the opposite sometimes happens. Among Pakistanis who have migrated to Britain since the 1950s, parents continue to arrange their children's marriages to cousins still living in Pakistan as a way of fulfilling their obligation to support kin (A. Shaw 2001). Having originally migrated to the labour markets of England to support their relatives, families look for spouses for their children among family members in Pakistan as a way to fulfil this obligation. In some cases, relatives are involved in transnational business together, and arranging for their children to marry one another consolidates these business relationships. These marriages help British Pakistanis maintain economic, social, and cultural connections to Pakistan and they potentially enable **chain migration**, in a context in which British immigration law has made it all but impossible for most Pakistanis to obtain immigrant visas through other methods.

While a few societies do not have any ritual that could be identified as a wedding, in most societies, the transition from an unmarried to a married state is marked with one. A wedding is a classic **rite of passage**, namely a more or less predictable and scripted event that marks a transition from one social status to another. But the relationship between weddings and marriage can differ across groups. In the Global North, it is increasingly rare for two people only to begin to live together after the wedding. In Britain, couples in the professional classes are more likely to wed and legalize their cohabitation than working-class couples, who often live together without marrying, even after children are born. Among many groups in southern Africa, marriage is a process: only after the husband has proven himself willing and able to provide bride-wealth to the wife's family over a period of time is the couple deemed truly married. The fulfilment of bridewealth obligations may be celebrated with a ceremony, but it is not the main marker of marriage.

Is marriage inevitable?

Marriage is a fundamental institution precisely because so many aspects of human existence depend on it. But there may be one exception to the universality of marriage. Prior to the establishment of the People's Republic of China in 1949, among the Mosuo or Na, a minority group in the Yunnan and Sichuan provinces, descent was matrilineal and households were headed by a matriarch (Shih 2010). Women and men had sexual relationships with one another that were called *tisese* (literally, 'walking back and forth'), in which women could invite or reject the sexual advances of different men at night. In the morning, men had to return to their own households. It was forbidden to talk about these relations in public, particularly in mixed company. Women could have children from different lovers if they wished. Women of the same household brought up their children together with little help from men. The *tisese* system kept sex and romance clearly separate from parenting, care, and the domestic economy. Mosuo morality did set some limits and did not condone all-out promiscuity. But the apparent lack of recognition of the institution of marriage indicates that the Mosuo were an exception to a number of widely held assumptions, including the notion that men are essential in bringing up children. At the same time, *tisese* did not preclude two people establishing an affective bond with one another that would closely resemble monogamous marriage.

After 1949, the communist government, eager to integrate ethnic minorities into the nation-state, exerted pressure on Mosuo men and women to marry and maintain male-centred households. This was not a successful project: many couples divorced and returned to their original matrilineal households. In the 1980s, as China shifted to market capitalism, state policy towards ethnic minorities changed from integration to a celebration of their diversity and uniqueness. But this turn unleashed a deluge of media attention on the Mosuo. Today, majority Han Chinese tourists flock to the area to participate in highly reified performances of an exoticized version of Mosuo 'culture' in theme parks, where Mosuo performers engage in sexual banter with tourists, violating the traditional norm of discretion (Walsh 2005). While they express annoyance at outsiders' prurient curiosity and lack of interest in other aspects of their lives, the Mosuo today depend on tourism for their livelihood. An exceptional practice has now become a commodity (Figure 4.5).

More generally, in all societies, one finds people who are adult but not married for a variety of reasons: widowhood, divorce, holding religious office that requires celibacy, the inability to find a marriage partner, or a lack of interest in married life. Yet many societies find people who are past marriage age but have never been married problematic. In Japan in the 1980s, for example, the derogatory term for an unmarried woman aged 25 or older was a 'Christmas cake', that is, a perishable product no longer sellable after 25 December (Takemaru 2010). But this stigma is not universal. In other societies, there are avenues for women to claim social status other than through their role as wives. In Tonga, South Pacific, for example, a woman has relatively low status compared to her husband and her in-laws, but ranks higher than her brothers, particularly if she is senior to them. While some stigma is attached to remaining unmarried, elderly single women can gain considerable respect and power, particularly if they are from a

Figure 4.5 Young Mosuo women working at the Yunnan Ethnic Village, a theme park in Kunming, China. (Courtesy of agefotostock/Alamy)

high-ranking family or if they can reinforce their status through success in education or by becoming guardians of valued traditional knowledge.

The situation of unmarried women may be further complicated if they have children. Some societies view children born out of wedlock as a problem, proof that the family has not sufficiently protected the unwed mother. Stories of backstreet abortions, newborns being put up for adoption, and unwed mothers being dispatched to institutions are all too common around the world. In such societies, the unwed mother, having become unmarriageable, is no longer available for the family to forge alliances with another family. The man who conceived the child, if he is known, is rarely the object of stigma, and the situation in fact may be interpreted as proof of his masculinity. In other societies, in contrast, having one or more children out of wedlock is a proof of fertility and can increase a woman's marriageability. In the Global North, an increasing number of women choose to have children through assisted reproductive technologies and remain single mothers. This choice is not devoid of practical difficulties (juggling child care with employment, for example), even if the mother is reasonably well to do, but nation-states are slowly beginning to make accommodation for it.

In yet other societies, women may have very good reasons to choose to remain unmarried, such as being able to take care of themselves and their children on their own more reliably than with a man in the house. In many parts of the Caribbean, where in the past black slave families were often forcibly broken up by their white masters and where discrimination continues to keep many in poverty, women may establish **matrifocal** families with their children, taking on male partners as long as these are able to contribute to the family's needs. In Barbados in the 1990s, women who were employed by offshore data-entry corporations, labour that was defined as 'feminine', led lives in which men were rather incidental because these women were much better able to support themselves and their children without relying on men, whose employment was generally much more precarious (Freeman 2000). While more privileged segments of the same societies may look down on these arrangements as morally problematic, they are in fact based on an unassailable logic.

While people throughout the world idealize marriage, there are many dark sides to married life, such as domestic violence, of which women are victims much more frequently than men. Most violence against women is committed by the men to whom they are married or with whom they are or were in a relationship with. Domestic violence can be physical and sexual, but it can also take other forms, including verbal violence, threat of abandonment, and financial and emotional abuse. We owe the recognition of violence in marriage to Marxist-inspired feminist critiques of the family, particularly since the 1960s, when a shift took place in the Global North in the definition of what counts as private and public. Prior to that time, what took place in the home was the prerogative of the male head of the household, and the law had no particular interest in it. When domestic violence was redefined as a matter of public concern, new laws, institutions, and movements emerged that sought to acknowledge the scale of the problem.

While people in the Global North may smile at descriptions of the pragmatic approach that people in other societies take to matters of marriage, acrid legal conflicts over property arise in the context of divorce in their own societies (Zelizer 2007). In divorce proceedings, proofs of unending love such as cooking and cleaning for the partner over the years, or gifts of jewellery and holidays taken together, are suddenly commodified, their worth tabulated to calculate how much one party owes to the other in the form of alimony, child support, and property division. Divorce reminds us in no uncertain terms that marriage in the Global North may after all not be that different from marriage practices that involve bridewealth, dowries, and other material concerns, despite an ideology that seeks to keep love and material interests separate.

Same-sex marriage

As we discussed in the opening vignette, one way in which marriage has been transformed in recent decades is the extension of the right to marry to same-sex couples. Whether historical or ethnographic precedents exist of the same gender marrying is unclear. Some historians have maintained that same-sex marriages were celebrated in Europe in the Middle Ages and perhaps before, but the evidence is circumstantial and we do not know if these unions were seen as on par with heterosexual marriage. In some societies and under some circumstances, women and men established marriage-like relationships with a person of the same gender. Among the Nandi of Kenya, for example, women who have not married or borne children and are beyond childbearing age can take a younger woman as wife, paying bridewealth to her family and taking part in rituals that are identical to **heteronormative** courtship (Oboler 1980). The younger partner is free to have sex with men and bear children, and the older partner, who takes on the social role of a man by assuming responsibilities otherwise associated with men, is considered to be their father, but the women do not have sexual relations. The practice is primarily designed to ensure that the childless older woman has heirs, and presupposes that the older woman is wealthy enough to pay bridewealth, bring up the children, and run the household.

In other contexts, a relationship between people of the same gender involves sexual and affective relations but it is contingent on specific circumstances. For example, in all-male mine workers' compounds in Apartheid South Africa, black migrant men of different ages had sexual and domestic relationships, in which the older man would take on the role of the husband by supporting his partner materially, and a younger man that of a wife by taking responsibility for household chores (Niehaus 2002). While these relationships formed because women were absent, they did involve sexual pleasure and emotional attachments. Comparable same-sex relationships involving people who would otherwise form heterosexual relationships are common in prisons throughout the world, where they are generally associated with power and protection from violence.

However, the lack of unequivocal precedent does not constitute an argument either for or against contemporary same-sex marriage. Many ideas that are uncontroversial in modern society have a shallow history and are not universal, such as accommodations to meet the needs of persons living with disability and considering slavery to be abhorrent. The first country to give legal status to same-sex marriage, that is the same rights and duties as heterosexual marriage, was the Netherlands in 2001. Since then, the list of countries and other law-making entities (states of federal countries, municipalities, tribal reservations) that have legally recognized same-sex unions has been growing at a rapid pace. Some political entities have established an alternative legal arrangement for same-sex couples, namely **civil unions**, which are also available to heterosexual couples who do not wish to marry.

At the same time, the opposition to it is also mounting. Some governments have instituted laws that specifically prohibit such unions, some by reworking the constitutional definitions of marriage that, when originally drafted at a time when same-sex marriage was beyond the realm of possibilities, did not specify that it had to be a contract between people of the opposite gender. In other cases, one finds a discrepancy between legal progressivism and the social conservatism that regulates everyday life. In South Africa, for instance, legalized same-sex marriage does not prevent, particularly in poor neighbourhoods, the everyday brutal repression of women and men who do not conform to gender norms and are assumed to be homosexual. In other African countries, people maintain (against ample evidence to the contrary) that homosexuality is 'un-African', that is, an imported Western depravity (Awondo, Geschiere, and Reid 2012). In Uganda, these ideas have been fuelled by conservative evangelical preachers from the United States, who push their own agendas and take advantage of the enduring wounds of **colonialism** in the country by encouraging many Ugandans' belief that homosexuality is yet another way in which Europe is damaging Africans.

Some lesbians and gays themselves oppose same-sex marriage and consider marriage to be a regressive and coercive institution. These opponents point out that most violence in society takes place within the family and that gays and lesbians should not emulate a practice that is at once the foundation of the **patriarchal** order and a deeply problematic institution.

Marriage as an ever-changing institution

Marriage is a social and cultural construct of central importance to virtually all societies. Yet it is defined differently across societies and it is constantly being redefined in the context of changing economic circumstances, political climates, and moral norms. It is at once a legal institution endorsed by state institutions and one that emerges through the practices and norms that guide people in their everyday lives. It is embedded in multiple aspects of human existence, including the production, consumption, and circulation of goods and services; the political interests of groups; the definition of what counts as 'us' and 'them'; the evaluation of what counts as moral; the circulation of ideas in a globalized world; and the weight of history, particularly of inequalities inherent in the colonial past. Many changes in marriage practices have taken place as a consequence of colonialism, missionization, economic change, and globalization.

We are living in a time when many institutions and practices that have never existed or have had a marginal status before are today considered normal or commonplace, such as people living on their own, women taking an active role in politics, and societies meeting the needs of people living with disabilities, and this is the ever-changing context in which same-sex marriage, once unthinkable, has become a reality in many nation-states.

Key thinkers mentioned in this chapter:

Claude Lévi-Strauss

Key terms mentioned in this chapter (see Glossary):

Affiliation; Affine; Arranged marriage; Avoidance practices; Bride service; Bridewealth; Caste; Civil unions; Clan; Companionate marriage; Complex marriage; Cross-cousin; Dowry; Elective marriage; Endogamy; Exogamy; Fraternal polyandry; Homosociality; Hypergamy; Hypogamy; Incest; Marriage; Moieties; Parallel cousin; Preferential marriage rules; Matrilocal residence; Monogamy; Neolocal residence; Patrilocal residence; Polygamy; Polyandry; Polygyny; Prescriptive marriage rules; Proscriptive marriage rules; Social reproduction; Rite of passage; Totem

Questions for discussion/review:

1   To what extent can one say that marriage is a universal social institution given that there are so many marriage forms?
2   What purpose do marriage rules permitting or forbidding marriages between particular people serve?
3   What does love have to do with marriage?
4   How does marriage articulate with other social institutions such as those concerned with economics and politics?
5   How has the institution of marriage changed over time?

Chapter 5

Gender, sex, and sexuality

When Elinor Ochs conducted fieldwork in the highlands of Madagascar in the 1970s, the island nation was a predominantly rural country and its people led largely local lives centred on agriculture, animal husbandry, and trade (E. Ochs 1974). Women and men had clearly differentiated work roles: men raised cattle, while women took care of growing and selling produce. Even though women's work was essential, men's work was more highly valued. In addition, men were in charge of ritual and political life, in which women were not allowed to participate. All important decisions for the village were reached in the public life that men controlled, while women wielded power in domestic settings and could only influence public life indirectly. Villagers, particularly men, justified these arrangements by explaining that women were brash, confrontational, and emotional, which helped them bargain and haggle in the marketplace but disqualified them from ritual and political life, where one had to be polite and level-headed, qualities that villagers attributed to men. In addition, men commanded the elaborate oratorical styles and esoteric knowledge that participating in public life required. This power differential was further reinforced by the fact that villagers considered politeness, indirection, and conciliation to be 'proper' normative behaviour, thus giving greater value to men's than to women's ways of acting.

Fast-forward to the 2000s, when Jennifer Cole conducted fieldwork in a port town of the same country (Cole 2014). By that time, Madagascar's economy had collapsed and many people were increasingly seeing emigrating overseas as the only solution to poverty. The ideological construction of gender demeanours remained, and young women were as brash and direct as their grandmothers, while men continued to be poised and composed, but the power was now reversed: while many men stagnated economically, some women became adept at marketing themselves to foreign visitors and using online dating sites to try to land a foreign husband, often from France, the former colonial power. Successful women migrated to Europe in hope of becoming wealthier. But the reality was often different: unskilled jobs available in Europe to migrant non-white women are poorly paid, the French husbands the women had met online often turned out to lead unglamorous lives, and French people treat the women like any other African immigrants, whom in this case they also suspect of being opportunists.

These two vignettes illustrate how gender can be constituted differently at different times in history. In the 1970s, gender relations in Madagascar were organized in terms of a local context, while three decades later globalization, migration, and social media played an important role in them. In both contexts, we witness the workings of **gender stratification**, the structures of inequality designed to maintain a power differential between the genders. Gender is not a state of being in itself, rather it is a state of being that exists in relation to other ways of being. But gender stratification has a different quality in the two situations: in the earlier one, men dominated women; in the latter situation, French people dominated women from

DOI: 10.4324/9781315737805-5

Madagascar, who in turn are sometimes better off than their male compatriots. Power dynamics operate not only between women and men, but within genders. Some women can have more power than other women and some men more than other men, while some women have more power than some men.

Gender stratification is based on the social and cultural evaluation of how women and men differ, including **gender roles**, namely the different tasks that society assigns to women and men, and **gender stereotypes**, namely the preconceived and often oversimplified ideologies of how women and men behave. Gender stratification has little to do with the physiological or other differences between women and men, as demonstrated by the fact that, in contrast to people in Madagascar, people in societies of the Global North tend to think that women are more polite than men. Even the one fundamental difference between women and men, the fact that only women can bear children, does not in and of itself explain why women and their activities are devalued; rather, it is how society constructs childbearing and child-rearing, as activities that are the primary responsibility and obligation of women, who should meet them without seeking wage work while being confined to the domestic sphere, leaving men free to attend to both domestic and public life (Rosaldo 1974).

Gender is stratified, but it is also crisscrossed by other forms of difference and inequality, including social class, wealth, race, ethnicity, religious affiliation, nationality, and a multitude of other ways in which we configure our and each other's lives, all of which can bestow upon people of both genders greater or lesser power. For example, a woman experiences her gender differently depending on whether she lives in a poor village in India or lives the life of an upper-middle-class urbanite in Australia: the former worries about whether she can get enough water for the family, how the weather will affect the crops, and where to find money for her daughter's dowry; the latter is concerned with how to find a good school for the children, how to make herself useful through volunteer work, and where to purchase organic food. Some white men in the Global North have been deeply affected by economic changes associated with **globalization** that have closed down the manufacturing industries where they used to find a particular male form of dignity. These men see themselves as lacking power and some may gravitate as a result to reactionary politics and conspiracy theories. All these dynamics require that we study gender in light of these other social dynamics, that is from an **intersectional** perspective in which all parameters of social difference intersect with one another to create the particular socio-cultural conditions within which people lead gendered lives.

Some core concepts

While gender is today widely recognized as a social concept, the term originated in the analysis of language. In many languages, nouns are assigned to a grammatical gender class (e.g., masculine or feminine in Romance languages, in addition to neuter in German and Russian) and word types like adjectives, articles, and pronouns must reflect the gender of the noun they modify. But this system has little to do with gender in the actual world, in that words can be assigned a grammatical gender that contradicts the real-life gender of the entities to which they refer; for example, in German, the word *Fraulein* 'young woman' is grammatically neuter.

Social scientists began to systematically develop the notion of **gender** as a social category in the early decades of the twentieth century. In anthropology, Margaret Mead conducted ethnographic fieldwork in 1928–29 in three small-scale societies of what is today Papua New Guinea and published in 1935 an influential book based on this fieldwork, *Sex and Temperament in Three*

Box 5.1   Waves of feminist thought

First-wave feminism refers to a socio-political movement that emerged in Victorian and Edwardian Britain and the United States, and later elsewhere. It refers principally to women activists who mobilized to obtain voting and property rights. Second-wave feminism emerged in the 1960s, when feminists in North America, Europe, and later elsewhere questioned and campaigned to eliminate enduring gender-based inequalities, not only in the law (e.g., the legalization of abortion and contraception, protection against domestic violence), but also in society at large, where for example women were paid less than men for doing the same work. This is when the influential expression 'the personal is political' emerged.

Second-wave feminism was later criticized, particularly by scholars in **postcolonial studies**, for assuming that all women in all societies share the same problems because of their gender and disregarding the fact that factors like poverty and racial discrimination may be just as problematic as gender discrimination. Third wave feminism took up this critique and theorized intersectionality, arguing that gender stratification can only be understood when it is contextualized in other forms of inequality. Beginning in the late 1990s in parts of Europe and Latin America, fourth-wave feminism continues to advocate for the rights of women as did second-wave feminism and to raise awareness of the intersectional oppression of women as in third-wave feminism, but does this by harnessing modern communication technologies such as Facebook, Twitter, and YouTube to denounce abusers of power on a global scale.

The metaphor of waves of feminism somewhat oversimplifies the fact that all the waves continue to exist in some form and that the different waves began at different times in different countries. To further complicate matters, there is no single feminism but rather multiple feminisms in each wave. Nonetheless, a broad historical understanding of how feminisms have developed over the twentieth and twenty-first centuries and how each new generation has defined itself in relation to previous generations remains important.

Primitive Societies. She argued that what she called 'temperament', roughly equivalent to what we call 'gender' today, is not biologically determined by a person's sex. Comparing the three societies, she claimed that, in one, both men and women had nurturing 'female' temperaments; in another, both had aggressive 'male' temperaments; and in the third, women were aggressive ('male') and men were meek and vain ('female'). Since there was considerable variation between these three neighbouring societies in how the two genders were expected to behave and relate to one another, gender could not possibly have universal characteristics rooted in biology.

Even though later scholars found many problems with her ethnography (Gewertz and Errington 1991), Mead was the first anthropologist to argue that sex as a biological fact must be separated from gender as a social and cultural concept. At the time, Mead's book caused a sensation among its readership in the Global North because it challenged widely held views that women were subordinate to men because they were 'naturally' weaker, more nurturing, and less assertive than men. While the vocabulary has changed, the basic insight of Mead's argument continues to be relevant to this day: we understand gender as being made up of the symbols, behaviours, roles, and statuses through which societies and cultures draw distinctions between women and men, which are learned and thus culturally variable.

In contrast to gender, **sex** is made up of genetic and physiological features of the body, which are more or less fixed at birth and define, in most but not all cases, male and female categories. Sex is the combined result of several physiological components and of the interaction between them. **Primary sexual characteristics** include chromosomes, hormones that the body produces and puts to use, the gonads (ovaries and testicles, which produce eggs and sperm, respectively) and the anatomy of other internal and external organs. **Secondary sexual characteristics** are other sex-marked body features such as the shape of breasts and of the pelvis and the distribution of hair, muscle, and fat. Sex is therefore a complex combination of biological factors, in which no single feature is more important than the others.

While gender and sex are not the same thing, they are intertwined with one another, in that we generally assume that people with male and female bodies (categories of sex) are men and women respectively (categories of gender). In many societies, people explain the attributes of women and men and the inequalities between them in terms of their sexual physiologies: for example, women are deemed not fit for certain jobs, such as heavy manual labour or military combat, on account of their alleged weaker bodies or the fact that they menstruate and give birth to children (Ortner 1974). Sex thus serves to justify the **gender hierarchies** that operate in all societies of the world, despite political and social efforts in some societies to rectify the inequalities inherent to these hierarchies. This led Gayle Rubin (1975) to argue that gender and sex form a unified system that transforms the biology of sex into human action and its products: women and men are quite similar to one another, yet societies go to considerable effort to emphasize the difference between them. One fundamental institution that performs this task is marriage (one could logically conceive of society without it), which is based on the social complementarity between the genders and which creates kinship and **patriarchy**.

In a similar vein, scholars inspired by Marx have demonstrated that, while society recognizes the labour that men perform as being 'real' work that supports families, the labour that is the responsibility of women is rarely if ever acknowledged as work: for example, women take care of the children, cook meals, do the shopping, clean the house, and wash the laundry, sometimes performing all these tasks as a 'second shift' before and after they have worked in a job where they are paid for their labour. Yet this work not considered to be labour, even though they support forms of labour that are recognized as such (men need to be fed when they return from the office or the factory). This is the insight of social reproduction theory, a Marx-inspired approach that emerged in the 1970s as an outcome of second-wave feminism (Federici 2018).

A third category, **sexuality**, refers to attractions and desires that are associated with the pleasure we derive from the stimulation of sexual organs and other parts of our bodies, often but not always in the company of one or more others, and the ways we arouse these desires. The open-endedness of this definition reflects the complexities of the concept. In the contemporary Global North, sexuality is commonly talked about as a binary contrast between **sexual orientations**, namely heterosexuality and homosexuality, with bisexuality sitting in the middle.

However, this distinction is not the only way to understand sexuality. Even in societies where this contrast is viewed as important, not everyone defines him- or herself in terms of these two categories. In the 1950s, the American sexologist Alfred Kinsey created an uproar when he documented that many North Americans engaged in all sorts of sexual activities publicly deemed 'immoral' at the time, and he proposed that sexual desire formed a continuum between different-sex and same-sex attraction, rather than discrete categories. Historical evidence shows that, in Western societies, homosexuality and heterosexuality are 'inventions' of the nineteenth century, when experts of various kinds, including legal professionals, psychologists and doctors, began classifying people in terms of their sexual proclivities, and ordinary people themselves began to understand themselves in terms of these categories and act accordingly, in the same way that we understand ourselves today in terms of certain popularized versions of psychology, such as 'introvert', 'type A', or 'addictive personality'.

The term 'homosexual' first appeared in 1869 in the writings of the now largely forgotten Hungarian scholar Karl-Maria Benkert; 'heterosexuality' is a later invention that originally meant what we today call 'bisexuality'. Of course, people had engaged in same-sex erotic activities probably since the dawn of humanity, often alongside opposite-sex activities, but these activities came to define a kind of person in the Global North only in relatively recent history. In many other societies, in contrast, 'the homosexual', and thus 'the heterosexual' as well, are not recognizable categories, and people have other ways of classifying people. Today, in the Global North at least, many millennials no longer find labels like 'gay', 'straight', or 'bisexual' useful in describing themselves, preferring to self-identify with terms like 'pansexual' and 'nonbinary'.

How many genders?

People in all societies assume that there are clear prototypes of what women and men should be, prototypes that are reproduced and maintained while children are socialized ('don't be such a sissy!') and in daily life and through popular culture celebrities such as Dwayne Johnson and Kim Kardashian, with equivalents in Bollywood and everywhere where popular culture is produced.

But not everyone abides by these stereotypes. Most obviously, within any society, some women are recognized as being 'feminine' while others are 'mannish', while some men are 'masculine' and others are found to be 'effeminate' or alternatively, in global popular culture since the 1990s, 'metrosexual'. In addition, many societies have what one can loosely call **transgender** people, namely people whose appearance and actions do not conform to the gender norms that society associates with the sex into which they were born, as they do for **cisgender** people who conform to normative expectations. 'Transgender' is an umbrella term that covers many kinds of people.

In the Global North, transgender people experience their gender in a way that is at odds with the gender ascribed to them on the basis of their sexual physiology. Some characterize themselves as 'a woman trapped in a man's body' or vice versa, an experience that was traditionally referred to as 'transsexuality'. Some may seek to **transition** to another gender identity with the help of hormone therapies and **sex-reassignment surgery**, in which surgeons transform female genitals into male-looking ones or vice versa. Others refashion themselves, with or without the assistance of medical technology, into another way of being gendered, not necessarily identifiable as female or male. For yet others, gender non-conformity is contextual, as is the case of persons whose interest is limited to adopting dress codes associated with another gender and sometimes seek to 'pass' in public (traditionally referred to as 'transvestism'). Lastly, drag queens and drag kings are persons whose gender-bending practices are confined to public performances designed as a serious critique of gender stereotypes or, more light-heartedly, for humorous effect.

Transgender identity in societies of the Global North is independent of sexual orientation, in that a transgender person is often not erotically attracted to persons of the same sex as the sex into which they were born. Consequently, people who experience transgender as an identity and 'come out' late in life have sometimes led **heteronormative** lives involving marriage and family, and thus have to negotiate their new gender identity with spouses, children, and other relatives. In some countries, transgender people have found it useful to form political alliances with lesbians, gays, and bisexuals, who together are often referred to with the acronym LGBTQ+, a term that is increasingly used globally. Even though transgenderism and homosexuality are completely separate experiences, people who identify with them recognize certain commonalities in their struggles for political and personal recognition.

Box 5.2   Changing terminologies: Queer

In English, the term '**queer**' originally meant 'odd, unusual', a meaning that, according to the Oxford English Dictionary, emerges in Middle English in the early 1500s. In the early twentieth century, it began to be used in the United States as a derogatory term for homosexuals, but in the 1980s, those who were denigrated by the term appropriated it and gave it a new meaning: a person whose attitudes, actions, or desires transcend and thus question traditional ideas about gender, sex, or sexuality. In the Global North, some lesbian, gay, or transgender people identify with the label 'queer', but one can also be a queer cisgender heterosexual if one is critical of gender and sex conventions. While this positive meaning originated in North America, it now has wide recognition in many parts of the urban industrial world and is spreading elsewhere.

In the Global North, transgender people's access to medical care is often predicated on their acceptance of their experience as a medical condition, 'gender dysphoria', which can have negative consequences in their lives. The self-understanding of many transgender people is that they are gender variant or gender non-conforming. As a result, transgender people often have difficult relationships with the medical world, and this is particularly aggravated in national contexts that do not offer universal health care, such as the United States. There, citizens have to rely on insurance companies, which are for-profit businesses, to pay for their medical care, and these companies often limit the range of medical services they are willing to cover for the insured. Many transgender people worldwide are poor because they suffer from discrimination in the job market and other contexts and, in the United States, they often cannot afford the kind of health insurance that would cover the medical care they need.

These matters concern not only the personal but also the political, as medical definitions of transgender have a determinative effect on gender-related law, policy, and politics. However, this effect is uneven across national contexts. For example, in Europe, one can legally change gender if one can secure medical evidence of one's transgender status, but the evidence required (e.g., levels of surgical or hormonal intervention, length of time spent under medical care) varies greatly between and even within countries. In other countries, the **medicalization** of transgender people can have unexpected consequences. In Japan, for example, transgender people are now legally classified as disabled, and thus entitled to political and social recognition and legal protection, in contrast to gays and lesbians, who remain socially marginalized.

In many societies of the Global South, the label 'transgender' has also been used to refer to people who do not conform to the normative expectations of women and men, but since the constitution of gender varies greatly across the world's societies, transgender categories take on many different forms, even within the same society. India's *hijra*, for example, are biological men of generally low social status who adopt a female-identified appearance and countenance, and often live in religious communities headed by a guru (Nanda 1998). Some claim origins as devotees of a Hindu goddess, to whom they sacrifice their masculinity by undergoing ritual castration. Yet many others diverge from these religious ideals and make a living by begging or as sex workers catering to heteronormative men. Their signature practice is the ritual blessing of new-born children, for which they demand payment, often aggressively. In other parts of the world, such as Indigenous Siberia and Southeast Asia, transgender people are ritual specialists, such as shamans or spirit mediums. This role may give them a certain amount of status, although it is not without problems: people believe that shamans, whether transgender or not, can use their supernatural powers for negative ends just as easily as they can to perform good deeds, and this suspicion leads people to mistrust and marginalize them.

In Tonga in the Pacific Islands, one finds a small but visible minority referred to as *fakaleitī* or *leitī*, a word that has been borrowed from the English word 'lady' and only applies to them (the prefix *faka-* means 'in the manner of'). While the category is difficult to define precisely, certain characteristics are stereotypically associated with their presentations of self, bodies, and contexts: a 'feminine' comportment (e.g., an emotional way of talking, a swishy walk, a love of drama), which stands out sharply against the hyper-masculine way in which normative men conduct themselves; a greater affinity with women than men (e.g., in friendship); being responsible for domestic work in the home (e.g., laundry, cooking, caring for elderly parents); in urban contexts, employment in professions regularly associated with women (e.g., seamstress, hairdresser); and the more or less frequent habit of wearing women's clothes, or at least gender-neutral outfits. However, the femininity that *leitī* embody is not the ordinary femininity of local women, but that of a cosmopolitan and glamorous femininity modelled on the kinds of images they find in international fashion magazines and emulate in their beauty pageants. With few exceptions, mainstream Tongans engage with *leitī* in a very matter-of-fact way, which always amazes outsider observers (Figure 5.1).

In contrast to transgender people in the Global North but like comparable categories of people in other non-Western societies, *leitī* are generally assumed to be erotically attracted to

Figure 5.1 Every year, *leitī* organize a beauty pageant, Miss Galaxy, in the best venue of Nukuʻalofa, the capital of Tonga, which attracts the cream of Tongan society coming to both admire their creativity and laugh at their antics. Here the winner of the 1997 pageant is surrounded by fellow competitors. (Courtesy of Niko Besnier)

persons of the same sex as that into which they were born (Besnier and Alexeyeff 2014). Unlike lesbians and gays of the industrial world, they are not sexually attracted to one another, but to men who identify as straight – the latter have no particular compunction about having sexual relations with *leitī* since the former are 'like women', but few are willing to turn the sexual liaison into a publicly visible relationship because marrying heterosexually and having children is fundamental to being considered an adult man. *Leitī* also differ from modern Western-style lesbians and gays in that their sexual orientation is not the defining feature of who they are, but only one of many aspects that define their identity. A few *leitī* abandon their transgender identification in mid-life, marry heterosexually, and have families.

Tongan *leitī* demonstrate a number of points. First, like many others, this society does not classify people in terms of sexual orientation, but in terms of how people are gendered, and it understands sexuality as the consequence of this gendering: if one acts like a woman, then one is erotically attracted to men. Second, people who display unconventional gendering do not suffer the same degree of stigmatization of which gays, lesbians, and transgender people have long been the target in the Global North. They continue to be viewed as an integral part of the kinship system and of the entire society, even though the respect in which others hold them depends on their contribution to family and society, rather than their gendering. Third, the people anthropologists characterize as 'transgender' in societies like Tonga share a few but not all features with the transgender in the Global North; for example, few *leitī* would consider changing sex medically, even if they could ever afford the procedure. So the category 'transgender' encompasses a broad spectrum of experiences worldwide.

Having said that, as we insist throughout this book, no society is an isolated entity, particularly in the globalizing age. Tongan people have migrated in large numbers to places like New Zealand, Australia, and the United States, where Tongan *leitī* are exposed to new ideas and new ways of thinking about themselves, and some become gay or lesbian when they migrate, thus redefining the basis of their identity from gender to sexuality, while others may adopt a Western-style transgender identity. In return, some transgender people in societies of the Global North look to groups like Tongan *leitī* for a legitimization of their personal experience. They argue that this experience is widespread throughout the world and that there is nothing inevitable about the marginal status to which they are relegated in their own society, although these arguments inevitably romanticize the lives of people in other societies (Towle and Morgan 2002).

Should we understand *leitī* and comparable categories as evidence of a 'third' gender in human societies? Probably not, because the kinship structure, the system of exchange, and all other dynamics that Tongans consider important only recognize women and men, and the contrast between women and men is fundamental to how the society is structured. For example, at ceremonial events (e.g., weddings, funerals), relatives of both genders make formal presentations of different objects: men offer agricultural products (e.g., yams, cooked pork), while women present plaited mats and large pieces of pounded and decorated barkcloth. Tongans view these practices as ways of affirming the fundamental role that gender and kinship play in their society. Yet there are no specific objects that *leitī* could produce at such events that would represent their gender as a separate category.

How many sexes?

While many people find it self-evident that there are two sexes and only two, the reality is more complex. Because sex is made up of many different factors, variants can arise when the components display nonstandard characteristics and the interaction between them does not work as expected. In all societies, a small number of people are born with ambiguous or non-standard sexual physiologies, described with the umbrella term **intersex**, which replaces pathologizing terms like 'hermaphroditism'. Medical professionals disagree as to what should be included in the category, a symptom of the fact that these judgements are ultimately cultural facts rather than medical ones. Intersex people themselves are less worried about what actually 'counts' as intersex than about the stigma that their physiology often carries and the poor treatment to which they have traditionally been subjected in medical institutions.

Variations in sexual physiology can be the result of chromosome structures that deviate from the usual 46,XX (female) and 46,XY (male) karyotypes, or structure of chromosomes. For example, people born with a 45,X karyotype ('Turner's Syndrome') have a female appearance but do not menstruate; while people born with a 47,XXY karyotype ('Klinefelter's Syndrome') have a taller-than-average male appearance with slightly feminized features (e.g., enlarged breasts and wide hips). Intersex bodies can result from disruptions in hormonal functions, such as androgen insensitivity syndrome (AIS), which can occur in people with normative XX and XY karyotypes when the body's response to androgen is impaired; in the case of AIS sufferers with a 46,XY karyotype, genitals appear smaller than expected or ambiguous. Many physiological features form a continuum rather than discrete categories, in the same way that some people can be very left-handed, somewhat left-handed, ambidextrous, or left-handed for some activities but not others. So the answer to the question, 'how many sexes are there in humans?' is not two, but not a specific number either. The two normative sexes are the product of subjective judgements about what 'normal' means.

It is only relatively recently that developments in genetics have shed light on the mechanisms of intersex, even though intersex people have existed throughout human history and in all societies. Until medical technologies such as chromosome testing were invented, intersex people were simply considered a little different from other people. For example, when the South African running star Caster Semenya, who has intersex traits, was growing up in a poor neighbourhood of Johannesburg, she was just a girl with boyish features and remarkable athletic abilities, until her extraordinary performance on the athletic world scene turned her into a 'medical problem'.

In the contemporary Global North, the birth of a baby who displays ambiguous sex is often cause for considerable anxiety for parents, who worry about how their child will fare against society's rigid ideas about sex and gender. In many cases, a team of medical experts is assembled, which includes paediatricians, endocrinologists, surgeons, and psychologists. Sociologist Suzanne Kessler conducted research in the 1980s in medical settings that dealt with intersex infants in the United States, and showed that treatment decisions were not only medical ones but also social (Kessler 1990). For example, when determining whether to turn the infant's ambiguous genitals surgically into something that looked like a penis or a vagina, doctors make judgements about the minimal size of a penis ('one inch', or 2.5cms). It takes little imagination to realize how socially subjective these decisions are, particularly since the medical professions in many societies are an essentially male world.

In the last decade of the twentieth century, intersex adults in many countries began to mobilize for a more reflective approach to the medical interventions on intersex children. Activists argue that these interventions often have traumatic consequences and that it is society, rather than intersex bodies, that needs to change. Bodies of ambiguous sex are often surrounded with secrecy and shame. The impetus for change was greatest in the United States, where activist Cheryl Chase founded the Intersex Trust of North America, which became a model for dialogues between medical professionals and intersex people worldwide (Chase 1998). But not all intersex people agree with this stance, in that some want to blend in and have their physiological difference rendered invisible.

In societies of the Global North, intersex activists share with the transgender people described in the previous section a fraught relationship to medicine, although in a contrasting way: while intersex activists mobilize to lessen medical intrusions, many transgender activists seek to increase their access to medical care, which is often out of reach because it is expensive and the medical professions in many countries consider medical interventions frivolous unless it concerns an intersex person.

Gender and race: how categories intersect

Earlier in this chapter, we noted that gender, as well as sex and sexuality, are always coloured by other aspects of identity, the basic insight that underlies the concept of intersectionality. Social traits that confer a disadvantage to people can be either alleviated or aggravated by other social traits. For example, gender, sexuality, and race are deeply intertwined, as is the case in Brazil, where people identify themselves and each other in terms of a substantial inventory of racial categories, which are the result of a long history of Indigenous subjugation, slavery, and immigration from Europe, Africa, Japan, and other parts of the world.

This was the case in the 1980s in Caruaru, a city of 210,000 inhabitants in the northeastern state of Pernambuco (Rebhun 2004). In contrast to global images of Brazil as sexually liberated and free of the strictures of morality, Caruaru was conservative. The town is far away from urban centres and strong divisions separated traditional land-owning families of European descent and their servants of African descent, whom they kept in conditions that were not very different from the slavery of the past.

But race is a process rather than a fixed identity, which means that it is based on highly context-dependent subjective evaluations. Someone's race, or more precisely people's evaluation of the person's race, can change over time, for example through a 'good marriage' or by becoming a charismatic Christian, both of which increase a person's respectability and thus 'whiten' her or him. Rebhun relates the anecdote of a young woman who, at her wedding, refused to get out of the limousine because the wedding photographer was running late. Her concern was not a matter of vanity; rather, she was anxious to have a photographic record of her wedding in white as proof of her respectability, which was potentially compromised by the fact that the groom was educated and had a good job but was dark-skinned, while she worked as a servant but was white-skinned.

In Caruaru, people based their assessment of women's moral worth on their sexual reputation. They categorized women, in descending order in terms of respectability, as the legal wife of a man, the mistress, the servant, and, at the bottom of the ladder, the sex worker. If a woman was a servant, elite men felt entitled to have sex with her with or without her consent. These categories all referred to the kinds of relationships a woman had with men, and a woman's identity was defined by these relationships.

There was a correlation between a woman's social status, her moral worth, and her race. Women who were perceived as 'darker' were also assumed to be promiscuous and thus morally stigmatized. 'Dark' was thus not only an assessment of skin pigmentation but also an evaluation of social status, particularly employment and moral worth, as well as race. Both moral worth and 'darkness' were social interpretations and neither determined the other. Both potentially produced social inequalities that had serious consequences for one's employability, marriageability, and access to medical care. For example, abortion at the time was legal only in the case of rape, but no one in a position of authority defined sex between a master and his servant as rape and so servants who became pregnant after being assaulted by their master were denied legal abortions. A woman could be 'lightened' or 'darkened' by life's circumstances, and conversely a woman could 'become' darker if her reputation was soiled, for example by having children out of wedlock.

This ethnography of how sexuality, gender, race, and social status are intertwined in northeast Brazil illustrates what social scientists mean by intersectionality. Gender is not independent of other ways in which people are classified and evaluated. Rather, multiple structures of social difference work together with gender to produce patterns of inequality that have enduring consequences for people's lives.

Gender, sex, and sexuality in colonial contexts

These patterns are particularly dramatic in the context of colonialism. Colonialism refers to the historical period during which Europe and later North America dominated the rest of the world, from Columbus' landing in the New World in 1492 to the decolonization era that began after World War II. As the ethnography of Caruacu illustrates, the effects of colonialism continue to inform many aspects of our lives, whether we live in former colonies or in former colonizing countries.

For example, during the colonial era, colonial powers throughout the world were concerned about 'rescuing' colonized women from what they viewed as the poor treatment to which their men subjected them. A telling example is the outlawing in 1829 by the British colonial administration in India of the ritual self-sacrifice of Hindu wives on the funeral pyre of their husbands, a practice called *sati* (Mani 1998). Whether the women mounted the funeral pyre of their own will is an unanswerable question. What is more significant is that the ritual was mostly limited to just two regions of India and it was practised by relatively few women who belonged to a small number of **castes**, yet colonial administrators were inordinately concerned with the welfare of these few women, and not with the poverty, poor health, and lack of education of the vast majority (Figure 5.2).

When colonizers worried about the welfare of 'natives', they often sought to rearrange gender roles to make them conform to what they saw as the 'proper' way of organizing men and women. Thus, in many parts of the colonial world at the height of colonial rule in the nineteenth century, administrators and in particular missionaries encouraged or forced women and men to conform to Victorian middle-class ideals of gender. For example, in some regions of Africa, they reorganized agricultural practices so as to increase men's participation and reduce the involvement of women, whom they redirected to domestic pursuits, with the effect of aggravating inequalities between the genders (Guyer 1991).

In fact, the very structure of colonialism, which is after all one of oppression and subjugation, was often justified in terms of gender and sexuality, although this could take different forms in different contexts. In Indochina (today's Vietnam, Cambodia, and Laos), French colonizers depicted colonized men as effete, degenerate, and effeminate, and thus in need of being virilized by the colonizer. But in other parts of the world, colonizers viewed colonized men as excessively masculine and recalcitrant to colonial subjugation; thus the Gurkhas of Nepal, the Zulus of South Africa, and the Māori of New Zealand had to be brought under control and the dangerous masculinity of their men channelled away from war and rebellion, into such activities as sport and the military. Gender and sexuality played different roles across different colonial contexts, but they were always of concern to the colonial powers. White men were particularly worried about the alleged dangers that colonized men presented for white women and used these anxieties to control their location, movements, and actions.

Colonialism was not only the imposition of the power of the colonizer onto colonized populations, but also involved more complex forms of power. In colonial-era legal and medical texts in British India, French Indochina, and the Dutch East Indies (now Indonesia), gender and sexuality were a source of tensions not only between colonizer and colonized, but also among

Figure 5.2 Handprints representing and commemorating royal wives and concubines who became *sati* in the Mehrangarh Fort in Jodhpur Rajasthan. (Courtesy of Schwiki/ Wikimedia, licensed under a Creative Commons Attribution-Share Alike 3.0 Unported licence)

colonizers (Stoler 1995). Men who were part of the colonial establishment, such as administrators, wealthy plantation owners, and businessmen, were troubled by what they saw as the depraved lifestyle of low-class colonists and other 'unofficial whites', such as small-scale traders, low-status workers, and ordinary soldiers, who were prone to 'go native' by cohabiting with local women, fathering children, and adapting to local conditions.

Relations between unofficial white men and colonized women endangered the ideology of white superiority and thus the legitimacy of the entire colonial project. They needed to be regulated somehow, even though many respectable men also had sexual relations with local women on the sly. A science of tropical health developed that was designed to warn against diseases, such as 'neurasthenia' (a combination of lethargy, depression, and anxiety), to which Europeans were supposedly exposed if they were in too close contact with colonized people. Child-rearing textbooks in the nineteenth century urged white parents in the colonies not to leave their children in the care of native servants for too long for fear that they become 'nativized'. Colonial authorities were particularly anxious about what to do with the offspring of unions between Western men and colonized women (creoles, mestizos, 'mixed raced', 'half-castes'), whose very existence defied the absolute difference between Westerners and non-Westerners that colonial ideology crucially rested on. In some cases, these children were forcibly taken away from their families and brought up in orphanages.

There was of course a great deal of variation in the ideologies and policies across the colonial world. Yet, from the early sixteenth century, gender and sex were at the foreground of social relations in the colonial world, in fact they defined the colonial context itself. Colonialism is never a simple story of political dominance, but always one in which the colonizers are arguing with the colonized, the colonizers are arguing with one another, and some colonizers are more similar to the colonized than to other colonizers.

Gender, sexuality, and global capitalism

Globalization has created new conditions for people's lives, such as new forms of labour, that also transform how they experience and express their gendered and sexual identities. India is well-known for the customer service and digital technology industries it has developed since the last decades of the twentieth century. Thanks to new communication technologies, such as highly efficient international telephone links, corporations in the English-speaking Global North have transferred their customer service departments to India, where labour is cheap and people speak English. The 'business processing outsourcing' (BPO) centres in Bengaluru, a south Indian city that has established a solid reputation as a high-tech global capital, employ a youthful labour force of both genders, who are attracted by generous salaries and promises of upward mobility (Mankekar and Gupta 2019). The centres are ultra-modern and impeccably clean, and the workers are expected to dress neatly and abide by a strict discipline, all of which exude middle-class status. Yet the 'virtual migrant' work in the BPOs is exhausting, partly because shifts have to conform to the different time zones where customers are located, which disrupts workers' cycles of waking and sleeping, and partly because the mentally draining **affective labour** it involves, is designed to make sometimes angry customers in faraway locations feel cared for and continue to give their business to the company. Not surprisingly, the turnover rate is high. And these conditions affect women and men differently.

While workers of both genders experience similar levels of exhaustion, women workers are under more pressure than men as their morality comes under the scrutiny of relatives, neighbours, and others because the work often takes place at night and in the company of men. Unlike men, women also perform a double shift, having to provide the affective labour expected of women at home in addition to the affective labour required on the job. Women's bodies are particularly affected by the work, as the punishing and irregular schedules play havoc with their menstrual cycles, and many fear that these disruptions will make them infertile. The global capitalism that the BPOs represent may offer the young worker new opportunities for social and economic advancement, but it does so at a cost and by creating new forms of gender inequality.

Cross-culturally, affective labour is particularly associated with women, who are stereotypically believed to be more attentive than men to other people's emotional needs because they bear and bring up children. Women in many parts of the Global South capitalize on these stereotypes to migrate to parts of the world where they can earn more than in their home countries. If they are lucky to have professional skills like nursing, they can find work in countries with a shortage of skilled health-related labour, but the vast majority who lack education have to make do with jobs as nannies, cleaners, care-facility workers, entertainers, bar hostesses, or sex workers, and are often vulnerable to abuse, exploitation, and violence. Women sometimes see their precarious jobs as a route to marriage (another form of affective labour) and thus greater legal and financial stability.

Such is the case of Filipina women who seek work in 'hostess clubs' in Japan. Many Japanese women, who grow up in rural areas of Japan, leave as soon as they reach adulthood for urban centres to find employment and marry white-collar men, which causes a marked gender imbalance (Faier 2009). Japanese hostess clubs employ women to entertain male customers, serving them drinks, lighting their cigarettes (when indoor smoking was still permitted), engaging them in small talk, flirting with them, and singing karaoke, but not necessarily having sex with them. Filipinas migrate to work in hostess clubs to earn money so that they can support their families back home. Many end up forming relationships with rural bachelors and marrying them. Many of these relationships are successful for both parties: the woman acquires financial stability and a long-term visa and the man finds a spouse who is willing to live in the countryside. But for others problems can arise. Both in the Philippines and Japan, club hostesses are stigmatized as sex workers and predatory husband-seekers. Some women are under pressure from their husbands and in-laws to 'act Japanese' and have to deal with isolation, homesickness, and their husbands' lack of enthusiasm for the **remittances** that their wives send to their families in the Philippines. For women of the Global South, the affective labour in which they are supposed to be experts thus represents a mixed resource, which can be useful to them as easily as it can denigrate them.

Some men also capitalize on gender to navigate global capitalism. Shipping corporations around the world, for example, like to employ men from countries of the Global South as seamen, a quintessentially male occupation, because they can pay them a fraction of what they would have to pay workers from the Global North and they do not have to worry about unionization. Filipino men are overrepresented in this market, and in small nation-states of the Pacific such as Tuvalu and Kiribati, becoming a seaman is one of the few viable sources of wage work. Since the early 1980s, these countries have established maritime schools, which young men aspire to join to learn how to work on ships. The schemes have serious social consequences, as the countries' young men are largely absent. The tediousness of working as a seaman drives many to alcoholism, and the sight of men spending their brief leaves in their home country between assignments in a drunken stupor has become common. The relations the men have with sex workers in the ports of the world have significantly increased the rate of sexually transmitted infections, causing some to become unable to father children, in societies where having descendants is essential. The global labour market may thus offer new gendered opportunities, but again at a cost.

Another field where masculinity figures prominently is the world of professional sport, which is largely based in the Global North. Many young men in the Global South watch the sporting success of a few of their compatriots and dream of the wealth, fame, and glory that sport dangles in front of their eyes. For example, many men from Fiji, Tonga, and Samoa in the Pacific Islands are talented at rugby, which most play from a very early age (Besnier, Guinness, Hann, and Kovač 2018). Increasingly, scouts working for rugby clubs in wealthy rugby-playing countries, principally Western Europe, Australia, New Zealand, and Japan, seek to recruit talented young players in the islands as they are the most promising, least expensive, and most malleable.

As a result, the sport has become the focus of young island men's hopes for the future, at the expense of formal education and other avenues of social advancement. Yet only the lucky and talented few manage to forge successful sport careers in a global profession characterized by cutthroat competition. While those who succeed have an enormous impact on families back home, sending remittances back to them of a magnitude unmatched by other migrant relatives, many others linger in third- or fourth-rate rugby clubs around the world, poorly paid and barely managing to make ends meet, yet unable to return home for fear of shame. Others never manage to leave their impoverished countries while having given up on other life possibilities. Sport migrations and the dreams that they engender have a profound impact on the relations between genders as well as on the relations between the few men who succeed and the many others who do not.

By facilitating mobility and communication across the world, globalization has given rise to new kinds of intimacies and has entangled them with the structures of capitalism. Among the more visible are transnational romance and marriage, sex tourism, and sex trafficking. Because they frequently involve encounters between the Global North and the Global South, and thus a differential in power and wealth, these developments tend to arouse intense emotions. Many NGOs make it their mission to eradicate what they see as the exploitation of women and other vulnerable people from the Global South who are forced into sex work in cities like Bangkok and Manila, or flown to cities in Europe or North America with false promises of employment and end up in sex slavery. There is no doubt that globalization has enabled new forms of sexual violence. However, the reality that anthropologists have uncovered through ethnographic fieldwork is sometimes much subtler than the sensational accounts that we read about on the internet or see on television.

Cuba, for example, became a gay tourist destination after the country opened up to tourism in the 1990s, and a lively underground homosexual sex scene has emerged, as Cuban men, who often have wives and children, offer their sexual services to male tourists (Stout 2015). The country has experienced a serious and prolonged economic downturn since the fall of the Soviet Union, which previously supplied the country with aid, and this is aggravated by the economic blockade enforced by the United States. As a result, many Cubans are poor and sex work is one in a range of strategies they employ to survive. There is considerable variation in the kinds of relationships that tourists and the sex worker establish. Some are limited to ephemeral encounters. In many other contexts, however, Cuban male sex workers bring their clients home and introduce them to their families, in contrast to sex workers of both genders elsewhere in the region who keep sex work and family life strictly separate. Family members establish bonds of **voluntary kinship**, at least nominally, with the tourist, calling them 'son' or 'uncle'.

These relationships benefit both parties. By making the tourist a family member, the sex workers and their families are entitled to expect that he will give them money and gifts, but in much greater quantity than they could expect from their own blood relatives. The tourist has an 'authentic' experience of Cuba that he would never have had if he had confined his visit to a tourist resort. Sometimes, the tourist does not pay directly for sexual services, and instead incorporates them in a long-term gift exchange, which can continue through return visits and in the form of remittances, thus blurring the boundary between affection and instrumentality. These relationships are not always problem-free, as the tourist can feel exploited and the Cuban family can be disappointed when the tourist's remittances shrink to a trickle and then dry up. But these problems are no different from those that arise between Cuban families and their relatives who have migrated overseas. Gay sex tourism to Cuba is thus not the categorically exploitative phenomenon, with the wealthy visitor as exploiter and the local sex worker as exploited, that it may appear to be at first glance.

Gender, sex, and sexuality as social, cultural, and political categories

Gender, sex, and sexuality present both considerable diversity across the world's societies and patterns that recur across different social contexts. As a social, cultural, and political category, gender is intersected by other forms of difference and inequality. While it is generally understood as the opposition between women and men, gender is in fact considerably more complex, as people in many societies do not fit neatly in this binary contrast. While we tend to think of sex as grounded in biology in contrast to gender, it is informed by the social and cultural meanings we attach to it. As the example of intersex people illustrates, sex is not constituted by a simple opposition between male and female physiologies, but by the mutual interaction of multiple biological functions that can contradict one another and that are the object of social evaluations. Sex is thus the product of both biology and the social and cultural processes of which it is the object. Similarly, sexuality, the attractions and desires for the pleasure associated with the stimulation of sexual organs, is always embedded in social relations, cultural norms, and political structures that give meaning to it.

As fundamental categories through which we understand ourselves and each other, gender, sex, and sexuality are deeply intertwined with one another and with other ways of classifying, understanding, and evaluating people. While at first glance they appear to be attributes of individuals, they are in fact implicated in the creation, maintenance, and contestation of inequalities in and across societies. They have played an important role in the ideologies and practices of colonialism and continue to figure prominently in relations between the Global North and the Global South.

Key thinkers mentioned in this chapter:

Margaret Mead; Sherry Ortner; Gayle Rubin

Key terms mentioned in this chapter (see Glossary):

Affective labour; Cisgender; Gender; Gender hierarchies; Gender roles; Gender stratification; Gender stereotypes; Heteronormative; Intersectionality; Intersex; Patriarchy; Primary sexual characteristics; Secondary sexual characteristics; Sex; Sexuality; Sexual orientations; Transgender

Questions for discussion/review:

1   Explain the differences between gender stratification, gender roles, and gender stereotypes.
2   Why do anthropologists consider it problematic to state that there are two genders and two sexes?
3   What can an intersectional approach to the study of gender, sex, and sexuality add to our understanding of these topics?
4   What do colonialism and globalization have to do with gender, sex, and sexuality?

Chapter 6

The body

Human beings throughout the world have remarkably similar bodies. Barring disabilities from birth, illness, or accident, or modifications resulting from medical or other kinds of intervention, we all have limbs, muscles, bones, skin, and internal organs that all look pretty much the same. There are of course some variations in body shapes and in skin, eye, and hair colour. Yet biological anthropologists have taught us that human beings' genetic makeup is remarkably uniform and only a tiny fraction of our genes produce differences in detail. We even share 99.6% of our genetic materials with our closest evolutionary cousins, the bonobos and chimpanzees (Marks 1992). This said, what distinguishes people across and within societies is how they see and understand the body as a unit and in relation to other bodies, how they move, feed, treat, adorn, and wash it. All these activities have repercussions on the body's appearance and on how it inhabits space. Thus, while bodies are obviously biological entities, they are also social and cultural constructs that are shaped by specific ideas and practices.

Writing in the 1930s, Marcel Mauss (1973) was the first social scientist to draw attention to the social and cultural constitution of bodies and their attributes. He provided many examples of how people used their body differently in different societies and in different times. For example, the soldiers in the French regiment to which he had been assigned during World War I were unable to march to English military music, because the music had been designed for a particular way of marching. While British and French people are very similar to one another in all sorts of ways, and while we expect soldiers on the same side of a war to march in identical fashion, almost imperceptible but consequential differences characterized how soldiers had been taught to march. On the basis of many such observations, Mauss suggested that we are all socialized into particular ways of inhabiting our bodies, which he termed **habitus**, ways that are deeply social, and yet perceived by those whose bodies are shaped by it as 'natural'.

Fat or plump, thin or sickly

Bodies everywhere are the object of constant concern. In the Global North, anxieties about body weight permeate everyday lives, the media, and institutions. In contrast to many societies of the world where people worry about having enough food to eat, in affluent societies, it is the over-availability of excessively rich food that is a concern. Combined with the sedentary lifestyle of many urban dwellers, the excessive consumption of food providing an abundance of certain nutrients (e.g., fat, sugar) creates panics about fat bodies. The injunction to be thin supports an enormous diet, cosmetic, and exercise industry.

For people who have difficulties controlling it, weight becomes the major concern in their life, which other people, the media, and the medical professions make them think about

DOI: 10.4324/9781315737805-6

constantly. Excess weight in the Global North is often viewed as a sign of moral deficiency. Even in societies where people are generally slim, there are obesity panics. In Japan, for example, women are avid consumers of diet pills, exercise programmes, and weight-loss regimes, and doctors frown upon slight increases in weight from one year's physical examination to the next (Miller 2006). In many societies of the Global South, in contrast, people see a thin body as evidence of illness or lack of food, or that the person's family does not care for her or him, and being thin is aesthetically undesirable. What constitutes an overweight and, for that matter, an underweight body are the product of social and cultural evaluations.

For those who have the time, the resources, and the interest, control of the body can take many forms, through such activities as dieting, exercising, accessorizing, waxing, or botoxing. Even though the imperative to control the body comes from society at large, articulated in the media, the fashion industries, the medical world, and government institutions, they become our own personal projects. Through our relationship to our bodies, we transform the dictates of society at large into activities that we see as our own personal projects. This is what French philosopher Michel Foucault (2008) in the 1980s called **biopower**, the transformation of structural forms of power into people's own personal desires for self-improvement. Through biopower, we internalize willingly the power structures that regulate our lives in ways that often escape our attention.

The ideal of a thin body in the Global North is a relatively recent phenomenon, which is tied to social class. Prior to the mid-twentieth century, as in the Global South, plumpness was a sign of wealth and thinness a sign of poverty. But these meanings were gradually switched around: watching one's weight became a middle-class concern, and today the lower the income and education, the greater the proportion of overweight people. These patterns can be understood historically. At the same time that urban industrial society was experiencing this shift, food production became increasingly industrialized. Certain synthetic ingredients high in calories but poor in nutritional value became widely available, and cheap food of often dubious quality became abundant because it was produced on an industrial scale that enabled producers to cut cost. This is true, for example, of chickens, which are raised in huge industrial complexes and processed by cheap, often migrant, labour, enabling food corporations to offer low-quality chicken to consumers at bargain prices (Schlosser 2001).

These dynamics mean that poorer people tend to consume cheap food high in sugar, sodium, and fat. Fatty and sweet food intake has the physiological effect of making people crave for more. The fast-food industry exploits this by offering large portions of high-fat meat, starch- and fat-rich accompaniments, and soft drinks for little money. Understandably, families watching their expenses relish these offerings, which enable them to feed many mouths on a budget. Food of high nutritional quality, such as organic, low-fat, low-sodium, and sugar-free products, are expensive. In some countries, poor people tend to live in areas called **food deserts**, where the only source of food are small convenience stores that sell low-quality food, because supermarket chains consider these areas too unprofitable to set up a franchise and yet they have put neighbourhood grocery shops out of business. All these factors contribute to the greater proportion of overweight people among the poor than among the rich.

In many other societies, being plump is considered beautiful, a sign of good health and, in women, a sign of fertility, just as it was not long ago in the Global North, and the stigma that is associated with fat bodies in the Global North is largely absent. In Pacific Island societies like Tonga, Samoa, and Fiji, the portly bodies of important people, such as chiefs, pastors, and politicians, signal the wealth of the village and the nation because they are evidence of the people's ability to provide them with ample food. In contrast to overweight people in the Global North, fat people in these societies treat the matter philosophically: cracking a joke at the expense of someone's excessive weight makes everyone laugh uproariously, including the target of the joke – a scenario that would be inconceivable in the Global North.

Yet one must be cautious about simplistically drawing a contrast between the 'fat-positive' Global South and the 'fat-negative' Global North. In Pacific Island societies again, women and particularly young men are muscular and fit when they are young because they are physically active, and they gain weight when they marry, have children, and become increasingly sedentary because they leave physical tasks to younger people. An overweight young man is thus different from an overweight older woman. In Samoa, Pentecostal Christians, who constitute a minority but are increasingly numerous, are critical of the commonly overweight pastors of mainstream Protestant denominations because they attribute their weight to their greed, lack of sincerity, and exploitation of the generosity of congregation members (Hardin 2019). In other contexts, body ideals have been made complicated by globalization, which has enabled the largely Western idealization of thin bodies to circulate to other parts of the world. It has been adopted in particular by members of privileged classes eager to emulate the cosmopolitan images they consume in fashion magazines and other globalized media. Thus fat can be simultaneously positive and negative in a particular society depending on its associations. It is not only body size that differs across groups, but also ideas about body size, that is, ways of thinking about and evaluating the body and its attributes.

The World Health Organization (WHO) defines obesity, namely weighing considerably more than is 'appropriate' for one's height, as a serious and increasing health problem that presents a risk factor for non-communicable (or 'lifestyle') diseases including heart conditions, diabetes, and chronic respiratory problems, resulting in high mortality. The organization has found that the problem is particularly acute in some societies. In countries like Samoa and Tonga, the proportion of inhabitants whom the WHO identifies as obese is very high, for many different reasons, none of which function as a single cause: the 'traditional' value placed on fat as a sign of health; increased sedentariness caused by urbanization and changes in the labour market; ill-understood genetic factors; and the increasing reliance on cheap but unhealthy imported food.

The last factor demonstrates that body weight is not only a local phenomenon but also one that is embedded in the global circulation of commodities. In the Pacific Islands, people traditionally ate root crops like taro and manioc, accompanied by leafy vegetables, and if they lived near the ocean, they had fish and shellfish; meat like chicken and pork was limited to special occasions. Sometime in the mid-twentieth century, businesses began importing frozen meat from New Zealand and Australia, two of the world's largest producers of meat, but the products that reached the islands were mostly mutton flaps, the fatty end of the animal's ribs, which no one in New Zealand or Australia would eat (Gewertz and Errington 2010). By the end of the century, mutton flaps in the islands featured in all daily meals, as people had turned away from agriculture and fishing, and no longer found the taste of fish, root crops, and vegetables appealing. Coupled with other factors such as an increasingly sedentary lifestyle and changes in people's tastes, the availability of poor quality food imported from the Global North, driven by business interests, has contributed to the prevalence of obesity, heart disease, and diabetes in the societies of the Pacific region.

Reading the body: race

The body is an object of evaluation of people's place in society and race is one of the most important ways in which this takes place. **Race** is the social classification of human beings according to their phenotype, namely their physical appearance, including skin colour, hair colour and texture, eye colour, facial features, and body structure. In addition, how people present themselves, their social position, and a myriad of similar factors, such as residence, work, wealth, and style of clothing, can all suggest different conclusions about the racial category in which people fall. These classifications are based on subjective assessments of people. There is no biological definition of race because, however one attempts to define a racial group according to biological factors, the variation within the group is always greater than the variation between it and other groups (American Anthropological Association 1998). Physical traits are genetically inherited independently of one another; thus the colour of someone's eyes may suggest one racial identity while skin tone may suggest another. There are people with pale skin who have frizzy hair and people with blue eyes and dark skin.

Furthermore, most aspects of physical appearance are on a continuum: it is impossible, for example, to determine objectively where in the colour spectrum the boundary between skin tones lies, so the boundary between pale skin and dark skin is entirely subjective. This is why people who lived under racially segregated regimes like Apartheid in South Africa could apply to legally change their racial classification (even though of course their appearance did not change), and people in multi-racial societies can claim a new racial identity under certain circumstances. In the early part of the twentieth century, Jewish European immigrants to the United States were not considered white, but were gradually 'whitened' as many became economically successful and rose in the class hierarchy (Brodkin 1998).

While race is a matter of subjective judgement, it becomes objectified in science, politics, law, media, and bureaucracy. These instruments of power transform it into a deeply consequential social and political process on which inequalities have long been and continue to be based, namely **racism**. Historically, the entire economy of such countries as Brazil and the United States was founded on centuries of slavery (as well as the dispossession of Indigenous people's land), which established an enduring hierarchy between white and black, as well as others, including Indigenous peoples. In Apartheid South Africa and pre-Civil Rights United States, racism was enshrined in laws that dictated what people classified into different race categories could do, where they could go, and how they could behave, with dark-skinned people experiencing punishing restrictions while light-skinned people were largely free to do what they wanted. Racism is not limited to the differences between people of European origin and people of African origin; although centuries of slavery around the world has given these categories particular salience, racism defines other categories of people as racially marked. For example, in the United Kingdom, people who descend from immigrants from the Indian subcontinent (primarily Pakistan, India, and Bangladesh) are defined as 'Asian' and often discriminated against. In 1882, the United States government passed a law that prevented people from China from immigrating, and in 1924 another law banned immigrants from other countries in Asia. These racist laws would not be abrogated until 1965.

Even though Apartheid has been abolished and the Civil Rights movement of the 1960s has forced governments in the United States to remove race-based laws from the books, race-based discrimination continues to pervade day-to-day existence. In many countries, police violence is far more likely to target people who are identified as 'black' than people who are identified as 'white', patterns that the Black Lives Matter movement, which emerged in the United States in 2013 and has since become global, has forcefully protested against. Statistically, black people are more likely to be poor, live in undesirable areas, have less education, and have more limited access to healthcare than white people. This became particularly evident in the disproportionate number of members of racial minorities in the United Kingdom, the United States, and elsewhere in the world who died during the Covid-19 pandemic that broke out in early 2020. In a sense, race is the product of racism, rather than the reverse.

While race is relevant to all societies of the world in one form or another, different societies have different understandings of it. In the United States, for example, race was long defined by what was termed the 'one drop rule', according to which people were considered black if they had one black ancestor. While this principle no longer has legal standing, relations between white and black Americans continue to bear the burden of the country's history of slavery and **settler colonialism**. In France, where racial minorities are migrants from the former colonial empire in Africa or the Caribbean and their descendants, the official ideology of republicanism dating back to the Revolution maintains that everyone is equal and that race is not a relevant category. As a result, state institutions are forbidden from asking directly someone's race, but they find roundabout ways of obtaining the information (e.g., by asking where the person's parents and grandparents were born). This ideology does not prevent rampant racism in French society.

Brazil's official ideology maintains that the country is a 'racial democracy', emphasizing the rainbow constitution of the population in which every shade of skin colour is represented (Roth-Gordon 2017). Many Brazilians, particularly privileged citizens, insist that social inequalities are based on social class rather than race, and that Brazil is free from the overt racism one finds in the United States. But this ideology does not explain why whites are overrepresented among privileged classes, blacks are concentrated in the lower rungs of the socio-economic hierarchy, while 'brown' people (shades of which are described by many terms in Brazilian Portuguese) occupy the middle ground. Even though Brazilians prefer not to call attention to race, they constantly 'read' each other's race through not only physical features but also subtle cues such as how one dresses, how one speaks, and where one lives and is employed.

Race is the product of a long history of bad science about bodies, in which early anthropology played a regrettable role. In the nineteenth century, some anthropologists were concerned with comparing the measurements of the bodies of people they attributed to different races, a project that came to be called **anthropometry**. This quest served their aim to classify people into racial categories and demonstrate evolutionary differences among them, with, unsurprisingly, white Europeans considered superior physically and intellectually to other 'races'. Mid-nineteenth-century Haitian anthropologist Anténor Firmin (2002) was an early critic of this unfortunate pseudoscience. In the United States, Franz Boas conducted studies that demonstrated that the shape of human bodies was as much the result of environmental factors as genetics (King 2019). Anthropometry supported racist politics including, most notoriously, those of Nazism, and continues to rear its head to this day.

The 'disabled' body

Disability is a cover term used to refer to the effects of impairments of the body, the mind, and the emotions. There are people with disabilities in all societies of the world and disability affects everyone: even people who are perfectly healthy in their youth experience a gradual reduction in their body and mental potential as they age, as muscles, bones, and organs lose their ability to perform and their memory, mental acuity, and other mental functions decline.

While disability is inherent to the human condition, what counts as a disability, what place society provides to people with disabilities, and how people treat those considered disabled varies greatly. In some societies, the presence of a person with a disability in a family is viewed as shameful and as a stigma for the family. In other societies, it is viewed as one of the many challenges of life that other people need to adapt to or tackle with the help of institutions, technologies, and human resources. In yet other contexts what is considered as a disability in

Box 6.1   Race, medicine, and science: an uneasy relationship

The fact that race is a social, cultural, and political category rather than a biological one presents a problem for many areas of science and medicine. For example, medical professionals long believed that sickle-cell disease, a genetic condition that reduces red-blood cell counts and may cause serious health problems, affected only black people. When they were confronted with white patients who suffered from the disease, rather than revising their assumptions about its racial distribution, they attributed it to an unknown black ancestor or to the alleged racial history of the population to which the patient belonged (Abu El-Haj 2007).

Advances in genomics since the late 1970s, particularly the Human Genome Project that mapped the genes of the human genome between 1990 and 2003, have been hailed as a breakthrough that makes it possible to trace individuals' genetic history and help identify their genetic vulnerability to specific diseases. But underlying these seemingly valuable aims are numerous problems. Many companies claim to provide individuals their genetic history in terms of geographical origins on the basis of a DNA analysis, but this claim rests on the assumption that, at one point in a hypothetical history, people with specific genetic characteristics were located in specific locations, from which they later migrated and intermarried with people of other genetic characteristics. It also does not take into consideration that, after a few generations, people share very little genetic information with their ancestors and their fellow descendants. These assumptions constitute a return to earlier and discredited concepts of race as a biological category grounded in different continents, black with Africa, white with Europe, yellow with Asia, and so on. Using DNA analysis to identify disease vulnerabilities is equally problematic, as the relationship between our genetic makeup and our physiologies is complex. Our physiological strengths and vulnerabilities are not the result of single genes, but of the immensely complex and unpredictable interactions among genes and between genes and the environment, which influence the expression of genes (a process known as 'epigenetics'). Scientists have even demonstrated that an expectant mother's genetic code can be modified by the genetic code of the foetus she carries, which thus introduces genetic materials into her body that she has not inherited.

Since the late 1980s, genetics have been increasingly used to investigate crime, and today it is viewed as a gold standard in identifying suspects and victims (M'charek 2020). Forensic investigators use genotypic data based on people's DNA to estimate the most likely hair colour, eye colour, and skin tone of people, thus claiming to establish a direct link between phenotype and genotype and returning race to a matter of genetics. While forensic DNA phenotyping aims to provide information about what individuals look like, it is in fact a clustering technology: it may indicate that a crime suspect is a man of dark skin tone with black hair and brown eyes, but this information is often interpreted in such a way that turns all men with these phenotypic characteristics into suspects, which is then narrowed down in sociological terms to all men with such characteristics who were present in the area of the crime. The possibility of over-determining the range of suspects is considerable. Race is thus alive and well among us.

one society may be viewed as a gift in others. This is the case for epilepsy, a terrible disease from the point of view of mainstream North Americans, but one which for the Shasth tribe of California marked a step towards socially valued shamanic knowledge and authority (Benedict 1934, 60). This is why anthropologists who study disability see it not as an inherent characteristic that makes some people different and less able to do things, but rather as a characteristic of human relationships, which determine what counts as 'normal' and what counts as something else (Ginsburg and Rapp 2020).

Since the end of the twentieth century, some people whom others would characterize as disabled have rejected the very label. Deaf people have been particularly active politically, arguing that they are not disabled but instead constitute a Deaf (capital D) subgroup, comparable to an ethnic minority, with its own culture and politics. This position emerged in particular from long-standing efforts to which deaf people have been subjected to encourage them to speak and discourage them to sign at the expense of teaching them skills and knowledge that they can use to improve their lives. Controversies continue about the usefulness of cochlear implants, a prosthetic device surgically implanted into the head to provide deaf people the ability to hear, although imperfectly and with great effort.

But questions about what counts as a disability, in the sense of being impaired from leading a normal life, go back far in time. In Europe, deaf people were historically assumed to be incapable of communicating and thus functioning in society. In the eighteenth century, a French Catholic priest, Charles-Michel de l'Épée, noticed that deaf people in Paris communicated with one another using hand signs. He learned the signs they were using, expanded and standardized them to manually sign the French language, and in 1760 founded the world's first school for the deaf, which continues to operate to this day. Students were taught what would later become French Sign Language, and thanks to the school sign language was gradually acknowledged as capable of expressing everything that oral language can convey and as having a structure just like any other language. Graduates of the school spread the concept to all corners of the world, founding schools and developing many of the sign languages that we know today.

But even without an institutional infrastructure supporting standardized national sign languages, deaf people in many societies have developed sign systems that fulfil their communicative needs. In the Al-Sayyid village of the Negev Desert in Israel, peopled by Muslim Bedouins who all descend from a single founding ancestor, about 3% of the population is genetically deaf (Kisch 2004). This high incidence is the result of the Al-Sayyid sharing great-grandparents who had a genetic mutation that causes deafness, which the preference of cousin marriage, a common practice in the Middle East, keeps in the population. But cousin marriage is also what makes the village a close-knit community and what keeps its deaf members tightly involved in village life.

In the early twentieth century, deaf villagers and their hearing relatives developed a local sign language that is used not only among themselves but also by many non-deaf villagers. Far from being a source of social isolation and marginalization, sign language is a point of pride for villagers, who see it simply as a feature of human difference that God has bestowed upon them. In the words of one Al-Sayyid man, 'When one plants seeds, one watermelon comes out like this [gesturing round] and another like that [gesturing oval]. Both are very good; a watermelon did come out, didn't it?' (Kisch 2004, 159).

The Israeli state, however, does not understand deafness as the villagers do and has instituted a programme of genetic intervention designed to lower the incidence of deafness, a process of **medicalization** that turns deaf people into a problem. The state has also had other effects. Compulsory schooling was established in the 1970s, sending hearing children to a nearby state school but deaf children had to commute to a school for the deaf in Beersheba, the regional centre, where they were taught Israeli Sign Language. The growing importance of reading and writing for such purposes as finding a job has also placed deaf people at a disadvantage because they received minimal literacy instruction. These changes have resulted in decreasing deaf villagers' communicative and social integration in the village and marking them as different from their hearing relatives. State intervention has thus created inequalities between hearing and deaf villagers where they did not exist before.

At the same time, it is important not to romanticize the position of people with disabilities in the Global South. In fact, in a neighbouring village to Al-Sayyid with fewer deaf people, the hearing-impaired may find life hard. Elsewhere, in Kinshasa, Democratic Republic of Congo, the state provides only minimal assistance to persons with disabilities (Devlieger 2018). People with disabilities have thus taken things into their own hands and organized themselves in groups that circulate around the city asking for money, often insistently, from shopkeepers, factory managers, politicians, and other people they consider able to give, providing them, in exchange for money, official-looking certificates adorned with the national flag at the top and various signatures and stamps. Calling themselves *documentaires*, they act just like agents of the state collecting taxes or NGO employees raising funds, thus making begging respectable and shielding beggars with disabilities from accusations of being opportunists. At the same time, the *documentaires* see the certificates as a criticism of the state's failure to support them.

Even where a welfare structure is in place, things often go wrong. For example, in the Russian city of Petrozavodsk, in the northwest of the country, the younger generations of people with disabilities are increasingly living at home rather than in the state institutions where they were housed during the Soviet era (Hartblay 2017). The state and private businesses have retrofitted buildings to accommodate the needs of people with disabilities, but many of these modifications are difficult or impossible to negotiate. In one case, a ramp leading to a post office was built next to the staircase, but wheelchair access to the door is blocked by a handrail. People with disabilities see these blunders not as the responsibility of a single corrupt or incompetent person or business, but as the outcome of many honest workers simply 'ticking boxes' and doing their job for a state system that is inherently corrupt.

As this example shows, efforts to accommodate persons with disabilities may be well-meaning on the surface, but when the perspective of the disabled persons themselves is not taken into consideration, the result can have the opposite effect and make their lives even more difficult. More generally, these ethnographic cases demonstrate that disability is not so much a feature of people's bodies but the result of the social, political, and physical environment in which they are located.

Wrapping the body

In other circumstances, one of the most basic things that people do to their body is to clothe it. Throughout history, humans have placed on and around their bodies clothing made from a broad variety of materials, from leaves and vines to bark, animal skin, animal hair, fur, fibre, metal, and paper. Clothes have many overlapping uses, including protecting the body from the elements or dangerous objects, creatures, or substances; beautifying it; camouflaging it; and emphasizing some of its features while hiding others. Clothing also creates similarities and distinctions. One of the first things that people do on the occasion of a national day or similar occasion is to don costumes that they consider to represent 'tradition': the distinctiveness that this creates marks them as different from members of other groups, and the fact that other

Box 6.2   Turkish disabled war veterans from the Turkish-Kurdish conflict

Throughout the world, war creates disabled bodies among both civilians and soldiers in a particularly efficient manner. Disabled war veterans generally have a complicated relationship with people whose disabilities stem from other causes and often do not participate in the latter's political mobilization. In Turkey, a protracted war with the Kurdish ethnic minority living in the east over the latter's claim for political autonomy has left a large number of people on both sides with permanent injuries, most because of landmine explosions, particularly as the conflict escalated in the 1990s (Açıksöz 2020). Turkish soldiers disabled in the conflict, many drawn from the working classes, are lionized by the state as national heroes and given the honorific title of *gazi*, a term with a long history endowed with religious and nationalist connotation that roughly translates as 'living martyr'. At the same time, their disabilities make their day-to-day lives very difficult in a country with limited infrastructure to accommodate the needs of people with disabilities. In particular, they represent a serious impediment to finding a spouse and starting a family, fundamental prerequisites in Turkey for men to be recognized as adults, and confine them to demeaning manual jobs like cleaning. The veterans are thus caught in a contradiction, exalted by the state for their sacrifice to the nation while having their working-class masculinity undermined, in this deeply masculinist society, by the very aspects of their bodies that give them symbolic status.

They negotiate this contradiction in a variety of ways. When they are together, gallows humour is a common coping strategy, one that downplays the seriousness of their conditions while implicitly critiquing the social position to which they are relegated. Most subscribe to an ultranationalist politics violently opposed at once to Kurdish separatism, the peace activism of intellectuals and many others, and the vacuousness of the state's glorification of their *gazi* status, which fails to attend to their material predicaments. Some stage political protests, dramatically removing their prosthetic limbs in public to provoke a visceral reaction mediated by the press and television.

Particularly poignant are instances in which *gazi* purchase on credit technologically sophisticated prostheses through private healthcare to replace the rudimentary and deteriorating prostheses that the state had provided them with. These situations emerged at the convergence of several transformations in the 1990s: as Turkey turned to **neoliberalism**, financial institutions began extending credit even to people of modest means; solidarity among veterans began eroding; and custom-fitted prostheses with robotic control devices became available. However, veterans who fell behind with their payments for these expensive objects became the victims of another aspect of the market, namely the repossession of their sophisticated artificial limbs and other belongings, creating a mediated spectacle that aggravated the veterans' abjection and fuelled ultranationalist sentiments.

Like other instances of disability, Turkish war veterans' disabilities are constructed by the interaction of bodies with the social, political, economic, and physical environment, but here politics is a particularly complex field characterized by deep ideological divisions over the ultimate meaning of war.

people who have the same identities wear similar outfits stresses their sense of belonging. What we use to adorn our bodies conveys messages to ourselves and to others about who we are (Figure 6.1).

Where we find considerable cross-cultural variation is in what body parts must be covered, how, and when. On the outer islands of Micronesia in the Northern Pacific, women are bare-breasted but must cover their thighs; in Western societies, in contrast, a woman generally only displays her breasts in public if she is at a beach where this is allowed or while breast-feeding, which she generally does discreetly. In most societies, women and men wear different clothes, which signal gender, and, because the onus of modesty is often placed on women, they are often expected to cover more of their bodies than men. Thus, throughout the Mediterranean region, women have traditionally covered their heads and faces to various degrees, a practice that still exists in the eastern part of the region and elsewhere in rural areas. But even this gender differ-ence is not absolute: among the Tuaregs of Niger and Mali, men cover their head and face while women do not.

During the colonial era, Christian missionaries and other agents of colonialism considered the lack of what they considered 'proper' clothing among the colonized to be a sign of their moral depravity and religious ignorance. They thought they needed to be saved through con-version to Christianity, generous applications of soap, and swaddling in trousers, shirts, and Mother-Hubbards, a long loose dress that covers as much of the body as it is possible to do. In South Africa, early nineteenth-century British Christian missionaries persuaded the Tswana

Figure 6.1 Men in body decorations at a moka pig exchange in the Nebilyer Valley, Western Highlands Province, Papua New Guinea, 1982; in the foreground is Thomas Nakinch, who studied anthropology at university and was then a member of parliament, and who operated skillfully in both local affairs and the political and business spheres. (Courtesy of Alan Rumsey)

whom they were converting to discard their leather garments in favour of textile clothing (Comaroff 1996). These efforts went hand in hand with missionaries' project to reconfigure the gender division of labour so that women would abandon farm work and take up sewing and laundering.

Because the local supply of clothing was limited, the missionaries shipped to South Africa clothes discarded by British middle-class families. The problem was that these often included ball gowns and starched collars, which were inappropriate in the local environment. By both necessity and taste, the Tswana improvised, transforming and wearing the clothes in combinations that would have surprised the original British owners of the garments, injecting their own creative aesthetics into the outfits. These experiments caused anxiety among the missionaries, who saw in them a lack of discipline and obedience. Clothes had become a subtle way of questioning the missionaries' authority and of the colonizing efforts of which they were part.

In societies that are **stratified** according to **rank**, **caste**, or **social class**, clothing frequently indicates the wearer's social position. In pre-modern Europe, for example, who could wear what was determined by **sumptuary laws** that prescribed that only members of particular social ranks were entitled to wear certain items of high-prestige consumption, which were out of bounds for other people. Thus, in Elizabethan England, only the royal family was allowed to wear purple clothes, a restriction that reflected the fact that purple dye, extracted from seashells harvested in Lebanon, was rare and expensive. Sumptuary laws are one way in which the powerful control others through **consumption**.

In the Global North today, the relationship between clothing and social identity is more complicated and less transparent. Of course, one can easily spot a construction worker, a nurse, or a barrister if they are wearing the outfits appropriate to their profession or trade, but in these cases clothing is a marker of position in the labour market, although it also indirectly marks social class. Members of different social classes may blur difference through strategic 'dressing up' and 'dressing down': the ubiquity of blue jeans; the country aristocrat wearing the same tweed jacket day in and day out; or a lower-middle-class person who over-dresses for a social event to compensate for her or his insecurity. Often, one can only infer social position from the clothes that people wear if one is particularly attentive to the quality of the cut of a suit or the maker of a dress.

Yet in many contexts clothing continues to mark social difference and collective belonging, and in some cases these dynamics are the object of conflict. What is popularly called the 'veil' refers to a variety of female garments associated with different cultures and contexts, from a head covering draping the wearer's hair (*hijab*) to a full-length garment that leaves only the eyes uncovered (*burka*). Head covers are generally associated with Islam, but until recently Christian women in Mediterranean countries also covered their heads in public, and some still do, particularly in religious contexts such as attending mass.

Head covers have generated intense emotions and political conflicts in European countries with Muslim minorities. In France and the Netherlands, the governments went as far as outlawing face coverings in public in 2010 and 2012, respectively, although the law is difficult to apply because of the general confusion about which garments are concerned and about what counts as 'public'. As is the case of any social practice relating to the body and its attributes, many different meanings can be attributed to head coverings, and debates about them often come down to confrontations of one interpretation with another. In the Netherlands, supporters of a legal ban on head coverings see in them a sign of the patriarchal and retrograde oppression of women. But young Dutch Muslim women cover their heads in increasingly larger numbers and for many different reasons, most of which have nothing to do with gender oppression: it can be a sign of religiosity, a demand for respect, or a sign of ethnic distinctiveness and of an 'authentic self' in a national context that celebrates self-expression, but in which their particular form of self-expression arouses public scorn.

Clothes, then, are serious business. They can communicate belonging and exclusion, similarity and difference, and be deeply embroiled in struggles over power and agency.

Modifying the body

Just as bodies can be covered and adorned, they can be modified. We casually modify our bodies and its attributes on an everyday basis, by trimming our nails or having a haircut, for example. But some forms of body modification can be imbued with great symbolic significance, particularly when they mark a **rite of passage**, that is, the transition of a person from one stage of life to another. Examples are a child's first haircut in Hindu India and among Hassidic Jews; the filing of adolescents' teeth in Bali or their sharpening among several groups in Central Africa; and the scarification of the skin among some groups in Papua New Guinea and East Africa. A particular form of body modification may have ritual significance in one society but not in another: among the Xhosa and Sotho of South Africa, boys are circumcised ritually as a marker of their transition into adulthood. In contrast, in countries like the United States and South Korea, circumcision was until recently routinely performed on male infants born in hospitals for its alleged health advantages, and not for any ritual purpose; the practice is now in decline in both countries. Others, like tattooing, may have different social and cultural meanings at different times of history and in different places.

Whether it is given ritual significance or not, body modification almost always has social and cultural meaning. Like clothing, it frequently helps distinguish one group from another. Male circumcision again is a very clear example. Jews attach important religious significance to it, believing that circumcising male infants is a ritual enactment of their covenant with God. It thus signals both difference and similarity, in that it marks male individuals as physically similar to one another within the group and different from members of other groups. Even where circumcision is not viewed as ritually meaningful, it can mark differences between groups. In the United States until recently, it presumed access to medical care and thus middle-class status, since medical care is not a right but a privilege in that country. Circumcision thus became a subtle marker of social class, as well as other forms of social difference that mapped closely onto class, such as a race, ethnicity, and urban vs. rural background.

Modifying the body is often about beauty. Physical attractiveness is unevenly distributed, and it can transcend other forms of inequality in ironic ways: a poor person might be beautiful and a rich person ugly. What also seems to be cross-culturally consistent is that people who are considered beautiful can use their looks to their advantage: they are viewed as better marriage partners, they attract more friends, and they get jobs more easily than people considered plain-looking. Beauty, thus, works as a kind of **capital**. Elective plastic surgery, namely surgical interventions primarily designed to improve the looks rather than the health of a person, is often considered to be the epitome of body modification. In the Global North, one generally thinks of it as a sign of the vanity of people with too much time and money on their hands. It is thus no wonder that people who have 'work done' tend to keep quiet about it.

By contrast in Brazil, where cosmetic surgery clinics are ubiquitous, people throw parties to celebrate their surgery-improved looks, and plastic surgery is not confined to rich and idle Brazilians but is also available to the less wealthy in public hospitals, where plastic surgeons

Box 6.3   Samoan tattooing in its local and global contexts

Tattooing, which consists in inscribing designs on the body by inserting ink or other liquids under the top layer of human skin, has been practised in different parts of the world since ancient times. Tattoos have been found on 5,000-year-old Egyptian mummies and on the body of a man nicknamed Ötzi, which was discovered in the Alps in 1991 after being preserved in ice for 5,300 years. In some Pacific Islands, tattooing carries considerable social and cultural significance. The word 'tattoo' in English is borrowed from the languages of the region. While Christian missionaries in the nineteenth century tried, and in some cases succeeded, in eradicating tattooing because they considered it sinful, it continued to flourish in Samoa, where most men and many women are tattooed (Mallon and Galliot 2018).

In Samoa, receiving a tattoo, or *tatau*, holds particular significance for men as a rite of passage: men's tattoos mark that they are eligible, in time, to become heads of their **households** and represent the family at village meetings, and it is a visible symbol of belonging to a specific lineage and village. Young men have elaborate designs called *pe'a* tattooed on their hips and thighs, a lengthy and painful procedure performed by hand with a mallet and a comb. Women's tattoos, called *malu*, are less elaborate in design and size, and the procedure carries less symbolic significance. Tattooing skills are the specialty of master craftsmen called *tufuga tā tatau* and are considered to 'belong' to particular families. People who receive a *tatau* from the *tufuga tā tatau* compensate him with gifts of food, traditional mats, and money, and the exchange is part and parcel of the **gift economy**.

Samoans consider *tatau* to be a timeless tradition, one that is central to what they call the *fa'a-Sāmoa*, or 'the Samoan way'. Yet *tatau* has undergone many transformations over time. In the first part of the twentieth century, it declined, but it experienced a revival at the time of Western Samoa's independence in 1962. Around that period, Samoans also began to migrate to New Zealand and the United States to look for work. Soon their overseas-born children began to search for their cultural roots, of which *tatau* is a strikingly visible symbol, and one that, with modern technology, can be quickly and cheaply acquired. Tourists and volunteers of the U.S. Peace Corps, who spent two or more years in villages teaching or doing development work, sought to obtain tattooed armbands (*taulima*) and anklets (*tauvae*) as souvenirs, which also helped the revival of the tradition. Samoan tattooists began to incorporate motifs from the Global North, such as American eagles and the Statue of Liberty (the eastern islands of Samoa are under U.S. control).

In the 1990s, two *tufuga tā tatau* families gradually gained particular national prominence and later international renown. In 2001, two brothers of one of these families began bestowing chiefly titles onto tattoo artists from the Global North whom they had trained and who had paid them substantial sums of money. This development created bitter conflicts with family members and other Samoans, who saw it as an unwelcome **commoditization** of the tradition. Today, some members of these families have gained global recognition, travelling widely to international tattoo conventions and tattooing people all over the world for substantial fees. Rather than remaining village master craftsmen, they are now globally recognized as 'tattoo artists', from whom urbanites in the Global North can acquire Samoan *tatau* without going to Samoa. They are undeniably beautiful in their intricacy and symmetry, but their aesthetic qualities have replaced the symbolism of belonging, rank, and **gift** exchange of *tatau* in Samoa. *Tatau* are now commodities bought and sold in a capitalist market, rather than gifts embedded in a long-term system of exchange in village settings (Figure 6.2).

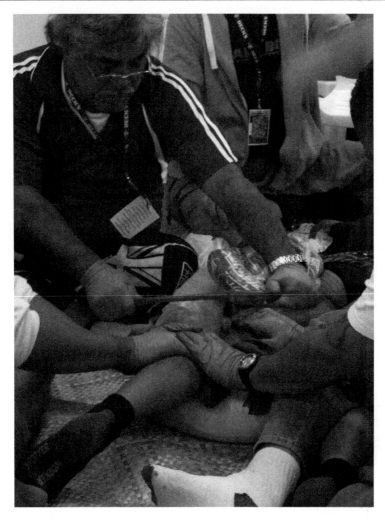

Figure 6.2 Samoan master tattooist (or *tufuga*) Su'a Sulu'ape Alaiva'a Petelo, who has developed an international reputation, at work at a tattooing convention in Auckland, New Zealand, 2009. (Courtesy of Sean Mallon)

provide pro bono services (Edmonds 2010). As one celebrity cosmetic surgeon put it, 'the poor have the right to be beautiful too'. Poor patients, overwhelmingly women, firmly believe that becoming better looking will help them materially, or at least that it will improve their self-esteem. There are other ways of doing so, such as psychotherapy, but only the wealthy can afford that. Plastic surgery, thus, is 'poor people's therapy' in an age when happiness is defined as the ability to buy things, including beauty. Plastic surgery in Brazil demonstrates the shifting nature of the boundary between medical necessity and elective interventions: if it helps improve poor Brazilians' lives, who is to say that the practice is frivolous? Here again, body modification is contingent on a specific ideology, which is historically and culturally situated.

In the twentieth century, until the 1970s, tattoos, piercing, and other forms of body modification in the Global North were largely confined to specific types of people, such as sailors and bikers, and the tattoo designs were largely predictable: an anchor, Mum's name, or a skull with wings. In the 1980s and 1990s, body modification became increasingly common and lost its marginal status. At the same time, tattoos acquired a different quality: people sought designs that they saw as reflecting some significant aspect of the self (Rosenblatt 1997). Even when people choose what in the tattoo world is referred to as a 'tribal design', that is, geometric designs inspired by Pacific Island or Southeast Asian tattoos, the wearer sees it as the result of a personal aesthetic decision removed from the social context in which the pattern originates but gives it a new meaning in the social context in which they live. Tattooing and fashionable body modification in urban centres of the Global North represent a visual statement of individuality that distinguishes the wearer from mainstream society, despite the fact that tattoos have become ubiquitous. In the U.K. today, about 20 per cent of the population has at least one tattoo and these are increasingly understood as going beyond mere fashion statements; rather, they mark important life events such as surviving cancer or domestic abuse, or helping to heal the trauma of bereavement by memorializing a deceased person on the body. By contrast, less mainstreamed forms of body modification, such as scarification, piercings, or face tattooing, can represent **resistance** to social conformity and protest against the values of modern capitalist society, even though they result from the same logic of consumption as everything else in contemporary society.

The marriage of technology and consumption has given rise to experiments that seek to enhance the capabilities of the body. Technologies designed to replace body parts and functions that have become limited or eliminated are of course not new, from wheelchairs for people who cannot walk to prosthetics for individuals who have lost a limb. Some experiments have stretched the limits of legality and ethics, such as injecting steroids into the bodies of athletes to enable them to overcome the physical limitations of the body. Yet other experiments have focused on the creation of cyborgs, bodies that are partly human, partly technological materials, such as computer-controlled body parts or exo-skeleta. Psychotropic drugs that make people feel better than they normally do also fit in this category. Extreme cases are experiments designed to preserve bodies after death by freezing them in hope that one day technology will enable them to be brought to life again. For anthropologists, the questions that these ventures raise are about the relationships among persons, technologies, the valuation of persons, healthcare infrastructures, political ideologies, and the market (Hogle 2005).

Body modifications can be the object of different interpretations: a particular practice can be viewed as beautifying by some but strange by others. The large pottery or wooden circular lip-plates worn by Mursi women in Ethiopia, which stretch their lower lip, have made them a magnet for tourists who flock to photograph them (Turton 2004). Tourists, however, do not take the photos because they appreciate their cultural significance for the Mursi, but because they consider them as evidence of the 'primitive' nature of the people. In contrast, Mursi women see the lip-plate as an expression of adulthood and fertility, and a way of distinguishing themselves from neighbouring societies. As the Mursi are now part of the cash economy, the women have little option, if they are to survive economically, but to allow tourists to take their picture in exchange for small sums of money. This commodified exchange demeans the Mursi women, who resent the tourists but need them for their money. In this instance, a body modification which symbolizes female reproductive capacity has been reduced to a sordid commercial exchange in which a small, poor, and relatively powerless group is preyed upon by wealthy foreign tourists eager for visual souvenirs of 'primitive' people.

Health, disease, and illness

As a biological entity, the body can succumb to illness, from the common cold to potentially serious diseases like cancer, AIDS, or Covid-19. Research in medical anthropology, which constitutes an important branch of socio-cultural anthropology, tells us that biological processes are always also social and cultural events. Medical anthropologists make a distinction between **disease** and **illness**: the former is a pathological event experienced by the body, while the latter is the social and cultural understanding of a health disruption. The two concepts often overlap but represent two ways of approaching the same phenomenon, yet there are occasions when an illness is not a disease, as when someone's health is affected by a psychological, religious, or social problem.

Like other matters that concern the body, health and illness are often tied to structures and ideologies of belonging and exclusion, and thus, more generally, power. There is a two-way relationship between illness and power, in that illness can be the basis upon which new forms of power are constructed, but it also can also justify pre-existing structures of power. Take leprosy or Hansen's disease, a disfiguring ailment caused by a bacterial infection that has almost disappeared today thanks to antibiotics. In historical times, people afflicted with the ailment were often ostracized, in part because of the horror that others felt when seeing the disfigurements that the illness caused, including deformed extremities, skin lesions, and blindness. It is no coincidence that the word 'leper' in English can be used as a synonym of 'outcast'. Yet we know today that the disease is not easily transmissible from person to person, so the exclusion that sufferers endured was the result of the social and cultural meanings attached to the disease, and not of any actual epidemiological condition (Figure 6.3).

Figure 6.3 Children patients and students at the North India Leper Hospital 1914. (Courtesy of Ernest Neve)

The social and cultural body

More than just flesh, bones and the complex biological mechanisms that keep it running, the body is a social and cultural entity, a medium through which humans negotiate their relationship with others and the social context at large. The body can be clothed, unclothed, inscribed, and modified in multiple ways. Marcel Mauss was right in the early twentieth century to recognize cross-cultural differences in the way people move their bodies; anthropologists have further developed his insight by showing that these differences can have political and social meaning within and across societies, which can generate conflicts over morality, ethics, agency, and power. The body, in other words, is one of the most basic sites where arguments about such matters as identity, politics, belonging, exclusion, entitlement, and the boundary between the human and non-human are waged.

Key thinkers mentioned in this chapter:

Franz Boas; Michel Foucault; Marcel Mauss

Key terms mentioned in this chapter (see Glossary):

Anthropometry; Biopower; Capital; Consumption; Disease; Habitus; Illness; Medicalization; Race; Racism; Rites of passage

Questions for discussion/review:

1 Why are normative ideals about body size always a matter of morality, social class, gender, and social values?
2 Explain why race, a social form of classification, continues to be so relevant to the life chances of individuals.
3 To what extent is disability the outcome of social, political, and physical environments rather than a matter of individual impairment?
4 Why do people modify their bodies in particular ways?

Chapter 7

The senses

When Liisa Malkki was conducting fieldwork in Tanzania in the mid-1980s among refugees who had escaped the Rwandan genocide, she noticed that she did not smell the same as the refugees (Cerwonka and Malkki 2007, 175). Her soap, deodorant, and perfume from the United States distinguished her smell from that of the refugees, who smelled of sweat, smoke from cooking fires, and a different type of soap. She discovered that the refugees made their own soap and she asked them to show her how to make it. Malkki's keen awareness of one sense, namely smell, made it possible for her to gain access to the lived experience of her research participants in a way that produced new methodological and theoretical insights. Information and knowledge, in this case soap making, is not the same as understanding. By making soap with others, the anthropologist not only learnt something useful, but also came to understand more profoundly the lives of refugees in an embodied process that drew on shared sensory experiences and took time and patience to learn.

The senses can tell us a great deal about other people's lives. All humans perceive physical phenomena through their senses because they all share the same basic physiology, yet their sensory perception is culturally shaped and, moreover, cultural values are transmitted through the senses. Aboriginal Australians distinguish by their smell people who belong to 'country', the original homeland they have inhabited for thousands of years, from people who do not (Merlan 2020). They sometimes rub rocks on their armpits and then throw them in water so that the landscape absorbs the smell of the people who belong there. Along with language, behaviour, and kinship, smell plays an important role in their relationship to the land and to each other.

Sight and sound

'Seeing is believing' is a popular saying that might just sum up not only what counts as evidence but also what counts as the best kind of evidence. And when people are in agreement with each other, they may say 'we see eye to eye'. Yet in particular societies, people may value one sense above others and in the process some senses that might help us understand the world are backgrounded. There is, in other words, nothing natural about the privileging of one sense over another. Whichever sense is prioritized is the result of local culture and history, as with the high value assigned in modern Western science to sight while other senses have come to be regarded as inferior modes of knowing the world. In contrast, in medical traditions such as traditional

DOI: 10.4324/9781315737805-7

Chinese acupuncture, practitioners pay considerable attention to touch and smell as they diagnose ailments and treat patients (Pritzker 2014, 40).

Expressions highlighting the preeminence of the visual do not make sense in all environments. For example, the Umeda people of the Sepik region in Papua New Guinea place high value on the senses of smell and hearing (Gell 1995). For them, navigating through the dense vegetation of the rainforest often makes seeing difficult, while listening to the sounds and taking in the smells of the rainforest can alert them to what is going on around them but is not visible. When making their way through the bush, the Umeda keep their gaze downwards to avoid thorns and obstacles on the paths as well as to look for animal tracks but it is with their ears that they 'survey' the territory to listen for the game animals they hunt. This is not to say that sight in hunting is irrelevant but simply that for the Umeda hearing may be more important in many contexts than seeing, and this is reflected in their language. For the Umeda, something is 'hidden' when it cannot be heard but is not considered concealed as long as it can be heard, even when not visible to the eyes.

The ranking of the senses in the modern Global North, with sight at the apex of the hierarchy, is the product of universal literacy and the rise of the scientific method. For literate societies, sight provides access to knowledge stored in visual form. The scientific method requires the close observation of the natural world to record in detail significant changes in experimental conditions, even if these days much science relies on technical machinery rather than the human eye to record data.

Scientists have long recognized that different people around the world prioritize different senses, but the way in which this recognition has been used has sometimes had a dark side. Lorenz Oken, a German nineteenth-century natural historian, divided humans into 'racial' groups based on what he thought were their sense priorities (Classen 1997, 405). According to him, Africans prioritized touch, which he thought was the most primitive of the senses and he placed them at the bottom of a human hierarchy; Aboriginal Australian people came next with taste; Native Americans apparently prioritized smell and Asians hearing; as could be predicted, at the top of the hierarchy came Europeans, with sight as their dominant sense. As one rose through the sense hierarchy, from touch at the bottom to sight at the top, the assumption was that the capacity for rational and civilized thought also increased. But he also thought that there were hierarchies within the racial groups; for example, he surmised that in European society women were more inclined than men towards the lower senses such as touch, reflecting their propensity to be less rational than men.

This is the kind of theorizing, now recognized as deeply flawed, that helped to justify a world in which colonial and gender oppression seemed natural. Yet, during the 1898 Torres Straits expedition, when A. C. Haddon and his researchers set out scientifically to record any possible differences in sensory perceptions between Westerners and others, they were unable to find any other than small physiological differences between groups but they did find differences at the cultural level (Goody 2002). For example, while people in all societies can see different colours, a physiological matter, how different cultures divide up the colour spectrum varies and this is a matter of culture. Indeed, the seven visible colours of the spectrum which Westerners are used to are seven in number because Isaac Newton, the seventeenth-century scientist who refracted light through a prism and was the first to understand the rainbow, considered the number seven to be a perfect number (Ardener 1971). And his decision to name one of the seven colours indigo reflected the economic importance of indigo dye in Europe in the seventeenth century more than any natural quality of the colour in question. How many colours we can name, and in some cases even the names given to colours, depend on our culture.

Box 7.1   Soundscapes of war

Martin Daughtry, an ethnomusicologist, conducted ethnographic research during the U.S. invasion of Iraq in 2003 and subsequent occupation on how U.S. military personnel and Iraqi civilians experience wartime sounds (Daughtry 2015). His work has taken the significance of sound into new areas, considering how people hear the violence of war, how they experience warfare through hearing, and how they survive the trauma of war, in some instances by memorializing violence in music. As Daughtry makes clear, soldiers, civilians, and others do not just 'see combat', they hear it as well.

In a war situation, being able to hear where gunfire is directed, what kind of weapon is being fired, or whether a helicopter is an enemy one may provide soldiers with enough information to save their own lives and those of others. These are sonic skills that soldiers and civilians learn in times of war but which, while increasing the individual's chances of immediate survival, nonetheless often lead to lasting trauma. Everyday sounds may trigger painful memories and compel those suffering from post-traumatic stress to relive past experiences of war long after the war is over.

Sound is a force that may be powerful enough to knock people off their feet or worse if they are too close to an explosion. However, the kind of extreme acoustic violence that occurs when one is close to a bomb blast is so intense as an embodied sensory experience that in the moment of the blast itself it overwhelms any culturally specific ways of experiencing sound. The noise and force of an explosion at close quarters is so overpowering as to shut out any way of thinking about it, it can only be felt. Only later, when dealing with the aftermath of violence and during the mourning that often follows, do the cultural resources of those caught up in the violence begin to reassert themselves (Figure 7.1).

The language that humans use to describe the senses can vary considerably. For example, in Tuvalu, spoken by Polynesian people in the Central Pacific, one term (*matea*) refers to 'seeing' and another term (*lagona*) refers to all other senses. This does not mean that speakers of that language are unable to distinguish between the other four senses or that they place little value on them, they simply use context to disambiguate the meaning of the term. In fact, they are particularly sensitive to smell: they prize the smell of garlands made from flowers like frangipani that they wear around the head, even when the flowers wilt and no longer look fresh but continue to be fragrant. Similarly, speakers of different languages can make more or less fine distinctions to describe different stimuli of the senses. For example, to the basic terms referring to taste that people in the Global North use (e.g., salty, sweet, bitter, sour), the Japanese add *umami*, a term now incorporated into English, which refers to a pleasant savoury taste found in foods such as parmesan cheese and mushrooms. The Maniq, a group of **hunter-gatherers** in southern Thailand, have a dozen different terms in their language that refer to different kinds of smell (Wnuk and Majid 2014).

In other societies, the senses and what they perceive are embedded in an elaborate system of correspondences that cut across various aspects of life. Traditional Chinese cosmology, for example, is organized according to five elements or *wuxing* (wood, fire, earth, metal, and water), each

Figure 7.1 Ethnomusicologist J. Martin Daughtry recording the sounds of military vehicles during the Iraq War, 2011. (Courtesy of J. Martin Daughtry)

of which corresponds to a particular smell, taste, sound, and sensory organ, as well as colour, cardinal direction, organ of the body, season, planet, and emotion (Hsu 2011). For example, the direction east is associated with wind, wood, sourness, the colour blue, anger, convulsions, and the liver. This cosmology, which is foundational to such pursuits as traditional Chinese medicine, astrology, and martial arts, integrates the senses into an all-encompassing theory about how the cosmos works, including the human body and the senses.

Even if members of a society consider one sense to be the key sense, people engage with the world around them using all their senses simultaneously. As cooks know well, people experience food through taste, smell, and sight. If food looks good but does not taste good or vice versa, a restaurant patron will be disappointed. In societies where food is eaten with the hands, touch is also thought to contribute to the taste of food. The sound of food being cooked or eaten can also add to our sensory experience of food. Experimental psychologists have shown that amplifying or muffling the sound of a potato chip as it is crunched alters people's perception of how fresh it is. Food can have its taste altered by sound alone.

In some cases, people have a neurological condition, known as **synaesthesia**, that enables them to process sensory information that usually stimulates one sense through the other senses. For a person with synaesthesia, a smell or sound can be felt as a colour or hearing a name can evoke a smell or taste. While some people appear to be born synaesthetes and frequently experience a sense through one or more other senses, others may achieve such an experience by consuming hallucinogens such as ayahuasca, a psychoactive plant-based brew that originated in South America. The Amahuaca of Peru, who were some of the original consumers of ayahuasca, say it enables them to separate out the individual notes of a bird song and taste each one in turn (Classen, Howes, and Synnott 1994, 156).

The taste of memory

For many of us, the connection between memory, smell, and taste is powerful. Modern neuroscience has shown that the senses of taste and smell are the only ones that connect directly to the hippocampus in the brain, where long-term memory is located. While science has provided the evidence for connections between individual memory and the senses of taste and smell, these connections have long been known to artists and used to explore the meaning of time, perception, and our developing consciousness of how embodied experiences shape us.

Marcel Proust, the French author of *In Search of Lost Time* (*À la recherche du temps perdu*), a seven-volume novel published between 1909 and 1921, produced what is perhaps the most famous literary example of how a sensory experience in the present can recall a long-forgotten mood and experience. The adult narrator, who is somewhat depressed as he sits down to tea with his mother, feels a sudden sense of exquisite pleasure at the taste of the petite madeleine, a small sponge cake shaped like a shell, dipped in tea and realizes that its taste had reawakened memories of happier times in his childhood. Without the childhood experience of eating cake dipped in tea, the man could not have recalled, through his sense of taste, his own early years and the moment of happiness consuming the cake gave him. The sensory experience in the present is necessary in this case to recall the past. And when all the people he recalls are dead, the places and objects gone, all that remains is the insubstantial taste and smell that both evokes and bears the weight of memory.

The smell or taste of a particular food can remind people of past occasions and gatherings when it was made or consumed. This may evoke personally and culturally important past moments, through sensory perceptions in the present, that serve to shape identity, make us who we are, and bind us to other people. The food we grow up with becomes a part of who we are and particular tastes and smells remind us of 'home', however this concept may be defined. For the many migrant labourers in the world who have had to leave behind families and homes in order to work in other places, recreating the food they grew up with, cooked, and fed to their children is an important means by which they continue to feel connected to their homeland. To share this food with others who have likewise had to leave their homes may become a way of creating a sense of community in an otherwise isolating and **alienating** living environment.

For example, Filipina women working as domestic servants in Hong Kong typically work six days a week, but on their one day off many congregate in a part of Hong Kong known as Central, turning it into a space they humorously call Little Manila (Law 2005). Here, they meet friends, exchange money and news, and taste, smell, and touch foods from home. Such practices performatively transport the women from Hong Kong back to the Philippines. Many are not allowed to cook their own food in the homes of their Chinese employers. In the Chinese media, the smell of Filipino food is described as having a 'filthy stench', but this description says more about Chinese people's racial prejudices of Filipina women as backward and lacking discipline than about the food itself. Filipina maids may lack the cultural capital to change these perceptions, but each Sunday they mark, in a small way, their rejection of Chinese prejudices by not using chopsticks to eat their food.

For others, the taste of food in the present may serve to heighten a sense of loss and evoke memories of foods that are no longer available. One example is that of a peach with a light white-pink skin, firm but moist flesh and sweet with a hint of sour taste known as 'the breast of Aphrodite' that is no longer found in Greece (Seremetakis 1996). This is the peach that anthropologist Nadia Seremetakis remembers from her childhood and which has been replaced in the markets with a softer, more watery, and less tasty peach whose flesh offers no resistance when one bites into it. The loss of this fruit denotes a loss of sensory knowledge and even history as the material objects that made up the everyday items of the past disappear from the present. And this disappearance is not accidental. It is part of a larger programme unifying and rationalizing food production and consumption across the European Union that results in the loss of distinctive regional tastes, textures, and smells.

The memories that taste evoke can have political implications, as powerfully witnessed by the recipes of home cooking that Jewish women from Germany, Czechoslovakia, and other parts of Europe compiled in the Terezín prison camp, where they had been deported during the Holocaust (De Silva 1996). The Nazi regime's propaganda machine showcased the camp as a model of the alleged comfortable conditions in which the Jewish deportees were kept, while in fact the camp was a transit point for Auschwitz. Some of the women inmates, many of whom had grown up in elite Jewish circles, wrote down recipes of the delicacies they used to cook, such as a dish of carp and potatoes, a goulash with sour cream and sauerkraut, and cakes filled with cheese, ground figs, and chocolate. They wrote the recipes, which survived them, on any piece of paper they could lay their hands on, including multiple copies of a propaganda leaflet exhorting the prisoners to stand and fight for the Führer. In the context of hunger, deprivation, and disease, these recipes and the sensory memories of home they represented were 'a revolt of the spirit', a way to use sensory memories of food as **resistance** against dehumanization.

Taste, food, and disgust

Everyone finds some foods simply repellent. Different groups of people have different ideas about what is disgusting and what is not. While in all societies individual tastes vary from person to person, they all fall into general patterns of food likes and dislikes that apply more or less uniformly within groups. Examples of food that is considered delicious in particular societies but not others abound. *Muktuk*, or raw blubber of whale and other sea mammals, is a delicacy among Inuit and Chukchi people in the Arctic and the taste for drinking warm cow blood among the East African Maasai is well documented. In contrast, most non-Japanese cannot stand the taste, smell, and texture of fermented soybeans (*nattō*) and many Muslims and Jews find the idea of eating pork disgusting.

Much research on these questions has been inspired by the work of Mary Douglas (2002), which was concerned in the 1960s with understanding how people in different societies classified things in the world. She defined anything that is not where it should be as 'dirt' which is, to put it simply, 'matter out of place'. For example, there is nothing inherently problematic about shoes, but when they are placed on the dining table in any European context or worn indoors in Finland or Japan, they become a problem. The problem stems from the fact that shoes are in their rightful place when worn on feet and used for walking outdoors, but when placed on a table or worn indoors they are out of place, and evoke a response of confusion, condemnation, or disgust. Many beliefs about when matters are out of place are specific to particular groups. For example, the British Traveller-Gypsies among whom Judith Okely conducted fieldwork in the 1970s held strong beliefs about how items should be cleaned: separate receptacles had to be used to wash the dishes, do the laundry, wash one's teeth, and bathe a baby, and the trailers in which they lived did not have sinks because water that has been used for cleaning anything should be discarded away from human habitation (Okely 1983, 82–3). When things are in their place, there is order; when they are not, there is pollution, chaos, confusion, and danger.

Douglas scaled up these ideas to a cosmological level in an analysis of the biblical abominations of the book of Leviticus in the Old Testament, which states, for example, that one should not eat pork or wear clothes that are made from more than one kind of fibre. Many earlier thinkers had tried to explain why the ancient Israelites considered pigs as 'dirt'. They had proposed, for example, that eating pork could make one ill, that it was a rich meat and therefore symbolized gluttony, that it was the diet of foreigners from which the Jews wanted to distance themselves, or that God forbade its consumption. For Douglas, none of these ad hoc explanations worked. The problem with pigs, as Douglas explains, is that they have cloven hooves but they do not chew the cud, and therefore they did not meet all the requirements to fit in the classification system as God had ordained, in which only animals with cloven hooves that chew the cud, such as cows and goats, are kosher, namely permitted to be eaten. Similarly, most sea animals that God created have scales, but oysters and shrimp are exceptions and are thus not kosher. People are repulsed by particular foods because they classify them as dirt. Ultimately, any disgust at the thought of eating pork a Jewish person may feel comes from a desire to keep to the classification system and to prevent the disruption and chaos that would result from not following this God-given cosmological order.

To disrupt the categories into which we sort everything is ultimately to challenge the very order of the cosmos. Dirt is always part of a system in which it is a byproduct of the system itself and anything can become dirt when it cannot be put into a clear category in whatever system of classification is in place. Dirt is therefore never found alone; it is always that which is ambiguous, anomalous, or rejected in relation to those things that belong clearly to one category or another.

However established classification categories are, they are nonetheless flexible, as individuals and groups adapt to fit new circumstances and contexts. What constitutes matter out of place at one moment or for one group of people may be incorporated into the realm of the normal at a different moment or by another group of people. For example, people have various approaches to religious prohibitions against particular food, drink, or ways of behaving, and some feel that abiding by moral norms, such as being a good person, is more important than following prescriptions and proscriptions. In other cases, circumstances call for flexibility and adaptation, and people often consume food that they otherwise find disgusting if the alternative is hunger or offending one's hosts.

In all societies, particular foods are considered desirable and often reserved for special occasions, but there is one potential food source that almost universally arouses disgust, namely human flesh, for most people the most taboo food imaginable. Yet tales of cannibalism abound, not least in European fairy tales, where wicked witches lure children into the woods to fatten them up as a succulent main course. Setting aside documented cases of cannibalism as a result of insanity or for survival in extreme circumstances, there were socially recognized ritual occasions when the flesh of human beings who are not members of one's own group, particularly enemies, was consumed, a practice called **exocannibalism** (from *exo-* 'outside'). Where it was practised, it was generally designed to demonstrate power over and hostility towards the vanquished, or to absorb their power. It took place in the past in parts of South America and the Pacific Islands. Some anthropologists have argued, however, that most accounts of cannibalism found in distant societies are based on hearsay or myths, and that they were part of Westerners' ideological construction of these societies as primitive and violent (Arens 1979). There may be some truth to this interpretation, although the evidence that some societies practised exocannibalism, some until the mid-twentieth century, is quite strong.

By contrast, the Wari', an Indigenous population in Brazil, used to practise **endocannibalism** (from *endo-* 'inside'), or the consumption of people in one's own group, as part of funerary ritual (Conklin 2001). They were forced to abandon the practice by Christian missionaries and government workers in the 1960s, when they first came into contact with the outside world. Prior to that, eating the roasted flesh, some organs, and the ground bones of the deceased honoured her or him, helped the mourners grieve, and facilitated the transformation of the spirit of the deceased into animals that could in turn be eaten. The Wari' were not motivated by a taste for human flesh or because their diet lacked protein. Only **affines**, with the exception of the spouse of the deceased, were expected to consume the bodies of the dead and they did it out of compassion for the deceased and their relatives. Relatives of the deceased would urge the affines to consume the flesh of their kin even when the flesh had decayed during the mourning period. Affines were obliged to eat at least part of the corpse, no matter how disgusted they felt, in order not to insult the family and the memory of the deceased. Burying the dead, which they have been forced to do since abandoning endocannibalism, was considered disrespectful because the earth is cold and dirty, and thus the opposite of the warmth of social togetherness.

The Wari' prioritize sight among the senses, and considered eating the dead to be a way of eliminating any visual reminders and painful visual memories of her or him. In contrast, they talked at great length about the smell of rotten flesh, which stuck to the mourners' bodies and hair. For a people who placed considerable value on being clean and fresh smelling, the experience was overwhelmingly powerful and memorable.

In other societies, the fear of cannibals or of being consumed was one way in which people conceptualized the exploitation and injustice to which they were subjected. This was a metaphorical use of ideas of cannibalism. During the first half of the twentieth century, the Toba, an Indigenous group in Argentina, were given the worst living and working conditions on the sugar plantations on which they laboured in order to survive (Gordillo 2002). Contemporary Toba remember the plantations as places of fear and death, and their bodies as literally consumed by hard labour and the appalling conditions. They transmit these memories from one generation to the next by describing spirits and people roaming the plantations in search of human flesh, but they paradoxically state that these cannibals found that Toba flesh had a bad taste because they were poor and did not eat nice things. They thus internalized through sensual memories their own low status and abjection on the plantations.

Cannibalism and witchcraft often go hand in hand. The Temne in Sierra Leone imagine witch-cannibals as people who are perverted by greed and other anti-social desires (R. Shaw 1997), beliefs that are widespread throughout west and central Africa. Their bodies lack a heart and they are capable of growing an additional stomach. No human stomach is capable of digesting human flesh as it is so disgusting that the body would reject human meat. Here the embodied and physical sensations of revulsion at the thought of consuming a person mark out the moral human being from the immoral and differently bodied cannibal-witch. In all cases where cannibalism is present or feared, the practice is always situated within a moral framework.

The taste of power

In most societies, people who are marginalized because of their gender, social class, or other aspect of their identity often find it difficult to have their concerns heard and addressed by those who occupy positions of relative power. In such situations, they may engage the senses to communicate messages which cannot be spoken or conveyed in any other way. Anthropologist Paul Stoller and sociologist Cheryl Olkes found this out the hard way while working with the Songhay in Niger, when they were served a thin tasteless sauce prepared by the youngest daughter-in-law of the **household** where they were guests, and which Stoller describes as so repulsive that it was 'the sociocultural equivalent of vomit' (Stoller and Olkes 1986, 341).

Among the Songhay, the burden of housework falls on the youngest daughter-in-law in the household and it involves an unremittingly exhausting routine of cleaning, cooking, washing, and drawing water from the well. When guests are present, the amount of work she has to do increases, particularly as it requires her to prepare the thick sauces deemed suitable for visitors. The Songhay have a hierarchy of sauces that index status and social distance: thick spicy sauces are served to socially distant guests while close family can expect to be served thin tasteless sauces. To serve a thin sauce to an outsider might be a sign that they are considered sufficiently close as to share in a family meal. In the case described by Stoller and Olkes, however, the thin sauce was the means by which an overburdened and unappreciated young wife communicated her discontent in the only form she had available to her. Needless to say, everyone present at the meal understood its meaning as both an insult to the guests and a silent but sensorily eloquent protest by the least powerful member of the household.

The taste of foods many of us take for granted today, such as sugar, may also be the outcome of centuries of complex international trade and commodity markets, exploitation, colonialism, and slavery. In this respect, a sweet tooth is not just the predilection of the individual but a taste that has been nurtured over time and is deeply enmeshed in histories of power, status, and politics.

In Europe, sugar was historically transformed from an expensive luxury good available only to the social elites of Europe to a cheap sweetener high in calories and low in nutrients that gave the workers of the industrial revolution in England enough energy to work long hours with little sustenance (Mintz 1985). The production of enough sugar to create and meet the demands of the populations of Europe was made possible by the Atlantic slave trade. When colonial slavery was officially abolished in various parts of the world over the course of the nineteenth century, poor people from countries such as China, India, and the Philippines migrated to work as both free and indentured labourers on plantations in the Caribbean and the Pacific.

When sugar first reached Europe from the Middle East, it was used in small quantities as an expensive medicine and spice purchased by royalty and the elites. In the early thirteenth century, King Henry III of England asked the mayor of Winchester to purchase three pounds of sugar and wondered if this much could even be bought at one time from merchants. It took several more centuries before sugar became an ingredient in its own right rather than a spice and it was only in the latter part of the nineteenth century that the price of sugar dropped sufficiently to turn it from luxury good to necessity for the working poor. In Britain, the annual per-capita consumption rose from 4lbs in 1704 to 90lbs in 1900. The increase in consumption of sugar as an energy source went hand in hand with the rise in consumption of bitter stimulants such as tea. Tea, made palatable with sugar, also made possible the increased productivity of workers without adding any nutritional benefit. Sugar-rich jams on bread became the fast food of the day for workers and hot tea with sugar replaced hot meals for factory workers as women now worked long hours in factories and finding the time to cook food at home became more difficult for them.

Sugar is a food many people around the world now take for granted, yet a fondness for the taste of sweet foods that developed over centuries has resulted in global economic, political, and social transformations, linking the West African coast where slaves were abducted to the plantations where slaves and indentured workers toiled in the Caribbean to the factories of Industrial Revolution England. As Sidney Mintz memorably argued, sweetness and power are inextricably enmeshed.

Smell

Smell can evoke memories, arouse expectations, or produce feelings ranging from rapturous pleasure to extreme disgust. A sense of smell can be refined and improved with training, but it becomes less sensitive with age. Just how this happens and how it differs from society to society and from person to person depends on many factors, with biology being only one.

In many societies, smells are seasonal and associated with particular emotions and ritual events. In Europe, for example, even though few people spend much time in winter pine forests, their aroma pervades the experience of Christmas that city dwellers associate with feasting, family gatherings, and good cheer. Other scents, such as cinnamon and spiced orange, not only conjure up Christmas, but are also part of a multi-million-pound industry in Britain, where sales of scented candles and diffusers have become a huge industry. Europeans may no longer bake gingerbread, but their homes can still smell as though they do if they can afford to pay for luxury-scented candles.

The Desana of the Amazonian rainforest of Colombia call themselves *wira* 'people who smell' because for them smell carries considerable cultural meaning (Classen, Howes, and Synnott 1994). Like the Australian Aboriginal people referred to earlier, they consider that the territory of a group is permeated with their odour and they compare this with animals that mark territory by scent. Different animals, people, and plants have distinct odours that are conditioned by where they live, what they grow, and what they eat. They are thought to emit a 'wind thread' that allows for them to be tracked and located. Because they are hunters, the Desana consider that they acquire the musky smell of the game they eat, while they find that their neighbours, the fisher Tapuya, smell of fish. Women and men within a group also smell differently. In rituals, Desana women are symbolized by the strong-smelling ants or worms that they are considered to smell like. They thus understand identity as a matter of smell. The Desana also have a complex and rich system of classification based on smell. Categories can bring together seemingly disparate fruits, animals, cultural values, and humans. For example, palm trees and one kind of deer belong to the same smell category because they are associated with male power and fertility.

Scents, and in particular perfumes, are often a key part of rituals, such as those designed to attract a romantic partner. The amount of advertisements throughout the world designed to persuade youth audiences that if only they could get their smell right, they could attract desirable mates makes clear just how important smells can be, or rather how masking the wrong ones and getting the right ones matters. The Trobrianders of Papua New Guinea made fragrances from coconut oil and mint, pronounced spells over them, and then anointed the person whom they desired with them (Malinowski 1929, 541–5). A man who had made the charmed perfume did not use it to make himself smell sweet but rather gave it to the one he desired in the hope that she would dream of him so that on waking she would be uncontrollably attracted to him. So powerful was the perfume that the Trobrianders told of how a brother and sister committed incest with disastrous consequences when the sister accidentally came into contact with the perfume her brother had prepared.

Some societies have strong norms about when certain smells are required or inappropriate. In the United Arab Emirates, for example, fragrance is an important part of everyday social interaction and guests invited to one's home are welcomed into a space in which the host has burnt incense (Kanafani 1983). Guests arrive wearing their own scent and, as they sit and share conversation and food, they absorb the scent of the home. When they leave, the host may offer them the opportunity to perfume their clothes with the host's fragrances. During a social visit, a guest is thus transformed from one who arrives bearing the scent of an outsider into one who has the scent of the insider. The quality of the perfumes offered reflects the position and status of the host and perfumes can signal social status; the most favoured perfumes, such as aloeswood, are very expensive.

In the Emirates, scent, attractiveness, and beauty are so closely intertwined that for a woman to be heavily perfumed in a public space where men unrelated to her are likely to be present is not acceptable. Nor is it acceptable for a woman to wear perfume when attending a mosque for prayer. In these settings, a scent that attracts attention to a woman is inappropriate.

Among Emiratis, different parts of the body such as hair and skin are scented with different perfumes and today in some households women continue to make their own perfumes from scents such as rose, sandalwood, jasmine, aloeswood, and musk. At weddings, special attention is given to the scenting of the bride's hair, and the groom's neck, ears, hands, and beard are scented with sweet-smelling oils and as he repeatedly steps over a censer of burning aloeswood the smell from the incense clings to him.

A funeral also requires perfumes. The body of the deceased is washed with sweet-smelling leaves and scented with oil. At the head and feet of the body, censers are placed to scent the body and the shroud is also perfumed. People say this is done so that the deceased will smell good when encountering God and so that the perfumes can attract angels and keep evil spirits away. By contrast, the mourners at a funeral do not wear perfume or perform the usual rituals of censing and perfume offering to guests. The use of perfumes on the deceased and not by the mourners marks the separation between the living and the dead and highlights the fact that the deceased is no longer able to take part in the social relations between the living that are ritualized through the exchange of perfumes.

Smells can be a marker of identity or difference. They can be an essential element in ritual and serve to organize space. Smells can arouse strong memories, either pleasant or unpleasant, and the moral worth of individuals and groups is often judged on the basis of smell.

Touching the past

Today, museum curators and designers increasingly encourage visitors to experience exhibitions and displays in ways that involve the senses. A visitor may be able to touch electronic displays to learn about a particular artefact or watch and listen to a video that shows how the objects on display are used or explains what they mean to the people who made them. Museums also incorporate attention to the visitor's sense of smell by adding scents to an exhibition when relevant. All this may seem to be innovative, but in fact museums in the seventeenth and eighteenth centuries allowed visitors to handle displayed objects (Howes 2014). The logic was that visitors could learn more about the objects through the senses other than sight alone. The texture, weight, and feel of an object makes a difference in how one understands it and adds to the enjoyment one experiences when holding something special. Through touch, a person can feel a connection to the creators of the object and, so thought the museum curators of the past, it can also lead to a sense of healing and well-being, in the same way that touching a religious relic might do for a pious person.

For Indigenous groups who remain today disadvantaged and marginalized because of a history of colonial oppression, touching objects made by their ancestors that are now preserved in ethnographic museums around the world can be a particularly important experience. It was during colonial times that many of the material artefacts of Indigenous groups were given or, as often as not, just taken from them eventually to find their way into museums, to which descendants of their original owners have had no access. Today, a new generation of museum curators is working with Indigenous people to help heal colonial traumas by connecting them with the artefacts made by their forebears. Through touch and other forms of sensory engagement, social relations are strengthened and well-being is enhanced, in addition to providing new knowledge to the museums about the use and meaning of the artefacts.

In 2010, the Pitt Rivers Museum in Oxford, England, sent five shirts collected in 1841 from the Blackfoot people, an Indigenous North American group, to museums in Canada so that tribal members could touch and examine them (Peers 2013). The shirts are not only important as heritage objects but also as objects that embody the spirits of the people who made and wore them. Touching the shirts, smelling them for the scent of home-tanned hide, examining the stitching and porcupine quill work, and putting their fingers directly on the painted finger marks of the artist who decorated them allowed the Blackfoot people to reconnect with their ancestors. For the participants, the experience aroused feelings of joy, grief, mourning, and anger, as well as gratitude that the ancestors had come back to visit. Finding ways to allow Indigenous and other groups to reconnect directly and at the sensorial level with items of their cultural heritage is a step forward in the decolonization process and one which can strengthen cultural identity and add to the knowledge and expertise of both the Indigenous people and the museum staff.

Sounds

Sounds we are familiar with make us feel secure in the auditory knowledge that we are in a place we understand, recognize, and belong to. Particular sounds, such as the call to prayer (*azan*) in Muslim countries or the ringing of church bells in Christian countries, may make us conscious of space and time. As ethnomusicologist Steven Feld puts it, 'as place is sensed, senses are placed; as places make sense, senses make place' (1996, 91). Hearing and listening shape how we interpret our experiences; understanding how people experience sound enables us to understand how people are shaped by sound.

The Kaluli, a group of about 2,000 people who live at the foot of Mount Bosavi in the Western Province of Papua New Guinea, sing in a way that echoes the sounds of the rainforest in which they live (Feld 2012). In the forest, sounds are not discrete, but rather they constantly intermingle, with some briefly standing out from others and then quickly receding. There is no silence and no unison. For the Kaluli, sound is a means to inhabit and understand their environment, the seasons, and the animals and birds in the environment. Birdsongs are the voices of spirits, which enable them to communicate with the ancestral spirits. Sounds also often reveal the presence of animals that may remain visually hidden. The aesthetics of Kaluli music reflects their auditory experiences of the rainforest. When singing, they avoid unison, yet their voices are always in synchrony with one another: some parts may be prominent and then recede, they can overlap or give way to other parts. The Kaluli utilize music to turn nature into culture.

Sound can also act as a tool for people to acclimate to new life conditions. This happens, for example, in hospitals in Britain (and other countries), institutions where the other senses are dulled or 'anaesthetized' to meet institutional requirements: patients' sight is limited to what they can see from a hospital bed, their sense of smell only catches the unpleasant scent of detergent, what they can touch is restricted, and the food is bland and tasteless (Rice 2003). Hearing is left as the sense through which patients experience the environment, but what they hear is the regular beep of monitoring machines, the shuffle of nurses in the corridor, and the muffled sound of voices and televisions. There is no silence here either, but unlike in the Kaluli rainforest, the hospital's constant noise is intrusive and inescapable. In order to get any rest, patients have to submit to the hospital's aural regime, and this submission to the sounds of the hospital is how patients get to understand the hospital environment and how they become familiar with its routines. At the same time, it forces them to conform to expected hospital behaviour and accept the role of patient.

Sensory impairment

Some people are born with sensory impairments, for example, with limited or no sight or hearing, but most people experience as they age some form of diminished sensory capacity or impairment. Others will experience temporary or permanent impairment from the use of drugs or alcohol, by participating in rituals which alter sensory perception, or because of illness or accident.

How the individual experiences and negotiates sensory impairment depends on the role that culture plays in mediating between the individual and the social and physical environment. Thus, while sensory impairment may be physiological or intellectual, the disability that derives from it is socially produced and results from conditions which exclude the person from access to aspects of social life readily available to those without impairments. When a blind or deaf person is denied employment because of the assumption that a physiological impairment signals an intellectual one, or when a blind person is not allowed to sit on a jury to hear a case because of the assumption that verbal statements require sight to evaluate the demeanor of witnesses, disability is the outcome. In these instances, the impairment of a single sense may lead to multiple forms of cultural impairment across several domains.

We all use our senses to perceive the environment and those with sensory impairment are no different. How we do so varies with the person, the level and type of impairment, and the ideologies which produce local understandings of what is considered to be 'normal'. Ideologies may include stereotypes about how those with physiological impairments perceive the world around them and how this sensory experience is mediated through language. For example, stereotypes about how the blind use touch to understand their environment privilege the hands as instruments of touch, whereas blind people may foreground instead how they encounter and understand the world from tactile sense impressions through their feet (Macpherson 2009).

The groups of blind and partially sighted walkers among whom human geographer Hannah Macpherson worked on nature trips to the Peak District and Lake District in Britain experience the beauty of the countryside they traverse in a number of ways. They hear what the sighted guides tell them about the landscape, and listen to the sounds of birds and other animals, they note the different smells as they cross the landscape and feel the touch of the breeze on skin. They also perceive the environment through concentration on the bodily experience of what they feel through their feet, the varying textures and slope of the ground as they walk. When one sense is impaired, people may experience the world around them through other senses. Touch is an active sense that requires people to engage physically and directly with their environment in order to perceive it. For the blind and partially sighted walkers, the feet in touch with the landscape added to their appreciation of the terrain and contributed to their enjoyment of the walk. For the walkers who had been sighted but were now blind, the texture of the ground beneath their feet allowed them to visualize memories of landscapes. Touching trees and rocks with the hands, in contrast, was not particularly important to them.

One of Macpherson's research participants described how she purposely chose to wear thin-soled shoes to walk in the city. She had developed greater foot and leg sensitivity since losing her sight and this facilitated her understanding of what she was walking over. That this is not an idiosyncratic position is made clear by blind sociologist Siegfried Saerberg (2010), who writes about how he gets a sense of his position in the environment by hearing and feeling what is beneath his feet: stone pavement, asphalt, or metal escalator steps.

Box 7.2   Feel the music

Evelyn Glennie, a British percussionist, started to learn to play the piano when she was eight years old and soon after took an interest in percussion but her hearing loss had already begun and by the time she was twelve she was diagnosed as profoundly deaf.

Although she was initially denied a place at the Royal Academy of Music because of her hearing impairment, she refused to accept this and insisted that she be considered for a place on the basis of her musical abilities alone. This marked a turning point for the acceptance of musicians with disabilities in the United Kingdom and elsewhere.

When learning a new piece of music, Glennie first practices 'internally' and once she has a visual memory of the piece she begins work with her instruments. For Glennie, hearing is a combination of sight, touch, and hearing (Glennie, Gilman, and Kim 2018, 322). She states that when the eye sees a movement it also registers it as a vibration on the body, with the vibrations on the ear causing the sensation of sound. By learning to link particular vibrations with what she sees and with where on her body she feels the vibration, Glennie can distinguish the higher pitches that she feels in her cheekbones, for example, from lower pitches that she feels in her abdomen. Glennie thus describes how she feels music through her body and how she can 'listen' to sounds by putting her hands on the wall of a music room. We all, in fact, 'hear' and 'feel' sounds through more than just our ears (Figure 7.2).

Figure 7.2 Percussionist Evelyn Glennie. (Courtesy of Caroline Purday)

The senses in human experience

While we understand our senses as natural responses to the world that surrounds us, these responses are shaped by culture and society. Different cultures and the same culture at different times in history place different levels of importance on different senses and give different meanings to sensory perceptions. Particular senses can structure social relations and can be associated with emotions that play an important role in these social relations, and thus the senses can act as a mechanism that bring together different aspects of human existence. At the same time, sensory perception and practices can become tools for the construction of inequalities among people of different social classes, religions, ethnicities, or genders. People in particular societies often associate certain sensory experiences with intense emotions of either pleasure or disgust, which in turn help them define themselves in relation to others. Sensory responses to food are a particularly revealing example: religious prohibitions of certain food items are experienced as revulsion, while 'food from back home' among migrants and other groups who have been disconnected from their original environments can inspire nostalgia and interpersonal closeness. Anthropologists have always followed their senses when they conduct fieldwork, as the senses can be powerful tools to understand the lives of others. Increasingly, they are explicitly incorporating into their work more complex and nuanced understandings of how the senses make us who we are and distinguish us from each other as cultural and social beings.

Key thinkers mentioned in this chapter:

Mary Douglas; Steven Feld; Sidney Mintz; Nadia Seremetakis; Paul Stoller

Key terms mentioned in this chapter (see Glossary):

Classification systems; Power; Senses; Sensory impairment; Synaesthesia

Questions for discussion/review:

1   Which sense is the most important to you? Explain your answer.
2   In what ways do the senses connect us to the past?
3   How is disgust at the thought of eating particular foods connected to how we classify the world?
4   How do people with sensory impairment perceive their environments?
5   To what extent are our senses cultural products?

Chapter 8

The life cycle

For the Beng people of Côte d'Ivoire, West Africa, babies are the spiritual reincarnation of people who had been dwelling among their friends and relatives in the afterlife, or *wrugbe*, a place of pleasure and abundance (Gottlieb 2004). They are born with memories, desires, and identities that parents and caregivers must respect and nurture to prevent them from growing homesick and being lured by spirits back to *wrugbe*. The baby must be carefully bathed, anointed with lotions, and adorned with amulets to protect it from the spirits. When babies cry for no apparent reason, it is a sign that they are missing their *wrugbe* relatives, and parents must apologize to them for having brought them back to life. Infant death, which happens frequently because the Beng are poor, is a sign that caregivers have not been careful enough to recognize the baby's connections to *wrugbe*. Babies are born with abundant memories and desires, and their task is to select which memories they will need for life on earth. Thus they do not need to acquire language because they speak all languages; rather, they must forget the languages they will not need.

The Beng demonstrate that we conceptualize and handle an infant in ways that are informed by our cosmology, which is easier to realize when we observe other people than when we observe our own practices. For the Beng, life on earth is only one stage in a long sequence of reincarnations that connect the living with the dead. The Beng's understanding of babies also shows that determining where life begins is not always straightforward: Beng babies are vulnerable because they occupy an ambiguous zone between death and life. We can recall that, in the Global North, people have different ideas on this question, as some people oppose abortion because they are convinced that life begins at conception, while others see life beginning at birth. As we will see presently, even medical scientists in different societies can have different views about when someone can be declared dead.

Categories of the life cycle

All human beings are born and eventually die. Most live to grow up and grow old. This is the **life cycle**, namely the sum total of the changes that humans go through from birth until death. While these changes are biologically driven, humans attribute meaning to them and turn a biological process into one that they understand in social and cultural terms. There are few clear physiological markers in the life cycle that mark transitions from one stage to the next: a baby's first tooth may be one and puberty another. But societies devise multiple ways of splicing the life cycle into discrete categories that help group people into social categories and ultimately organize society and culture. Different stages of the life cycle are associated with different rights and duties and thus, as people go through life, their position in society changes. Categories of

DOI: 10.4324/9781315737805-8

the life cycle are some of the most fundamental ways in which people in all societies of the world understand human diversity.

Life cycle categories are of three types: age, generation, and life stage. **Age** is a measure of how long a person has lived, often reckoned in years but always in tacit comparison with other people who are younger, older, or the same age. Where people reckon age numerically, they often think of birthdays, particularly significant ones, as important ways of reckoning age. In societies where infant mortality is high, people celebrate a child's first birthday as a significant achievement because it means that the child has survived infancy, but they may not pay much attention to subsequent birthdays. **Generation** is defined in terms of the experiences that people share. We can think of generation as an abstract social category or as a concrete group of persons. For example, in the Global North, we talk about the 1960s generation and the millennials: members of the former experienced social upheaval such as the sexual revolution and the civil rights movement, and millennials have lived through the explosion of information technology and deal with an uncertain future because of growing economic and environmental insecurity.

A **life stage** is defined in terms of the social, cultural, and economic status of people: whether they are economically and socially dependent on others (childhood, adolescence), independent and taking care of others (married adulthood with children), or no longer productive and increasingly dependent on others or the state (elderly). As social and cultural categories, life stages can differ widely across cultural contexts. They are sometimes marked by events that people consider important, which can be of many different types: for example, a child's first haircut, a boy's circumcision, a girl's first menstruation, initiation, school graduation, military service, marriage, the birth of a first child, and retirement. But transitions need not be marked in any particular way.

There is considerable overlap between the three ways of thinking about the life cycle. In the Global North, people of the post–World War II generations, a time of general economic security and abundance, were expected to become economically productive and partnered (life stage) when they were in their 20s (age). The idea that life stages should closely map onto chronological age (e.g., that most 18-year-olds graduate from secondary school) is a product of the growing importance of formal institutions like schooling, work, and pensions in Europe and North America in the nineteenth and twentieth centuries. But life-cycle categories can be mismatched: prior to the nineteenth century, aristocratic families of Europe married their children before they reached puberty, and thus before they were physiologically capable of consummating the marriage, because marriage was primarily designed to make dynastic alliances. In many societies of the Global North today, many people try to look young well into old age, as witnessed by the enormous amount of money spent on products to keep flesh from sagging and hair from turning grey. We can understand these concerns as efforts to create a discrepancy between age and life stage.

Not all societies consider age, generation, and life stage equally important. In some societies of East Africa, Amazonia, and New Guinea, people pay little attention to chronological age but considerable attention to **generation sets** (sometimes called 'age sets'), which are hierarchically organized categories of men (less frequently women) who are thought to belong together according to certain criteria, usually determined by the generation set to which their fathers belong. Generation sets can sometimes include people of very different chronological ages. A man is admitted to a particular generation set when he has experienced a certain event, such as an **initiation ritual**, and membership in the generation set determines many aspects of people's lives, such as the clothes they wear and the work they do. Membership is obligatory and these systems ensure the social separation of members of different generations, which prevents conflicts between them, at least in theory. Generation sets are always grounded in many other aspects of society and culture, such as property, kinship, residence, and cosmology. In societies that are structured in this way, membership in a generation set determines how old a person is considered to be.

Transitions from one life stage to another are frequently marked by **rituals**. Rituals that are performed at transitions between life stages are called **rites of passage**, a concept that was theorized by Arnold van Gennep, a Belgian ethnographer and folklorist, at the beginning of the twentieth century. People who undergo a rite of passage take on a new identity and status; for example, school graduation transforms a student into someone with a diploma and a wedding transforms two individuals into a married couple. The new status confers new rights and duties on the persons who undergo the rite.

Rites of passage vary greatly in intensity, length, and importance, but they all share a number of characteristics. They are organized in three stages, the first of which is **separation**, during which the person who undergoes the rite is separated from the rest of society, sometimes completely isolated from it. The second is **liminality**, during which persons have an ambiguous, 'betwixt and between' status: neither what they previously were nor what they will become. The third stage is **incorporation**, the return of the person to society, with a new status.

Infancy

Across the world, people greet the birth of a baby in different ways. The practices that surround a new infant are the result of how people conceptualize the infant and its relationship to the world in which it is born, as the example of the Beng at the beginning of this chapter demonstrates, but also of the material conditions into which the infant is born. For example, in many societies, adults may refrain from naming the infant for some time because they believe that it is not yet a fully human being. Where healthcare is rudimentary and life is hard, this may well be a sound strategy until one can be sure that the baby will survive infancy.

In many places, a newborn and its mother are often viewed as being in a liminal state and as a result they are kept in seclusion, sometimes surrounded by a few other women who take care of them. People explain the need to seclude the mother and baby in different ways, including the need to shield the baby from witchcraft, the fact that the baby and the mother are potentially polluting to other people (specially men), or the requirement that the mother be exempted from work so she can focus on taking care of the baby.

Once the mother is reintegrated and the newborn is welcomed into society, the mother returns to normal life. Attending to the baby is often only one of many other tasks to which she must attend. For example, among the Gusii of southwestern Kenya, women are in charge of tending the fields, taking care of the cattle, preparing food for the family, and selling produce at the market (LeVine 2004). Mothers keep infants in close physical contact, sleeping with them and holding them, but they do not play with them, talk to them, or respond to their babbling, although they pay attention to babies when they show signs of distress. In fact, Gusii babies cry less often than babies born to middle-class families in the Global North. A Gusii mother often delegates infant care to her other children, who are expected to know early in life how to handle babies. As children grow up, mothers expect them to comply with their wishes and they rarely praise them.

Gusii child-rearing practices contrast with those of middle-class urban people in the Global North. When a child is born in a middle-class urban family in Western Europe and North America, the family is entirely focused on the child: the home is child-proofed; family members have to keep quiet when the infant sleeps; the infant is surrounded with toys and other expensive accoutrements (e.g., prams, clothing, utensils); and people believe that interacting with the child, through play and conversation, for example, is essential to its development. Mothers rarely delegate child care to an older sibling, for the simple reason that in an urban nuclear family there may be no siblings present or if there are they may be at school. In the Global North, a large body of theory and practical advice turn what is only one of many cultural models of child rearing into universal precepts. According to these theories, Gusii child-rearing practices are pathological; yet there is no evidence that Gusii children grow up with any of the psychological problems that the theories predict they would.

Other aspects of how adults deal with infants demonstrate that the practices that people in the Global North assumed, at least from the mid-twentieth century until very recently, to be self-evident are not. For example, in many societies of the Global South, mothers breastfeed their babies whenever the need arises rather than on a schedule, since babies are with their mothers all the time, often strapped to their backs while mothers are working. Weaning sometimes does not take place until the child is deemed 'ready', which can be well into childhood, unless a new infant takes priority. Likewise, potty training in many societies happens casually. Until recently in villages in Tonga, where store-bought diapers were beyond the means of most families, small children often walked around with no clothes on. Little fuss was made if accidents happened and the bodily waste was quickly mopped up (Morton 1996, 136).

Sometime during the second year of their life, barring physiological or cognitive impairment, children throughout the world begin to develop the ability to speak. Of course, some children are more precocious than others and children use different strategies in their language development. But by about age two and a half, all children are able to express themselves in simple sentences in the language or languages spoken around them and to produce utterances that they have never heard before. This is because the capacity for language is imprinted in the human brain, much like the ability to see. As they grow older, children's vocabularies expand very quickly and their utterances become increasingly complex. They also quickly come to understand a considerable amount of the language that is addressed to them or that they overhear. We refer to children's development of language in their early years as **language acquisition**. This process is different from the language learning that we undertake with considerable effort when we learn a foreign language later in life. Language acquisition is also different from learning to write: writing is a technology, a representation of language, which also requires effort to learn. Young children acquire their native language or languages with much less effort.

Children acquire their first language or languages by interacting with others, such as their parents, caregivers, and siblings, and these interactions are rich in socializing lessons for the child. While language acquisition refers to children's growing knowledge of the structure of language (e.g., vocabulary, sentence structure), **language socialization** is the process by which children learn to use language in particular social situations and in which they learn to become a social person through verbal interactions. While language acquisition is primarily studied by linguists, language socialization is a social and cultural process that primarily interests anthropologists, particularly linguistic anthropologists.

For example, in the village in Samoa where linguistic anthropologist Elinor Ochs (1988) conducted fieldwork in the late 1970s, people lived in large families in houses that were generally full of activity, and this was the setting in which children were brought up. Adults treated babies lovingly, passing them around from one person to the other, and children of either gender from the age of five were often expected to take care of babies, carrying them as well as they could as they played or attended to chores. Babies were born into a lively and crowded environment that contrasted with the common middle-class nuclear family in the Global North, where babies interact mostly with their mothers or paid caregivers, sometimes with their fathers, and occasionally with other children. In Samoa, older children and adults frequently held babies outward to face the centre of the home and rarely addressed them, yet this had no visible effect on the child's language development. The message the babies got from these practices is that they should pay attention to other people and their needs, in a society in which individualism is devalued, in contrast to, for example, middle-class North American and European society.

As Samoan children grew a little older and began to speak, they tried to make themselves understood to older children and adults, as young children do everywhere, but Samoan adults did not try to make sense of small children's sometimes unclear utterances; rather, they expected the child to continue trying to make her- or himself understood. These interactional practices have an underlying message: do not expect the world around you to adapt to your needs, but rather adapt to the needs of others around you.

This may seem harsh to readers who grew up in homes where parents' lives revolved around the needs of children. In other words, in contrast to societies in which bringing up children represents a project for parents and where children expect to be the centre of attention, social-izing children in Samoa and many other societies is just another aspect of life: children must learn to fend for themselves and adapt to others. And one of the many ways in which they learn how to be in the society in which they will grow up is through the structure of the interactions in which they take part.

Different child-rearing practices produce different kinds of persons. Children who grow up in middle-class families in the Global North become independent individuals who expect their surroundings to adapt to their needs. With this individualism comes a free-thinking and poten-tially assertive attitude that parents and others value in children and later in young adults. In contrast, children who grow up in societies that socialize them to be attentive to the needs of others and to adapt to circumstances develop what is referred to as a **dividual** notion of the person (M. Strathern 1988, 13–15). The individual person values autonomy, consistency across contexts, and differentiates the self from others. The dividual person, in contrast, orients her- or himself to contexts and social relations and values adaptability to situations. Both of these ways of conceptualizing the person are found in all societies, but societies differ in terms of the value they place on one or the other.

Childhood

Some historians and social scientists maintain that, in the Global North, the very concept of childhood did not emerge until the nineteenth century. A landmark work by French historian Philippe Ariès (1962) argued that during the Middle Ages and the Renaissance, children were considered to be little adults who led independent lives and were expected to contribute to the economy of the **household**. Because child mortality was high, parents did not form strong emotional attachments to children. They did not feel that children had to be protected from danger or from the activities of adults, such as sexual relations. It was only when new institutions like compulsory schooling came into being in some countries in the nineteenth century that children were recognized as different from adults and in need of protection and special accommodations.

While subsequent historians have challenged Ariès's theories, he made an important con-tribution by recognizing that age categories like childhood have had different meanings in history. He also demonstrated that age categories may be characteristic of persons and the relationships between them, but they are also embedded in cultural beliefs about what it means to be a person. For example, institutions like compulsory formal education today

---

Box 8.1   Colonialism and child-rearing practices

During the colonial era, the child-rearing practices of colonized peoples often came under scrutiny. In the Philippines, which was a colony of the United States between 1898 and 1946, infant mortality ran at about 400 in 1,000 births at the turn of the twentieth century (McElhinny 2005). We know today that this very high rate was the result of the combined effects of poverty, poor healthcare, and the switch from subsistence agriculture to cash crops, which meant that people had turned away from locally cultivated rice rich in nutrients and now consumed low-quality imported rice, particularly in urban areas.

To respond to this alarming situation, the U.S. colonial administration made public health a high priority, which they presented as benevolent and humanitarian. Yet, rather than attributing the high infant mortality to structural factors like poverty, U.S. authorities and Filipino colonial elites blamed poor Filipinos' child-rearing practices such as cuddling small children, kissing them on the mouth, and having them sleep alongside adults, all of which, according to colonial medical authorities, exposed the children to infections. In the words of one Filipino physician, these practices amounted to 'superstitious and faulty maternity practices based on the ignorance of the people' (2005, 187).

These representations in turn justified colonialism, which the United States thought of as a project to educate and civilize Filipinos, particularly mothers, and until this goal was reached, the country could not gain independence. Different theories about how children should be raised clashed, but in this case, one theory was backed up with considerable power and this power difference was used to justify it. This kind of power differs from the military, political, and economic power that supports colonialism, but it is just as effective. It is an example of what Michel Foucault called **biopower**, which refers to the control of people through intimate aspects of their lives.

Regulating people by declaring their child-rearing practices faulty is a common strategy in many other contexts. For example, state authorities in many countries of the Global North often depict mothers among ethnic and Indigenous groups as deficient to justify placing their children in foster care. Similarly, poor working mothers who must leave their children in the care of neighbours or older children constantly worry about the risk of losing custody of their children.

---

remove children from the sphere of the family for significant portions of their waking hours, under the assumption that children need special care, thus identifying childhood as a separate stage of life.

In many places, children are expected to contribute to household chores early in life. Among the Matsigenka Indians of the Peruvian Amazon, a society of about 8,000 people who live in small villages dispersed in the forest, parents aim to bring up small children who are calm, responsible, and hardworking (Ochs and Izquierdo 2009). Children quickly become independent and self-reliant, although they are also expected to conform to ideals of sharing and sociability. As they grow older, they are expected to contribute an increasing amount of labour, including fetching and carrying objects. By the age of five or six, when tasks become gender specific, girls help out with childcare and cooking, while boys accompany their father to the gardens. They are expected to take the initiative and learn to perform tasks on their own, because showing them would violate their autonomy. As the

Figure 8.1 This Matsigenka little girl has learned how to handle dangerous objects like large knives early in life in order to contribute to the labour of the household, 2004. (Courtesy of Carolina Izquierdo)

children are generally cooperative, few conflicts arise with adults over the children's work contribution (Figure 8.1).

In the Global North, in contrast, middle-class children are not expected to contribute to labour beyond taking care of specific tasks such as washing the dishes and tidying their own rooms, and even these are often the object of protracted negotiations with parents. But the idea that children should not work is relatively recent; for example, it was only in 1933 that Britain outlawed paid work for children younger than 14. Among less-privileged social classes of both the Global North and the Global South, children become apprentices early in life, learn a trade, and begin a work life that lasts many decades. Work often competes with school in children's lives. This is not because parents do not value schooling, but because there is no choice: the household needs money in order to survive. This is one way in which social inequalities are reproduced from one generation to the next: poor children can devote less time to schooling,

Figure 8.2 Hide carrier, tanneries, Ain al-Sira, Cairo, 1999. Child and adolescent labour is still an everyday reality for many of those born into the poor and working classes around the world. (Courtesy of Yasser Alwan)

which is a common precondition for upward mobility later in life, than children who grow up in privileged families, where household chores are taken care of by technological means (e.g., running water, dishwashers) or by paid helpers and where there is no need for extra income (Figure 8.2).

Youth and adulthood

Just as childhood is a product of historical and social contexts, youth and adulthood vary considerably in their definition. Nevertheless, in the recent history of the Global North, youth and adulthood have been increasingly delineated through laws and other institutions that determine when one can vote, drive, drink alcohol, or have sex (not necessarily in that order), as well as when one should attend school or perform military duties. These norms have spread through the globalization of ideas about what is appropriate and necessary for people occupying particular age categories, as set out for example in United Nations conventions and declarations. The result is that in most if not all societies of the world, people recognize youth and adulthood as globalized categories, even though they might assign different meaning to them.

Coming of age is the object of rites of passage in many societies. For example, in Cuba and throughout the Latino world of North America (and increasingly elsewhere in Latin America), a girl's 15th birthday is often marked with a celebration called the *quinceañera*. In Havana, girls look forward to their *quinceañera* for years before their 15th birthday, and it is the object of considerable and costly preparations (Härkönen 2014): a live band is hired, food and drinks are in abundance, and a particularly extravagant wardrobe must be purchased, as the girl changes clothes several times during the celebration. An elaborate photo and video shoot is a central aspect of the event, as the images will circulate among relatives for many years to come.

The ritual is a celebration of the girl's sexual maturity and beauty, and of her mother's care in bringing her up. The photographs emphasize her seductiveness and mark the attainment of sexual adulthood. (Elsewhere in the Latino world, this aspect may be given less overt emphasis, and other aspects, such as virginity, may be given greater importance.) Separated and placed at the centre of attention of the celebration, which is a liminal phase, the girl is paraded around the city in either a classic convertible car or a horse-drawn carriage. Of particular importance is the girl's relationship to her matrilineal relatives, primarily her mother, who is the main organizer and whose achievements are celebrated in the *quinceañera*, and then other relatives on the mother's side. The girl's father and patrilineal relatives play a more marginal role. At the end of the *quinceañera*, the girl is reintegrated into society as a young adult, having been presented as such by her family to the community, but she is primarily integrated into her matriline.

While the *quinceañera* is most obviously a rite of passage to mark the girl's transition from childhood to adulthood, it is also a ritual of gender: the emphasis on the girl's beauty, sexual and reproductive maturity, and place in the matriline all focus on the fact that she is a woman. There is no equivalent for boys, who become men without any ritual to mark this achievement. The simultaneous meaning of the *quinceañera* as both a marker of a life-stage transition and a marker of gender illustrates a common feature of rites of passage and rituals in general: they are always rich in meaning (Figure 8.3).

Rites of passage frequently have consequences beyond their effects on the specific people who undergo them and are often suffused with cosmological meaning of importance to the entire society. A dramatic example of this are the initiation practices of some societies of the Highlands of Papua New Guinea prior to their conversion to Christianity and their increased contact with the outside world in the 1960s. These are best known through the work of U.S. anthropologist Gilbert Herdt (2005), who conducted fieldwork among a group he called the Sambia a couple of decades after they had abandoned the initiation rituals. Sambia society was ordered by a strong segregation between the genders: men and women interacted minimally, and while they believed that female children could grow up successfully by being fed by their mothers, male children required more than mother's milk in order to grow into the strong warriors they were expected to become. What they needed was men's fluid that resembled most closely breast milk, namely semen. When boys reached their teens, they were separated from the women and brought to a clearing in the forest, where they had to perform fellatio on men. The men who performed this service had to be in a particular kinship relation to the boys, usually the mother's brother or the sister's husband. The ritual, which we refer to as **ritualized**

Figure 8.3 Coming-of-age day in Japan (*seijin no hi*) is an occasion when young people, particularly women, who are turning 20 during the year put on outfits considered
traditional, such as the *furisode*, or long-sleeved kimono, that these young women
are wearing in Tokyo in January 2011. (Courtesy of Nikita Shulga)

homosexuality, was accompanied by other rituals designed to terrify the initiate and persuade
him to abide by the segregation of genders.

When the initiation was over, the boy was an adult, could marry a woman, and in turn take
part in the initiation of boys of the next generation. But the rite of passage also solidified the
gender segregation that was so fundamental to the Sambia, and thus was more than just about
'growing' a new generation of men. Today, the Sambia have been taught by missionaries and
other external agents that their rituals are the object of shame, and they strongly deny that they
ever existed. They are now more interested in what modernity can bring them than what their
forefathers did in the past.

Common rites of passage that mark the transition from youth to adulthood are marriage and
the birth of children. Another is economic productivity, and through this lens, youth is a period
of increased productivity that enables people to marry. Among the middle classes in the Global
North, productivity is thought of as 'economic independence', although in most cases independence is more a matter of ideology than economic reality: children are expected to move out of
the family home in their late teens or early 20s, but frequently continue to receive financial
assistance from their parents, although this is framed as helping them become independent individuals rather than loans that need to be paid back or gifts that demand return gifts. People in
other societies are expected to become economically productive as early as possible in order to
support their parents, younger siblings and extended families, and thus take over from the older
generation the duty of providing for others.

For many young people in the contemporary world, however, the transition to adulthood has become problematic, as economic downturns in the late twentieth century have limited the provisioning opportunities that were available to previous generations: it is today difficult to make ends meet in agriculture, and in cities jobs are scarce and the competition for them fierce. These are situations where the only solution is to migrate to wealthy economies, despite the legal barriers that governments in the Global North have erected to prevent poor people from immigrating.

Young men have been particularly affected by changes in the world's economy. For example, Uttar Pradesh, a state in northern India, experienced a population explosion between the 1960s and the 1980s, which resulted in large numbers of young people coming of age in the 1980s (Jeffrey 2010). At the same time, middle-class and middle-caste agricultural families became wealthier through government subsidies, and were able to send their sons to university and look forward to coveted employment in the state bureaucracy, which offered job security and status. However, in the 1990s, following **neoliberal** policies, the state reduced the bureaucracy, abolished subsidies, and privatized many services. Large numbers of educated youth could no longer find public-service jobs and the private sector did not grow enough to open up new employment opportunities. Unable to find local jobs, lacking the connections and skills to seek employment in larger cities, and disillusioned by their studies on topics they felt were disconnected from reality, young men spent their days in what they called *timepass*, sitting together in tea stalls, smoking, chatting, and whiling the time away. Their sense of failure, disillusionment, and anxiety is the other side of the coin of the widespread images of India as an emerging economic world power, which only benefits the most privileged.

In societies in which young people have similar experiences, marriage and having children, which were once important markers of adulthood, have become unreachable goals, again particularly for young men, who have to prove to the families of prospective spouses that they are able to support a family. As a result, young people remain single longer, unable to demonstrate that they are mature adults. Young men in urban Ethiopia have experienced shifts in the same ways as their Indian agemates: the increased availability and status of formal education, the hope of landing a job with the government, a reduction in employment opportunities, and a glut of unemployed educated youth, who would rather remain unemployed than take on low-status jobs as carpenters or blacksmiths (Mains 2012). They continue living with their parents, yet they cannot conceive of marriage until they have moved into a home of their own and secured a job. Even the first step of married life, the wedding, involves considerable expense, as all the neighbours must be invited to a lavish celebration, or else they risk becoming the subject of shaming gossip.

Even in societies of the Global North, where most people have enough to eat and a roof over their heads, young people experience the malaise of economic downturns. In urban Japan, for example, a society that until recently was one of the wealthiest superpowers of the world, an economic crisis that has lingered since the early 1990s has eroded a post–World War II system in which people could live a middle-class life thanks to men's lifetime employment in industry, commerce, or finance. Today, large numbers of youth survive on insecure employment with little hope of a better life (Allison 2013).

Despite these pessimistic scenarios, even in the most precarious circumstances, young people find ways to survive economically and reclaim a sense of dignity. For example, poor young women and men in Dakar, the capital of Senegal, acquire and sell fashionable clothes in an intense urban informal economy (Scheld 2007). Many are from rural backgrounds and have migrated to the city to try to make money to send back to their families in the villages, but work is scarce and they must develop inventive ways of earning a living. Dakar residents' fascination with fashion offers them the opportunity to do so. Large amounts of second-hand clothing are imported from the Global North, which are then sold and resold at flea markets or within social networks. The boundary between stealing, borrowing, buying, and selling is somewhat blurred on an economic scene where competition is fierce. The youth rely on one another's help, sometimes pooling their resources to buy particularly fashionable outfits that they wear in turn. A favourite trick is to lure potential customers to a display of clothing, onto which a group of the seller's friends descend and create a commotion, forcing customers to quickly buy something to get out of the potentially unpleasant situation.

Changing socio-economic conditions around the world have affected how generations interact with one another. Among the nomadic pastoralist Samburu of Kenya, for instance, men were organized in generation sets and acquired status as they progressed up the age-set hierarchy and as they accumulated wealth in cattle, acquired wives, and fathered children (Meiu 2017). Tensions arose between the generations, however, as older men prevented younger men from acquiring cattle for as long as possible, which did not allow them to marry, while younger men did their best to undermine the older men's efforts. In the twentieth century, colonialism offered the young men new opportunities to circumvent the age-grade system by joining the army or the police force, and earning money to buy cattle rather than wait for their fathers to give it to them. After independence, new opportunities for business and political power also reconfigured power relations.

One major change that took place from the 1980s was tourism and Samburu young men began traveling to tourist areas of the country to sell souvenirs to wealthy visitors from the Global North. An economy of sexual relations quickly developed, particularly between older female tourists and younger Samburu men, as the former found the men exotic and the latter enjoyed the wealth that they acquired from these relationships. Some members of junior generation sets became wealthy 'young big men', building large houses in their home villages and launching political careers. In contrast, some Samburu elders hard on their luck tried to cash in on the same global opportunities, becoming 'beach-boy elders' who sold souvenirs on beaches and attempted to form relationships with foreign women.

The Samburu generation set system had never been stable, as members of different generation sets were always in competition with one another, but colonialism and then independence and globalization introduced new ways for the less powerful to undermine the system. Yet the age-set system has not disappeared: people constantly talk about young big men and beach-boy elders, finding them both contemptible. The morality of the age-set system thus lives on even while it is being undermined.

Ageing

As they grow older, all human beings experience a decline in their physical and cognitive functions. However, the experience of ageing varies across societies and cultures and within them, as it is dependent on such matters as access to healthcare, the structure of families and communities, and cultural ways of thinking about the elderly (Figure 8.4).

Throughout the world, advances in medical knowledge, better nutrition, and the improvement of sanitation have contributed to dramatically lengthening people's life expectancy. Between 2000 and 2016, the global life expectancy rose by 5.5 years to 72.0 years (World Health Organization 2019). But there are blatant inequalities: while in wealthy countries people live much longer than ever before, in other places torn by war, famine, political turmoil, and displacement, life expectancy is in fact declining. In Russia, for example, life expectancy for men

Figure 8.4 In most societies, old age is a time when work has given way to leisure, as illustrated by these senior men enjoying a game of chess in Washington Square Park, New York, 2015. (Courtesy of Deborah Williams)

declined dramatically after the fall of communism because of rising unemployment, a deteriorating healthcare system, and increased alcohol and tobacco consumption.

In many societies, the elderly are seen as sources of wisdom deserving of respect and attention. The thought that one could move elderly parents into a paid care facility, where children and grandchildren occasionally visit them, is horrifying to many people around the world, where taking care of elderly relatives is the moral duty of adult children. In northern Thailand, for example, when a woman in her 80s had a stroke and was discharged from hospital in a permanent coma, her daughters took on the arduous task of caring for her (Aulino 2016). Their actions can be explained in terms of Buddhist beliefs in karma, whereby one acquires merit for future life by doing good things to others in this life, but they are not solely a matter of belief. Rather, caring for an incapacitated elderly person is simply what one does.

However, one should not idealize how small-scale or rural societies treat their elders. While it is true that many societies do not see the elderly as the burden that they often represent in capitalist countries in the Global North, old people are not always treated with kindness and respect. In addition, the burden of elderly care invariably falls on women, thus reinforcing gender-based inequalities that are already created by the fact that women are overwhelmingly responsible for unremunerated and devalued domestic work. Nevertheless, it is true that the nuclearization of families, the intensification of urban living, and the increasing commoditization of such services as healthcare have introduced problems in the Global North that did not exist in the past.

In Japan, the country with the highest life expectancy in the world (estimated by the Organisation for Economic Co-operation and Development at 84 years) but a birth rate that has long been declining, many elderly people live alone. Some remain independent and active, as Japanese people value not being a burden on others, and one sees many more elderly people in the streets of Japanese cities than in Europe or North America. However, the state is struggling to care for the increasing numbers of the elderly in the context of a prolonged economic crisis (Danely 2014). Japanese newspapers periodically carry stories about old people being found dead in their small apartments as no one enquired about them for days or weeks.

In societies in which people find themselves unable to care for elderly relatives, new forms of inequality arise. People who are employed to take care of the elderly, whether in private homes or in institutions, invariably earn very little and are often exploited. Many are migrant workers from poor countries or poor regions of the same country. They often have few qualifications and thus only have their caring skills to market for a living.

In North America, Europe, and increasingly other places, the late twentieth century saw the emergence of new ways of thinking about ageing. In the United States, for example, there is no better compliment to elderly persons than to tell them that 'they don't look their age', which at other times in history would have sounded absurd. Elderly people are increasingly expected, and expect of themselves, to 'age successfully' by remaining independent and physically and intellectually active (Lamb 2019). Newspapers periodically publish stories about 90-year-olds running marathons, which readers consume admiringly. These trends have also given rise to an enormous industry of cosmetics, plastic surgery, and travel and education programmes for the elderly, all designed to keep them active and youthful. These changes result from people internalizing neoliberal imperatives that people be responsible for their own lives rather than depending on others. But these imperatives are predicated on people's ability to consume, leaving poor people unable to 'age successfully', particularly if they live in a country like the United States where healthcare is very expensive. Here as elsewhere, culture, economics, and politics all work in tandem.

Death

Few things are more certain than death. Yet death is more complicated than this cliché assumes: death is at once a biological event, during which the body's functions shut down and begin decaying, as well as a social and cultural event, during which the mourners reconfigure their social relations with the dead and with one another. This is where death can have different configurations across the world's societies. Even as a biological event, death is not straightforward. Medical scientists, who base their understanding of the difference between life and death on 'facts', abide by different practices in different societies, which suggests that science, like everything else, is embedded in culture. For example, in Europe and North America, doctors today declare people to be 'brain dead', and thus no longer alive, when they can no longer breathe on their own, and most members of the public accept their expertise, except in highly publicized cases involving deeply religious relatives or conflicts within families (Lock 2001). This understanding emerged in the 1950s, in tandem with advances in intensive-care and organ transplant technology. In Japan, in contrast, people see death as an event that is primarily the family's responsibility, and they distrust biomedicine. The dead body must be carefully cared for and the deceased memorialized as an ancestor. The implications are important: the organs of a brain-dead person in Europe and North America can be harvested for organ donation while in Japan few families agree to organs being removed from the body of a dead relative. The cross-cultural difference is rooted in different levels of public trust in and authority of the medical professions, as well as different understandings of what constitutes a person.

Box 8.2   Biological death and social death

As a biological event, death is the result of interrelated processes: organs no longer function as they should because of disease, decay due to old age or trauma, as in the case of accidents, and they affect one another, causing the body to shut down. But there are other ways in which people can 'die': when they no longer have interactions with other human beings, when they are abandoned by those around them, or when their life is declared dispensable by those in positions of authority. This is termed 'social death', namely death within life, just as life can exist within death in the form of spirits and ghosts. Social death happens, for example, to Alzheimer's patients as the disease progresses, but it can also happen for non-physiological reasons.

Anthropologist João Biehl (2005) tells the story of a woman he named Catarina who lived in a rehabilitation centre in Porto Alegre, Brazil, which was in fact a place to which people are brought to die. The increasing marketization of medical services, the reckless use of psychiatric drugs to treat people considered mentally ill, and the complicity of a poor family who were unwilling and unable to take care of an unproductive relative all led to Catarina's abandonment in this facility, where she lived disconnected from meaningful interactions, waiting to die. As it turned out, Catarina was not mentally ill, as her relatives had concluded, but rather suffered from a rare genetically transmitted neurological disease that made her unable to stand and later sit. Yet, in her state of abandonment, Catarina managed to find meaning by compiling what she called her 'dictionary', a series of notebooks in which she drew and wrote notes.

Social death can take many forms and has often affected not only individuals like Catarina but also entire categories of people. Inspired by Michel Foucault's work, Cameroonian philosopher and political theorist Achille Mbembe (2003) introduced the term **necropolitics** to refer to the political decisions that bring about social death to particular types of persons. Slavery, for example, rendered members of enslaved populations socially dead, in that their life was reduced to the labour they could provide and to their ability to supply more slaves by reproducing. In the 1980s, the unwillingness of many governments around the world to deal with the HIV pandemic condemned entire segments of populations to social death before they were physically dead. Today, the Australian government's incarceration of refugees for indefinite time on Manus Island and Nauru and systematic police violence in the United States and elsewhere against black people are examples of necropolitics.

In all societies of the world, people mourn the dead in a variety of ways: crying, wailing, keening, praying, wearing special clothing, and so on. Funerals are events in which many things happen. They are often viewed as commemorations of the deceased and designed for the mourners to express emotions and deal with the paradox constituted by one life ending while other lives need to continue. Beliefs in reincarnation or resurrection, memorials, ancestor worship, reburials, embalming, and other attempts to preserve the body can all be seen as ways in which humans try to cope with the paradox of the simultaneous end and continuation of life.

However heart-felt expressions of grief are, they are socially organized. For example, in many societies, how one behaves on the occasion of someone's death is determined by one's social relation to the deceased: crying and wailing may be expected of close relatives, but be inappropriate in a distant relative; in contrast, if people close to the dead person fail to express sorrow in a particular way, they may become the object of criticism. But other concerns can take precedence at funerals or in the rituals which follow. Commonly, people bring objects, food, money, and other valuables, which are redistributed according to the rules of kinship; the wealth of the dead person is distributed; people determine who inherits the political or social roles of the deceased; and social hierarchies and power differences can be reaffirmed or challenged.

Funerals can take many different forms. Some can be very simple affairs with little or no ritual, as is the case among secular humanists in the Global North. Others are elaborate gatherings lasting several days or weeks, during which entire families or clans get together. Generally speaking, the more important the person is, the more elaborate the funeral: the funeral of heads of states and other public figures are the occasion for solemn processions and religious services that are broadcast on television and watched by millions. In Britain, the death of Princess Diana in 1997 led to a national outpouring of collective grief and public mourning that brought out all kinds of reconsiderations about social class and the relationship of the state to the people, and for a while lowered the suicide rate significantly (Figure 8.5).

Figure 8.5 Funeral rituals continue even in the context of global events such as the 2020 Covid-19 pandemic; this funeral in the Philippines is attended by a limited number of mourners all wearing face masks as required by law. (Courtesy of Judge Florentino Floro)

How societies commemorate the dead articulates with the social, political, and religious dynamics at play in the society in which the deceased lived and the mourners continue to live. For example, the Ga of Ghana bury the dead in elaborately artistic coffins, known as *abebuu adekai*, literally 'receptacles of proverbs' (Bonetti 2012). These coffins, in the shape of cars, canoes, swords, or animals, known as 'fantasy coffins', are prized throughout the art world for their artistic qualities, but for the Ga they have a much more complex meaning. They symbolize the wealth and status of the deceased. At the funeral, which must be video recorded, the coffin is paraded through the streets, pausing in front of the homes of important families to mark the dead person's social relations. Coffins in the shape of high-status objects or animals, such as lions or chiefly stools, are ways of making claims on the land in the context of the tense conflicts over land ownership that play out in the region where the Ga live.

Bodies can be buried, cremated, mummified, donated for organ harvesting or medical teaching, turned to compost, placed in caves (as among the Toraja of Indonesia), hung in trees for birds to eat (as among Zoroastrians in South Asia and some Tibetans), or in rare cases eaten (as the Wari' in Amazonia formerly practised). All practices reflect and contribute to cosmological beliefs, as well as ideologies of the self and its relation to society. The idea, for example, that one can choose how one's body is to be disposed of reflects an ideology of individuality that would have no meaning in many societies. Funerals are so important as contexts in which kinship is foregrounded, politics is fought over, and exchange is prominent, that their configuration cannot be left to the whim of the deceased. A radical manifestation of the seeming individuality of societies in the Global North is cryonics, namely the freezing of a recently dead body in liquid nitrogen in the hope that one day technology will be able to revive it and grant it immortality. While in the United States cryonics is associated with a few wealthy self-absorbed people with fringe libertarian ideas, in post-Soviet Russia, where there is a long history of debates about prolonging life, it attracts a variety of people with different agendas: some see it as a sort of insurance policy against death, others as an expression of care for one's close kin (Bernstein 2019). At least in theory, cryonics represents a challenge to the finality of death.

Anthropologists not only study death and its rituals during fieldwork, but they also sometimes have to deal with death in an immediate fashion and share this experience with the people among whom they conduct fieldwork. In this sense, the work of anthropology can be extremely intimate, and like all intimate experiences it can be filled with complexities. Such was the experience of Deborah Gewertz, a U.S. anthropologist who has conducted decades of fieldwork among the Chambri, who live along the Sepik River in Papua New Guinea (Gewertz and Errington 2002). In 1998, Gewertz's adult daughter Alexis was knocked over on her bicycle by a truck and killed in the United States. Gewertz and her anthropologist husband Fred Errington returned to Chambri a few months later at the villagers' request, who wanted to bring closure to the death of the young woman, whom they had known from childhood. But there the anthropologists were confronted with different understandings of death and different ways of thinking about people's place in their society.

Death rituals bring people together in a pan-human experience of grief, but rituals, whether among the Chambri or anywhere else, also bring out tensions and conflicts. In this case, conflicts arose over who was to preside over the funeral, with different people claiming Alexis as their kin. Chambri villagers performed rituals to ensure that the dead woman would return to the world of ancestors, but they were also anxious to find the 'real' cause of Alexis's death: did her parents examine the body for signs of sorcery, did they ask for compensation from the truck driver, who will answer for Alexis's death? Which clan was entitled to claim the spirit of the dead woman? These and other questions demonstrate the complexities of death and its rituals:

they express grief, but this grief is never divorced from cultural and social meaning, which Alexis's funeral among the Chambri brought out in a particularly stark way.

The life cycle as social and cultural process

Humans are born, mature, and grow old, and so far no human has managed to avoid dying. Yet what defines the stages of life can vary across the world's societies and at different periods of history, and they can become the object of conflicts within the same society. Even the boundaries of life, that is where life begins and ends, are subject to different definitions.

Understanding the life cycle requires more than simply following people as they transition from one stage of life to another. It requires us to be attentive to the political and economic context in which people live, to the cosmological world through which people seek explanations, to the course of history, and to the different perspectives that people in the same society can bring. It also requires us to pay attention to the commonalities between people who fall in the same age, life cycle, and generation categories, as well as the relationship between people who belong to different categories.

Key thinkers mentioned in this chapter:

Philippe Ariès; Arnold van Gennep; Achille Mbembe

Key terms mentioned in this chapter (see Glossary):

Age; Dividual; Generation; Generation sets; Language acquisition; Language socialization; Life cycle; Life stage; Necropolitics; Rites of passage; Ritual; Social death

Questions for discussion/review:

1   What are the three life cycle categories and how are they distinguished from each other?
2   How are social values reflected in child-rearing practices?
3   What are rites of passage and why do we need them?
4   To what extent have global socio-economic developments in recent decades made it more challenging for young people to fulfil the expectations of adulthood?
5   How can a person be socially dead yet still be alive?

Chapter 9

Gifts and exchange

As the Danish novelist Isak Dinesen (Karen Blixen's *nom de plume*) was dying of a disease that made it impossible for her to eat, she wrote in 1958 a short story about food titled *Babette's Feast* (Dinesen 2015). In the story, Babette, a penniless French Catholic refugee from the horrors of the Paris Commune in 1870, arrives in a small austere Lutheran village in Norway. She is taken in by two pious, unmarried sisters. Though the sisters are concerned about taking in a stranger, their sympathy and charity overcomes their doubts. In return for board and lodging, Babette works for the sisters as cook and housekeeper. In time, the sisters and other villagers come to depend on Babette and accept her presence. When Babette unexpectedly wins the lottery, the sisters fear that she will leave them to return to her native France. Instead, Babette prepares a feast for them and the members of their church.

In preparing the feast, Babette is revealed as having been a master chef in her former life. The meal is her way of repaying the debt she owes to the sisters and the villagers for their kindness. Babette's feast is a return gift, in other words a gift that is given in return for a previous gift. The exchange of gifts creates a relationship of **reciprocity** that binds together Babette and the sisters and bridges social, cultural, and religious differences. To accept, and in this case literally to consume, Babette's gift of food is an act of communion, a shared meal uniting a group.

However, gift exchange is not the only kind of exchange Dinesen describes. When Babette buys the supplies to prepare the feast, she participates in a different kind of exchange. These supplies are commodities purchased for money from shopkeepers. This is a financial transaction that, in contrast to the gift, does not create reciprocity and interpersonal connection. Babette transforms the commodities into gifts and in the process uses up all her lottery proceeds. But she is untroubled by her return to poverty because for her the material loss of wealth is outweighed by what she has gained through the giving of her gift.

As *Babette's Feast* illustrates, exchanges can be material or symbolic and are often a complex combination of both. Alliances between people, groups, and nations can be sealed by gift and **commodity exchange**. Friendships are maintained through ritualized exchanges of greetings and gifts, and enemies can be turned into allies through trade agreements. But alliances can also be broken off by the refusal to exchange. Some gifts are given in the expectation of a return while others are given altruistically. The sisters in Dinesen's short story do not expect anything in return for their kindness. Yet, even anonymous gifts of charity may bring a return to their donors, for instance by affirming their self-image of generosity, or in some countries a tax deduction.

Gifts and exchange have been the concerns of economic anthropology since the early twentieth century. How is the circulation of objects and services among people imbued with moral

DOI: 10.4324/9781315737805-9

and symbolic significance, and how does it serve to strengthen or endanger social relations between people? In other words, how do economic relations articulate with many other aspects of human existence?

The gift

In the Global North, people think of gifts as personal tokens of appreciation that people offer one another on special occasions such as Christmas and anniversaries. But in other societies, gift giving plays a central role in every aspect of social life, structuring social relations and defining the meaning of social events; an economic system based on gift giving is a **gift economy**. In such societies, far from being a pleasant demonstration of affection, gift giving is often a serious event filled with anxiety and tension.

Bronislaw Malinowski was the first anthropologist to document in detail the workings of a gift economy when he conducted fieldwork in the early twentieth century in the Trobriand Islands, in what is today Papua New Guinea. The Trobriand men among whom he lived made perilous sea voyages by canoe to exchange valuables, called *vaygu'a*, with their counterparts on different islands (they still do today, although they now travel by plane). The objects in question were adornments, namely necklaces made from red shells (*soulava*) and armbands made from white shells (*mwali*), which were of no practical use and were not even often worn, but some became famous for having been owned by illustrious men. The voyages that Trobriand men made to exchange these objects formed a vast circular network across many islands in a large archipelago, which they called the *kula* (Figure 9.1).

Figure 9.1 Shell necklace used for kula exchange (*soulava*), Trobriand Islands, late nineteenth century, George Brown Collection. (Courtesy of Norio Niwa/National Museum of Ethnology Osaka)

Box 9.1   White traders and the *kula*

Malinowski's groundbreaking study of *kula* presented Western readers with a description of what appeared to be a traditional and internally coherent exchange system. However, before Malinowski arrived in the Trobriand Islands, white traders had been there, some as early as the 1860s, even before colonial law was established (Lepowsky 2019). They had radically altered the *kula* by bartering muskets and rifles with the islanders for pearls and pearl shells. Among Trobrianders, the increased availability of weapons led to a predictable rise in killings, which had to be compensated in shell valuables and one way of obtaining such shells was through *kula*. In addition, the white traders were now manufacturing shell-disc necklaces and greenstone axeblades with metal tools, which meant that the valuables were more plentiful than ever. All these factors had fundamentally altered the *kula*.

After 1888, Britain gradually established colonial control over New Guinea, which it transferred to Australia in 1902. This control included the suppression of armed conflict and punishment of homicide, making *kula* voyages much safer. By then, Trobrianders were acquiring valuables from the white traders by working for them. So the *kula* that Malinowski witnessed was the product of a colonial history that was well underway by the time he conducted fieldwork. When he witnessed the *kula*, he appeared to have been unsure what it meant until he persuaded some of the white traders to help to explain to him what he was seeing. In contrast to the traders' pragmatic and extractive approach, Malinowski provided a holistic account of the *kula* as a social institution but did so in terms that suggested stability and tradition.

The direction of the voyages depended on which objects were exchanged. On a map, men who exchanged *soulava* necklaces travelled in a clockwise direction, but they travelled in a counterclockwise direction if they exchanged *mwali* armbands. Malinowski described the *kula* as a ring and each man in the exchange system as part of a circuit; if he was imagined as facing the centre of the ring, he had *kula* partners to his left, from whom he received *soulava* and to whom he gave *mwali*, and to his right, from whom he received *mwali* and to whom he gave *soulava*. No man knew all the participants in the *kula*. Rather, he knew only his own immediate exchange partners and perhaps some of their exchange partners. *Kula* valuables never stopped circulating. A man who received a famous *kula* valuable might try to hold on to it for as long as possible, but his partners would scheme and use magic to get him to give it to them. Men became famous when they exchanged with partners at the top of their game. Men were ranked according to who their partners were and how successful they were in acquiring famous objects. Less successful men gave their *kula* valuables away and found their partners quick to receive them but slow to reciprocate.

Every detail of the *kula* exchange was subject to strict rules of etiquette and involved a great deal of ritual and magic. The exchanges themselves were formal affairs conducted in public, a man did not haggle with his *kula* partner over the gift he received nor could he complain about it. A man who did not behave accordingly would be accused of treating *kula* as though it were a simple trade exchange. Alliances between *kula* partners were long-lasting and came with both **rights** and **duties**. They enabled individual men to gain fame by attracting famous valuables to their village. The *kula* helped to keep the peace between villages and islands and paved the way for more ordinary trade relations. It was central to the life of the Trobrianders and had symbolic, ritual, economic, and political significance.

Malinowski's ethnography of the *kula*, *Argonauts of the Western Pacific* (1922), was instantly recognized as a major contribution to anthropology. While Malinowski described one complex exchange system in great detail, Marcel Mauss, in his classic text on *The Gift* published in 1923–24 (Mauss 2016), placed Malinowski's findings in a theoretical and comparative context of gift exchange in other societies. For Mauss, gift exchange was an early form of contract. Two parties, often representing larger groups, entered into an exchange that involved both trust and risk. The exchange establishes a relationship between parties, which comes with obligations, including hospitality, and a willingness to enter into other kinds of exchange, such as trade. People are subject to three obligations: the obligation to give, otherwise one is a social outcast; the obligation to accept the gift, otherwise one is behaving in a hostile manner to the giver; and the obligation to return the gift, otherwise one is forever in debt and loses status.

One has to trust that if one gives a gift, one will receive a return gift in the future. However, there is always a risk that the recipient may not complete the exchange and so put an end to the relationship, even possibly signaling the beginning of hostilities. By contrast, one way to establish peace at the end of a period of hostility between groups is to resume the exchange of gifts. The refusal to give and the refusal to accept a gift are hostile acts. Equally, gift exchange may be viewed as 'war by other means'. For example, the exchange practices of the Kawelka people in Papua New Guinea, in which **big men** (or *bigman* in the lingua franca, Tok Pisin) seek to outdo their rivals by the sheer scale and size of their gift, is sublimated warfare (A. Strathern 2008). The same is true of the **potlatch** practised by some Indigenous peoples in North America, which we discussed in Chapter 1.

Time is another important element in gift exchange. If the recipient of a gift reciprocates immediately, the gift loses its purpose, namely to establish an enduring relationship between giver and receiver. Such an exchange is **barter**, which takes place in contexts where typically people do not find it necessary or useful to establish a lasting relationship (Figure 9.2).

Figure 9.2 Eugene von Guérard, 'Aborigines [sic] met on the road to the diggings' (1854), oil on canvas. (Courtesy of Geelong Gallery, Australia.)

Gift exchange figures centrally in ritual life: people give gifts to spirits, the dead, or the gods so that they may protect and bless them with wealth and good fortune. Another aspect of the ritual power of the gift is the fact that it remains mystically attached to its original owner, and thus it is **inalienable** despite the fact that it changes hands. Mauss used the New Zealand Māori term *hau*, which translates roughly as 'spirit', to describe the giver's essence that remains in the gift. For Mauss, this is why a gift must be reciprocated. But later anthropologists argued instead that the obligation to return a gift was not mystical; rather, persons in traditional societies did not think it acceptable to profit from gifts they received and so they returned gifts of greater value (Sahlins 1972). In other situations, gifts must never be returned: at Hindu funerals, family members give the officiating priest gifts that are said to contain the sins of the deceased, which logically they do not want returned (Parry 1989).

Even if a gift contains the spirit of its owner, the original owner of an object can keep it but grant another person the right to use it to make yet other gifts (Godelier 1992). Such gifts can be understood to be both inalienable, as the property of the owner, and alienated while circulating in gift exchanges. For example, in the Trobriands, *kitoum* are objects owned by individuals or lineages, such as shells or axe blades, that can be used in a variety of ways: for exchange, as **bridewealth**, or today for sale to tourists. Some may be used in *kula* when they are launched on an exchange path known as a *keda*. As soon as the first recipient of the *kitoum* accepts the gift, it becomes a *vaygu'a* and from then can only be used for *kula* exchanges. But the original owner of the gift continues to own it, and he can thus theoretically withdraw it from the *kula* at any time, although in practice this rarely happens. Rather, if a necklace or armband has been put into circulation in the *kula*, the original owner waits for it to come back along the *keda* path and then takes it back as *kitoum*, which closes the *keda* path. It is thus possible to keep an object and also give it in gift exchange.

There is another category of objects that are too sacred to be exchanged, sold, or gifted, and these are the objects that are the source of the identity and origin of the group itself. These sacred objects may have originated as gifts, but the givers were the gods or the ancestors, and they must be preserved because they mark the origins of the group. Among the Baruya in Papua New Guinea, with whom Maurice Godelier (1986) conducted fieldwork, sacred objects represent the powers of life and death and thus are material objects that refer to the origins of all things, the beginning of time, and the order of the world.

There are therefore three categories of objects: those that can be given, namely inalienable and alienated gifts; those that can be sold or bartered, namely commodities; and those that must never be given or sold, namely sacred objects. Together, the three forms of giving and keeping produce society.

Women and gift exchange

Malinowski's fieldwork in the Trobriands focused principally on men's gift exchanges. Fifty years later, North American anthropologist Annette Weiner also conducted fieldwork in the Trobriands but focused instead on women's gift exchanges (Weiner 1996). While men compete for status and fame in the *kula*, women engage in the competitive exchange of women's wealth, namely banana- and pandanus-fibre skirts and bundles of dried banana leaves, known as *doba*. Making these items represents hard work: women have to cut down and dry banana leaves, decorate them, and stitch them together; pandanus is even more labour-intensive as pandanus leaves have thorny edges that must be cut out. These items figure prominently in the exchange during *sagali*, mortuary rituals held for a deceased member of the women's **matrilineal** clan. Women who are rich in *doba* are 'strong women' and gain the respect of other women, as well

Box 9.2   Reciprocity as social lubricant: *guanxi* in a Chinese village

In some societies, gift giving can be so institutionalized that their members recognize it as a fundamental cultural feature. In rural China, for example, *guanxi* refers to networks of personal connections, members of which are expected to exchange gifts on diverse occasions, some specific and others not, some associated with specific rituals while others have no such associations (Yan 1996). *Guanxi* is both the social matrix for gift exchange and its outcome. In the small village in Manchuria where Yunxiang Yan spent part of his childhood during the Cultural Revolution and to which he returned as an anthropologist to conduct fieldwork, social life is compact, as the people with whom one works are the same as those one spends moments of leisure with. People have *guanxi* relations with close relatives, affines, neighbours, friends, distant relatives, and colleagues, and patterns of gift exchange outline a map of a person's social networks. *Guanxi* networks are organized into different zones: one's personal core consists of close relatives and affines, on whom one can always rely and with whom one exchanges gifts most frequently; one's reliable zone is made up of one's close friends and somewhat distant relatives, who can be counted on for help if needed; and in one's effective zone fit distant relatives and villagers who are not kin, who can potentially assist.

Villagers are attentive to the fact that different gifts are appropriate for different occasions and for different people. Giving a gift on an inappropriate occasion or giving a gift that is not of the expected value are serious breaches of social and moral convention, and someone who routinely violates these conventions is eventually marginalized and ostracized. *Guanxi* and gift exchange can just as easily reinforce social bonds as they can create inequality. Social relations that are not supported by *guanxi* have relatively little meaning.

Gift exchange in *guanxi* networks come into play in four spheres of life, which work hand in hand. First, it organizes economic life, because all labour, such as agriculture and house building, must rely on the cooperation of people outside the household, and thus can only be accomplished if one relies on one's *guanxi*. Hiring labourers would be shameful because it implies that one does not have an adequate *guanxi* network, and thus that one is not a moral and responsible member of the community. Second, gift exchange creates a social support system when personal emergencies arise and at critical times, such as when food is in short supply. Those who do not have a good *guanxi* suffer more than those who have a good *guanxi*, even though the latter may be in greater need. Third, gift exchange comes into play during life-cycle rituals such as weddings and funerals, which require other villagers' participation; if a deceased person is not mourned properly, her or his soul will not fare well. Finally, *guanxi* is a political instrument: it is important to cultivate good relations through gift exchange with politically influential people, and political ambitions can only be fulfilled if one has good *guanxi*.

Guanxi is important at all levels of Chinese society: for example, it is very difficult to start a business without exchanging gifts and politicians can only be successful if they have a strong gift-exchange *guanxi* network. Uninformed observers often characterize and the flow of gifts in *guanxi* networks as favouritism, cronyism, patronage, or 'corruption'. Chinese people take a different view: they regard the flow of gifts as the very essence of society. It is the lubricant that makes life possible, it affects how one fares materially, it is the basis of morality, and it ensures that one's soul is well taken care of in the afterlife.

as men. Like *kula* valuables, women's valuables rarely have any specific use; rather, they materialize the hard work that women put into their production and the social relations they make
possible, by symbolizing the strength and continuity of the matrilineal clan after the death of
one of its members. Women's valuables embody the clan's identity and ancestral power that
women, as the conduit of matrilineal kinship, reproduce over the generations (Figure 9.3).

Women who are the most active contributors at the mortuary distributions may not have had
the time to manufacture *doba* and instead depend on their male kin to help them purchase them
from other women. Women act independently of men, but politically ambitious men will

Figure 9.3 Mortuary ceremony, Omarakana, Trobriand Islands; mourning women count
banana leaf bundles for ritual exchange. A woman in the centre wears a decorated
fibre skirt, 1976. (Courtesy of Edwin Hutchins and Dona Hutchins Collection,
University of California San Diego)

actively support their kinswomen's efforts to become 'strong women'. Women's wealth production in the form of *doba* contributions are given full public recognition and are central to the society, a point that Malinowski overlooked.

At funerals, women of the matriline of the deceased person give *doba* to members of the matrilines with which the deceased had exchange relations, in particular the deceased's spouse and father, who belong to different matrilines. The *doba* are repayment for the care they took of the deceased during her or his lifetime and they sever the social ties the deceased had in life with these matrilines. Women who successfully give away large amounts of *doba* and are left with nothing at the end of the *sagali* can be satisfied that they are indeed women of wealth.

Today, in addition to the banana leaf skirts and bundles, women also give cloth as part of the *sagali*, which they have to pay for in cash (Lepani 2017). Cash is in short supply in the islands and people must obtain it from relatives working for wages elsewhere in Papua New Guinea or abroad. This may seem to represent the commodification of the *sagali* and the lessening of the value of *doba*, but in fact Trobriand women view this as an extension of the power and resourcefulness of women who, rather than simply seeking economic independence through wage labour, use their earnings and remittances to fulfil their social obligations and those of their fellow clan members.

However, the labour and time required to make sufficient *doba* for a *sagali* has in recent decades become a matter of discussion among some Trobrianders, who argue that it diverts women's energies from more pressing tasks, such as cooking for their families, and takes hard-earned cash away from buying useful commodities. These views reflect Christian values about where women's work should be directed, namely to the home. They also reflect the increasing encroachment of capitalist forms of commodity exchange. In the 1990s, one Trobriand village took the decision to end *sagali* exchange. Yet the villagers continued to attend *sagali* in other villages and young women from other villages now do not wish to marry into the village because they no longer hold *sagali*. For women, economic considerations based on commodity markets have not displaced the value of their wealth and their ability to demonstrate in mortuary rituals their commitment to reproduce the matriline.

Other innovations demonstrate the continued vitality of *sagali* distributions and the agency of Trobriand women. At one *sagali* that Katherine Lepani attended in 2003, the women collectively decided to wear trousers instead of traditional skirts. This was to honour the deceased, a woman who had been a successful school principal. The trousers worn by the women made a striking visual statement about the power and agency of women in the modern world.

Women's skirts continue to symbolize female power and sexuality, and the banana leaf bundles to symbolize the milk with which women nurture their children. Women's wealth thus not only reflects the power of individual women but also represents the value of women and their power to reproduce the clan. The increasing involvement of Trobrianders in the capitalist economy has not undermined the importance of women's wealth as the gendered labour required to make *doba* continues to materialize the social relations connecting individuals to each other and to their matrilines.

Reciprocity and morality

The give and take of goods and services between individuals and groups is known as **reciprocity**. Anthropologists use this concept to understand different forms of exchange. In the 1960s, Marshall Sahlins (2004) developed a schema of types of reciprocity taking the kinds of social relations that they create as a point of departure, in contrast to Malinowski and Mauss, who were more interested in what was exchanged and how. Sahlins's schema identifies three types of reciprocity. One is **generalized reciprocity**, which occurs when people give without keeping an account of who gave to whom. Givers are not particularly interested in whether and when they will receive a return gift and may be content with simply giving to others, motivated by generosity and altruism. An example is giving a present to someone for his or her birthday in many societies of the Global North. The giver has a vague expectation that the receiver will also give a present for the giver's own birthday, but if this does not happen it is not a tragedy because the present was primarily a thoughtful act. Other examples of generalized reciprocity are acts of sharing and pooling. It can also be motivated by the expectation that others will be equally generous; for example, people give blood to a blood bank with the expectation that blood will be made available to them should they need it. The typical context in which generalized reciprocity takes place is within the family or between close friends, as well as charity.

Balanced reciprocity takes place when one party gives something to a recipient with the expectation that the recipient will reciprocate either at the moment or in the future with a gift of comparable value. It represents a continuum, with at one end buying something from a shop, where the 'giver' (i.e., the merchant) expects the 'recipient' (i.e., the customer) to provide the amount owed for the transaction at the point of exchange; and at the other end gifts given with the understanding that the recipient will return a gift of comparable value at some point in the future, as in *kula* exchange. Sometimes these exchanges are publicly witnessed so that both parties can be held to account for what is given and what will be given in return. Balanced reciprocity takes place between relative equals, but equals who are in competition with each other, and generally involves non-kin, with the possible exception of **affines** and potential future affines.

Negative reciprocity refers to trying to get something for nothing or for less than the value of the object. Examples include haggling, theft, the imposition of tariffs, and exploitative labour situations in which an employer tries to keep wages as low as possible so that she or he can maximize profit. There is no relation of trust between two parties and there is often distrust. Negative reciprocity takes place between non-kin, often between strangers or enemies when kinship obligations are lacking and violence more likely. For example, witches, who are often conceptualized as mystically consuming the organs of their victims which ultimately results in their deaths, take what does not belong to them and give nothing in return.

Central to this schema are questions of morality, which is to say socially recognized norms of behaviour that apply across social contexts. Sahlins' three types of reciprocity are associated with different applications of moral norms, and thus different kinds of social relations. In generalized reciprocity, exchange is motivated by affection, duty, or altruism. In balanced reciprocity, the nature of the exchange is dictated by rules or norms. In negative reciprocity, what dominates is immorality, ruthlessness, and distrust.

Yet the immorality of negative reciprocity can be mitigated by other factors. For example, in the Auschwitz concentration camp during World War II, prisoners had to take what they needed in order to survive (Narotzky and Moreno 2002). Food, and even the spoons and bowls the prisoners needed in order to eat, were extremely scarce. Prisoners who were most likely to survive were those who could 'organize', which is to say take what they needed. Yet standards of morality persisted: some prisoners were willing to steal from the warehouses containing the belongings that the guards had confiscated from inmates when they first arrived at the camp, but they were not prepared to steal from fellow prisoners. Those who worked in the medical facilities were prepared to take clothes and food from the dead, but would not steal from those who were still alive, even if they were likely to die soon. Even in this extreme context of negative reciprocity, prisoners followed an unspoken moral code they had devised for themselves, which we call a **moral economy**.

The dead today can give others the gift of life when they agreed to organ donation while still alive. The transplantation of organs from a person who has recently died to an ill person, one of the most extraordinary achievements of modern medicine, involves the mobilization of cutting-edge technological expertise and a complex operation of matching donor and recipient under time pressure. It also involves social processes like mourning the deceased donor and celebrating the receiver's new lease on life. It is a particularly dramatic instance of what anthropologists have long analyzed as the gift, in which the gifted object is a living organ.

Organ donation evokes strong emotions, bringing the giver and the receiver into a close relationship on a certain level. Yet medical institutions do their utmost to ensure that the families of the donor and the recipient do not find out each other's identity or meet, although in some cases families manage to defy this injunction. While donors' relatives must maintain a front of dignified altruism in the public eye, they often harbour feelings that they have not received sufficient gratitude for their extraordinary gift. And while recipients and their kin are expected to show appreciation and good health, they have to keep quiet about the harsher realities that they often also confront, such as destitution, unemployment, and disrupted family relations.

Body parts are scarce and valuable, and professionals involved in their procurement evaluate them in reference to their origin. This takes the form of a medical assessment of the quality of the tissue, but it is also a social evaluation (Sharp 2006). The most prized body parts are those of young people who have met an untimely accidental death: their organs are thought to be least affected by aging, lifestyle, and illness. At the other end of the spectrum are organs harvested from dead prisoners, which are thought to be diseased and morally tainted. In the United States, where the murder rate is one of the highest in the world and where many donated organs come from murder victims, transplant professionals are often silent about the cause of death of organ donors. Even after death, bodies are evaluated according to social and moral standards.

Even more dramatic is the valuation of body parts when they are procured through an illegal and often transnational traffic, in which people sell their non-essential body parts, such as a kidney, in a desperate attempt to alleviate poverty (Scheper-Hughes 2000). Organ trafficking is often sensationalized and its extent is difficult to assess, but it is certainly implicated in global inequalities. Equally controversial is commercial surrogacy, when a woman bears a child for money. In spite of the payments made for the service, it is often represented as the gift of a child to a person or couple who might otherwise remain childless. It raises complex moral and ethical questions, particularly when the surrogacy involves a carrier who lives in a poor country and carries a child for money (Deomampo 2016). Some see transnational commercial surrogacy as exploitative of poor women in the Global South and think that it should be illegal; others see it in a larger context in which many countries deny access to assisted reproductive technologies to some groups (e.g., gays and lesbians, unmarried individuals), and argue that surrogacy provides poor surrogate women the opportunity to lift themselves out of poverty.

Exchange serves to reproduce people and society. From the most intimate and interpersonal exchanges to trade deals between states, giving and taking underpin what we are entitled to expect from others, what we are obliged to give to others, and our sense of who we are. The different forms that exchange takes, however, depend not simply on understanding what exchange is but also on a shared understanding of what constitutes a gift, and this is not as obvious as it may first appear.

When a gift is not a gift

For Mauss, people in pre-capitalist societies always exchange the gift with the expectation that they will receive a return gift in due time. Thus, in those societies, there is no such thing as a free gift. A free gift would deny the possibility of social relations. This led French philosopher Jacques Derrida (1992) to argue that a free gift is impossible because if one gives a gift expecting a return gift, then it is not a gift. Derrida's abstract ruminations may seem removed from real

---

Box 9.3   Food banks in twenty-first-century Britain

Britain is one of the wealthiest countries in the world and yet over 20% of the population lives below the poverty line, some in dire poverty. Successive governments' austerity
measures and cuts in welfare provision have exacerbated the divide between rich and
poor and resulted in a dramatic increase in the need for food banks, to which people who
cannot afford to buy food turn for emergency food supplies.

Many food banks are run by churches and other religious institutions and the mostly
middle-class volunteers who staff them see their role as an extension of their Christian duty
to help those in need (Caplan 2016). While the volunteers treat the recipients of food aid
with respect, few seem to consider that a more permanent solution to the problem of food
poverty might have to do with tackling unemployment and low salaries, and providing a level
of welfare support that would allow people to manage without needing to depend on food
banks. The volunteers have absorbed the messages of austerity promulgated by the government and no longer think of food insecurity as the failure to provide a basic entitlement, but
rather as the unfortunate outcome of individual circumstances that have afflicted their clients.

In the language of the gift, the food that clients receive is donated without expectation
of return and is hence close to a pure gift that does not create lasting relations between
giver and receiver. As a result, the clients often feel stigmatized. As recipients who cannot
reciprocate, they remain in debt with a permanently lowered status. Some will rectify this
situation as soon as they are able to by donating food or working as volunteers and so
change their status from that of recipient to that of donor.

---

life, but they offer a way of understanding the lengths to which some may go to avoid forming
reciprocal relations based on exchange, by trying to give up exchange altogether.

Among the Jains, a religious group in Northern India of about two to three millions, some
people become renouncers, namely monks and nuns who devote their lives to spiritual pursuits
and give up all earthly possessions (Laidlaw 2000). The renouncers wander the streets everyday
around noon carrying bowls and wait to be called into the kitchens of Jain families who give
them food. This wandering is called *gocari*, literally 'grazing' as cows do, suggesting that their
movement is random. Each family gives such a tiny amount of food to each renouncer that they
barely notice that any food has gone, and so the renouncers go from house to house until they
have collected enough food for the day. The renouncers are clear that they are not begging and
therefore the food is not charity, so they are not in anyone's debt. They do not return a word of
thanks for the food they receive and they do not return to the same **households** each day to
ensure that they do not form relationships with particular families. Once they have obtained the
food they need, the renouncers come together and mix all the food together so that the donations from individual families' become indistinguishable. All these practices serve to deny sociality and thus ensure the success of the renouncers' ascetic pursuits.

The food that the renouncers receive is as close an example of a pure gift as we can find.
However, Jain householders consider that they do give a gift because giving to worthy recipients
is an act of religious merit. While they are not supposed to expect a return on the gift, the gift
may bring them rewards in future reincarnations. Some form of reciprocity is inevitable even if
it is deferred to some unknown future point and even if people go to great lengths to deny it.

Gift, commodity, and exchange

Gift exchange plays a particularly important role in societies that have not been totally absorbed into a capitalist economy, as was the case of the Trobriands at the time of Malinowski's fieldwork. In economies based on commodity exchange, money, first invented over 5,000 years ago, is essential. Money has two effects. One is that it allows its users to compare the value of resources that can be of a radically different nature, such as labour, food, transportation, education, and corporate stocks. Some resources, such as love, friendship, and loyalty, cannot be bought with money, although they can be strengthened with money and other gifts. The other effect of money is that it enables exchange over great distances and between large numbers of people, and thus it makes large-scale societies, in which social relations do not depend on face-to-face contact, possible. Exchanging an object for money constitutes the object as a **commodity**, in contrast to the exchanges we have described so far, which constitute the exchanged object as a gift.

Gift exchange is a transaction between people designed to nurture their relationship; in contrast, commodity exchange is a transaction of one object for another through the mediation of money, which does not form the basis for a relationship between the exchange partners (Gregory 1982). As we saw earlier, gifts frequently retain a connection to the giver; for example, we cherish a present from a loved one because the object reminds us of its giver, and *kula* valuables become important when they have been owned by famous men. In contrast, an object we purchase in a shop retains nothing of the shopkeeper who sold it to us. Thus gifts are **inalienable** (from the giver) while commodities are **alienable**.

In actual practice, gift and commodity exchange are often entangled with one another. For example, in Dinesen's short story, Babette procured food with the lottery money she had won, and thus the food was a commodity, but when she turned it into a feast, it became a gift, with all the moral and affective associations of the gift. The beautiful carpets historically woven by women in what is today Turkmenistan were originally part of the intimate furnishing of the families of the women who wove them (Spooner 1988). Often, they were an important feature of dowries, they featured symbolically important motifs, and carpets woven by important women bore the reputation of their creator. When they are sold to dealers and exported to the Global North, they become 'authentic' commodities that can fetch hefty prices. Thus commodities can be transformed into gifts and vice versa.

The contrast between gift and commodity is deeply embedded in a history of transformations from a world in which the gift played a central role in life to a world in which commodity transactions dominate. In pre-industrial society, the household was typically a unit of both production and consumption. For example, households grew vegetables for their own consumption and preserved, pickled, and stored them at home. This is still the subsistence model found in many societies of the Global South. But households could not grow and make everything they needed, and thus exchanged goods with other households. With industrialization, production has increasingly moved out of the home and into the factory.

Over time, the household in the Global North became less a place of production and more one to which individuals returned after work to recover from increasingly **alienating** forms of labour. As economic historian Karl Polanyi describes it, economic production and social life became disembedded from one another, which is to say, increasingly distinct and separate from one another. In this context, the home and relations between kin were increasingly based on sentiment alone, rather than on the shared labour needed to meet the needs of the household. What the household consumed was no longer the product of its members' labour, but rather commodities purchased outside the home and in the global era frequently manufactured thousands of kilometres from the household that consumes them. Work became associated with the sphere of calculation, alienation, and exploitation, while home was imagined as the opposite, a sanctuary where people cared for each other and exchanged with each other without calculating and keeping track of who did what for whom.

As society and economy grew more separate, so did gifts and commodities. In fact, the widespread contemporary idea of a gift as 'free' and not being the product of calculation (as in the expression 'it's the thought that counts') depends on the idea of a commodity understood as the opposite, producing no relationship between buyer and seller. Gift and commodity can only be understood in opposition to each other. In the *kula* or the potlatch, or in pre-industrial Europe, the idea of a free gift with no expectation of a return gift would have made no sense, as the whole point of gift exchanges in these contexts was to give in order to receive a return gift in the future.

In many societies, however, the economy has not become as disembedded from other spheres of existence as it has in the Global North. There, gift exchange continues to be very important to social life. For example, families continue to grow food, fish, or hunt, and redistributing the surplus to other families in the form of gifts is a common activity. But capitalism and commodities have penetrated almost all societies of the world, and gift exchange takes place side-by-side with commodity exchange, sometimes uneasily. Different groups can prioritize one form of exchange over the other. While the poor must be able to count on gift exchange and the mutual support that derives from it, the wealthy are often eager to distance themselves from the gift economy, and thus to rely on commodity purchases, which enables them to free themselves from expectations of reciprocity and indebtedness from kin, neighbours, and others. In the Global North, for some middle-class people who are disillusioned with capitalism and consumerism, the gift economy represents a nostalgic return to a simpler life. Such is the case of 'neo-rurals', urbanites who abandon their middle-class lives and 'return' to farm life.

For those who have difficulties making ends meet in a world of wage labour and commodity exchange, the gift economy represents a means of survival. Bonds between exchange partners forming dense social networks offer a kind of insurance against future wants. It makes good sense to make alliances by giving gifts to many exchange partners so that when a need arises a return gift can be expected. In poor neighbourhoods in Chile, affected by the national and global economic reforms and **austerity** measures that have eroded poor people's economic security, women offer support to each other, for example, by feeding the child of a close neighbour who has lost her job (Han 2003). They do so with tact and grace, as when a woman invites her unemployed neighbour's child over for dinner saying that she has cooked too much food. Through small acts of mutual help, frequently repeated, people develop a sense that they share their hardship.

General and special purpose money

Money can be used in multiple ways: it can be a store of wealth, a means of exchange, or a measure of value. General purpose money of the kind most people are used to today does all of these things and makes it possible to quantify anything that can be bought and sold according to a single scale of value, including labour. Special purpose money, by contrast, only serves one or two of these functions and can only be used for a restricted set of exchanges. For example, coupons and vouchers are a form of special purpose money and can be exchanged for particular goods and services but not for cash or any goods or services that are not part of the voucher scheme.

Special purpose money is found in many parts of the world. Among the Tiv of Nigeria, until the early decades of the twentieth century, the economy was divided into three hierarchically ranked spheres of exchange each with its own special purpose money (Bohannan 1959). The lowest sphere was market exchange in which people bartered for subsistence goods. This sphere was morally neutral. Next came the sphere of prestige goods including cattle, slaves, medicines, magic, brass rods, and a locally produced white cloth called *tugudu*. Within the prestige sphere, brass rods served as a limited general-purpose money for reckoning value and as a means of payment. The highest sphere of exchange was made up of rights over women other than slaves. The simplest form of exchange in the highest sphere was an exchange of sisters for marriage by two men. In practice, however, men who shared a common male ancestor, and were thus **agnatically** related, would form ward-sharing groups with rights in the daughters of the group so that each man could have a female ward to exchange for a wife. The only morally acceptable exchange for a woman given in marriage by one lineage was another woman from the lineage who had received the first woman.

Exchanges within spheres were morally neutral while those across spheres were evaluated as morally charged, either positively or negatively. For example, if a person used brass rods from the prestige sphere to purchase goods from the lower sphere, as might happen when someone was in need, the person was in a 'bad' position, while the person who obtained the brass rods in the exchange was in a 'good' position. However, when the colonial administration introduced general purpose money to the Tiv, all commodities could be measured on a single scale and made them exchangeable for cash. The result was to undermine the separate spheres of exchange and the moral economy that had distinguished market transactions from prestige ones.

However, the model of the three spheres was less bounded than the anthropologist Paul Bohannan first described it (Guyer 2004). The Tiv did not only exchange among themselves, but also in regional trade networks, for example by exchanging prestige sphere *tugudu* cloth with the Hausa to the north and brass rods with traders in the south who brought in European goods. Thus they were already engaged in economic transactions with parties who did not have any commitment to their moral economy. In fact, the Tiv used their transactions with these other traders to obtain the special purpose currency for exchanges in their prestige sphere of exchange.

In addition, when the colonial authorities outlawed exchange marriages in the highest sphere, a man could no longer exchange his daughter or sister for a bride, but could now use brass rods, a prestige currency, to pay the bridewealth. This effectively undermined the highest sphere of exchange in Tiv society (Parry and Bloch 1989). For this reason, Tiv elders mistrusted money and viewed it as a negative force undermining the moral social order. In contrast, younger Tiv men welcomed the new system as it undermined the senior men's control over access to women and the power they had wielded over the younger men through this control.

Money-mediated market transactions are not simply economic but also social and cultural. Not everything can be bought and sold and people will make different judgements about the relative morality of any given exchange.

Neoliberalism and austerity

In the last chapter of *The Gift*, Mauss suggested that, in contemporary society, traditional forms of exchange and the reciprocity that they formed had been lost. But in the aftermath of World War I, when Mauss was writing, they were beginning to be replaced in the Global North by new state institutions such as benefits for the sick and unemployed, social housing for the working classes, and pensions for retirees. Mauss viewed them as the obligation that the state owed to workers who had, by their labour, created the wealth of their countries.

Underpinning these developments in social welfare was a new sense of morality in which the state guaranteed a minimum level of subsistence and support to all citizens. These developments in the Global North came into full bloom after World War II and the generations that came of age in the second half of the twentieth century were granted greater opportunities for education, better healthcare, and a higher material standard of living than any previous generation in history, except perhaps in Bolshevik Russia in the 1920s. While these policies varied from one country to the other (e.g., the United States never established universal health care), they guaranteed important safety nets for citizens. Of course workers paid for these benefits in taxes, so the benefits were the product of an exchange between the state and the citizens, mediated through employers and financial institutions. While the income gap between rich and poor did not disappear, welfare policies helped reduce extreme poverty and helped the upward mobility of many families. For example, lower-middle-class families could hope that their children would get an education and thus secure better jobs than their parents.

In the 1980s, many governments reversed these developments by reducing or eliminating welfare and a new way of thinking about citizenship emerged. In this changing ideology, citizens were supposed to be responsible for their own destiny and that of their close kin without relying on the government for help. Prime minister Margaret Thatcher in the United Kingdom and President Ronald Reagan in the United States played major roles in transforming this new way of thinking into practice, which then spread to many other countries of the world. This ideology, which came to be known as **neoliberalism**, advocates the deregulation of markets, the privatization of state institutions, and the reduction of government infrastructures. The neoliberal state has one responsibility: to ensure that private enterprise takes over the responsibilities of the state.

As part of the new way of thinking about the citizen as self-sufficient, large numbers of urban working people in Britain and the United States were encouraged to buy homes rather than rent, and take out mortgage loans even when they were not in a position to pay them back, from which finance capitalists profited hugely. In Britain, for example, the state encouraged local councils to put social housing up for sale to their occupants. What took place, however, is that wealthy entrepreneurs bought large numbers of these housing units and turned them into rental properties or sold them again at a profit. For a while, house prices kept rising, mortgages were in demand, and banks were more than willing to lend; it seemed as though everyone was a winner. This is what is called an economic bubble.

In 2006, economic anthropologist Gillian Tett, an assistant editor at *The Financial Times*, warned of an impending financial crash because too many mortgages were being mis-sold to people who would default on their debts. Yet, she was ignored or denounced for her efforts. In 2008, a financial crash on a global scale happened, just as Tett had predicted, though most governments and financial institutions claimed that they were taken by surprise. Many banks in the Global North were on the verge of collapse and governments bailed them out, thus diverting public money into corporate hands. Businesses retrenched and cut jobs. Homeowners saddled with mortgage debts lost their jobs and their homes, many families became homeless, and millions of lives were shattered.

In Europe, the countries most affected by the global economic financial crisis were Greece, Spain, Portugal, Italy, and Ireland. These countries received large bailouts to help them through the crisis from the European Central Bank, the European Commission, and the International Monetary Fund (nicknamed 'the Troika'), but the bailouts were tied to conditions, namely the implementation of strict **austerity** measures cutting deeply into welfare, health, education, and pensions. Austerity led to more job losses and increased poverty, and its human cost was steep. For example, the suicide rate in Greece increased by 35% between 2010 and 2012, mostly among men of working age (Rachiotis et al. 2015) (Figure 9.4).

As a result of austerity measures, in many parts of Europe, the ideal of the autonomous individual able to live independently has been seriously undermined. Adults who have lost their jobs and homes have had to return to live with their parents on the latter's pensions, a situation

Figure 9.4 Athenians protesting in 2011 against austerity measures imposed on Greece by the Troika, which led to major cutbacks in social welfare provisions and caused widespread impoverishment. (Courtesy of Susan Brownell)

that reverses the expectation that working adults support the elderly. Many people had to start depending on food banks to feed themselves and their children. In Ferrol in northwest Spain, which was devastated economically by the closure of ship-building industries, people organized cooperatives to collect and redistribute clothes and food (Narotzky 2016). In one of these cooperatives, people bypass the cash economy by exchanging food, labour, or used clothes for points, which they can use in turn to obtain what they need from the collective. Those who receive food are asked to join the cooperative to help with the work so that everyone who receives also gives, which maintains people's dignity despite being cash poor. These are some of the ways which people have found to work together and share labour, skills, and goods in order to survive under austerity. These kinds of exchanges helped develop a moral critique of the institutions that caused the crisis and resulted in hardship.

Other responses to the financial crisis include **social movements** that take on the banks that repossess homes and make families homeless. One such group in Spain, the *Plataforma de afectados por la hipoteca*, 'Coalition of People Affected by Mortgages' (PAH), provides support to those in debt and at risk of losing their home (Sabaté 2016). PAH activists physically block bank employees from repossessing homes and instruct mortgage defaulters to turn their shame into moral indignation at this widespread social problem resulting from real-estate speculation and predatory lending, thus reframing the crisis in terms of a moral economy.

The Occupy movement, which started in 2011, is another social movement that has focused on the immorality, inequality, and injustice of the increasing wealth gap between the richest 1%

of the population and the rest (Graeber 2013). Participants in this leaderless movement began by setting up an encampment in a park in New York City's financial centre. The movement, which spread to over 1,500 cities throughout the world, argued that the actions of financiers and states in one country affected the lives of workers across the globe. One of the movement's demands was that everyone receive a living wage, an idea with a long history known as **universal basic income**, namely a sum of money that the state provides regularly and unconditionally to every person regardless of wealth and income, to guarantee that everyone has enough to live on and alleviate poverty. This idea is based on the recognition that, under capitalism, half of all work performed, including care work and domestic labour, is not waged. Universal basic income would replace the welfare system that only serves to fuel the poverty trap: people stay on welfare because if they go to work they lose their benefits, but do not make enough money to stay out of poverty. Mauss would have considered the idea of universal basic income as a form of redistribution by the state of wealth derived from taxes to all citizens (Figure 9.5).

Figure 9.5 Occupy Pittsburgh. (Courtesy of Poitrus/Wikimedia, licensed under a Creative Commons Attribution-Share Alike 3.0 Unported licence)

Gifts and commodities: thinking about social relations

People in all societies exchange things. In many societies, the exchange of gifts is fundamental to the creation and maintenance of social relations because it creates reciprocity and indebtedness that continue over time, keeping people connected to one another. Gift exchange is the practice that makes society possible. By contrast, commodity exchange is important in keeping goods circulating and is thus fundamental to the economy, particularly in capitalist systems. But commodity exchange is impersonal in that it does not create bonds between people. Different kinds of exchange can be understood in terms of different forms of reciprocity that have divergent effects on social relations.

While gift exchange and commodity exchange create different kinds of social relations, they often coexist. In capitalist societies, where the commodity is central, poverty forces people at the lower end of the economy to rely on one another's help as a kind of insurance in case of future need. The economy, whether primarily gift-based or commodity-based, is always as complex as the social systems in which it is an integral aspect.

Economic crisis can transform the way in which people exchange and the way they think about exchange. The global financial crash of 2008 provides one instance of how a dramatic change in economic circumstances has made many people around the world raise questions about the disparities in wealth between the majority and those who control the resources, and to examine anew how we think about social justice.

Key thinkers mentioned in this chapter:

Paul Bohannan; Bronislaw Malinowski; Marcel Mauss; Marshall Sahlins; Annette Weiner

Key terms mentioned in this chapter (see Glossary):

Alienable; Austerity; Balanced reciprocity; Barter; Big men; Commodity; Economic anthropology; Generalized reciprocity; Gift; Gift economy; Inalienable; Kula; Moral economy; Neoliberalism; Potlatch; Negative reciprocity; Reciprocity; Social movement

Questions for discussion/review:

1   How do gift economies differ from those based on commodity exchange?
2   What does reciprocity have to do with morality?
3   Is it ever possible to give a gift with no expectation of return?
4   How does special purpose money work?
5   How did different groups of people around the world respond to the financial crisis of 2008?

Chapter 10

Religion

Like many other countries with a Muslim majority, Malaysia experienced a religious revival during the 1970s and 1980s. Some Malaysians sought to reverse a perceived decline of religion that many attributed to the economic development and social transformation of the country (Kloos 2019). The movement was spearheaded by a new urban and educated middle class that saw Islam as an all-encompassing way of life that should be integrated into politics and society, rather than as a religion that one practises in private.

Middle-class professional women, including doctors, lawyers, and psychologists, have played a central role in the revival. Some appeared on television debating topics such as gender, sexuality, and morality, and became media celebrities who merged their professional expertise with religious authority in ways that challenged the authority of male religious figures. Dr. Harlina Siraj, for example, argued against conservative patriarchal views that sought to forbid sex education, but maintained that such education should encompass not only technical information about the body but also concerns for spiritual and psychological well-being.

As these celebrity women demonstrate, far from representing a return to regressive forms of Islam in which men dominate women, the Islamic revival in Malaysia is both a conservative and a progressive reform movement that asserts gender equality, although in ways that are different from how gender equality is understood in Western contexts. The celebrity professionals bring together secular and religious authority, illustrating the blurred and unstable boundary between them (Figure 10.1).

Religion: a complicated concept

As the opening vignette illustrates, religion can play a central role in people's lives, but this role is subject to different and sometimes conflicting perspectives. Indeed, how to define the very concept of religion has been a thorny problem for generations of social scientists. Commonsense definitions often do not work. For example, one could propose that religion is what people turn to in order to ease suffering caused by such conditions as poverty, loneliness, or the inevitability of death. While religion may serve this purpose in some circumstances, in other contexts religion aggravates suffering instead. For example, Shi'i Muslims in Iran self-flagellate to commemorate the martyrdom of the Prophet's grandson Hussain and some Catholics carry heavy crosses and endure other painful rituals on Good Friday. In these instances, people embrace suffering through religion. Conversely, people find many ways of easing suffering that are not religious, for example, by visiting psychotherapists, watching television, or drinking alcohol.

In a classic work of nineteenth-century evolutionary anthropology, E. B. Tylor proposed a definition of religion as 'the belief in Spiritual Beings' (1871, 1, 383), which had two

DOI: 10.4324/9781315737805-10

Figure 10.1 Islamic teacher and popular preacher Ustazah Fatimah Syarha with one of her regular study groups. International Islamic University Malaysia campus, Gombak, Selangor, Malaysia, February 2017. (Courtesy of David Kloos)

components: the conviction that humans have souls that continue to exist after death and a belief in supernatural entities such as spirits, ghosts, gods, or God. This simple definition had the merit of being inclusive of most faiths past and present (except perhaps some forms of Buddhism). Yet it is problematic in that it says nothing about what people do with religion, what role it plays in their lives, and how it interacts with other aspects of life such as politics, culture, and society. It also assumes that the distinction between 'supernatural' and 'natural' is self-evident, which is not the case. For example, for Rock Cree Indians of Manitoba, Canada, animals lead intellectual, emotional, and spiritual lives not unlike those of humans, and hunting them requires considerable religious ritual to appease these qualities (Brightman 1993). What is 'supernatural' from one perspective is everyday reality from another.

In contrast to Tylor, Émile Durkheim (1912) proposed that religion is a social phenomenon: it is external to the individual, it pre-exists and outlasts everyone, and it enables and constrains behaviour. Through religion, practitioners classify everything in the world as sacred or profane, which enables them to make sense of their experiences. In addition, the repetition of **rituals** reinforces and validates shared beliefs. Durkheim arrived at this analysis by considering the totems that Australian Aboriginal people worshipped, which represented different clans and, when brought together, offered an image of the society as a whole: 'if [the totem] is at once the symbol of the god and of the society', he wrote, 'is that not because the god and the society are only one?' (Durkheim 1915, 206). He surmised that the same applied to complex societies: people go to church, the mosque, the temple, or the synagogue, where they participate in rituals (prayers, offerings, prostration, etc.). These acts, which everyone performs at the same time and in the same location, create strong emotions of togetherness, which he termed **effervescence**, and strengthen their belief in their commonality. Durkheim understood religion as a social institution designed to overcome social divisions and generate a sense of cohesion and belonging.

This idea certainly resonates in the contemporary world, although in some cases in ways that Durkheim could not have predicted. For example, one of the first things that many migrants do on arriving in a new country is to locate a church, mosque, or temple associated with the religion they practised in their homeland. For example, in Nigerian Pentecostal churches in Amsterdam, pastors work to create a sense of solidarity and unity among Nigerian migrants, who come from diverse social and economic backgrounds (Andrikopoulos 2013). The church is where newcomers gather information about employment, housing, and the law. There they can also find a marriage partner and, if they are undocumented, 'borrow' identity documents from people whose identity photo looks vaguely like them to help them secure employment, since Dutch authorities have trouble distinguishing the features of different dark-skin people. Through religion, migrants find mutual support and a sense of belonging.

An important aspect of religion that Durkheim's account overlooked is the fact that religion is an individual experience, in addition to a collective one. This is what Clifford Geertz (1966), later in the twentieth century, explained by arguing that religion is constituted by the meaningful **symbols** that organize believers' religious feelings. These include the aesthetic and emotional power of belief that manifests itself in rituals. Religion offers believers explanations about the nature of existence that they recognize as true. Religious symbols make meaningful statements about the way the world is, our place in it, and how we should conduct ourselves.

This view was later criticized by Talal Asad (1993), who argued that while Geertz had stressed the importance of symbols, he had not explained how symbols become important. What a worshipper should believe or reject is always the result of what an authority decides, be it the scriptures, a religious specialist, a spirit medium, or other worshippers, and thus power is intrinsic to religion. What counts as religion or as the 'true' religion is frequently the subject of (sometimes acrimonious) debate: believers in one religious tradition sometimes critique adherents of other religions as worshippers of illegitimate deities and believers in erroneous ideas. One cannot understand religion independently of these power struggles. Even where religious pluralism and mutual tolerance reigns, there is frequently a powerful entity (e.g., the law, the state) that exerts its authority to ensure coexistence. Religion is thus inseparable from the larger social and political context in which it is practised.

Ritual: religious and secular

Religion becomes particularly visible in rituals, such as prayers, temple visits, holy feasts, and pilgrimages. Our understanding of rituals owes much to the foundational work of Victor Turner (1979), who defined a ritual as a sequence of activities that are scripted (e.g., involving specific language and comportment); that take place in a **liminal** space and time, apart from the flow of everyday life; and that 'do work', namely bring about change. Some rituals also reinforce an unstructured sense of egalitarianism and togetherness among participants, which Turner termed **communitas.** To Turner's definition we can add that rituals affirm and construct power structures: a religious ceremony displays the power of a church or a religious expert (Figure 10.2).

Our lives are saturated with rituals. Rituals can also be non-religious, such as those associated with politics, leisure, or the life cycle. Examples include national day celebrations, carnival, and rites of passage. Yet religion often lurks in the background of rituals participants consider secular. While *carnaval* in Rio de Janeiro is a festival of dance, music, and costumes, the ritual on which

Figure 10.2 A re-enactment in 2008 of a late-nineteenth-century Grand Sacrifice to Heaven at the Temple of Heaven in Beijing, a ritual performed since ancient times by the emperor to reinforce his claim to be the man who connected the cosmos by linking heaven and earth and ensured fruitful harvests, illustrating that a ritual can have political, religious, and economic meanings at the same time. (Courtesy of Susan Brownell)

it is historically based, namely carnival in medieval Europe, was rooted in the religious calendar, between Epiphany and Lent. Life-cycle rituals like a *quinceañera* in Latin America or a Bar- or Bat-Mitzvah in Jewish communities celebrate a young person's coming of age, a secular event, but the former often begins with a church service and the latter is officiated by a rabbi.

Events like concerts, sporting events, and other types of performances are also ritualized. For example, the Olympic Games are scripted events that stand apart from the flow of everyday life, they are held at a specific time and in a specific place, and they bring people together. While the Parade of Nations held during the opening ceremonies is organized around the idea that marching athletes identify with a specific nation-state, it also emphasizes a global commonality in which every nation, however big or small, has a place in the ritual. But what sport events lack is the transformative effect and the dimension of power of religious ritual (Brownell 1993). People participate in the Catholic mass, in Friday prayer, or in temple offerings because they think it does something to them and because they see it as a religious obligation, but no one feels obliged to attend a football match and it does not transform who one is. In addition, rather than affirming a power structure, sport events create communitas among spectators. Of course they display the power of athletes' bodies and of the hosting city, but this is different from the structural power that religious rituals showcase.

The term 'ritual' is often used to refer to everyday activities like brushing one's teeth or washing the dishes. Here again, these activities resemble rituals in that they are scripted, but calling them ritual stretches the category to the point that it is no longer useful in distinguishing activities that 'do work', like religious rituals, from mundane or routine activities that have no such effect.

A classic example of a religious ritual is the pilgrimage. Pilgrims undertake pilgrimages for different reasons, including fulfilling a vow, asking for blessings, and doing penance. Some pilgrimages last a few hours while others involve a substantial investment of time. Some only have local significance while others are global events in which millions of people participate, like the yearly Muslim Hajj to Mecca, one of the five pillars of Islam. Yet there are also commonalities, which Victor Turner (1974), by extending the pioneering work of Van Gennep (1960), was the first to theorize. Pilgrimages display all the characteristics that he attributes to rituals: they follow a script, stand apart from the ordinariness of life, take place in specific locations and at specific times, have a transformative effect, and enable communitas to emerge among pilgrims.

What takes place during a pilgrimage explains why it has a transformative effect. At least in principle, a pilgrimage erases differences among pilgrims, who all become religious subjects in search of the sacred, regardless of age, race, or social standing. This effect may be reinforced by requirements that pilgrims wear the same clothes, share food, or perform the same actions. For example, the Hajj begins with the ritual of the *tawaf*, during which huge crowds of people all dressed in the same clothing walk seven times counterclockwise around the Kaaba, a stone structure at the centre of the Grand Mosque of Mecca that symbolizes the house of God. Taking part in this ritual together on an equal footing symbolizes the pilgrims' belief in the same God and creates communitas, which corresponds closely to the Classical Arabic term *umma* 'those who are bound to God' (Figure 10.3).

Figure 10.3 Many hundreds of pilgrims throng around the Kaaba at the start of Hajj, August 2018. (Courtesy of Adli Wahid)

But Turner ignored the role that power can play in a pilgrimage. For example, in the Hajj, the government of Saudi Arabia, which controls the sites of the pilgrimage, determines who can attend through quotas that are widely thought to be based on political factors (Bianchi 2017). The Saudi government is also known for treating non-white pilgrims, women, and Shiʻi Muslims poorly, while privileging wealthy pilgrims who travel in style. Communitas and liminality are important characteristics of an idealized version of pilgrimages, but in practice all pilgrimages are shaped by social, political, and economic conditions and differences.

Precisely because rituals, whether religious or secular, are expected to 'do work', they can also fail for various reasons: the person in charge may lack expertise, the intended outcome may not be realized, or the conditions of the ritual as a liminal event are not met. For example, pilgrims undertake pilgrimages for many reasons, including healing, renewing their faith in the religion, and the hope that a relative will convert; but the healing, the renewal, or the conversion may not happen as hoped, and thus the pilgrimage is not a success because it does not deliver on its promises (Kaell 2016). Rituals are thus potentially fragile events.

World religions, local religions, and local practices

One problem that anthropologists face in their attempt to define religion abstractly is that the concept brings together under one label many kinds of systems and practices. Major world religions like Christianity, Islam, Judaism, Buddhism, and Hinduism, practised by hundreds of millions of people, are different from what one can loosely call 'local' religions, which are limited to particular social groups. World religions are based on scriptures that provide rules of worship and behaviour followed by people in many different parts of the world. In contrast, the religious beliefs and practices of the Rock Cree Indians described earlier are specifically tied to the ecological and social environment of one society and would have no meaning in other contexts.

There is considerable diversity both between and within world religions. For example, some religions easily allow, even encourage, new converts, while others are exclusive. Christian missionaries have roamed the earth for two thousand years converting people, and from the sixteenth century onwards these efforts came to be an integral part of the colonial subjugation by Europe of the rest of the world. By contrast, mainstream Hinduism has traditionally been considerably less enthusiastic about converting outsiders in part because it is so tightly intertwined with the 'traditional' social structure of Indian society, namely its caste system.

Within world religions, furthermore, there are differences in how people interpret scriptures, conceptualize deities, and think about the world. The more than two billion people worldwide who identify as Christian may all refer to the Old and New Testaments as foundational texts, but disagree on such matters as how they should worship God, how churches should be organized, and how they should conduct their lives. Many adherents of world religions do not see religion as a concept that exists independently of other realms of life such as politics, society, science, and art, as the opening vignette of this chapter illustrates. For centuries, Confucianism in China consisted of assorted philosophical precepts about ethics and duty based on the Analects, which Confucius (Kong Fuzi) wrote in the sixth century BCE; only in the nineteenth century were these precepts standardized and codified into something akin to a religion under the influence of Buddhism and as a reaction to the Christianity that missionaries were introducing (Bayly 2004, 341). In the West, the idea of religion as a sphere of activity that was separate from other aspects of life arose in Europe during the Reformation, during which people became aware that it was possible to live as a Christian but follow different

Box 10.1   Burning Man: a spiritual non-religious pilgrimage

In 1986, a couple of friends in San Francisco got the idea of building a wooden effigy of a man, transporting it to a small beach below the famed Golden Gate bridge, and setting fire to it. The event drew a small crowd, who enjoyed the impromptu event's aesthetic and spiritual qualities. They repeated it every year, building a larger structure each time and attracting increasing numbers of participants. In 1990, because participant numbers had become unwieldy, they moved it to a stretch of the desolate Black Rock Desert in northwestern Nevada. Burning Man has been held there every year since, except in 2020, when it was canceled because of the Covid-19 pandemic (in 2021, it was held in cyberspace).

In 2019, the effigy that was set on fire at the end of the event, along with the temple that accompanies it, stood at 19m. That year, the event attracted almost 80,000 people from all over the world, who camped in the desert during the week and a half that preceded the ritual bonfire, in a highly organized temporary city in the form of a horseshoe. Participants bring all their food, water, and other necessities, and they must leave nothing behind. The event has multiple facets: some participants, or Burners, construct and display art installations, many of which are extravagant structures that variously showcase art, playfulness, and subversion, inviting other Burners to not only see but also experience in assorted ways; others dress up in costumes or walk around with little or no clothing; 'mutant vehicles' are elaborate creations that focus on aesthetics more than on their transportation potential; emphasis is placed on sharing, giving, and non-monetary exchange; hedonism, pleasure, inclusiveness, ecological consciousness, and community participation are all prioritized; and numerous events are on offer, such as classes, workshops, performances, and parties.

The governing body of Burning Man insists that the ritual is not a festival, in that it is not designed to entertain participants, but rather expect them to be the agents of their experience (Lucia 2020). For many Burners, Burning Man is a spiritual non-religious experience: it is transformative in that it takes people out of their ordinary materialist and anxiety-driven realities and places them in a context where interactions are meaningful even between complete strangers, and beauty and inventiveness take precedence over profit making and consumption. They arrive in a remote location, where the ecology is radically different from their home environment (e.g., sandstorms are frequent), spend time set apart from their daily life, and leave again having experienced something special that they feel makes them a different person. It thus meets Victor Turner's characterization of a pilgrimage (Gilmore 2010). Of course not everyone has the same idea of what a spiritual experience is: for some, it is consciousness-raising catharsis, for others it is hedonistic pleasure.

Many veteran Burners bemoan the fact that the event has become too mainstreamed and commercialized, despite its overt opposition to capitalism. Because the event is so fascinating it has attracted celebrities who fly in in private aircrafts and camp out in high style, which defeats the counter-cultural foundation of the event. The cost of tickets has risen considerably over the years, to which participants must add the expense of covering all their camping and transportation needs. As a result, Burning Man attracts predominantly well-to-do mainstream participants who have the means to undertake this spiritual non-religious pilgrimage and the privilege that enables them to participate in the first place.

doctrines; this awareness also created the possibility that one could lead a 'secular' existence (Asad 1993). The term 'religion' in fact hardly appears in the English translation of the Bible. The Reformation and later the Enlightenment transformed religion in Europe into a matter of private practice and personal choice, although some forms of Christianity continue to oppose this view.

Even in religions whose adherents insist on the authority of scriptures, such as the Vedas, the Sutras, the Qur'an, the Torah, or the Bible, believers organize their religious lives in many different ways. Some see the scriptures as a literal code for worship and the conduct of one's life, an approach known as **orthodoxy**. While orthodoxy is generally associated with a power structure in which religious authorities define the 'correct' way one should worship, this is not necessarily the case. For example, in the women's mosque movement in Cairo that Saba Mahmood (2005) studied in the late 1990s, women of diverse social backgrounds organized weekly meetings in mosques to read and explain the Qur'an and other religious texts to each other. The women were reacting to what they saw as the marginalization of Islam in secular Egypt, which was transforming it into an abstract belief system with no relevance to daily life. They insisted that religion had to inform all aspects of their lives, including how they understood their bodies, social relationships, and everyday conduct. But by claiming the authority to interpret the scriptures, they were indirectly challenging the authority of male theologians. To an uninformed observer, the women's mosque movement seemed to practice a conservative and subservient version of Islam, yet Mahmood argued that the women were in fact claiming **agency**, although of a different kind from how it is generally understood in Western contexts.

In other contexts, people practise rituals associated with different religions even though authority figures may define these religions as incompatible with one another. For example, in rural northeast Brazil, three main clusters of religious practices compete for adherents: the Catholic church, charismatic Protestant churches, and Afro-Brazilian religions that have roots in African religious practices, the best known of which is Candomblé. There is no love lost between charismatic churches and Afro-Brazilian religions, as the former accuse the latter of consorting with the devil and promoting immorality, while the latter criticize charismatics' intolerance and lack of respect for cultural traditions and practices (Selka 2010). Adherents of the two religious groups see each other's morality as incompatible (Figure 10.4).

Yet, in this part of Brazil, the two religions draw adherents from the same social strata, namely working-class Afro-Brazilians with little education or political influence, and many belong to the two religious groups, sometimes in secret, simultaneously or at different times. Some find little contradiction in the charismatic Christian and Candomblé recognition of the power of a higher spirit; others are afraid that the Candomblé spirits might punish them for failing to honour them; yet others simply enjoy the musical and other practices of each religion. In contrast to official discourses, they find that the moralities advocated by the two religions are not incompatible. What they all share is a sense of being marginal to mainstream Brazilian society.

One can think about such situations in various ways. Some social scientists use the term **religious pluralism** to refer to the coexistence of well-differentiated religious traditions in the same place at the same time. In Japan, few people identify as 'religious', yet many regularly pray in Buddhist temples and honour the gods in Shinto shrines. **Households** generally have a Buddhist altar to bring blessings to the family and a Shinto altar that commemorates the ancestors. Many Japanese couples marry in a Christian chapel, followed by a Shinto ceremony. But

Figure 10.4 Candomblé offerings to Exu, a deity of crossroads and passages, which must open all ceremonies to ensure the success of the ceremony. Normally, these offerings cannot be photographed; in this case, the image was photographed at an event organized by activists in Salvador da Bahia in 2009 that sought to expand Candomblé's public visibility and recognition. (Courtesy of Elina Hartikainen)

when people die, they commonly are given a Buddhist funeral. People may thus align different religious traditions with different purposes.

In other contexts, religious pluralism is not a matter of integrating different religions into one's life but rather a matter of people of different religious persuasions having to live side by side. In Jos, a city in central Nigeria with a history of religious violence between and among Muslims and Christians, religious messages associated with the two religions, in the form of prayers, sermons, and other forms of address, constantly fill the air over loudspeakers (Larkin 2014). But because these messages address no one in particular, people simply ignore the cacophony as they go about their daily routines. However, when a Christian group translated their own religious pamphlets into Arabic and tried to distribute them to Muslims, violence erupted because the pamphlets suddenly addressed Muslims specifically.

In other situations, a particular belief or practice not associated with any single religious tradition may coexist with orthodox religion. Such is the case of the evil eye, namely the belief that an envious person can magically cause harm to the object of their envy. People ward off the evil eye by behaving modestly, wearing protective objects, or reciting particular formulas. This belief is widespread throughout the Mediterranean, the Middle East, South Asia, and sub-Saharan Africa, as well as Central and South America, where it coexists with various forms of Christianity, Islam, Hinduism, Judaism, and other religions.

The term **religious syncretism** refers to the blending and incorporation of beliefs and ritual practices from different religious traditions. It is somewhat flawed because it assumes that religions are well-defined and separate before people combine them, while practitioners may not see them that way. For example, in Iran since the early 2000s, a renewed interest in the occult, blending Islamic mysticism with Western New Age metaphysics, has developed among the middle classes (Doostdar 2019). Middle-class Iranians who are interested in getting rich, regaining a lost partner, or harming an unfair landlord seek the services of self-appointed experts who claim to be able to interpret centuries-old texts and dispense amulets, write cures, or perform exorcisms. This interest is part of a broader disillusionment with Islamic nationalism since the 1979 Iranian revolution and a turn to self-care in the context of ongoing economic uncertainty. At the same time, people try to ensure that the occult practices remain true to both scientific methods and the precepts of Shi'i Islam. Orthodox religious authorities condemn these practices as idolatrous superstition, invoking the Qur'an's prohibition of sorcery, but what counts as such and what does not is difficult to establish. Those who engage in the occult do not find that it is in any way antithetical to their Muslim devotion (Figure 10.5).

Even within religious communities that self-define as orthodox, different norms may apply to different community members. Hasidic Jews in Brooklyn, New York City, form 'non-liberal' religious communities, meaning that their religious beliefs are more important to them than the secular life around them, which they label as 'liberal' (Fader 2009). Yet boys and girls have different experiences of growing up: the former devote their time and energy to studying the Torah, while the latter are charged with negotiating the community's relationship with the outside world, so that the boys may remain free to study. While the young women are critical of the materialism of the outside world, they selectively incorporate aspects of it by taking pleasure in the experience of shopping for clothes, for example, as long as their purchases abide by Hasidic standards of modesty. Boys and girls speak different languages: boys use Hasidic Yiddish, close to the language of European Hasidic Jews, while girls use Hasidic English, namely English peppered with Yiddish features. Girls are familiar with many aspects of mainstream American culture, such as gender equality and fashion, but they constantly stress that they are different from this culture and affirm their moral superiority to it, insisting that freedom and self-actualization are only possible through Jewish religious practices.

To understand religion, anthropologists focus on the social practices that people engage in as they enact their religious beliefs, what can be called their 'lived religion', rather than concentrating on texts, doctrines, and official attempts by authorities to separate the sacred from the profane, or the permitted from the forbidden. The latter are important, of course, but they are only one aspect among many of what constitutes religion.

The religious and the secular

In the late nineteenth and early twentieth centuries, many social theorists thought that the role of religion would wane in the modern world as science was increasingly providing the answers to some of the questions that were traditionally the domain of religion. They predicted that, in this process of **secularization**, religion would become a matter of personal choice rather than a social imperative and would become disconnected from other aspects of human existence

Figure 10.5 Talismans sold in the Tajrish bazaar in northern Tehran, with instructions on how to use them, July 2008; the sign above lists their functions as 'sorcery cancellation, problem solving, sustenance, love and affection, deflecting calamities, the evil eye'. (Courtesy of Elham Mireshghi)

such as law, politics, the economy, and the arts. Max Weber in particular lamented this process because it would lead to the **disenchantment** of the world, the loss of a sense of wonder and mystery as people increasingly lived their life according to rational principles. Yet religion remains alive and well today and in some cases has increased in importance.

The secular position maintains that religion should not dictate how public life is conducted. Moral codes are needed to ensure that people and their needs are respected, but these are no longer associated with any religious tradition. Individuals are free to pursue their religious convictions, but this pursuit is an individual choice. **Secularism** is a state policy that turns the secular into law. It takes different forms in different nation-states. The distinct form that France has developed since the Revolution in the eighteenth century, known as *laïcité*, sets limits on the expression of religion (e.g., in clothing or ornaments) in the **public sphere**. In the United Kingdom, in contrast, the state is secular but the monarch has the official title of Defender of the Faith and Supreme Governor of the Church of England. This form of secularism recognizes all forms of religious expression as equally valid in public institutions.

While secular nation-states in Europe and the Americas present secularism as a policy designed to protect individual freedom and equality, it is in fact a Christian doctrine in new clothes (Asad 2003). They continue to celebrate Christian holy days as national holidays (e.g., Christmas but not Eid or Diwali). Secularism allows people to be religious, but only if they do so in their private lives, conforming to the way of being Christian that emerged in the Enlightenment and effectively excluding other ways of being religious. This explains the clash between Western secular democracies and migrants and citizens who practise their religion, such as Islam, in ways that go beyond a private experience. While mainstream citizens in secular society believe that secularism is universally encompassing and that those Muslim citizens who see religion differently are intolerant, the former do not realize that secularism only tolerates certain ways of being religious. Secularism can thus become a form of oppression, as illustrated by laws that Western states have implemented against minarets, the call to prayer, headscarves, and other public ways of being Muslim. Secularism is thus not necessarily a benevolent system.

The globalization of religion: Pentecostal and charismatic Christianity

One striking counterexample to the prediction that religion would wane in the modern world is the global spread of Pentecostal and charismatic Christianity since the 1980s. This approach to Protestantism emerged in the United States at the beginning of the twentieth century as revivalist movements driven by people seeking to return to Christianity in what they saw as an increasingly secular world. Pentecostal Christianity and charismatic Christianity differ slightly from one another: for example, Pentecostals form independent congregations, while charismatic Christians can remain members of older and more established churches like Methodism and Catholicism. Both movements, however, share many characteristics: believers emphasize the need to be 'born again', individuals' responsibility for their own salvation, and their direct personal experience of God and the Holy Spirit without the mediation of priests or pastors (Robbins 2004). Pentecostal and charismatic Christians may experience ecstatic gifts such as the power to heal or exorcize, speak in tongues, and receive prophecies. Church services are exuberant events, with dancing, singing, and dramatic prayers, often supported by technological tools such as electronic musical instruments and video transmission. In their daily life, adherents abide by strict codes of moral conduct, abstaining from drinking, smoking, gambling, and extra-marital sexual relations, and by encouraging humility and modesty.

During most of the twentieth century, Pentecostal and charismatic Christianity was largely confined to North America. In the last quarter of the century, however, it experienced exponential growth, particularly in the Global South, at the expense of traditional forms of Christianity. Today, hundreds of millions of people identify as Pentecostal or charismatic, particularly in sub-Saharan Africa, Latin America, Oceania, and the United States. Because the churches are independent, they can proliferate as one does not need to submit to the authority of a regulating organization to establish a new church. Some churches preach the prosperity gospel, which offers believers the promise that, if they are genuine in their faith, God will provide them with health and wealth in this life, prefiguring their salvation in the afterlife. In some cases, church leaders take advantage of this promise, convincing believers that they must give generously to the church to prove their faith.

A common-sense account of why Pentecostal and charismatic Christianity is so globally successful is that it offers people who lead precarious lives a solution to their problems: a tight-knit
community of believers, hope for a better life on earth, and salvation in the afterlife. It is indeed
the case that many poor people are attracted to Pentecostal and charismatic Christianity,
although many others are as well. There is no single explanation for this success, but a number
of characteristics stand out. One is the church's emphasis on egalitarianism: everyone is a child
of God with the same chance of salvation, regardless of social class, race, gender, or expertise.
Anyone can walk to the front of the church and address the congregation.

Rather than just being wedded to local community structures, adherents feel that they are
part of a global family of true believers, and it is thus not surprising that the explosion of
Pentecostal and charismatic Christianity has coincided with globalization in the late twentieth
century. Because they are one with God, believers often develop an individualism that resembles
the autonomous self that **neoliberal** capitalism promotes. Pentecostal and charismatic
Christianity has the paradoxical ability to both adapt to and break away from local contexts.
Churches are run by local people and anyone can become a pastor, at least in theory. At the same
time, it puts considerable effort into breaking away from symbols and images associated with the
past. This explains the hostility, described above, of charismatic churches in Brazil towards
Candomblé spirits.

This radical break with the past is particularly evident when people convert and become
new kinds of persons. They learn to see life before conversion as immoral and without purpose, and conversion as a transformation into a present full of joy and hope. Converts are
often expected to avoid contact with people they knew before conversion, including kin, to
avoid a return to past ways. In Samoa, for example, women develop friendships with new
converts to whom they are not related and guide them through their conversion, nurturing
them in ways that mirror how senior women traditionally treat younger family members,
feeding and mentoring them (Hardin 2019). They cushion the rupture that conversion
involves (potentially breaking away from spouses, relatives, and former lives) with familiar
forms of care.

In societies where kinship, reciprocity, and social cohesion are important, conversion can
be socially costly because converts still need to function in a social system in which people
depend on one another. Breaking away from kinship-based reciprocity presupposes that
converts have the means to live independently or that they can quickly secure new networks to help them survive. For example, among Zapotec people, an Indigenous group of
the state of Oaxaca, Mexico, converts tend to be people who have weak connections to
village life in the first place, such as newcomers who lack relationships of *compadrazgo*, or
god-parenthood to children of other adults that bind them economically and socially (Gross
2012). Converts refrain from taking part in feasts celebrating the Catholic patron saint of
the community, which they consider idolatrous, and this further marginalizes them.
Sometimes, they return to Catholicism because they find their social isolation in the village
too difficult.

Across the world, Pentecostal and charismatic Christianity is particularly appealing to
women, for several reasons. The church offers them a morally safe space in which to interact with other women beyond the household, for which they may otherwise have few such
opportunities. They also gain respect when they demonstrate that they have the gifts of the
Spirit by speaking in tongues or for their leadership in prayer groups. In addition, the
morality expected of church members improves women's lives: men are encouraged to
reject unacceptable behaviours such as adultery and to develop new forms of masculinity
centred on responsibility and domesticity. While this morality also enforces a patriarchal

Figure 10.6 Worship at a mega-church near Houston, Texas. (Courtesy of Julian J. Rossig/
iStock)

order and women are still expected to subordinate themselves to their husbands and
church leaders, it can still reconfigure gendered power relations to the benefit of women
(Eriksen 2016).

For Pentecostal and charismatic Christians, faith is a response to a powerful message from
God. But anthropologists also need to explain why so many people began to answer this message towards the end of the twentieth century. As we have seen, many factors are involved,
including the effects and possibilities of globalization, changing social and economic circumstances, and the growth of a secularism that some find wanting (Figure 10.6).

Humans and spirits: animism and shamanism

For many people around the world, spirits and other non-human entities interact with humans
in significant ways. People who subscribe to such beliefs do not see humans as categorically
different from spirits, but rather as part of a continuum that can encompass ghosts, spirits, ancestors, animals, or features of the landscape. While some aspects of such belief systems resemble
religion, they are better described as ways of relating to the world. They are commonly anchored
in specific natural environments and do not make sense outside of them. To describe them, in
the nineteenth century, E. B. Tylor coined the term **animism** (from Latin *animus* 'life, soul').
Drawing on the theories of his time, he proposed that animism was the most 'primitive' form of
religion. Primitive people, he argued, assigned human-like attributes to animals, plants, and features of the landscape, but abandoned these errors as they moved up the evolutionary hierarchy
to greater civilization. They 'progressed' first to **polytheism**, the worship of multiple gods, and
finally to **monotheism**, the belief in a single God. Today, many anthropologists are cautious
when using the term 'animism' because of its associations with an ethically problematic nineteenth-century evolutionism.

Animism is difficult to come to terms with because it radically questions fundamental tenets
of the modern Western consciousness which most anthropologists grow up with, including the
conviction that there is a fundamental distinction between humans and non-humans. Animism
is not a matter of simply projecting human qualities onto animals and objects. Rather, animists

Box 10.2   The revival of religion in China

Religion never exists independently of other aspects of social life, such as economics and politics. For example, in China during the Maoist era, the state suppressed all religions and religious practices as 'backward superstitions'. When the state overhauled its economic and political structure in 1978 and inaugurated what it called 'socialism with Chinese characteristics', a blend of free market economy and centralized political control, the country experienced an explosion of religious practices of all kinds, including Buddhist, Daoist, Christian, Muslim, and folk religious practices. This phenomenon can only be understood in the context of the social, political, and economic transformations that Chinese society has experienced.

In Wenzhou, a city that during the reform era was transformed from a sleepy rural town into a bustling industrial centre, where everyone is engaged in some kind of capitalist entrepreneurial activity, people have turned to religion with great fervour (Yang 2008). They build temples and ancestral halls, organize rituals and festivals, and stage elaborate funerals, the most important life-cycle ritual. All this activity is designed to ensure good fortune for themselves, their descendants, and the community at large. The revival is ecumenical: in addition to reviving ancestor worship and popular practices concerned with demons, spirits, and gods, people donate to Christian churches and Buddhist temples, hire Daoist and Buddhist priests and nuns to perform rituals, and seek the services of fortune tellers. All these activities are costly, and the wealthy in particular spend large amounts of the money that they have earned through their business activities. The religious revival supports large numbers of craftsmen, architects, and religious specialists, strengthening the local economy.

China's religious revival can be explained in a number of ways. First, religion fills the moral vacuum that was left when people lost faith in communist ideology and the materialism of the communist regime. It is also an attempt to counter what Max Weber called **disenchantment** by 're-enchanting' the modern world. In particular, the violent excesses of the Cultural Revolution (1966–76), when citizens were pitted against one another, intellectuals and wealthy people were tortured, imprisoned, or killed, and student-led paramilitary groups attacked traditional cultural practices, constitute a dramatic background for the search for a different social order. Second, the revival is a reaction to the profit-seeking, individualism, and materialism that lie at the core of capitalism, which threaten the cohesion of the family and the moral fabric of the community. Because they are enabled by the generosity of people who can afford to finance them, religious activities ensure that wealth is redistributed. Lastly, religion is a way of affirming a local identity independent of the central state: the gods, goddesses, spirits, and ancestors that people worship are local entities, and rituals and festivals are occasions on which people come together and experience what Turner called **communitas**.

In response to the revival of religion, the central state has generally looked the other way, except when religious movements become too organized and threaten state power. For example, in 1992, a martial art master called Li Hongzhi invented a new practice called Falun Gong, a form of exercise inspired by Buddhist morality, which quickly drew millions of adherents, in part because the exercise component enabled people to stay healthy at a time when state-funded medical care was being drastically cut down

(Besnier, Brownell, and Carter 2018, 88). While they originally supported Falun Gong, state officials became concerned that it was becoming a political movement with ties to the West, and outlawed it. Massive protests ensued, which the state repressed harshly. Today, the movement has largely moved to the United States and Europe, where it has aligned itself with right-wing groups that oppose communism. Likewise, the state claims that the revival of Islam among Turkic-speaking Uyghur people in Xinjiang is associated with Islamic fundamentalism and separatism and has relentlessly persecuted them since 2014, including large-scale violations of human rights that have been denounced internationally.

see themselves as part of a broad cosmological world that includes everything around them. For example, for the Yukhagir in Siberia, humans behave like animals when they interact with them and vice versa (Willerslev 2007). The Yukhagir are an Indigenous group of **hunter-gatherers** who were once incorporated into the socio-economic structure of the Soviet Union but, after its collapse, have returned to a subsistence existence, including hunting. When they hunt an elk, humans mimic it, donning its fur, emulating its movements and sounds, and see situations through its eyes; they become an elk. At the same time, people are perfectly aware that animals and humans are not the same. Hunters know they walk on two legs and carry a gun, and they only behave like animals during the hunt and not in other circumstances. Rather, humans and animals form a continuum of life forms. Humans, animals, and objects are embroiled in a cycle of endless reincarnation. Spirits penetrate the bodies of animals and humans and return to a different world at death, where they wait to become the soul of another animal or human.

Like other belief systems, animism often coexists with different belief systems. For example, for the Yukhagir, there is room in the world of spirits for Jesus, God, and Lenin. Animism also undergoes transformations as people's lives change. Because it is so closely grounded in the specific natural environment in which people live, animism can easily lose its concreteness when people stop interacting with this environment. For example, among Australian Aboriginal groups of Arnhem Land in northern Australia, old people who grew up in what they call 'country', namely the landscape in which their group has lived for millennia, have a strong sensory connection to specific features of the landscape, which is imbued with the **Dreaming**, the world of spirits that interact with humans (Merlan 2020). For an elderly woman, the water level of a rockpool changes over the seasons because they host spirits of her dead relatives, who cause the water to sink into the sand. Younger people continue to lead lives informed by spirits, but because they no longer interact with the environment as intimately as their elders (e.g., they no longer depend on hunting and gathering for food), for them the spirits have become abstract and generic.

One social type who is closely associated with animism is the **shaman**, a ritual specialist capable of mediating between humans and spirits and curing illnesses. The term derives from a word meaning 'to know' in Tungus, an Indigenous language of Siberia. While shamanism is associated with societies of northeast Asia, shamans are also found in various forms in other societies. Elements of shamanism characterize certain practices within world religions such as Buddhism, Christianity, and Islam, although these practices are often condemned by mainstream religious authorities. In some societies, shamans have powers that may run in families and that other people do not have; in other societies, everyone can communicate with spirits but shamans do it particularly well. In some cases, shamans go into trances in well-defined rituals, sometimes after ingesting mind-altering substances, while in other cases they exert their skills casually. In short, there is considerable variety in shamanistic practices.

Shamanism is often risky. In exchange for their powers, shamans may have to forgo certain privileges, such as being able to have children. Shamans are often both sought after and feared, and in some societies are obliged to live on the margin of communities because they are dangerous. Among the Waorani, an Indigenous group of eastern Ecuador, the shaman is the adopted parent of the spirit-jaguar and as such is able to tell others where in the forest they can find game to hunt (High 2012). But the Waorani shaman can also make people ill or command real-life jaguars to kill people, and they are thus a threat to peace. Elsewhere, shamans are accused of being charlatans or anti-social characters. During the Soviet era, Indigenous Siberian shamans were persecuted for being remnants of traditions that prevented Indigenous people from becoming proper Soviet citizens. Among some groups, shamans disappeared completely, and today many still view them as a source of shame (Figure 10.7).

As shamanism has waned in Indigenous societies, since the 1960s, it has become the object of considerable interest in the Global North, as part of what is called the 'New Age', namely a turn to 'traditional' ritual and spiritual practices by people seeking an alternative to the **disenchantment** of the modern world. The generation of the 1960s and 1970s rejected the materialism and conservative and imperialistic politics of the post–World War II decades, and saw Indigenous peoples as their inspiration for a spirituality that brought humans back to innocent purity.

Figure 10.7 Prayer flags flutter in the wind on Laji Mountain (Gongmaole in Tibetan), Qinghai Province, China, in 2010 to carry blessings to people and the environment around them. Prayer flags originated in Bon shamanism but were integrated into Tibetan Buddhism, a history that illustrates the permeability of religious practices. (Courtesy of Susan Brownell)

Shamanism came to occupy an important place in the New Age, in which the work of anthropologist Michael Harner was instrumental. Harner had originally conducted fieldwork among the Shuar people of eastern Ecuador before establishing in the 1980s a well-funded foundation that combined the various shamanistic practices of Indigenous peoples around the world. Needless to say, 'global shamanism' is different from the shamanism that Indigenous peoples practised and sometimes still do. A common criticism of the New Age is that it has appropriated the belief systems and practices of Indigenous peoples with no regard to their plight as impoverished groups fighting the encroachment of corporate and state interests into their territories (Ivakhiv 2001).

Witchcraft, sorcery, and magic

Charismatic Christians may consider witchcraft to be the work of the devil and thus the antithesis of religion, yet witchcraft shares many features with religion. For example, it is based on humans connecting with spiritual beings, it involves rituals, it is based on symbols, and it involves power relations. However, its aim, namely to bring about a change of some sort with the help of a non-human, 'occult' agent, is different from that of religion. In some cases, practices that once qualified as witchcraft have become religion, as in the case of Candomblé in Brazil. Charismatic Christians' anxiety about witchcraft may be a symptom of its potential threat as an alternative religious system.

Witchcraft, sorcery, and magic are overlapping concepts that are not always distinguishable. Historically, in some societies, sorcerers were thought to be intentionally motivated to perform sorcery, while witches just had occult powers. However, other societies did not make this distinction because they were not particularly concerned with whether people acted intentionally. Magic is action directed at a specific task and involves the use of objects and words to perform acts that are not possible through other means, as the practices of middle-class Iranians described earlier illustrate. Malinowski (1948) noted that Trobriand Islanders in Papua New Guinea performed magic when they went fishing on the open ocean, which is dangerous, but not when they fished on the reef, which is predictable and safe. He thus proposed that people use magic to relieve anxiety when confronted with unpredictable circumstances, whereas people practise religion without a specific practical purpose in mind.

Witchcraft and sorcery explain events that otherwise have no other explanation. A classic work by Edward Evans-Pritchard, *Witchcraft, Oracles and Magic among the Azande* (1976), based on his fieldwork among the Azande of the southern Sudan in the late 1920s and 1930s, demonstrated that, contrary to the theories of the day, witchcraft was rational and logical, even if it did not conform to the laws of science. For the Azande, all misfortunes, including accidents, illness, and death, had to be explained. For example, grain-stores, under which people often gathered to relax, would sometimes collapse because the wood they were built from had been damaged by termites; the Azande understood perfectly well that old buildings did not last, but they wanted to explain why a grain-store collapsed at a particular moment so as to hurt specific individuals. The only possible explanation was that a witch had caused the accident to happen.

Witches acted because they were angry at their victims or envious of them. Because stinginess and bearing grudges would make others suspect that one was a witch, the Azande did their best to appear kind, generous, and sociable. Only commoners could be witches; chiefs, who traditionally presided over witchcraft trials, could never be accused of witchcraft, and thus the rank hierarchy was not open to challenge. Witchcraft was inherited from one's same-gender parent, and thus no man would accuse his own father of witchcraft and no woman her own mother, because this would have been tantamount to admitting being a witch by implication. This allowed parents to maintain authority over their children. For Evans-Pritchard, who as a **structural functionalist** was concerned with how societies maintained their stability, the social organization of Zande witchcraft was a social mechanism that ensured peace and cohesion in the society.

At the time Evans-Pritchard wrote, the general assumption was that, with increasing urbanization, education, and development, beliefs in witchcraft, sorcery, and magic would disappear. This has proved not to be the case: in many societies, they are on the rise. The dynamics of witchcraft and sorcery in the contemporary world share similarities with those of the Azande in the 1930s, such as the role attributed to envy and spite. But, in contrast to their predecessors, anthropologists today ask how these emotions emerge in social and economic conditions in a global context, and these questions lead them to recognize witchcraft as a modern phenomenon rather than as an exotic and archaic belief system.

For example, in Cameroon in the years that followed independence in 1960, speaking openly about witchcraft was in bad taste; by the end of the millennium, talk of witchcraft was all over the media, in politics, and in courtrooms (Geschiere 1997). While the *nganga*, traditional healers who protect people against witches, used to cut a low profile in the past, living on the edge of villages, they now openly sell their services, advertising their expertise in 'Rosicrucian knowledge' or 'secrets of the Orient' on large banners. Witchcraft helps Cameroonians make sense of a rapidly changing social order in which some people seem to miraculously get rich while the lives of many others continue to be mired in poverty. In contrast to the old days, when witches simply ate their victims, they now put them to work on invisible plantations in the service of the wealthy people who dominate the national economy, echoing the slave trade of the past but in a new guise. Witches procure their victims by making them indebted to them and compelling the debtor to supply a relative to cancel the debt. Displays of extravagant consumption (cars, houses, household goods, etc.) bring suspicions that someone is benefiting from witches who supply them with workers. Like capitalism, witchcraft involves selling, debt, and the ability to control the labour of others, and it operates just as mysteriously.

Capitalism and witchcraft were similarly entangled in Ghana in the 1990s, when young Akan men from rural backgrounds were trying to become wealthy by tapping into the global circulation of commodities and finance (Parish 2000). With credit cards, they imported desirable commodities for resale from Europe like watches and cars, but they despaired that these dealings did not seem to make them rich, which they attributed to two types of witchcraft. One was enacted by women in their home villages with whom they had sexual relations and who could bewitch them because they were envious of their money and resentful that they did not redistribute it as expected in village **gift economies**. This witchcraft remained local because, in the young men's opinion, the women did not understand the complexities of international credit card transactions; yet it could make young men ill or impotent.

The other type of witchcraft was caused by male relatives who had succeeded in migrating to Europe and could mysteriously remove money from the young men's bank accounts and misuse their credit cards. This was witchcraft on a global scale, implicated in the mysterious workings of capitalism. The young men feared these two types of witchcraft because of the position in which they found themselves, caught between two irreconcilable economic systems: a village-based economy of **reciprocity**, which they were unable to satisfy; and a global economy of individual capitalist accumulation, which also left them frustrated because no matter how hard they worked they did not become rich.

Box 10.3   Witchcraft in the contemporary Global North

Magic and witchcraft are alive and well in the contemporary Global North in the form of Wicca, modern paganism, channeling, spiritualism, and other practices. In England in the 1980s, people who belonged to a variety of groups that practised witchcraft in different forms numbered several thousands (Luhrmann 1989). They drew inspiration from a wide variety of sources that they often blended together, including the Kabbalah, Rosicrucianism, Druidism, and particular interpretations of ancient and 'primitive' religions, some with a feminist angle that took the form of the worship of goddesses or Mother Earth. While they formed different groups with different agendas whose memberships partly overlap, they all shared a belief in magic. Contrary to the expectation that people are attracted to secretive groups because they are socially or materially disenfranchised, most modern magicians (the generic term that Tanya Luhrmann used to refer to members of different groups) were in fact predominantly well-educated middle-class people.

They held beliefs that other people would find irrational and saw these beliefs as on par with science. For example, where ordinary people would see a coincidence between two events, modern magicians would see logical connections. Their activities were replete with ritual, which were necessary to give meaning to them. For example, suddenly talking about the presence of an ancient goddess in the room would have been a strange thing to do, but if one did so in a candle-lit room decorated with drapes in which people were all wearing robes, the goddess's presence became credible. Ritual, thus, played an important role in modern magicians' practices: they often involved meditation and visualization that induced powerful spiritual experiences.

Modern magicians acquired these beliefs through a process of initiation into the groups to which they belonged, during which they learned knowledge that the group considered secret. Secrecy confirmed that the knowledge to which the magicians were privy and which others did not have was important and special. They alone had access to a reality that could affect their own lives positively, for example by making them stronger and more assertive. Secrecy gave modern magicians a sense of control over their lives and thus had a therapeutic effect: ideas that might seem terrifying, such as the inevitability of death, could become less terrifying when viewed through the lens of secret knowledge, particularly if this knowledge was shared only among a highly selective group of like-minded people.

Religion as an anthropological subject

For anthropologists, religion is not just beliefs or doctrines, but also practices and institutions that bring religious experience to life for believers and that connect religious life to the social, cultural, and political realms. Through religion, individuals and groups come to understand, accept, or challenge their place in the world. Religion can foster community and compassion just as easily as it can lead to violence and conflict. Yet firmly held and seemingly unchanging beliefs do change over time as religious people respond to historical transformations, including the rise of secularism, the collapse of colonialism, and the different experiences of modernity around the globe. The position of Malaysian Muslim women with which this chapter opened captures many of the complexities inherent in religion, as the postcolonial rise of a successful nation-state created a new urban middle class and gave women access to secular education. This, paradoxically, empowered women to reject secularism and to advocate a 'return' to a faith-based society. And while the rejection of secular modernity fuelled by economic success may appear, from one perspective, to be the reassertion of an old conservatism, from another perspective the religious authority that the women claim is a radical challenge to the gender hierarchies that have long structured Malaysian society and orthodox Islam. The turn, or return, to religion is, in this case, inextricable from the complex social and political histories of a nation.

Key thinkers mentioned in this chapter:

Talal Asad; Émile Durkheim; Edward Evans-Pritchard; Clifford Geertz; Saba Mahmood; Victor Turner; E. B. Tylor; Max Weber

Key terms mentioned in this chapter (see Glossary):

Animism; Agency; Communitas; Disenchantment; Dreaming; Liminal; Monotheism; Orthodoxy; Polytheism; Religious pluralism; Religious syncretism; Ritual; Secularization; Shaman; Symbol

Questions for discussion/review:

1   Why is religion so difficult to define?
2   What do you understand by secularism?
3   How do rituals work?
4   What factors explain the globalization of Pentecostal and charismatic Christianity?
5   Why do witchcraft beliefs continue to be held by so many people across the world?

Chapter 11

Rank, caste, and social class

In early 2011, huge demonstrations took place on Tahrir Square in the centre of Cairo, Egypt. The authoritarian government of president Hosni Mubarak first responded with lethal violence but, on 11 February, unable to contain the upheaval, Mubarak was forced to resign and the initial enthusiasm of the revolution received global press coverage. But Egyptians were not unified in their vision of how the revolution should be implemented. What did not catch the attention of the international press were the well-dressed young people who descended on the square on 12 February. Armed with brooms, dustpans, rubbish bags, and paintbrushes, they set out to clean up the square and organize the crowds, to the initial amazement of anthropologist Jessica Winegar (2016), who was there to witness the events. For the young people, the revolution was ushering in a new era of cleanliness and orderliness. The household rubbish that the corrupt regime had routinely failed to collect, despite imposing new taxes for this purpose, would finally be taken care of. Similarly, the proverbial chaos of Cairo's metro would be, symbolically and practically, a thing of the past.

But not everyone shared in the enthusiasm for these efforts. For example, heated arguments broke out between people from the countryside who had set up camp in front of the Museum of National Antiquities and city sophisticates who tried to get them to leave. The villagers retorted loudly that they were the ones who had protected the museum and they would only leave when the revolution was over. When a young urbanite in fashionable clothes started lecturing metro riders about entering and leaving the cars in an orderly fashion, older working-class women in headscarves scoffed. The revolution thus had different meanings for different segments of the population. The middle classes' concern for order and respectability was an attempt to control the disorder and lack of hygiene they associated with the working classes. Cleanliness had become a battleground over which the social classes were contesting the terms of the Arab Spring.

Differences among members of the same society are quick to emerge even when they are coming together in political solidarity, and sometimes these differences take unexpected forms. Most societies around the world are organized internally in groups that are dependent on one another but occupy different positions with respect to their members' access to food, property, education, healthcare, relationships, and other life necessities and privileges. But societies differ in terms of how these groups are organized: in some, privilege or the lack of it is determined by which lineage one belongs to, while in others it is a function of the labour and services one performs, and in yet others it is a matter of whether or not one owns property. There are many overlaps between these various ways of organizing social groups, but they share one characteristic: they are all instances of people converting differences (in birth, wealth, position, skills, etc.) into **inequality** by giving greater value to certain characteristics and lesser value to others. When inequality distinguishes groups of people, it gives rise to **social stratification**, namely

DOI: 10.4324/9781315737805-11

the structuring of society into groups that are unequal in relation to one another. While social stratification is grounded in inequality, people find all sorts of ways of rationalizing it and ensuring its continuity over time.

Egalitarianism and social stratification

Social stratification seems to have existed throughout history and is the norm in perhaps all societies today. So is it inevitable? In other words, have there been, at some point in the past, societies in which people had roughly the same resources and opportunities, and do such societies exist today? There is a long history in Western scholarship of thinking that in some distant past society was egalitarian, and that inequality and stratification came about as society grew in size as men began dominating women and other men, or as people began thinking of property as individual rather than communal. There is of course no way to prove or disprove these conjectures, although some societies in both the past and the present are better examples of **egalitarianism** than others. For example, if we compare nation-states, those that impose high taxes on citizens, like Norway or Denmark, tend to exhibit less extreme wealth disparity than those whose tax code allows rich people to find more or less legal ways of paying little tax, such as the United States. Taxes are one form of wealth **redistribution**, which, if the state manages it well, ensures that rich and poor have the same access to healthcare, education, benefits, infrastructure, and other aspects of the **commons**, resources to which everyone should have access.

Political philosophers draw a distinction that helps makes sense of what we mean when we talk about egalitarianism and its opposite, namely the distinction between **equality of opportunity** and **equality of outcome**: the former is the notion that everyone should be given the same chances in the job market or before the law, for example, with no one being disadvantaged because of who they are or what they have (e.g., their race, gender, religion, or wealth); the latter is the situation in which everyone in society is equally wealthy, powerful, healthy, and happy. It takes little reflection to realize that equality of outcome is an ideal that is impossible to achieve in practice. For example, some people enjoy better health than others, which gives them a clear advantage in life over less healthy people. Even equality of opportunity, which is a prominent ideal in liberal democracies, is difficult to achieve, although society can strive for it. For example, age will have a determinative effect on whether applicants for some jobs will be taken seriously: only young healthy people can perform demanding physical labour, but young people lack experience for positions of responsibility, such as the management of a business.

Anthropologists have documented societies in which everyone, or at least every adult man, is more or less equal, or in which people maintain an ideology that views equality as desirable and important. Small-scale societies are more likely to be able to maintain relative equality than those that have many people. This is because in large-scale societies, authority is generally centralized, which creates inequalities between people as some have more authority than others. Small-scale societies in rural Papua New Guinea, an extremely diverse country (more than 800 different languages are spoken there) where many ethnolinguistic groups consist of only a few hundred people, maintain a strong ideology that adult men should be equal to one another and ensure egalitarianism through exchange: someone who has more of something is under the moral obligation to share it with others. But this does not mean that everyone has the same **status**. Some men have more pigs, land, food, and wives than others, and women and younger men have invariably lower status than adult men. Yet some men simply have more than what others also have, rather than having things that others do not have, which is an important distinction. In contrast, wealthy people in highly unequal societies own yachts, airplanes, and real estate that poor people can only dream of.

But even in societies that value egalitarianism, other dynamics can come into play that create substantial inequalities among people and kinds of people. Among many societies in Papua New Guinea, women are thought to be inferior to men and young people to older people. In some of these societies, this was traditionally enforced by **initiation rituals** that imparted secret cosmological knowledge to male initiates, who were absolutely forbidden to share this knowledge with women – although many ethnographers have documented that women were no fools and knew perfectly well what was going on. These rituals were a means of creating inequalities between women and men and between non-initiates and initiates through religion, which in turn bestowed greater social authority on male initiates, even in the relative absence of serious wealth disparities. Since the 1980s, as they have adopted Christianity, many groups in Papua New Guinea have abandoned the initiation rituals and the cosmological belief systems that underlay them, yet the gender- and age-based inequality perdures.

In ancient Greece, which today is widely recognized as the cradle of the idea of democracy, deep inequalities were in fact produced and maintained by the complex intersection of which family one was born into, how much wealth one had access to, whether one owned land, and factors like gender, age, citizenship, and place of birth. Aristocratic men from privileged families held citizenship rights (e.g., to vote, speak in public, hold office), owned productive and easily accessible land, employed labourers, and owned slaves. Less privileged citizens owned property of lesser quality and quantity, and generally had to live in villages outside the city in order to tend to their fields, which were located far away from the city. Merchants were also citizens but did not own land, and aristocrats generally did their best to exclude them from political power. Labourers were theoretically free but depended on selling their labour to wealthier families to survive. Finally, the large population of non-citizens included all women, children, adolescents, foreigners, and, at the bottom of the social ladder, slaves, many of whom were from defeated enemy city-states. So, while the principles of democracy dictate that everyone is on an equal footing, in the cradle of democracy these principles only applied to male citizens.

What the examples of egalitarian societies in Papua New Guinea and democratic societies like ancient Greece demonstrate is that ideals of egalitarianism are difficult to put into practice. The vast majority of societies in the world are stratified according to various principles. Where people's social status and power is determined by birth, such as the lineage, clan, or group into which they are born, status is said to be **ascribed**. Ascribed status contrasts with **achieved** status, which is the product of a person's individual qualities, such as charisma, courage, dignity, or personal achievements. **Meritocracy**, namely the belief that personal merit is the basis of one's position in society, is an ideology commonly associated with achieved status. Ascribed status is theoretically unchangeable, in that a person can expect to keep it throughout life and pass it on to her or his descendants. In contrast, achieved status can be increased, for example, when someone earns a lot of money or acquires power in some manner in the course of her or his life.

While the distinction between ascription and achievement is useful, in practice everyone's status all over the world is a mixture of ascription and achievement. For example, if high-ranking persons in a rank-based system do not behave in ways expected of them, they may lose the status and prestige associated with their ascribed status; in contrast, in systems in which status is achieved, as in class-based societies, the family one is born into has a very strong effect on the status one achieves in life. Meritocracy, which is so elaborated in the modern world, ultimately turns out to be a fiction that hides inequalities based on ascription.

Rank

An example of a social organization in which status is ascribed is **rank**, which places people in stratified groups according to the lineage in which they were born. European societies up to the Enlightenment and the political transformations of the nineteenth century were rank-based societies: the sovereign and the sovereign's family occupied the most important position in society; they were surrounded by aristocratic families, which were themselves ranked in terms of their relative importance and wealth; and commoners constituted the bulk of the population, with the clergy forming a group that straddled both. In theory, the king or queen ensured the country's safety and well-being; the aristocracy required peasants, who until the rise of cities were the largest group of commoners, to cultivate their land but also to give part of their produce to the aristocrats, who were supposed to protect them in exchange.

Classic examples of rank-based societies are those of many Pacific Islands and those of Indigenous peoples in the Pacific Northwest of North America. For example, in Tonga, an island nation-state of the Western Pacific, a rank system operates that is patterned in part on an ancient chiefly system and in part on British social structure of the early nineteenth century. At that time, the country, which formerly consisted of small autonomous chiefdoms, was conquered and unified by one chief, Tāufaʻāhau Tupou, who established himself as the king of the group, converted to Christianity under the influence of British missionaries, and took the name Siaosi, the transliteration of 'George', after King George III of Britain. He rewarded the chiefs who had sided with him with titles of nobility, and his descendants continue to rule the country, supported by the aristocratic families.

The royal family and aristocrats today still own most of the land and expect commoners to pay tributes to them, which traditionally consisted of agricultural products but now include money and consumer goods. In theory at least, high ranking people are not expected to keep this wealth but instead should redistribute it to the people. This takes place during huge feasts on the occasion of important weddings and funerals, to which people bring cooked pigs, large yams, valuable plaited mats, decorated barkcloth, consumer goods, and money, and expect to receive some of these resources in return.

The sovereign and the high-ranking are believed to have the ability to ensure that the country prospers, the land is fertile, the weather stays predictable, and people live in peace. This belief harks back to ancient times, when chiefs, as descendants from the gods, harnessed supernatural forces, although today this is framed in Christian terms. In theory at least, the sovereign, the aristocrats, and the commoners form a social structure in which everyone is dependent on everyone else for the production and circulation of wealth. Rank permeates all aspects of life, and there are also rank differences within families: older siblings hold higher rank than younger siblings and thus have more decision-making power, and women's rank is higher than their brothers. Women are not allowed to own land, but their brothers and male cousins have a life-long moral duty to keep them supplied with produce from the land as a demonstration of respect for their rank – thus, while the situation may seem to be unfair when seen from the outside, it is predicated on values that bind people together and ensure that everyone receives what they have the right to.

However, from the second half of the twentieth century, things started changing (Besnier 2011). The royal family and the aristocrats have not always attended to their redistributive duties and instead have accumulated wealth according to capitalist principles, losing touch with the commoners and leaving them to fend for themselves, which has encouraged many to emigrate. At the same time, because so many have left the country, subsistence agriculture has lost its prestige and economic importance, and people have become increasingly dependent on

Box 11.1   Kingship in India: the commodification of rank, tourism, and innovation

Wealthy tourists who travel to India and stay in the royal palaces now converted into luxury hotels may be surprised to realize that the maharajas they may meet and whose colourful ceremonies they may attend are not officially royal at all. In 1971, the central government of India passed the Deregulation of Princes Act, abolishing the aristocratic titles, privy purses, and privileges of the 565 rulers of the princely states that were home to a quarter of the country's population at independence in 1947. As a result, most former rulers could no longer maintain their lavish properties and lifestyles. For some, international tourism was an opportunity to preserve royal palaces as hotels, wedding venues, museums, and stops on sightseeing tours.

Such is the case of former Maharaja Gaj Singh II, whose Rajput ancestors ruled over the desert state of Jodhpur in Rajasthan (Balzani 2003). They traced their origins to Surya, the sun god, and from him to Rama, the righteous king whose exploits are recounted in the Sanskrit epic, the *Ramayana*. Gaj Singh II, who became Maharaja of Jodhpur in 1952, oversaw the conversion of his palace after the Deregulation of Princes Act into the Umaid Bhavan Palace Hotel. A key attraction of the hotel is the fact that the former ruler continues to live in the palace and perform rituals on religious and festive occasions at the *darbars*, formal gatherings of aristocrats and others who pay homage to him in the great halls of the palace hotel.

From the perspective of the participants, these *darbars* are important occasions on which to don formal clothes, festive turbans, and decorated swords, be greeted by a king who is no longer king, and offer fealty to him. Most tourists do not understand the details of the ceremonies, but they can watch from balconies reserved for the purpose, as priests chant prayers and perform blessings, and different categories of former royals, palace officers, and guests rise in turn to process towards the Maharaja seated at the centre of the hall on his richly embroidered *gaddi* (throne). For the tourists, 'tradition' has here become 'heritage', but it lacks historical contextualization and has become an essentialized and selective spectacle of **commodified** culture displaying a romanticized vision of Rajput chivalry, honour, and hospitality.

One Jodhpur royal family member, Raghavendra Rathore, has commodified his aristocratic lineage to market a line of fashion products. Such entrepreneurship capitalizes on royal birth as inspiration for his modern yet traditional luxury clothing, exclusively regal yet available for a price. Images of sophisticated living also sell royal luxury hotels and the former Maharaja himself is regularly photographed promoting the hotel and Jodhpur tourist sites, several of which he owns, including the imposing Mehrangarh fort.

The former Maharaja of Jodhpur has encouraged tourism in other ways. Since 2007, an annual Rajasthan International Folk Festival has been held at the Mehrangarh Fort, with the former Maharaja as chief patron and Sir Mick Jagger as international patron. Other initiatives include the Centre for Flamenco and Rajasthani Music, created in 2013 to celebrate the historical relation between Rajasthani folklore and Spanish Flamenco, which is said to have been brought to Spain by gypsies from Rajasthan. These initiatives allow Gaj Singh II to continue to perform his kingly functions as patron of the arts, but in a distinctly modern form. They are also a continuation of the cosmopolitan engagements of Rajput rulers, who have a long history of surviving political and economic challenges through adaptation and innovation (Figure 11.1).

Figure 11.1 The 347-room Umaid Bhavan Palace, Jodhpur, which was commissioned by the Maharaja as a famine relief project in the late 1920s and was at one time the largest private residence in the world, is now run as a luxury hotel. (Courtesy of Pradeep717/ Wikimedia, licensed under a Creative Commons Attribution-Share Alike 4.0 International license)

imported, rather than locally produced food. These social, cultural, and economic changes have generated political discontent: unhappy with a political process that favours high-ranking people, commoners have demanded greater political participation. This example demonstrates that the delicate balance of a ranking system based on mutual obligation can easily be challenged by other forces, such as capitalism.

Caste in India and beyond

A society can be stratified by **castes**. The English language borrowed the term 'caste' from Romance languages, where it originally meant 'lineage, race, breed', and the anthropological meaning of the English term partially overlaps with these original meanings. A caste is a social group that is often characterized by the labour that its members traditionally performed at some point in the past. Caste distinctions are supported by religious, moral, and cultural beliefs that justify the inequalities of the system by invoking the allegedly inherent attributes of its members. Caste membership is theoretically fixed over time, in that people are not able to move from one caste to another during their lifetime and children belong to the same caste as their parents. Thus societies that are organized in terms of castes are a clear example of a system in which status is ascribed. In addition, a caste is **endogamous**, meaning that people marry within their caste.

The classic example of a caste system is that of colonial India, aspects of which survive to this day. Hindu Indian society was organized into four *varna*, or clusters of castes, in descending order of status: the priestly and scholarly castes, or Brahmin; the warrior and ruler castes, or Kshatriya; the merchant and peasant castes, or Vaishya; and the castes of labourers, artisans, and providers of other services, or Shudra. Outside of and below this hierarchy were the 'untouchables', who are today referred to as Dalit, who were traditionally assigned labour that was considered degrading and unclean, including collecting rubbish and excrement and working with leather, which was abhorrent to many in a society that was traditionally vegetarian. While different occupations are accorded different levels of prestige, everyone depends on the labour and services that members of other castes provide: members of the priestly caste need artisans to supply them with household furnishings, while rulers need the priests to perform religious rituals, and without the Dalit's labour, life would become impossible.

The four *varna* groups were subdivided into hundreds of local caste categories, or *jāti*, which were in fact more important than the *varna* in people's daily lives. They varied by region and were associated with much more specific forms of labour than the *varna*. But because British colonial authorities needed a simplified and standardized system to classify colonized Indians for the censuses that were designed to enumerate and control them, they focused on the *varna* categories, which have since constituted the backbone of the system. Thus, while the principles of the caste system date back to ancient times, the particular configuration it has today is, in large part, the product of colonialism (Dirks 2001).

Hindu beliefs about purity and **pollution** provided a moral framework that explained and justified the caste system. Brahmins were ritually purer than everyone else, and this is why they held religious office, while Dalits were the most impure group, hence the unpleasant work to which they were assigned and that defined them. Members of the higher castes could not touch, accept food from, or be around lower-caste people or Dalits for fear of being polluted by them; if this accidentally happened, they had to perform religious rituals in order to regain their purity. In French anthropologist Louis Dumont's (1980) classical analysis of social structure in India, caste is a totalizing system, legitimating Hindu beliefs about purity and pollution, that determines social relations, the economy, and culture.

Dumont's analysis is somewhat problematic in that castes can exist without Hinduism and Hinduism exists outside of the caste system. In India, all groups, including Christians, Jains, Sikhs, Buddhists, Muslims, and the Indigenous groups that inhabit many regions (the so-called 'scheduled tribes') are treated as if they are part of the caste system. Similarly, there can be Hinduism without castes: Hindu Indians who emigrated during the late nineteenth and early twentieth centuries as indentured labourers to sugar plantations in Fiji, Mauritius, Guyana, and Trinidad and Tobago abandoned caste distinctions for most practical purposes, 'encouraged' by British colonial authorities anxious to get them to work hard without being encumbered by 'superstitions'.

Even though people today are no longer expected to stick to the kind of labour that their caste membership dictates, the religious beliefs that formed the basis of the Indian caste system justified prejudices and inequalities that survive to this day. In particular, even though untouchability was officially abolished in 1955, the Dalit continue to be discriminated against, and many have mobilized politically. Many have converted to Christianity or Buddhism to escape the social marginalization that Hinduism justifies. The Indian state has established affirmative action programmes to counter discrimination, which have enabled a few Dalit to achieve considerable political and economic power. There are strong moves afoot in some quarters to eradicate the caste system completely. In urban India, people pay greater attention to social class differences associated with wealth and international mobility than to caste differences. Where caste continues to play an important role is in the choice of a spouse.

If we define a caste system as being made up of endogamous and hierarchically ordered groups responsible for different forms of labour, but in need of each other's products and services, then some societies in sub-Saharan Africa, such as the Wolof of Senegal, meet this description. In the 1970s, when linguistic anthropologist Judith Irvine (1989) conducted fieldwork in rural Senegal, the top of the caste hierarchy was occupied by nobles while at the bottom were

griots, people who specialized in making music and delivering oratorical performances. The nobles and the griots were interdependent: in ritual contexts, the griots sang the praises of the nobles, recited their genealogies, and recounted the noble deeds of their ancestors, thus affirming the noble's prestige and political power. The nobles, for whom singing their own praises would have been inconceivable, rewarded the griots with gifts. The more beautiful and convincing the praise song, the more generous the noble was expected to be – if he was not, the griot could actually turn nasty and criticize the noble in public, which would have been deeply shameful for the noble.

One of the most visible markers of caste among rural Wolof was how people presented themselves in public. The nobles were impassive and dignified, and said very little. This is an interesting counterexample of the widespread belief that, cross-culturally, the powerful are those who speak the loudest and most effectively. If they really had to speak in public, they did so in a low, slow, and hesitant voice. Most of the time, they would let the articulate griots speak on their behalf. For example, at a noble's funeral, it was the griots who wailed on behalf of the bereaved family members, expressing the nobles' sadness and loss. In daily life, griots were recognizable for their talkativeness and the wide range of emotions they expressed: they tended to speak very fast and use emphatic, colourful, and creative language. Thus the mutually dependent division of labour among castes went beyond goods and services; it was also a division of linguistic and emotional labour in which the language and emotions that members of different castes produced complemented each other. Today, castes have largely disappeared in Senegal as many people have migrated to the cities and the state encourages people to think of themselves primarily as citizens. Thus who belongs to what caste is often no longer clear, yet here again, marriage is one area where concerns about caste survive.

Social class in the Global North

While caste-based organization is deeply enmeshed with religion, at least in its South Asian version, the organization of society into social classes is embedded in an economic system, namely capitalism. The thinker whose work is fundamental to any analysis of social class is the German political theorist Karl Marx. Along with his friend and co-author Frederik Engels, Marx wrote his most important works in England during the Industrial Revolution, when the economic and social landscape was radically restructured. The Industrial Revolution was made possible by a number of convergent events. By the mid-nineteenth century, Britain and other European powers had colonized much of the rest of the world, and they encouraged or forced colonial subjects to cultivate crops for export to Europe, such as sugar and cotton. At the same time, peasants in Britain were fleeing the countryside as it could no longer support their needs, in large part because a series of laws passed in earlier centuries enabled landowners to force peasants off common land on which they had previously grazed their cattle and gathered food and firewood. This development, known as **enclosure**, also took place in other countries at different times. Peasants thus moved to the cities, where they had little choice but to offer their labour to the factories owned by wealthy industrialists that manufactured products from raw materials, many of which were imported from the colonies. Capitalism thus emerged in a broad context of land enclosure, colonial expansion, and technological development (Mintz 1985; Wolf 1982).

These developments transformed the world. Prior to the Industrial Revolution, British society was made up of many different social groups, including aristocrats, tradesmen, artisans, and peasants. The Industrial Revolution collapsed many of these into two **social classes**: the

---

Box 11.2   The transformation of griots in Mali

Griots, or praise-singers, are common throughout West Africa. In Mali, where they are called *jeliw* (singular form *jeli*), griots were traditionally part of specific families attached to high-ranking or powerful families, whose praises they were responsible for singing on important public occasions. The practice is still followed in some rural areas. In urban areas, however, *jeliw* have reinvented themselves as singers of popular songs that are broadcast on radio, which appeared in 1957, and television since 1985, and in the late 1990s were circulated on cassette tapes (Schultz 2001).

Clear continuities connect *jeli* pop singers of today to the traditional roles they played in the past. In traditional rural contexts, female *jeliw* often sang the praises of their high-ranking female patrons by praising their modesty, patience, and subservience to their husbands and in-laws, features of a conservative morality. Modern *jeliw* also sing about the value of these qualities but in a generalized fashion that does not focus on a particular person but pitch them instead in a general way against the corrupting influences of modern urban living, where social relations are governed by money and everybody is out for themselves.

The pop songs lack the depth of knowledge of older praise songs, and many local commentators criticize them for lacking 'authenticity'. But they have enormous appeal to urban generations, particularly young women, and have given a new role to an old social category. For their female fans, the pop songs, performed by sophisticated celebrity *jeliw*, articulate a Malian morality dressed in the fashionable attires of the contemporary world, thus providing a model of how to be local and global at the same time. Although some male *jeliw* have become international stars of the 'world music' circuit, it is women singers who are most popular in Mali.

---

bourgeoisie, who owned the **means of production**, primarily the factories, from which they derive **capital**; and the **proletariat**, who owned only their labour, which they sold to the factories in order to survive. At the root of capitalism is the accumulation of wealth; this contrasts sharply with the principles on which other economic systems are founded, such as the imperative to redistribute in **gift economies**. The inequalities between the bourgeoisie and the proletariat were dramatic, and Marx and other commentators of the time wrote passionately about the terrible conditions in which the proletariat lived, with young children working in factories and people living short and brutal lives. Marx hoped that the proletariat would develop 'class consciousness', the realization that their misery was not inevitable but the product of a particular economic structure. This realization, he believed, would enable them to mobilize politically and redress the stark inequalities of capitalism by abolishing social classes through revolution (Figure 11.2).

In Europe, some social groups stood outside of both the bourgeoisie and the proletariat. One was the aristocracy, which continued to derive wealth from land and sometimes intermarried with the wealthy bourgeoisie. Another consisted of beggars, criminals, sex workers, the homeless, the unemployed, and other disadvantaged groups, which Marx labelled **lumpenproletariat** (*lumpen* in German means 'rags'). Yet another were small-scale traders and craftspeople, which Marx called the **petty bourgeoisie**; he predicted that most such people would become

Figure 11.2 In the last decades of the twentieth century, factory work has increasingly moved to the Global South, although some industries remain in the Global North, such as this Ford final assembly plant in Dearborn, Michigan, United States, 2009. (Courtesy of Spencer Grant/Alamy)

too poor to sustain their economic activities and would join the ranks of the factory workers, or in a few lucky cases would become wealthy and melt into the bourgeoisie.

On this point, history proved more complicated: as the nineteenth century unfolded, the petty bourgeoisie in Europe and North America became more important as the increasingly complex bureaucratic organization of society required their services as accountants, teachers, civil servants, engineers, technicians, and supervisors. By the beginning of the twentieth century, many had acquired property, including urban homes. Neither wealthy nor destitute, they became what we know today as the middle classes. **Consumption** plays a central role in the life of members of this social class, who define themselves in terms of the consumer goods they can buy and display. For example, at the beginning of the twentieth century, they bought automobiles as these were becoming affordable and they shopped in the department stores that emerged in cities of the industrialized world.

Fifty years after Marx, these developments prompted another German social theorist, Max Weber, to propose a different theory of social classes and capitalism. For Weber (1992), capitalism was the result of the transformation of the Protestant bourgeoisie's emphasis on asceticism and frugality as a way of showing that one may be among the chosen few who would enter paradise (this was called predestination). Protestants took seriously the frugality that the Scriptures encouraged (as spelled out in the New Testament in such passages as 'it is easier for a camel to go through the eye of a needle than for a rich man to enter the kingdom of God') and neglected other scriptural injunctions that encouraged altruism ('A generous person will prosper'), and this enabled them to accumulate wealth.

Weber's approach to social classes is different from Marx's approach: for him, a social class is made up of people who think and act in similar ways and their class status is defined by lifestyle, affinity, and prestige, in addition to economic position. He saw society as organized into **status groups** rather than social class. In contrast to Marx's **materialist** theory, based on whether or not people owned property, Weber's **ideational** theory of social class was more successful in accounting for how the members of the middle classes that emerged in the late nineteenth century think alike, in their interest in consumption for example, but display little of the political consciousness that Marx saw as central to the organization of social classes. If anything, far from experiencing class solidarity, middle-class people feel they are in competition with one another.

Integrating materialist and ideational approaches

Marx and Weber each captured different but important aspects of social class. One's social class depends on capital (Marx), but it is also predicated on one's education, who one knows, and what one likes to do (Weber). The integration of these approaches formed the basis of the work of French sociologist Pierre Bourdieu, whose writings have exerted considerable influence on Anglophone anthropology since the 1980s. His integrative approach resonates with anthropology's emphasis on **holism**, which seeks to capture different perspectives of a particular phenomenon, and it lends itself well to ethnographic investigation.

For Bourdieu, social class is a matter of both material and ideational forces, which can work in unison just as easily as they can contradict each other. For example, people who find themselves transported from a life of modest means to a life of wealth (e.g., entrepreneurs, elite athletes, lottery winners) are often looked down upon, particularly by other wealthy people, as not 'really' belonging to the social class to which their new wealth enables them to aspire. They may be wealthy, but they lack the knowledge, the refinement, and the outlook on life that other people with older wealth value. These *nouveaux riches* are caught between material and ideational criteria for social class, which normally should align, and their predicament confirms, rather than disrupts, this alignment.

Language provides a vivid example that everyone can relate to (Bourdieu 1991). In all class-based societies of the world, knowing how to speak (or write) in complex sentences, with a rich vocabulary and allusions to thinkers and writers, is a skill one acquires through an elite education: a private secondary school, for example, which gives one access to a good university, which in turn gives one a good crack at landing a career that offers money and a future. But this way of speaking is looked upon as elitist by people who did not have the same opportunities in life; in order to be accepted by them, one needs to speak in a different way, with a different accent and a different vocabulary.

This example demonstrates how material, social, and cultural dynamics are interdependent. To attend a private school and a good university, one needs to have the means to pay fees in countries where education is not free, and, in all countries, to have the means to delay getting a job, rather than doing so immediately after secondary school in order to support one's parents and siblings. These material resources enable one to access social resources, such as friendship ties with influential people, and cultural resources, such as knowledge of philosophy, literature, and the arts. This is what Bourdieu (2010) in the 1980s termed **distinction**. In this model, all these resources constitute forms of capital: one can 'exchange' material capital for social capital, i.e., one's social networks, or cultural capital, namely one's ability to display refinement, and vice-versa. For example, 'speaking well' gains one entry into prestigious institutions and circles, where it is deemed to be a sign of intelligence and refinement. And the fact that people who lack material capital do not care for the social and cultural capital of those who have material capital keeps the system in place and ensures its **reproduction**: the children of those who have social and cultural capital in turn control the value system, and the children of those who lack this capital are materially disadvantaged but find comfort in their own circles that share their values.

Bourdieu's model of social class thus combines Marx's emphasis on the material basis of social class, whereby those who control wealth belong to the ruling class and those who do not belong to the ruled class, with Weber's understanding of social class as a matter of lifestyle, affinity, and prestige. At the same time, social class is always complicated by other kinds of divisions in society, such as gender and age. For example, classical music in the Global North tends to be a marker of middle-class status, but young people of all social classes generally prefer to listen to other musical styles like hip hop and electronic music. This is another manifestation of the **intersectionality** discussed in Chapter 5.

The middle classes in a globalized world

As social-class stratification is so closely embedded in capitalism and capitalism emerged principally in Europe and North America, in many societies that have traditionally been organized according to principles other than capitalism, social classes are a much more recent phenomenon. By the end of the twentieth century, capitalism had spread to all corners of the world, to the extent that today few societies if any have not been affected by it. Since the 1980s, globalization has further accelerated this process, as people living in the remotest corners of the world are now exposed to consumer goods and are seeing wage employment as inevitable. Because some people do better than others in this system, it creates class inequalities.

Situations in which the middle classes are new are particularly interesting to anthropologists because they can teach us about how different contexts give them specific configurations. For example, in China, for most of the period from the Communist Revolution in 1949 to the end of the Cultural Revolution in 1976, private property was illegal and the economy was under the centralized control of the state. Beginning in 1978, however, the state implemented drastic economic reforms that introduced market principles, decentralized the economy, and opened the country to global trade and industry. The result was a massive increase in wealth, but also sharp new inequalities, as some people have become very wealthy while the bulk of the population in cities and the countryside are impoverished. In between, a new urban middle class has emerged, made up of managers, business owners, and professionals and their families, often with ties to state officials, whom they rely on in their ambitions to do well.

Consumption plays an important role in the lives of members of this new middle class, and housing is one way in which they display this consumption (Zhang 2010). In 1998, the state allowed individuals to own homes for the first time in 50 years, and since then housing has become a visible marker of social class. In contrast to the overcrowded, cramped, and shoddily built apartment buildings where poor people have to live, spacious upscale complexes surrounded by gardens are the housing of choice for the new middle class. 'Gated communities', protected by fences, cameras, and guards that give residents a sense of privacy and safety, are visible ways in which the new middle classes distinguish themselves from the rest of the population. But, within the complexes, people rarely socialize and feel little solidarity with one another. Like the *nouveaux riches* elsewhere in the world, they often feel insecure about their new class status.

In other places, the new middle classes have similar concerns about marking themselves out as different from others. In Papua New Guinea, for example, most societies were until relatively recently small-scale, tightly organized, and fiercely egalitarian, with complex systems of reciprocity that straddled the generations and ensured that no one could rise above others. However, since the 1990s, a middle class has emerged in the urban centres, consisting of people whose parents became, after the country's independence from Australia in 1975, government officials or business owners and who took the place of the white colonizers (Gewertz and Errington 1999).

Members of this urban elite distance themselves from their rural relatives for fear that the latter may make claims on their money and resources. They reject the obligations of kinship that organize the lives of villagers. Instead, they seek to develop social relations based on friendship and common aspirations, which they cultivate, for example, by becoming members of private clubs and civic organizations like the Rotary Club. They assert that villagers have only themselves to blame for their poverty because they are unable to hang on to their resources. This view echoes former colonial discourses and recasts social and economic differences in a moral frame. The middle classes see their privilege as the result of having done well in a meritocratic system.

These ethnographic examples illustrate the fact that economic and cultural dynamics are tightly intertwined in creating and maintaining social stratification. What is for one group of people an important cultural expectation, namely participating in exchange and redistribution, is redefined by another group as a sign of moral deficiency and a lack of planning.

In many societies where social-class stratification is relatively new, one factor that plays an important role in creating social-class differences is the extent to which one can count on the material assistance of relatives living in wealthier countries. This is the case, for example, of Tonga. In the 1970s, Tongans began migrating to New Zealand on temporary visas, where they filled the need for labour in such sectors as meat-processing plants, agriculture, and the service industries. Since then, they have also migrated in increasing numbers to Australia and the United States. Today, Tongan migrants form an extensive **diaspora**, now in its third generation. There now are many more people of Tongan descent overseas than in Tonga, a situation that is common among other small nation-states of the world.

Many diasporic Tongans continue to maintain contacts with their families back in the islands and feel a strong sense of duty to support them – in fact, migration has always been explained in terms of 'helping the family' (Besnier 2011). They send **remittances** on a more or less regular basis to their relatives in the form of money or consumer goods, such as clothing and household furnishings. In exchange, families in the islands take care of the family land and homes and, if practical, send food, mats, decorated barkcloth, and other island goods to their relatives overseas.

The monetization of the economy, the growing importance of consumption, and the diasporic dispersal of the population have given rise to a market economy, and with it to a growing middle class. This middle class is composed of people who can tap into resources in wealthier countries or have relatives in the diaspora on whom they can count. It is superimposed onto the rank system described earlier: it has arisen primarily in the non-aristocratic population that has become wealthy through transnational ties, but its most successful members are aristocrats who combine local privilege with global connections. Successful middle-class entrepreneurs and their families distance themselves from others by presenting themselves as cosmopolitan citizens at ease in urban industrial contexts, and are somewhat impatient with rural and poorer Tongans. Many speak English to one another, while at the same time they still strive to speak Tongan in appropriate contexts so that they will not be criticized for being pretentious.

The capitalist economy based on ties to the outside world coexists with the non-capitalist exchange practices that bind families together which Tongans consider to be fundamental to local identity. Local and global dynamics are deeply intertwined.

The neoliberal transformation of social class

The concept of social class that Marx, Weber, and Bourdieu strove to make sense of was embedded in the context of capitalism as it had emerged during the Industrial Revolution. Since the 1980s, however, capitalism has undergone radical transformations. No longer contained in the nation-state, it is today globalized. Money flows more easily than ever across national boundaries and workers in very different parts of the globe are now connected to one another, as production and service provision can quickly move across vast distances: a corporation can decide to close a plant in Europe and open one in China, and a bank to offshore its IT or customer services to India, suddenly eliminating jobs in one part of the world and creating jobs in another.

The state has also transformed itself in this globalized context, privatizing its operations, opening its markets to new interests, and reducing its responsibilities to citizens. These are the developments that are referred to as **neoliberalism**. They have had major effects on the structure of social classes throughout the world, particularly since the 2008 global financial crisis which, many have argued, was a consequence of neoliberal policies. Because citizens of countries that had previously offered a welfare system could no longer count on this safety net, many people, including those who belonged to the middle classes, experience increasing **precarity**, namely job insecurity and difficulties in maintaining their class status. Entire neighbourhoods and towns have been turned into communities where unemployment, poverty, and ill-health reign. In the United States, where ordinary people were particularly affected by the 2008 crash because so many had been coaxed by financial institutions into buying houses they could not afford, many lost their homes or were desperately trying to seek financial assistance, only to find that their only recourse was to try to negotiate with the banks that had lied to them in the first place, and in many cases continued to lie to them by faking their signatures on documents (Stout 2016). Iceland went so far as to declare the country bankrupt (Loftsdóttir 2010).

In the United States again, corporations have lobbied vigorously to reduce government restrictions on environmental pollution and as a result people in many areas of the country are living in toxic environments. These are often the same areas where corporations have closed down industrial plants, which means that they also suffer from widespread unemployment (Walley 2013). Throughout the world, neoliberalism has transformed the structure of social classes: wealth and income are now concentrated in the hands of a small, very wealthy class, the middle class has shrunk, and the number of people living precariously has increased. In many countries, homelessness has skyrocketed as a result of government privatizing or eliminating assistance for the poor and unemployed and treatment for addiction and mental illness (Bourgois and Schonberg 2009). People have had to rethink how they can make a living, what their position is in the social structure, and how they organize their lives (Figure 11.3).

In Japan after World War II, the middle class had grown at a remarkable pace and its poster image was that of the 'salaryman' (*sararīman*), the male employee of a company who devoted his life to white-collar work, while wives took care of the home and brought up the children (Allison 1994). The corporation rather than the state took care of employees and their families, and did so for life in exchange for the employees' hard work and loyalty. This was hardly a perfect system: it enforced a rigidly gendered division of labour, encouraged conformity, and created a punishing work schedule for men, who were expected to devote all their waking hours to work and were expected to socialize with co-workers after work, leaving little time for family life and sleep. But it enabled the emergence of a vast and well-to-do middle class and the country to rise out of the ashes of World War II as an economic world power (Figure 11.4).

Japan then experienced an economic downturn that started in the early 1990s, earlier than in Western countries, and was aggravated by the 2008 crisis. It has changed the life

Figure 11.3 Industrial deregulation during the Trump administration in the United States authorized oil drilling right next to homes in Carlsbad, New Mexico, where noxious fumes, nonstop industrial noise, and chemical spills have caused serious health problems. (Courtesy of Justin Hamel)

configuration of many young people. Today, many fewer corporations guarantee permanent employment than in the past, forcing an entire generation to reinvent itself. Many young people now survive on multiple, part-time, and insecure jobs, the iconic example of which is as a cashier in a convenience store (*konbini*). The luckier ones can earmark time to pursue their interests in fashion, performance, or the arts, but they often face the ire of the older generations for what the latter see as their lack of responsibility, maturity, and conformity to bygone cultural values (Cook 2016).

The global poster children of the neoliberal age are employees of startup companies in Silicon Valley and comparable high-tech regions of the world (Gershon 2017). To be successful in the global neoliberal economy, workers must be flexible, inventive, and risk-taking, and be able to blur the lines between working and personal lives. In Silicon Valley, workshops teach people how to present themselves to potential employers like a business, with adaptable skills and the willingness to accept insecure, temporary, and conditional employment, and sometimes be remunerated with promises of company shares rather than income. Prospective employers view a history of employment in the same firm for longer than two years as problematic evidence that the job applicant lacks ambition. In this context, Bourdieu's characterization of social class as a matter of social, cultural, and material capital seems to describe another age.

Neoliberalism has also transformed the day-to-day lives in the Global South. In poorer countries, the state has never provided many social services to citizens, but neoliberal policies have further reduced even the little that states used to provide. Neoliberalism has affected people's lives in two major ways. One, it has deregulated markets, which means that the state can no

Figure 11.4 Japanese *sararīman* not only have to work long hours but also are required to socialize with their co-workers after work, which often involves copious alcohol consumption and forces them to sleep in public places when they have missed the last train home to the suburbs; Setagaya, Tokyo, 2007. (Courtesy of Anneke Beerkens)

longer subsidize small-scale producers or protect them from the potentially wide fluctuations in the price of goods caused by unpredictable weather and speculation in the world's financial markets. This has had a profound effect on small-scale farmers, among others, who cannot compete with large farming interests. In rural areas of India, the rate of suicide has increased dramatically among farmers unable to cope with debt and drought. Two, neoliberal policies have considerably reduced state bureaucracies, which in the postcolonial world was the main source of employment for the well-educated and the foundation of the middle classes. Rich countries and world institutions like the World Bank and the International Monetary Fund have played a crucial role in these transformations: as many national economies in sub-Saharan Africa, Asia, and elsewhere collapsed in the 1980s, they offered these countries loans on condition that they implement **structural adjustment** policies to reduce the bureaucracy and liberalize markets.

In the countryside, large numbers of people were no longer able to survive on agriculture and migrated to cities, where they made a living with whatever means they could. For example, in urban Vietnam, poor migrants from rural areas collect and recycle used home furnishings for a living, yet they stress that they are performing a socially valuable service and demand recognition for their contribution to society (Nguyen 2016). In Abidjan, Côte d'Ivoire, unemployed young men from families that have migrated from the country's hinterlands or neighbouring countries develop all kinds of techniques to make money on the edge of legality, including setting up phone booths with a stolen mobile phone, extorting money by pretending to be a police officer, or selling stolen goods (Newell 2012). They ostentatiously display their wealth by wearing expensive-looking clothes and buying large quantities of drinks in bars, to project an image of themselves as worthy of dignity in the eyes of others. Even the urban middle classes in countries of the Global South find it difficult to find work. In many parts of Africa, it is not unusual to find doctors and lawyers driving taxis to supplement their income.

The economic, social, and political changes that the world has experienced since the end of the twentieth century have had profound effects on the structure of society and on people's lives. Globalization connects people throughout the world, but these connections do not always improve people's lives; sometimes they damage them.

Hierarchy and inequality in the structure of society

In many societies in the past and the present, ideologies of egalitarianism have encouraged people to downplay economic and social inequalities, although equality has always proven difficult to achieve and maintain over time. More frequently, societies have been stratified according to different principles. Rank, caste, and social class are based on different principles and are associated with different kinds of societies: while rank and caste are associated with pre-capitalist social structures, social class arose with capitalism in the nineteenth-century Global North and its later global spread. They nevertheless overlap, and in many societies social stratification is the effect of rank or caste and social class simultaneously. In all three systems, status can be ascribed and achieved. For example, even in a caste or rank system, which appears to ascribe people to specific social categories in a rigid way, people find ways of moving up and down the social hierarchy. All three systems have been profoundly affected by neoliberalism and globalization.

Key thinkers mentioned in this chapter:

Pierre Bourdieu; Louis Dumont; Frederik Engels; Karl Marx; Max Weber

Key terms mentioned in this chapter (see Glossary):

Achieved status; Ascribed status; Bourgeoisie; Capital; Caste; Commons; Consumption; Diaspora; Distinction; Egalitarianism; Equality of opportunity; Equality of outcome; Griots; Idealist; Inequality; Intersectionality; Materialist; Means of production; Meritocracy; Neoliberalism; Precarity; Proletariat; Rank; Redistribution; Remittances; Social class; Social stratification; Status groups; Structural adjustment

Questions for discussion/review:

1   How can inequality be conceptualized?
2   What are the defining features of caste systems?
3   What did Bourdieu contribute to materialist and ideational understandings of social class?
4   In what ways has neoliberalism altered earlier models of social class?

Chapter 12

State, nation, and citizenship

In the contemporary world, one of the most ubiquitous documents that people carry is a passport. Yet the requirement to have a passport to travel internationally dates back only to World War I (Torpey 2000). Prior to that, the only people who were required to carry state-issued documents to cross national borders were diplomats and other high-status people. The booklet with which we are familiar today was established at the Conference on Passports and Customs Formalities and Through Tickets of 1920, held by the League of Nations in Paris. Passports issued by wealthy countries allow much freer cross-border mobility than passports issued by poor countries or those caught up in conflicts. Nowadays, passports contain biometric information about the bearer stored in a microprocessor chip, which allows authorities to exert considerable control over people.

Passports are a striking example of the importance of the role that the state plays in contemporary lives. They are at once an enabling tool and an instrument of control and surveillance. They create hierarchies between the inhabitants of the Global North and the Global South, between people who have valued passports and those who do not, and those who can have a passport and those who cannot. The passport plays an important role in how we constitute ourselves as citizens, an essential aspect of our identity. The entity that issues passports, namely the state, may appear distant and abstract, yet it pervades our lives.

Some core concepts

The concept of the **state** has existed for about 5,000 years, although in different forms. Some states conquered other states to become empires, and history is replete with accounts of empires like the Roman Empire and the Ottoman Empire. In the Middle Ages, Europe was divided into more than 1,000 states, which held various degrees of autonomy and allegiance to one another. The concept has undergone many transformations over the centuries, one of which was the consolidation of the plethora of states in Europe enacted by the Peace of Westphalia, a series of treaties that European powers signed in 1648, ending the Thirty Years' War (1618–48). This event institutionalized the notion that states must have clear boundaries within which the government has unchallenged jurisdiction, although in actual practice this notion only became a reality in the nineteenth century. While the notion may seem self-evident in the world in which we currently live, it was not in the past and is still the object of considerable contentions in many contexts.

In the early twentieth century, social theorist Max Weber (1978) defined the state as a continuously operating compulsory political organization that secures the sovereignty of a territory, governs its population, and claims a monopoly on the legitimate use of force to enact its laws. The state governs through powerful bureaucratic institutions staffed by specialists, such as politicians and civil servants. It imposes its authority through such institutions as the police, courts of law, and

DOI: 10.4324/9781315737805-12

tax authorities. In return, in theory at least, the state is expected to look after people by protecting them against invasions, looking after the ill and the unemployed, and maintaining roads and train lines. In practice, no state manages to achieve these idealized goals all at once.

A closely related concept is the **nation**. In contrast to the state, the nation is made up of people, not institutions. The concept is much more recent than that of the state, emerging in the eighteenth century and refined in the course of the nineteenth century. It is the product of post-Enlightenment intellectual debates. German romantic philosopher Johann Gottfried Herder (1744–1803) contends that people define themselves in terms of an 'essential character' that made them part of a greater whole made up of others who felt the same; folklore, religion, and language all contributed to these feelings. For French historian Ernest Renan (1823–92), neither shared language nor religion was sufficient to produce a nation. Rather, collectively shared needs are the basis for solidarity, and national identity is based as much on forgetting as it is on celebrating shared ideals.

Nationalism refers to the beliefs held by members of a nation that the nation matters. As a concept, it is rooted in the rise of nationalism in nineteenth-century Europe and the Americas, which spread to other parts of the world in the twentieth century. Nationalist beliefs can take many forms, from hanging a flag from the window of one's home to going to war. Even people who do not feel strongly about being part of the nation will occasionally experience a sense of bonding with their co-nationals. For example, every four years, when athletes enter an Olympic stadium in the Parade of Athletes, even people who do not think of themselves as patriotic may feel butterflies in their stomach as they watch their country's team on television (Figure 12.1).

Figure 12.1 Mega sport events bring out nationalist feelings as well as a sense of belonging to humanity, as demonstrated by these citizens of Japan, the United States, Croatia, and Russia celebrating together watching the live broadcast of the opening ceremonies of the 2018 Winter Olympic Games in PyeongChang, South Korea. (Courtesy of Susan Brownell)

Whatever we feel about nationalism, it surrounds us all: flags in government offices; leaders' portraits and other emblems on coins and banknotes; and references to leaders as *the* president or *the* prime minister are all forms of what sociologist Michael Billig (1995) terms 'banal nationalism'. Banal nationalism is particularly effective in making us believe in the importance of feeling that we are part of a nation because it is so ubiquitous, which means that it acts upon us while we are going about our everyday life. It also encourages particular forms of consumption, as illustrated by the association of cigarette smoking with nationalist pride in China that we mentioned in Chapter 1.

Another category is **citizenship**. Most simply, citizenship is a legal set of conditions that refers to the rights and duties involved in taking part in the workings of the state, such as voting in elections. Even though the concept is recent, it has considerable power, so that people who are stateless because they do not have a citizenship encounter many problems in their daily lives. But the legal concept is only one aspect of what citizenship actually entails, because rights and duties are distributed differently among citizens.

The state

In contexts such as the United Nations General Assembly, each state has equal representation, no matter how large or small. But there is considerable variation among the states of the world. For example, the state in India governs over 1.3 billion people, namely 18% of the world's population, living on more than 3Mkm^2 of land, while Tuvalu has a population of just 12,000 people and an area of 25km^2. Some states, like Norway and the United Arab Emirates, are extraordinarily wealthy, while others are desperately poor, and some states redistribute their wealth to citizens while others do not. Thus people's relations to and expectations of the state can vary widely.

A state is the product of two processes: it must be recognized by other states, with which it can have diplomatic relations, and it must be legitimized by the citizens of the country. Some states, like Tibet's government in exile, exist in a state of limbo because they do not have jurisdiction over the people they purport to govern. In other cases, a population that shares a language and identity lives in different states. Such is the predicament of the Kurds, who occupy a territory divided among Iraq, Iran, Turkey, and Syria, a situation that resulted from the colonial division of the Middle East at the end of World War I and that the Kurds have contested ever since. Palestine is a state that is partly occupied, partly blockaded by Israel, and some Palestinians live in Israel as citizens of that country. In Nigeria and Papua New Guinea, the state governs populations of such diversity that it is a miracle that they can function at all. Yet in many cases, the nation and the state overlap, however imperfectly, and the term **nation–state** captures the idea that the nation is encompassed within the territory over which the state that governs it has jurisdiction.

According to James Scott (1998), the modern state is based on the need to make populations 'legible' by classifying people, places, and practices. Cities are planned on rational lines, 'scientific' agriculture is imposed on farmers, weights and measures are standardized, people are counted, and places are mapped. While these endeavours are designed to improve life, many fail. For example, planned collectivized agriculture in the Soviet Union had disastrous consequences. In other cases, the drive for legibility leads to repressive practices. The Chinese government's current system of social credit is one example: people are assigned a value through artificial intelligence technology, losing points if they commit a road infraction or associate with suspect people, gaining points if they donate blood or praise the government on social media. Their ability to travel, shop, work, and study depends on their social credit value. This system is an example of how the state's efforts to make citizens legible can lead to sinister results.

Rather than being a distant and **alienated** site of power, ordinary citizens encounter the state in their everyday lives and forge ideas about how it works (Gupta 1995). The most obvious context in which citizens experience the state is bureaucracy. People interact with bureaucracy when they apply for an identity card, mail a letter, pay taxes, or register a newborn baby. These interactions have consequences, as it is through them that people construct the state 'from below'. A common stereotype of bureaucracy is that it is a rational bearer of power that is indifferent to ordinary people's concerns: citizens must approach state employees with the right kind of documents, and bureaucrats seem to take pleasure in finding fault with the documents they submit and refuse the required services. This is the picture that Max Weber attributed to the workings of the modern state, where following procedure is more important than accomplishing tasks. But citizens are not dupes and are often capable of navigating the complexities of the state to get what they want and make bureaucracies work for them (Herzfeld 1992).

One phenomenon often associated with agents of the state is corruption. The World Bank defines corruption as 'the abuse of public office for private gain', a definition that seems uncontroversial but is in fact far from straightforward. Underlying it is the assumption that public and the private spheres of life can easily be kept separate and that the distinction is fundamental to the proper functioning of the state. In actual practice, this is often not the case. In the Global North, for example, kinship, friendship, and other types of personal connections play a crucial role in the making of public careers. Yet governments in the Global North and international organizations often accuse governments in the Global South of being corrupt, demanding that the latter demonstrate efforts to implement 'good governance' as a condition for receiving development and other kinds of aid.

In Indonesia, for example, under pressure from international organizations, the state has launched anti-corruption campaigns since the fall of the dictator General Suharto in 1998. But Indonesian bureaucrats are often perplexed about what categories like 'corruption', 'collusion', and 'nepotism' actually mean (Tidey 2016). To obtain coveted public sector jobs, ambitious young people must rely on the support of their families, who often pool their resources to help them finance their studies and overcome other costly obstacles. This places them in a difficult position in that, in the **gift economy** that pervades kinship relations, they are then indebted to their relatives, who expect the newly minted bureaucrat to provide return gifts in the form of favours. Civil servants are thus caught in a situation in which the professional imperative to refrain from corrupt practices is at odds with the expectations of the gift system. This is further complicated by the Indonesian state's long history of defining the nation-state as a large family, an image that further contributes to the blurring of the boundary between the public and the private.

Two important aspects of how Max Weber theorized the state are its monopoly on the legitimate use of force and its responsibility to protect the nation-state's borders. The military plays a prominent role in these tasks. In highly militarized countries like the United States, Russia, Israel, Turkey, and China, the military is conspicuous in daily life: separation walls, checkpoints, military bases, museums, monuments, commemorations, emergencies, and so on. In some cases, the state convinces its citizens that the nation-state is under threat and that the only possible response to this threat is a strong military presence.

In Israel, for example, security is an integral part of people's daily existence and of their actions, words, and emotions (J. Ochs 2011). Security guards are so prevalent in the urban landscape that ordinary citizens hardly notice them. Because lengthy military service is compulsory for both men and women (three years for men, two for women), soldiers are everywhere and having spent time as a soldier is a significant aspect of citizens' lives. People have internalized a culture of fear and security without always being aware of its political grounding. While most of them rarely encounter the 'enemy', largely defined as Palestinian, they participate in the construction of this elusive enemy as a danger that must be controlled through the militarization of the nation-state. Militarization thus not only protects the sovereignty of the nation-state, but it is also a cultural practice that permeates everyday life.

In many cases around the world, however, the state does not manage to function as Weber characterized it. In the public imagination in the Global North, state failure is generally attributed to civil war, insurrection, famine, population displacement, economic collapse, or pandemics, events that contribute to the state not being able to maintain its sovereignty over people and territories. While states have failed throughout history all over the world, failed states today are stereotypically located in the Global South, and for a good reason: frequently their failure is historically rooted in the fact that they were created arbitrarily at decolonization and through the geopolitical maneuverings of world powers.

For example, as Afghan anthropologist Nazif Shahrani (2002) explains, Afghanistan's territory was created in the 1880s by the United Kingdom and the Russian Empire, which split up the territories of various ethnic groups between and among various neighbouring states. This placed fragments of different ethnic groups within the territory of the newly created nation-state, which was headed by rulers who had, at best, an uneasy relationship with the population. The Soviet Union's invasion of the country in 1979 was followed by a war between different groups, which was a proxy for the Cold War tensions between the Soviet Union and the United States, from which the Taliban emerged. The end of the Soviet presence in 1989 left the country in a state of economic, political, and social chaos, which subsequent events, such as the invasion by the United States, only aggravated. Far from resulting from a nation's inability to organize itself under a central government, as it is often represented in public discourse in the Global North, Afghanistan's status as a 'failed state' results from a long history of interventions by world powers.

Despite the image represented on world maps, in which every piece of land on earth is governed by a state, some states exert power over their territories and populations only with great difficulty. Such is the case of the area known as the 'Golden Triangle', where Burma, Thailand, and China meet, and where people do not recognize the authority of any state, do not pay taxes, and cross national borders with little regard for them. Similarly, the Western Sahara in northwest Africa, which was colonized by Spain until 1975, has been contested by an independence movement called the Polisario Front, as well as by its three neighbouring countries, Morocco, Algeria, and Mauritania (Wilson 2017). Sahrawi who live in the Western Sahara are wary of any state authority, and whenever government representatives make demands on them, they quickly leave for the desert, taking with them their property, animals, and resources, against the regulations of both the Polisario and the countries that lay competing claims on their territory. Mobility is thus one way of evading the authority of the state, which is predicated on people remaining anchored in place (Figure 12.2).

The state is an entity that affects the daily lives of most people in the world and acts independently of the nation, and sometimes against its best interests, but it is also one that people in certain circumstances can circumvent. It is a complex institution, whose various manifestations can act in contradictory ways, and because the institutions of the state are operated by people, the tools of anthropology can be usefully applied to an understanding of the state.

Figure 12.2 A group of Sahrawi refugees take a break to enjoy tea in the pastures near Afraijat Albashir, Western Sahara, April 2008. (Courtesy of Alice Wilson)

Nation and nationalism

Prior to the nineteenth century, ordinary people in Europe and elsewhere led localized lives dominated by kinship and religion, and there was little use for them to develop a sense of belonging to a nation as they were largely unaware of the people who lived outside their immediate sphere of life. Industrialization and urbanization in the nineteenth century changed all this, as Ernest Gellner (2006) argued. Society became more complex and anonymous, states became bureaucratized, most people had access to education, and national languages supplanted regional dialects. The inhabitants of a country now needed to emphasize their commonalities, including a shared culture and past, which were fostered by widespread literacy, and nationalism emerged out of these dynamics. While nationalism rests on the belief that it is rooted in the past, it is in fact the product of modernity.

While pioneering, Gellner's ideas are problematic, particularly because they do not account for the rise of nationalism outside the Global North. This is the problem that Benedict Anderson sought to address on the basis of his fieldwork in Indonesia, a vast insular country that had been a Dutch colony before it gained independence shortly after World War II. Indonesia is not only large but also culturally and ethnically diverse, with over 700 languages, although most Indonesians also speak a **lingua franca**, Bahasa Indonesia, which developed during the colonial era. 90% of its population is Muslim, but there are also Christians, Buddhists, Confucianists, and adherents of local religions. The problem that Anderson posed is, how can citizens of a postcolonial country with so much diversity and no unified history develop a sense of belonging to the same nation?

The title of Anderson's book, *Imagined Communities* (2016a), gives the answer away. People need to *imagine* that they are part of a *community* in the sense that nineteenth-century social scientists conceptualized it, even though most will never meet face to face. An **imagined community**, which is the basis of nationalism, has three characteristics: it is *limited*, that is it has boundaries and does not include all of humanity; it is *sovereign* because the nation governs itself, rather than being ruled by royal dynasties with a mandate from God; and it is *imagined*, namely people must think of themselves as belonging to the same community as large numbers of other people whom they are unlikely to ever meet. Nationalism emerges as people come to believe that they have a common history, such as a struggle for independence, a repertoire of common symbols, such as a national anthem and a flag, and a set of common institutions, including the educational system. Like Gellner, Anderson attributes an important role to widespread literacy, particularly what he called print capitalism, namely the production of books and newspapers by private companies for public consumption. The simultaneous consumption of the same printed materials by people living very different lives not only encouraged them to think about the same issues but also encouraged them to use a single, standardized language.

Imagined Communities became one of the great books of the twentieth century and was translated into multiple languages. But Anderson's theory of nationalism has its shortcomings. For example, the assumption that literacy makes people think in a certain fashion overlooks the fact that people use reading and writing in many different ways, some in line with the intentions of those who produce written texts, others in opposition to them, and yet others that have nothing to do with the construction of the nation: for example, they write letters, post comments online, and publish articles designed for many purposes other than developing a common sense of national belonging. Literacy is thus what people make of it, rather than what it imposes on people.

Traditions play a very important role in the construction of the nation. But traditions are themselves the object of manipulations for political ends, which is what the notion of **invented tradition** seeks to capture. How a tradition may come to represent the nation is sometimes surprising. For example, in most people's minds, the tango is inextricably associated with Argentina and its passionate, seductive, and elegant culture. But tango's history is in fact complicated (Savigliano 1995). In late nineteenth-century Argentina, it was danced by poor women and men, particularly sex workers, and sometimes by middle- and upper-class men in search of a titillating experience. Respectable society looked down on it for its overt sexuality. But in the early twentieth century, it became a craze in London, Paris, and New York, and this is when Argentinian elites started paying attention, reimporting the dance and making it into an important national tradition and a symbol of the nation.

While Gellner's and Anderson's works have broken ground in our understanding of how nations are constructed, many authors have taken exception to their assumption that everyone is equally involved in the construction of nationalism. One particular statement from *Imagined Community* has provoked considerable reanalysis, namely the claim that the nation is always understood as a fraternity (2016a, 7). Anderson was attempting to capture the contradiction between the fact that the nation is a product of the imagination and the fact that people are willing to go to war for it. But his use of the term 'fraternity' is not haphazard. An imagined community is primarily a masculine project and women are expected to take on a secondary role as wives, mothers, and sisters.

Nationalism is embroiled in other forms of inclusion and marginalization. This is the insight developed by George Mosse (1985), a historian of modern Germany. For Mosse, nationalism in nineteenth-century Germany, an important case because the country was only unified at the end of the century, rose as a new middle-class morality about gender and sexuality was emerging. Both developed simultaneously in all-male institutions like fraternities, secret societies, and the armed forces, institutions that excluded many kinds of people whom mainstream German men saw as morally deficient, most obviously women, but also Jews, homosexuals, socialists, and ethnic minorities. In the early twentieth century, these ideas were incorporated as central to fascism, with tragic results.

While these ideas are about European history, they illuminate the fact that nationalism is grounded in ideas about morality and constructed in opposition to part of the population. For example, in Fiji, an island nation in the southwest Pacific, more than half of the population today consists of Indigenous people, the i-Taukei (literally, 'owners'), who have inhabited the island since prehistory. The rest of the population largely consists of Indo-Fijians, descendants of immigrants from South Asia brought as sugarcane labourers in the late nineteenth and early twentieth centuries, while the islands were a British colony. While the two groups led peaceable but separate lives until the late 1980s, i-Taukei have since staged a series of military coups that have marginalized Indo-Fijians. In response, many Indo-Fijians have chosen to emigrate and their numbers in Fiji have steadily declined.

One very important marker of Fiji's national identity is the sport of rugby (Guinness and Besnier 2016). Today, Fijian teams are extraordinarily successful internationally and many Fijian men forge careers playing for teams all over the rugby world, enabling them to secure jobs, which are otherwise few and far between in Fiji. Rugby gives the country a world visibility that it cannot claim in other ways because of its relative economic and political insignificance. Many in Fiji see the success of i-Taukei migrant players as a way of showing the world what Fijians are capable of, and the sport plays an important role in constructing Fijian nationalism. But rugby is only played by i-Taukei, as Indo-Fijians are seen as too thin and weak to play it. When some try to play, they are ridiculed, and the country's sports authorities do not encourage Indo-Fijians to play. While the i-Taukei majority welcomes them as supporters, spectators, and sponsors, Indo-Fijians are relegated, in subtle yet consequential ways, to a marginal position in one of the fundamental elements of national identity, illustrating Mosse's argument that nationalism is constructed through the exclusion of part of the citizenry (Figure 12.3).

Nationalism can take on sinister forms, as the history of the twentieth century has demonstrated dramatically. Since the turn of the millennium, radical forms of nationalism have emerged once again. New nationalist ideologies, such as those associated with political parties like the United Kingdom Independence Party, the National Rally in France, the Freedom Party in the Netherlands, and One Nation in Australia, react against what they perceive as the threatening influx of migrants, the arrogance of elite cosmopolitans, and the deterioration of the material conditions of ordinary people. The 2016 'Brexit' referendum in the United Kingdom that decided the country's departure from the European Union and the 2016 election of the populist Donald Trump to the presidency of the United States for one term were two key events that have propelled new forms of nationalism to the world stage.

What Australian anthropologist Ghassan Hage calls 'paranoid nationalism' (2003) is a nostalgic longing for an earlier time when society was imagined as homogeneous, factories offered secure employment, and the state could be depended on to take care of vulnerable citizens. Supporters do not see climate change and world poverty as problems that concern every human being and are opposed to what they see as the relinquishing of national sovereignty to supranational bodies like the European Union and the United Nations. Far from having been erased by the forces of globalization, radical nationalism is alive and well in the contemporary world.

However, nationalism also competes with other ways in which people choose to define themselves. Even Anderson later wrote in his autobiography that he realized that people could identify with dynamics other than the nation, including 'Hollywood movies, neoliberalism, a

Figure 12.3 A member of the Fijian Rugby Sevens national team deflects a tackle by a player on the British national team at the 2016 Olympic Games in Rio de Janeiro. The Fijian team went on to win the gold medal after crushing the team that represented their old colonial masters. This was the first Olympic gold medal ever won by any Pacific Island nation. (Courtesy of Niko Besnier)

taste for manga, human rights, impending ecological disaster, fashion, science, anarchism, post-coloniality, "democracy", indigenous peoples' movements, chatrooms, astrology, supranational languages like Spanish and Arabic and so on' (2016b, 127–8). Globalization in particular has facilitated new forms of identification, and some people no longer feel particularly attached to the country where they were born or where they live.

Citizenship

In its classic definition, citizenship consists in the **rights** and **duties** involved in taking part in the workings of the state, such as voting and paying taxes. In theory, citizenship provides the basis upon which the state treats people fairly and looks after them when the need arises. This definition can be traced back to the city-states of ancient Greece, when citizenship was the privilege of male property-owning warriors who had been born in the city-state, and excluded many people, including women, slaves, children, craftsmen, merchants, and people who were not born locally.

There are different ways of thinking about citizenship. One is to think of it as a legal and social status available to those who satisfy certain criteria. Viewed in this manner, people can be citizens if at least one of their parents (or in some cases an ancestor) is a citizen, a principle termed **jus sanguinis**, or if they were born within the boundaries of the state, a principle termed **jus soli**. Jus soli citizenship is common in North and South America, while jus sanguinis laws apply in most of the rest of the world. Sometimes scholars add a third category, **jus domicilii**, to refer to people being eligible for citizenship in a country on the basis of permanent residence.

In practice, however, the rights and duties of citizenship are distributed unevenly. For example, most middle-class white citizens in Europe and the Americas are confident that the police can be entrusted to keep the peace and look after law-abiding people and their property. But for members of racial or ethnic minorities, the police are often a repressive institution that will enact violence upon them for little or no reason. At different times and in different places, institutions have provided a legal basis for the marginalization of certain kinds of citizens. Examples of such discriminatory practices abound, including examples like Nazi Germany's requirement that Jews wear a star of David and Jim Crow segregation laws in force in the southern United States until the Civil Rights era. Discriminatory practices persist in many countries today, sometimes in subtle form. Palestinian citizens of Israel, who descend from survivors of the massacres and expulsions perpetrated by Jewish immigrants at the founding of Israel in 1948, may have in principle full citizenship rights, yet they are exempt from compulsory military service, while many desirable educational and employment opportunities require applicants to have completed military service.

These situations suggest that citizenship is not a status but a practice, namely the outcome of actions, be they by the state, as the previous examples illustrate, or by citizens themselves. People act as citizens by paying taxes, obeying laws, serving in the military, attending meetings, volunteering for causes, taking part in protests, or simply nurturing relationships with neighbours. Some of these acts, like participating in protests, are explicitly political, while others, like staying out of trouble, look like simple surviving strategies but ultimately have consequences for one's participation in the nation-state as a citizen. Citizenship as status and citizenship as practice do not always overlap: one can pay taxes and serve in the military in a country without having formal citizenship status. One can thus think of citizenship as made up of all the ways in which people encounter the state in different contexts and on different scales. In daily life, some acts are more consequential than others (González and Sigona 2017).

Citizenship has had different meanings at different times in history and in different locations, but it has always had the effect of both including some people and excluding others. For example, the end of the twentieth and the beginning of the twenty-first century have been marked by increased restrictions on poor people's attempts to cross national borders in search of a better life. Citizenship becomes a particularly salient problem for them, particularly **undocumented migrants**, people whose official documentation is not recognized by authorities as allowing them to reside in the country where they live. Minor encounters with the state, such as being fined for parking illegally, can result in deportation, which have the result of splitting families up, causing economic hardship, and ruining lives.

Undocumented families hoping to legalize their status cling to fragments of hope, as they deal with capricious immigration bureaucracies and legislation that can change at the whim of politicians. In California, undocumented Latinos feverishly collect official documents, such as school identification cards, tax returns, and medical records, to demonstrate to the authorities that they have been in the country for a long time as law-abiding residents (Abarca and Coutin 2018). Bureaucracies' obsession with documents becomes their own, as they affirm '*los papeles hablan*', 'papers speak'. Even though they may have lived many years in the country, contributed to its economy, and participated in civil life, they remain vulnerable to exploitation and discrimination, against which they have no legal recourse, and they live in constant fear of being

Box 12.1   Black Lives Matter, social media, and citizenship

One of the most visible social movements to dominate the global **public sphere** in the 2010s is Black Lives Matter (BLM). It originated in 2013 as a grassroots decentralized movement on social media with the hashtag #BlackLivesMatter, following the acquittal of George Zimmerman, who shot and killed unarmed black teenager Trayvon Martin in Florida because he thought he did not belong in the neighbourhood where he was walking. Repeated instances of violence perpetrated with impunity by police officers on black people throughout the United States gave it momentum, often because bystanders were able to film them with their mobile phones. A point of high tension was the acquittal in 2014 of a policeman who killed another teenager in Ferguson, Missouri. The hashtag #Ferguson quickly spread on social media and protesters flocked to Ferguson and staged demonstrations (Bonilla and Rosa 2015). Social media played multiple roles: amplifying the protests and the anger that motivated them, enabling people to participate while not being physically there, and associating racist violence with other forms of violence around the world. Social media provided an 'eventfulness' to the events that would not have been possible with traditional media coverage and added an important dimension to acts of citizenship.

But social media has other effects. While there was nothing new about police violence against racial minorities in the United States and beyond, the presidency of Donald Trump, a frenetic Twitter user, from 2016 to 2020 had a particularly aggravating effect on racial tensions in the United States, as he repeatedly tweeted or retweeted criticisms of BLM protests and tacitly supported white supremacists who staged counter-protests.

Black people in rural areas of the United States are less commonly victims of race-based physical violence than black people in cities, but still routinely have to deal with racial discrimination in their daily lives. In a small and relatively poor area in rural Tennessee, for example, where church is an important focus of people's lives, the BLM movement has inspired church leaders, particularly prominent women, to organize prayer meetings and workshops to place racism at the forefront of the local public sphere (Henderson and Louis 2017). While this mobilization is motivated by the same events as the urban BLM movement, it is couched in Christian and socially conservative terms that differ from those of BLM, eschewing **intersectional** questions of gender and social-class discrimination.

What is novel to our times is how social media have enabled the BLM movement to spread to other nation-states of the world, where the targets of racism may differ but the effects remain the same. Britain has a large population whose ancestors migrated from across the colonial empire, such as South Asia, Africa, and the Caribbean. In France, racism principally targets people of Maghrebi, West and Central African, and Caribbean origins. Racists in the Netherlands and Germany target descendants of Moroccan and Turkish migrants. The globalization of BLM demonstrates how acts of citizenship can emanate from one national context and take different forms as they spread globally.

deported. The problem they face is that they can fulfill the duties of a citizen, such as paying taxes, but they benefit from none of the rights.

These are the paradoxes that have prompted some groups of undocumented migrants to mobilize politically. For example, in France in the mid-1990s, a group that called itself the *Sans-Papiers* ('without papers') claimed that their ongoing contributions to French society entitled them to citizenship (McNevin 2006). Many had moved to France legally but had become *sans-papiers* because immigration laws had changed. A similar logic underlies the activism of the 'Dreamers' in the United States, children who immigrated with their undocumented parents and have spent their entire lives in the country, but find themselves threatened with deportation to their parents' country of origin, to which they have no connection. While they can attend primary and secondary school, they are prevented from getting a university education because they are ineligible for financial aid (Martínez, Muñoz, Nuñez-Janes, Pavey, Rodríguez, and Saavedra 2020). While well-meaning politicians depict the brightest among them as model citizens who 'deserve' legal status, ultimately their struggles are no different from those of other undocumented migrants.

These movements question the logic according to which the state assigns citizenship to some and denies it to others. While the orthodox view sees citizenship as something that has gradually been expanded in the course of history to previously excluded categories like women, non-landholders, and racial minorities, these movements demonstrate that laws about citizenship continue to exclude some people from the nation.

Minorities and majorities: ethnicity, Indigeneity, and autochthony

While nationalism is based on the imagination of a community of equals, people within the nation find all kinds of ways in practice of accentuating differences among themselves. One of these is **ethnicity**, a form of identification based on the ideology of a common history and common social and cultural practices, which may include language, religion, social conventions, kinship, and ways of organizing daily life. Conceptually, an ethnic group differs from a nation, in that it is defined in contrast to a larger whole, usually the identity of a national majority or that of other ethnic groups within the nation-state. Thus ethnicity only emerges in the context of a nation-state. Ethnicity also differs from **race**, in that the physical features of members of an ethnic group do not necessarily distinguish them from members of the majority. In addition, an ethnic group can be racially diverse: Latinas and Latinos in the United States officially form an ethnic category, but they are racially diverse.

Ethnicity may be the basis of political claims to nationhood, as is the case of the Kurds, the Catalans, or the Uighurs. Terrible wars have been fought in the name of ethnic identity, such as the Biafran war of independence in the 1970s, the wars that led to the independence of Eritrea and South Sudan in 1993 and 2011, respectively, and the various wars that marked the breakup of Yugoslavia in 1991–92. In all cases, however, ethnic struggles are embroiled with other factors, particularly the control of resources.

Ethnicity has different manifestations. For example, in **settler colonial** nations like the United States and Australia, where all inhabitants other than Indigenous people trace their ancestry to immigrants (voluntary or forced), ethnicity has different meanings according to the circumstances. For example, Irish Americans may wear green during St Patrick's Day celebrations, but being of Irish descent has little meaning otherwise. This is what sociologist Herbert Gans (1979) called 'symbolic ethnicity'. In contrast, being Latina or Latino means potentially being exposed to discrimination, which makes ethnicity more consequential. Religious convictions can form the basis upon which an ethnic group emphasizes its distinction. Such is the case of Orthodox Hasidic Jews in New York City, who see themselves as morally superior to the society in which they are embedded. They strive to create a religious modernity that contrasts with the secularism around them but that also engages with it through religious practices, as well as dress, body comportment, the use of Yiddish, and other markers of difference (Fader 2009).

Ethnicity is as much about showcasing the internal commonality of the group as about establishing difference with others. This important insight was the aim of a landmark work by Norwegian anthropologist Fredrik Barth (1998), who had conducted fieldwork in the Swat Valley of Northern Pakistan, where ethnic affiliation plays a central role in how people identify. They constantly emphasize their difference from other groups and hold negative stereotypes of them. Barth proposed that ethnicity is constructed through interactions with others and is an ongoing process of difference making. This is why the school of thought of which Barth was a founder is called **transactionalism**, a term that emphasizes that culture emerges from the interpersonal interactions in which people engage.

Another form of identification is **Indigeneity**, a status based on an ancestral belonging to the land and self-identification as a minority with distinct customary social, cultural, and political institutions. Indigenous groups generally live in settler colonial states, surrounded by members of a majority descended from immigrants who colonized their lands. Examples are Native Americans in the United States, First Nations in Canada, Māori people in New Zealand, Aboriginal people in Australia, Native Hawaiians in Hawaii, Amerindian groups in Amazonia, and Siberian peoples in Russia. Indigenous peoples have often endured histories of displacement, massacres, land confiscation, treaties that were subsequently violated, and other forms of economic, political, and cultural violence. In some cases, the colonizers' violence was so systematic that the groups simply died out, victims of genocides and newly imported diseases and poverty, as in the case of the Beothuk of Newfoundland. In other cases, Indigenous groups inhabit areas that have been occupied by the dominant majority for a considerable time and thus cannot be considered to be a settler colony, such is the case of the Orang Asli of Malaysia, the Ainu of Northern Japan, and the so-called 'scheduled tribes' of India. Many Indigenous groups around the world suffer from poverty, addiction, unemployment, and poor health.

Inspired by the civil rights movement of the 1960s, many Indigenous groups have mobilized politically to reclaim the resources that had been taken away from them. Some groups have done better than others. For example, the government of New Zealand in 1975 established a tribunal to examine Māori claims on property that was supposed to have been protected under the 1840 Treaty of Waitangi signed by the British Crown and Māori chiefs. The tribunal has ordered the restitution of land and other resources to Māori tribes. In the United States, where Native American reservations are not subject to the laws of the state and local jurisdictions in which they are located (but they are subject to federal laws), some tribes have established since the 1970s lucrative casinos and other gambling establishments, which in many states are otherwise prohibited (Cattelino 2008). Tribes that were until then mired in poverty became wealthy, funding social services, medical services, and cultural projects, and redistributing the earnings from gambling among their registered members. Nevertheless, these developments have also given rise to new patterns of inequality, as some are able to benefit from these resources better than others.

Some Indigenous peoples, such as Native American nations, Hawaiians, and Aboriginal Australians, consider the state in which they are legally embedded fraudulent because it has systematically violated the sovereignty of their groups or has disrespected historical commitments. Anthropologist Audra Simpson (2014), a member of the Kahnawà:ke Mohawk Nation,

Box 12.2   Language endangerment and language revitalization

About 5 to 6,000 languages are spoken in the world today. However, they are unevenly distributed: while 20 languages are the mother tongue of 50% of the world's population, most other languages have fewer than 10,000 speakers. Linguists estimate that about half of these languages will have disappeared by the end of the twenty-first century because they are not being transmitted to younger generations. In Australia, when Europeans began colonizing the country at the end of the eighteenth century, Aboriginal inhabitants spoke 250 different languages; two centuries of colonialism later, only about half have survived. While many languages have become extinct in the past, **endangered languages** are disappearing today at an unprecedented rate, particularly in Australia, the Pacific Islands, South and Southeast Asia, Siberia, and the Americas.

Indigenous languages are over-represented among endangered languages because many Indigenous peoples have endured colonial rule, dispossession, and genocide, and are today often economically disadvantaged and socially marginalized. In North America and Australia, Indigenous children throughout the twentieth century were sent to boarding schools where they were punished for speaking their native languages. In their attempts to survive in a hostile world, Indigenous people have moved to cities or married **exogamously**, which has accelerated the disappearance of Indigenous languages. Just as television and the Internet can encourage children to learn world languages like English and Spanish, it can also dissuade them from speaking their own language.

Efforts to reverse the disappearance of endangered languages are part of a growing global trend of **language revitalization**. It began at the end of the twentieth century, as scholars and others realized that, when a language disappears, an entire body of knowledge also disappears (Nettle and Romaine 2000). In addition, Indigenous peoples around the world see the revitalization of the language of their heritage as an essential aspect of reclaiming an identity to which colonialism has caused so much harm.

However, language revitalization efforts are always complicated. Even in the best of circumstances, learning or relearning a language requires time and resources, and when people are struggling with economic and social problems, it may not be their first priority. Linguists are often involved in revitalization programmes, but even when the scholars come with the best of intentions, Indigenous people may consider them to be yet another form of colonial intrusion into their lives.

Revitalization programmes can become embroiled in community conflicts about unrelated matters. Where different dialects of the same language are spoken, revitalization efforts generally focus on the dialect that is deemed to be the standard form and the revitalization programme may have the unintended effect of making speakers of other dialects feel that what they speak is an inferior form. Revitalization programmes sometimes focus on what some people consider the 'authentic' form of the language, which may be different from what people use on a daily basis; this is akin to assuming that Shakespeare's English is 'authentic' English. Literacy presents its own problems, as there may be different ways of representing the sounds of a language that has previously not been written or used in writing only for limited purposes; each may have different histories and associations, and people may not agree on the best orthography.

In short, revitalizing endangered languages in Indigenous contexts is an important endeavour, but one that calls for caution.

which extends across the national border between Canada and the United States, writes that some of her compatriots adopt a 'politics of refusal' to engage with the terms of citizenship defined by the state in power. Refusal is distinct from **resistance**, in that the latter is a political action that attempts to fight back against power according to the terms set by power; refusal, in contrast, ignores these terms. She tells the story of a Kahnawà:ke lacrosse team that attempted to travel to the United Kingdom for the World Lacrosse Championship in 2010. (The Mohawk invented lacrosse.) Rather than state-sanctioned passports, they brought with them tribal identification documents and copious evidence of the historical treaties that their forefathers signed with the British Crown, which have been violated by Canada. They were allowed to leave the United States but the United Kingdom refused to let them in.

Indigenous activism is not without pitfalls. In the same way that ethnicity is constructed in the interaction of ethnic groups with others, Indigeneity is the product of a mutual construction that can involve local, state-level, and global agents, but Indigenous politics can also be derailed by this multiplicity of stakeholders. Indigenous Amazonians, for example, continue to be explicitly threatened by the encroachment of the state and the market seeking to build dams, dump radioactive waste on their territory, or exploit its natural resources.

In Amazonia, the Kayapó and the Xavante, who number between 10,000 and 15,000 people, were once encouraged by missionaries and other agents to become 'civilized' and stop wearing their culturally distinctive paints, feathers, earrings, and headdresses. In the 1980s, as they began to protest the encroachments on their land by the state and corporations, they began wearing these adornments for public events like political protests and courtroom appearances (Conklin 1997). The symbolic markers they chose to revive helped them gain the support of global environmentalist movements and celebrities, who held romanticized images of them as natural guardians of an endangered ecosystem. The groups were careful to wear adornments that reflected these images and to put aside others, such as jaguar-tooth necklaces, that they had worn in the past but which could undermine their image as conservationists. But this strategy backfired, as unsympathetic media disseminated photos of individuals wearing ordinary shorts and t-shirts in their home environments, thus claiming that they were not 'real' Indians. When the legitimacy of cultural identity is determined by others, those for whom this cultural identity represents one of the few political tools at their disposal are particularly vulnerable.

A different way of making political claims rests on the concept of **autochthony**. This concept refers to being born in the land in which one resides, and it goes back in history to ancient Greece. Autochthony is the opposite of **allochthony**, the identification of a person as a recent arrival. The difference between autochthony and Indigeneity is that the former is a claim to political power, while the latter is a claim of resistance against the power of the majority or a refusal of this power (although a few groups claim both Indigenous and autochthonous status).

As Dutch anthropologist Peter Geschiere (2009) demonstrates, these concepts have gained prominence in vastly different contexts in the context of struggles over who belongs to the nation. In the Netherlands, for example, starting in the 1960s, the country invited 'guest workers' from Morocco and Turkey to fill gaps in the lower rungs of the labour market. While they were expected to stay only as long as their labour contracts lasted, they predictably remained in the country and now their descendants constitute ethnic minorities that comprise 4.5% of the population. In the 1980s, the terms 'autochthone' and 'allochthone' gained currency as euphemisms for 'native' and 'immigrant', but they remained bureaucratic terms and today mainstream Dutch people still continue to refer to members of the ethnic minority as 'Moroccans' and 'Turks', even though they are Dutch citizens, often speak only Dutch and English, and many do not practise Islam.

What is interesting is that similar dynamics are at play in a very different part of the world. In Côte d'Ivoire, Cameroon, Congo, and South Africa, violence has periodically erupted since the 1990s targeting people from rural areas of the country or neighbouring countries, who may have long settled in the more desirable regions of the country but have been redefined as 'immigrants' and blamed for all the ills of society, from violence to labour and housing shortages. These events are often embroiled with rivalries between political parties and tensions over the control of resources. While Western commentators often dismissively describe these conflicts in Africa as 'tribal', they are in fact similar to the political tensions over immigrants and their descendants in Europe.

State, nation, and citizenship as forms of organization

Even though the state, the nation, and citizenship are relatively recent concepts, they dominate the lives of virtually everyone in the contemporary world. Few people today live outside the reach of the state, as most have to pay taxes, carry identification documents, and abide by national laws. However, in situations where the state has little control over people, they may find ways of evading unwanted state intrusion into their lives. Nations are a mode of belonging held together by nationalism, as people emphasize their commonalities and gloss over their differences, but nationalism is also a matter of excluding certain types of people that those in power deem deficient. Citizenship is a legal set of conditions that are constructed in the encounter between state institutions and the person. Because the state is complex and its various manifestations produce different and sometimes contradictory regimes, for many people citizenship is contingent on the criteria that state institutions apply in determining their rights.

There are many ways other than the nation through which people can forge a sense of belonging to a larger unit. One is ethnicity, grounded in a sense of commonality within a nation that is distinct from a political or numerical majority. Indigenous groups assert their distinct identity on the basis of being the original inhabitants of a territory, and in settler colonial societies some challenge the legitimacy of a state that they deem illegal. Increased mobility since the twentieth century has raised new questions about belonging and new forms of politicized nationalism that favour the strengthening of national borders and assertions of autochthony that question other people's right to live and belong. For the same reasons, these movements often oppose the nation-state's participation in supra-national bodies such as the European Union and the United Nations.

Some commentators have argued that international bodies such as the European Union and the United Nations, as well as globalization and neoliberalism, have undermined the authority of the state. It is true that states have had to ensure that their laws conform to supranational bodies, sometimes to good effect, as in the case of European Union member states having to eliminate discriminatory laws against minorities. At the same time, states have strengthened their control over who crosses borders, as we will see in the next chapter, and continue to exert considerable power to strengthen the market, for example, in the form of tax breaks and other favourable conditions for transnational corporations and wealthy individuals. The state is thus far from being a thing of the past.

Key thinkers mentioned in this chapter:

Benedict Anderson; Fredrik Barth; Ernest Gellner; George Mosse; James Scott; Max Weber

Key terms mentioned in this chapter (see Glossary):

Autochthony; Allochthony; Citizenship; Ethnicity; Gift economy; Indigeneity; Invented tradition; Nation; Nationalism; Nation-state; Race; Settler colonial states; State; Transactionalism

Questions for Discussion/Review:

1   How can the state and the nation be distinguished?
2   In what ways are communities 'imagined'?
3   Explain why nationalism is always, in part, based on the exclusion of part of the citizenry.
4   Outline some of the complexities involved in understanding what citizenship entails.

Chapter 13

Mobility and transnationalism

People have always journeyed from one place to another for many reasons. Migrants and transnationals, people who move from one country to another but retain ties with their country of origin, are just two types of persons who move. Refugees, expatriates, cosmopolitans and tourists are some others, each with particular outlooks on and experiences of mobility. While those from the Global North may migrate, sometimes temporarily, to enjoy life and work in a new country, others such as asylum seekers, may find barriers, both physical and bureaucratic, impede their journeys. Somewhere between the categories of the privileged expatriate and the refugee are the hundreds of thousands of workers from the Global South who migrate to work in mostly low-paid jobs to support their families. Migration is today a topic of intense political debate, often linked to issues of economic and political security and cultural integrity.

The Circassians, who call themselves Adyghe, are a people whose original homeland was in the northeast of the Caucasus Mountains. They tend to be fair skinned, with light hair and eyes. Many converted to Islam in the fifteenth century. Their territory was invaded by the Russian Empire and between 1763 and 1864, 90% of them were killed. Survivors were exiled to regions of the Ottoman Empire that are today parts of Turkey, Jordan, and Israel (Shami 2000). It is estimated that one in seven Circassians now lives outside the Caucasus region, spread across 50 countries.

In some countries where the Circassians have settled, they have been allowed to preserve their language and culture, while in others there have been coordinated efforts to **assimilate** them into the broader population to promote the modern fiction of a single national identity. For example, in Jordan, members of the 90,000-strong Circassian community speak both Circassian and Arabic, are supporters of the Jordanian monarchy, and many are politically opposed to the state of Israel. In contrast, Circassians in Israel, who number about 4,000, speak Hebrew, generally support the Jewish state, and serve in the military. However, they also promote their own language and are permitted to fly their own flag. They are **endogamous** and have tailored their education system to resist assimilation into either the Jewish majority or the Palestinian minority. But as Muslims they are the object of discrimination, although not as severe as that which Israeli Palestinians experience because they can 'pass' easily in a country where the majority is of European descent.

Since 1989, partly as a consequence of the end of the Cold War and later the spread of the Internet, there has been a growth of Circassian **nationalism**. The Circassian **diaspora** has lobbied to have the killings by Russians in the nineteenth century officially recognized as a **genocide**. Circassians have also strategically used global events such as the 2014 winter Olympic Games in Sochi to draw attention to their cause. Sochi is symbolically important for Circassians as it was the port from which they were deported, it is named after a Circassian ethnic subgroup, the Shache, and it was the last capital of independent Circassia (Zhemukhov 2012) (Figure 13.1).

DOI: 10.4324/9781315737805-13

Figure 13.1 Circassians living in Turkey gather in front of the Russian Consulate in Istanbul on 2 February 2014 to protest against the 2014 Sochi Winter Olympics. (Courtesy of Sedat Suna/EPA/Shutterstock)

Circassian activists seek to promote an image of Circassians dispersed around the world as a **transnational** community by foregrounding their cultural heritage and ties to the ancestral homeland. But many Circassians who have integrated into the societies in which they live do not share this position: they take part in ritual events only occasionally, eat Circassian food only on special occasions, and no longer speak Circassian. Transnational activists essentialize Circassian culture as frozen in time, constructing a sense of community from an idealized notion of what it means to be Circassian. This idealization is thus a mix of memory, nostalgia, and practice, and is quite different from how Circassians who remain in the ancestral homeland construct their lives today. When some Circassians visit this homeland, they are disappointed by what they see as modern Caucasus Circassians' lack of modesty, loose sexual practices, and assimilation into mainstream Russian society.

Migration past and present

Circassian history illustrates how the mass movements of human beings have often been enmeshed in histories of genocide, forced exile, and ethnic and religious persecution. The Circassian case is unfortunately all too common an experience for many minority groups in the colonial and modern eras. But it is also the case that from the time our human ancestors began their long walk out of Africa and across the globe over 60,000 years ago, humans have always been on the move. Our scientific understanding of prehistoric migrations is changing rapidly as new findings and recent research have revealed that different populations of early humans migrated from Africa at different times. When they encountered each other again, they inter-bred. For example, modern Europeans have up to 2% DNA from Neanderthals, an extinct population that lived in Europe and Asia. Our human ancestors took many different routes as they journeyed to make their new homes in every inhabitable place on earth. One such route connects modern Melanesians in the western Pacific with an extinct human group that lived

40,000 years ago, whose remains, consisting of two teeth and one finger bone, have been found in Siberia and are referred to as the Denisovians (Stringer 2012).

As human beings settled in different locations, they altered their environments, sometimes depleting natural resources and creating environmental pressures that made it impossible to survive, compelling them to move. Social, political and economic factors such as population growth, war, and famine have also motivated humans to migrate. Humans today migrate for reasons similar to those of their ancestors throughout prehistory and history.

Over time, humans have developed increasingly powerful technological means of extracting resources, aggravating the problems that these activities cause to an unprecedented extent and creating new global inequalities. In the current geological age that some refer to as the **Anthropocene**, human activity has been the dominant cause of climate change, altering weather patterns and ecological systems on earth. While humans have always migrated, today they migrate in a different context from the past, across a world that is densely populated and burdened with environmental, political, and social problems.

Mobility, migration, and transnationalism

Humans migrate for many different reasons: some move on a temporary basis while others move permanently to a different location; some move because they want to and others because they have to; for some social groups, mobility is part of life while for others it is exceptional. All these forms of movement can be described with the umbrella term **mobility**. Economic migrants, migrant retirees, asylum seekers, indentured labourers, refugees, political exiles, guest workers, tourists, reporters, globe-trotting celebrities, business people, exchange students, diplomats, and airline crew members are all examples of people who move. **Migration**, namely mobility of a more or less permanent nature motivated by education, work, marriage, the desire for a better life or to escape unfavourable circumstances, constitutes one type of mobility. Many forms of migration are the direct result of centuries of **colonialism**, which has created lasting global inequalities, even though most colonies around the world have gained independence. Some aspects of migration are shared by other kinds of mobilities, but not all: for example, tourists are mobile but only for a bounded period of time at the end of which they return home, while refugees and asylum seekers migrate against their will and may never be able to return home.

Across the world, people have been migrating from rural to urban areas in increasing numbers. The deregulation of international markets for commodities like food has made it difficult for peasants and small-scale farmers to compete with the economic and technological power of large agricultural corporations. Disasters like floods and droughts, as well as dispossession of land by developers, drive rural people away from their land. Socio-economic inequalities between rural and urban areas are increasing everywhere. In 2008, for the first time in history, more than half of humanity lived in cities.

In China, it is estimated that close to 300 million people have moved from the countryside to cities since the 1980s, history's biggest-ever population shift from countryside to city. Yet the state has made these migrations illegal by instituting a registration system called *hukou* that regulates, in theory, where individuals can live, but in practice does not prevent people from migrating (Xiang 2005). A *hukou* that authorizes one to live in cities, particularly in desirable neighbourhoods, is only available to people who can prove that they are employed there and that they have a steady income. The *hukou* system has contributed to creating some of the most extreme social inequalities in the country.

These restrictions have created a large 'floating population' of poor people who eke out a living in sub-standard housing on the margins of cities and often go back-and-forth between their urban dwellings and their villages of origin, where their elderly relatives have remained. Because they migrate illegally, they cannot access healthcare, education, housing, and other social services. Some engage in petty trade, such as selling goods on the side of the road or renting rooms to new migrants. Others work in construction, rubbish collection, and domestic work. Yet others join the ranks of the throngs of workers labouring in factories, which depend on their labour, which is cheap, unregulated, and unprotected. Permanent city dwellers view these migrants with suspicion and disdain, and tensions frequently arise between these groups. Migrants nevertheless manage to form communities of sorts in the cities, for example by setting up unofficial schools that cater to children of families not allowed to send their children to city state schools because they lack the proper *hukou*.

Many factory workers are young women who migrate from villages in hope of putting some distance between themselves and the potentially oppressive patriarchal structure of their rural communities; they support their families through **remittances**, but find themselves overworked and exploited (Pun 2005). Others become karaoke bar hostesses; they are paid to entertain male customers and generally expected to have sex with them (Zheng 2009). Yet this occupation has some advantages over factory work, in that the hostesses can claim at least some dignity by wearing fashionable clothes and thus undermining urban stereotypes of rural migrants as poorly dressed ruffians. Their glamorous looks and much greater consumption power mark them as superior to migrant factory workers. Rural to urban migrations in China have therefore created new patterns of inequalities as well as new social aspirations.

The second part of the nineteenth century and the early twentieth century were marked by large-scale worldwide migrations. The potato famine in Ireland forced almost two million people to move to the United States in the 1840s and 1850s. Millions of Europeans sought a better life in North and South America; for example, 1.3 million Swedes migrated for reasons that ranged from rural poverty to religious repression. Likewise, millions of Italians, Germans, and East Europeans moved across the Atlantic, fleeing poverty and violence in their home countries and attracted by the economic opportunities. Yet, while the United States saw itself as a country of immigration in the early twentieth century, it did not welcome all immigrants: in 1924, Congress passed an Immigration Act, which prevented people from Asia from immigrating and set quotas for Southern and Eastern European immigrants. After World War I, Turkey and Greece 'exchanged' 1.6 million people and at the Partition of India and Pakistan in 1947, between 10 and 12 million people were forced to move because their religion in the new nation in which they found themselves was no longer that of the majority and they feared persecution.

However, the boundary between voluntary and involuntary migration is blurred. In the Philippines, for example, jobs are scarce and many people since the 1970s have migrated voluntarily to the Middle East, East Asia, North America, Australia, and other parts of the world to seek employment as manual workers, domestic workers, and healthcare professionals. In 2015, the United Nations estimated that there were 5.3 million temporary, irregular, or permanent Filipino migrants around the world, representing 5.3% of the country's population (Organisation for Economic Cooperation and Development 2017). The remittances they sent back home to support their families and communities amounted to US$30 billion, some 14% of the country's GDP. The government has hailed Filipino migrant workers as the 'new national heroes'. But critics have argued that, far from being heroes, they are victims of the global capitalist economy and have criticized their exploitation by their government, which relies on labour migration instead of focusing on developing the national economy.

In Hong Kong, there were more than 100,000 Filipina temporary migrant domestic workers in the early 1990s, a figure that has since doubled. Some are integrated into the lives of the families they cook and clean for, sharing in family birthday celebrations, receiving gifts from them, and even going on foreign holidays with them (Constable 2007). Others talk of being shouted at, constantly criticized, denied free time, and forced to submit to rigid work schedules. Dealing with employers is not the only issue Filipina domestic workers have faced: the Philippine government has tried to impose customs taxes and controls on their employment opportunities and even on what they can do with their earnings. For example, in the early 1980s, it introduced a policy of mandatory remittances, forcing workers to send 50% of their earnings back to the Philippines. In response, domestic worker groups in Hong Kong united to protest, arguing that they wanted to send remittances on their own terms, and by 1985 the order was officially lifted.

The lives of Filipina domestic workers in Hong Kong illustrate what migration scholars have termed **transnationalism**, namely the simultaneous organization of social, economic, and political relations in different locations (Basch, Glick Schiller, and Szanton Blanc 1994). Some migrants negotiate their place in the host country and their social relations with their employers, other local people, and fellow migrants, while at the same time they nurture close relations with family members, friends, and neighbours in their country of origin through remittances, regular phone calls, and participation in community, regional, and national politics. In other words, transnationalism captures the fact that migrants who settle in a new place, whether temporarily or permanently, maintain contacts with their society of origin and sometimes with other places where fellow migrants have settled. But not all migrants lead transnational lives; some experience a clear break with their past lives in their country of origin and integrate into the host society, learning the dominant language and adapting to the lifeways of the majority population. This was the case of many migrants from Europe who settled in North America in the nineteenth and twentieth centuries, who discouraged their children from speaking anything other than English and taking an interest in the societies from which they had migrated.

The extent to which migrants are inclined to feel part of their host societies depends crucially on the policies of state institutions and the attitudes of the majority population. Too often, in the contemporary world, migrants are not well treated in their host countries, particularly if they are poor and look different. Legal residence rights are difficult to obtain unless one is wealthy, privileged, and of the 'right' race. In some nation-states, immigrants never qualify for permanent residence. Such is the case of the oil-rich United Arab Emirates, where labour migrants from South and Southeast Asia, other countries of the Middle East, and many other locations outnumber citizens by a ten-to-one ratio and shoulder the bulk of the economy in sectors such as construction, the service industries, domestic work, and other sectors of low-level employment. Some remain in the country for decades, yet their presence in the country is contingent on their remaining employed, through a sponsorship system called *kalafa*. It is fertile ground for labour abuse as employers know that the migrants have little choice but to remain in their employ. There is virtually no way immigrants can apply for permanent legal residence or citizenship, and the children of immigrants may grow up in the country but only qualify to remain there as long as one of their parents is working (Figure 13.2).

Reactionary politicians frequently use the 'problem' of immigration to deflect citizens' attention away from real socio-economic problems, such as declining economies and growing inequalities, and implement sometimes draconian policies of exclusion. In the United States, the raids on workplaces, the mass incarcerations, and the separation of children from their parents that have taken place since 2016 are dramatic examples of these exclusion policies based on the demonization of migrants, many of whom have fled violent situations that are often the direct result of U.S. foreign policies.

In some countries, **integration** policies are designed to encourage or oblige immigrants to conform to the majority population by requiring them to take language or civic tests as a

Figure 13.2 Migrant workers in the Blue Valley supermarket at the checkout bagging groceries for local Emirati women, United Arab Emirates, 2016. (Courtesy of Deborah Williams)

condition for legal residence; ironically, these policies frequently have the opposite effect and work much less well than policies based on **multiculturalism**, namely the legal recognition and appreciation of social and cultural diversity in a country.

One country where integration figures prominently in public discourse is the Netherlands. As we saw in Chapter 12, the country has a substantial ethnic minority descended from Moroccan (as well as Turkish) guest workers. Even though members of this minority have lived in the Netherlands for over half a century and are Dutch citizens, they continue to be referred to by the mainstream population as 'Moroccans' and they often encounter discrimination in education, the labour market, and other situations, much of which is fueled by **Islamophobia**. Xenophobic right-wing politicians present the 'immigrant problem' (particularly concerning young men) not as the outcome of discrimination but as evidence of their inability and unwillingness to integrate into mainstream Dutch society.

Box 13.1   The culturalization of citizenship and the complexities of intersectionality

Many Dutch people are proud of the early progressive accomplishments of their country in the realm of gender and sexuality, the Netherlands being for example the first country in the world to legalize same-sex marriage in 2001. However, reactionary political figures that lobby against immigration and the rights of Muslim Dutch minorities, such as the right to wear head scarves in public, have taken gender and sexual rights as a way of justifying their politics. They construct new immigrants from Islamic countries and Muslim minorities as sexist and homophobic and thus as threatening the 'freedoms' of Dutch society with respect to gender and sexuality. Some LGBTQ+ organizations have railed against Muslims, arguing that Islam, and therefore the ethnic minorities of Moroccan and Turkish origins, is hostile towards them. Needless to say, the reality is considerably more complex, and most Muslim Dutch are concerned by other matters than gender and sexual rights in their daily lives, such as how to evade police harassment and how to feed their families. But in a reversal from politics in most other countries, the protection of lesbians and gay men has now become a right-wing platform in the Netherlands.

In the mid-2000s, a particularly reactionary Minister of Immigration and Integration, Rita Verdonk, instituted new laws for prospective immigrants from outside the 'West', which was defined as Europe, North America, Australia, New Zealand, and, surprisingly, Japan. The prospective migrants now had to take civic and language exams as part of their application to immigrate and had to answer questions on a film that stressed that Dutch society was 'tolerant' but not particularly welcoming of newcomers (Geschiere 2009, 161–2). The film also depicted brief scenes of a topless woman on a beach and two men kissing in a field of flowers, which the immigration authorities thought would be particularly shocking to Muslims and deter them from applying for residency. In actual fact, few people from outside the Global North other than prospective spouses of Dutch nationals and highly qualified individuals qualify for permanent residence in the Netherlands.

These politics have the effect of constructing Dutch society as uniform (so that it can be depicted in a film) and the Muslim Other as culturally backwards, thereby fueling Islamophobia among mainstream Dutch people. They are an example of what has been termed the **culturalization of citizenship**, namely an understanding of citizenship as a matter of beliefs and attitudes. One upshot is the rather strange division in official statistics of migrants into Western and non-Western categories, with the Japanese classed as 'Western' while Turkish people, many of whom are physically very similar to Europeans, are 'non-Western' (2009, 150–1). One group that these conflicts leave in a precarious position are people who are both Muslim and LGBTQ+, who may find themselves excluded from acceptance by Islamophobic elements among LGBTQ+-identified Dutch people and equally unwelcome among some Muslim groups, who may see them as aligned with Islamophobia. These dilemmas exemplify what is meant by **intersectionality**, social categorizations that may result in overlapping and interdependent systems of disadvantage.

Government policies towards immigrants and popular opinion about them can sometimes be at odds with one another. Nor is popular opinion monolithic. Thus, in the summer of 2015, when over 350,000 migrants fleeing war in the Middle East and poverty in South Asia arrived in Hungary on their way to Germany, the Hungarian state deployed a discourse of crisis, depicting the migrants as criminals, and sought to stop and incarcerate them (Kallius, Monterescu, and Rajaram 2016). But many citizens in Hungary simply ignored the state's authority and groups mobilized to provide humanitarian help to the migrants. One, Migrant Aid, a large and well-organized group, offered help but kept the migrants' growing protests against the state's policies at arm's length; another, Migszol, a small grassroot organization, took an approach that showcased solidarity, joining in the protests and providing assistance to disadvantaged groups already based in Hungary, such as the homeless and the Roma, who are also discriminated against. The state and the nation, and different groups within the nation, may act in divergent ways (Figure 13.3).

While the Hungarian government's policy is an example of a state trying to keep migrants out, in other situations the state's inability to provide for its citizens forces people to leave. In some countries, people have abandoned hope of making a living at home because of dwindling economic opportunities: agriculture and fishing are no longer viable ways of making a living, education no longer delivers on its promises and labour markets in the cities have collapsed. For example, in Togo, one of the poorest countries of West Africa that became even poorer at the end of the Cold War when overseas aid dried up, everyone is trying to leave, and the United

Figure 13.3 Migrants walk from Hungary towards Austria at the beginning of what came to be known as the March of Hope, 4 September 2015. (Courtesy of Migszol Csoport)

States is the preferred destination (Piot 2010). Every year, the U.S. government runs what is informally referred to as a 'Green Card Lottery', a random drawing of applications for permanent resident status, and a large portion of Togolese have tried their luck. Even if one's application is drawn, prospective migrants have to go through stringent embassy interviews and provide official documents. A vibrant industry has emerged in Togo providing falsified documents, doctored photographs, interview coaching, and witchcraft services to meet these needs. Fictitious marriages and made-up kinship relations are alternative ways of attempting to emigrate, while Pentecostal churches, to which people flock, offer promises of prosperity and a better future.

Migrants from poor countries dream of a better future not only for themselves but also, and perhaps even more so, for the relatives they have left behind. One reason is that migrants often have to rely on relatives for help in putting together the funds to help them migrate (e.g., for airfares, visas, smugglers, settlement expenses), and thus migrants are indebted to people in their home country even before they set out. In addition, success in societies where a **gift economy** operates is not measured in terms of individual economic accumulation, but in terms of the **redistribution** of wealth, which migrants in some cases see as a duty, and not sending money would be considered deeply shameful. Remittances also ensure that the migrant will be welcome again in the home country in case things do not work out. Like gifts in a gift economy, remittances thus represent more than money: they are embedded in long-term social relations of **reciprocity** (Figure 13.4).

But problems frequently arise in the gap between migrants' precarious existence in the host country and their families' expectations in the home country. For example, many Somali

Figure 13.4 Small business in Haines City, Florida, offering services to immigrant Latinx workers including money transfers, flight booking, package mailing, bill payment, as well as photocopying, faxing, shoe repair, and beer, November 2013 (Courtesy of Ian Dagnall/Alamy)

migrants in London, who left Somalia as it descended into civil war in the late 1980s, often having spent years in refugee camps in countries bordering Somalia, eke out a living as taxi drivers, healthcare workers, security guards, and other menial workers, if they find employment at all (Lindley 2010). Their relatives in Somalia have little idea of the hardships of migrant life and assume that their migrant relatives are wealthy and should thus remit generously. They sometimes place their migrant relatives under enormous pressure, bombarding them with phone calls at strategic times of the day, which migrants sometimes choose not to answer. Migrants who struggle to make enough money to send back home or even to keep a roof over their own heads complain that their relatives think that in London 'money grows on trees', a cliché heard in migrant communities the world over. They sometimes find out to their dismay that folks back home are misspending the money they send. Among Somali migrants in London as well as migrants everywhere, remittances become the catalyst of sometimes tense negotiations over what kinship relations entail.

Refugees and asylum seekers

The examples of Filipino, Somali, and other migrants represent economic migration. In contrast, refugees migrate for different reasons. In 1951, the United Nations Refugee Convention defined **refugees** as persons who have left their country of origin because of persecution on the basis of race, religion, nationality, political opinion, or membership in a particular social group; are not protected by their home country's laws; and would risk persecution if they were to return home. Refugees may apply for **asylum** in the first safe country to which they have fled and have the right to remain there until their claim for refugee status has been decided. The convention originally applied to Europeans displaced by World War II and as a consequence of events that occurred before 1 January 1951, but in 1967, an additional protocol removed the dateline and extended these rights to non-Europeans.

Both the 1951 Convention and the 1967 Protocol exclude from the definition of a refugee people who leave their country because they are poor or those who are protected by their country's laws. Internally displaced people who have left their home but not crossed national borders do not count as refugees, even though their plight may be just as desperate. At the end of World War II, large populations in Europe were displaced and became refugees. But the world has experienced an enormous increase in the number of displaced persons in the twentieth century because of war, political repression, religious and ethnic conflict, and poverty, only some of whom are legally considered refugees. Relatively few reach the Global North and most only manage to reach a neighbouring country, which explains why the countries that hosted most refugees in the world in 2019 were Turkey, Pakistan, Uganda, and Sudan.

Countries in the Global North have set up refugee courts charged with determining whether a person's plight falls within the international definition of a refugee and therefore whether they qualify to legally remain in the host country. However, this determination takes place in a complex bureaucratic context rife with cross-cultural misunderstandings. In the United Kingdom, asylum courts handle large numbers of cases with little time to process them. They sometimes rely on the services of experts, including anthropologists who have relevant knowledge of the asylum seeker's country of origin. For example, Marzia Balzani (2011) served as an expert in the cases of Pakistani women seeking refugee status to escape forced marriage. To succeed, the women had to present their stories, in the little time they are accorded, in a way that judges will consider credible. They had to argue that they were forced into marriage and not that they simply refused to accept an arranged marriage. They also had to show that they could not have escaped the marriage by moving to another part of the country and leading independent lives in safety. The role of the anthropologist was to provide detailed background information to help the judge reach a decision.

Sometimes people whose refugee claims do not succeed are allowed to remain in the host country on humanitarian grounds. In France, for example, the state passed a law in 1998 that provided temporary legal status to people suffering from a life-threatening illness, such as AIDS, for which there was no treatment in their country of origin (Ticktin 2011). While well-meaning in principle, these humanitarian laws coexisted with brutal immigration policies. Undocumented migrants who could not prove that they qualified for refugee status were summarily imprisoned and deported. So other experts employed by the state, such as doctors, had to determine whose suffering was deserving and whose was not, and as the application of the law became increasingly restrictive in the 2000s, people whose predicaments were just as terrible as those of others but did not meet the authorities' definition of suffering were drawn to take drastic action. For example, some stopped their treatment so that they became ill enough to be deemed 'deserving', while others considered becoming infected on purpose. This created new forms of inequality based on the hierarchies of deservingness that state policies created.

Borders, walls, and barriers

Borders are territorial boundaries that divide one sovereign state from another. Border zones are spaces where people, vehicles, goods, and valuables are allowed or prevented passage from one country to another. They are regulated by the migration regimes of governments, enforced on the ground by immigration officers who have the power to deny entry to and detain anyone whom they find suspicious or undesirable, decisions they base on the documents that people carry and also often on their physical appearance.

The basic document that border crossers must carry is the passport, which as we saw in Chapter 12 first became required during World War I and was standardized in 1920, an aspect of **governmentality** through which states exercise control over citizens and non-citizens. Passports do not all have equal value: holders of passports issued by wealthy countries like Japan, South Korea, Denmark, Italy, and Luxembourg are allowed to visit 188 or 187 countries without a visa, while the holder of a passport issued by Afghanistan and Iraq is only allowed without a visa in 25 and 27 countries, respectively, even for brief visits.

Over the course of the twentieth century, border bureaucracies became increasingly complex, with the successive requirements that people apply for visas, be fingerprinted and photographed, carry passports with microchips and submit to iris and facial recognition. Some of these technologies prevent people from even getting as far as the border: applying for a visa may require accessing and filling out forms online (which assumes access to the Internet and the required know-how), paying fees, and travelling to a consulate for an interview. Borders are thus multi-layered and sort through people in multiple locations.

At the same time, borders are imposed by states as artificial divisions that cut across regions otherwise characterized by continuity and sameness. The Greek-Albanian border, for example, was closed for most of the second half of the twentieth century as Albania was a communist fortress, yet there were constant cross-border movements of traders, shepherds, workers, families, and sheep along a continuous landscape (Green 2005). Today, people who live in the region move homes across this border depending on the seasons and forge identities that transcend those imposed by the two nation-states. Borders can be porous under some circumstances just as easily as they can act as formidable barriers to movement in other circumstances.

Box 13.2 Ahmadiyya Muslims in Britain: a complex and internally differentiated migrant group

The Ahmadiyya Muslim community in Britain, numbering about 25,000 people, may appear to be a homogeneous group. Most British Ahmadis are of South Asian heritage and follow the teachings of their founder, Mirza Ghulam Ahmad, a nineteenth-century charismatic prophet from the Indian Punjab. This, however, conceals the different migration histories of subgroups within the community and the different paths they took on their journey to Britain.

Ahmadiyya Islam was founded in colonial India in 1889, in part in reaction to the aggressive proselytizing campaigns of Christian missionaries. The Ahmadis were active in spreading their faith and in 1926 inaugurated the first purpose built mosque in London, at the heart of the British colonial empire (Balzani 2020). There were few Muslims in Britain at that time and the event was so unusual that it was reported in the national press and a film of the opening, attended by British social and political leaders and foreign dignitaries, was screened across the country as an exotic curiosity.

In 1913, there were just six Ahmadis in Britain, three students and three missionaries working to convert the British. It was only in the middle of the century that single men from South Asia, including some Ahmadis, began to arrive in larger numbers, expecting to work for a few years to send remittances back to their families before returning home. Then, from the mid-1960s, as a consequence of the Africanization policies in countries such as Kenya, Ahmadis who had settled in East Africa during colonial times and had a right to enter the United Kingdom were forced to migrate. Some chose to go to India or Pakistan, countries their ancestors had left generations earlier, but many migrated to Britain, where they hoped their children would benefit from the education system. In addition, in the 1960s, women and children arrived from Pakistan to join husbands and fathers who were already settled in Britain.

In the 1970s, the Pakistan government declared Ahmadis non-Muslim and discrimination against them increased. A further blow came in 1984, when legislation was passed in Pakistan effectively criminalizing the Ahmadiyya faith. Many Ahmadis, finding themselves threatened and sometimes persecuted, sought asylum in other countries such as Britain. The spiritual head of the Ahmadiyya Muslims left Pakistan in 1984 to live in exile in London. The arrival of asylum seekers in the late twentieth century, however, was not greeted with the same positive interest by the media as the opening of the Ahmadiyya mosque had been six decades earlier.

While many Ahmadi migrants from East Africa were professionals and business people, and were fluent in English, most Ahmadi migrants who came directly from Pakistan had few qualifications and often spoke little or no English. East African Ahmadis also held more liberal ideas about women's education and employment.

What these patterns show is that the Ahmadi Muslims in Britain constitute a complex and varied group. The outwardly homogeneous community of people who share a faith conceals an internal diversity resulting from different migration histories and different experiences, outlooks, and attitudes.

States can deploy another kind of barrier beyond border checks and legal quotas in the repertoire of strategies against unwanted border crossers: the environment. In recent times, the environment has played an increasingly important role in making migration more difficult, expensive, and dangerous. Since the 1990s, tens of thousands of potential refugees have attempted to cross the Mediterranean from Africa to Europe under extremely dangerous circumstances, and many have died. The Sonoran Desert between the United States and Mexico is a dry, barren, and harsh environment. Yet it is one of the few routes left that migrants from Mexico and Central America can take to reach the United States in hope of escaping poverty and violence and finding a better life, paying human traffickers (*coyotes*) to guide them across. This is because the U.S. government's anti-immigration policy, known as Prevention Through Deterrence, now prevents migrants from crossing the border through towns. The desert has become an open grave for many migrants who do not survive the journey, dying of dehydration or hyperthermia (De León 2015). The desert erases the migrants' very existence as their bodies are eaten by animals and bones are bleached by the sun. Hundreds are now catalogued by just numbers when all that is found are skeletal remains or pieces of clothing picked up by the Tucson Samaritans, a volunteer humanitarian group based in Tucson, Arizona, as they try to bring closure to families. Terms that authorities use to refer to migrants, such as 'illegals' or 'undocumented migrants', dehumanize them and erase their diversity. Official documents have explicitly stated that this policy would lead to deaths but that these could be blamed on environmental exposure and human traffickers, rather than on the government. States can thus co-opt the environment to serve as a form of immigration control.

Borders not only control movement across national boundaries but can also be erected within national territories. The Palestinian West Bank is crisscrossed by a labyrinth of walls, checkpoints, fences, turnstiles, and other barriers that Israel has erected since the Second Intifada uprising of 2000. Israel justifies its policies by arguing that these barriers help it control Palestinian terrorism. For ordinary Palestinians, such as anthropologist Reema Hammami (2019), they represent a daily impediment to their movements to and from home, school, work, friends, and relatives. New walls and checkpoints spring up constantly: neighbours who can reach each other's homes in a few minutes at one moment are suddenly obliged to make hours-long detours through checkpoints in order to visit one another (Figure 13.5).

Controlled by young Israeli soldiers, both women and men, checkpoints in Palestine are violent settings, both physically and symbolically. Ambulances taking critically ill patients are held up, people are routinely turned back for not having the right papers, young women are commonly harassed by male soldiers (and treated with contempt by female soldiers), and Palestinians, especially young men, are often interrogated, beaten, and humiliated. Between 2000 and 2006, 68 women gave birth at checkpoints while waiting for their turn to be interrogated. Soldiers routinely separate small children from their parents, interrogating them separately.

Despite the increased sophistication of the technology that the Israeli state has implemented at checkpoints in the West Bank, such as x-ray machines and smart identification cards, decisions about Palestinians' right of movement within their own territory continues to be largely at the whim of ordinary Israeli soldiers. Thus, far from being governed by a coherent, rational, and sophisticated system, encounters at checkpoints are highly personalized, and it is their unpredictability that makes them effective tools of colonial policing, as those who are policed can never know what their fate will be.

As a matter of principle, **neoliberal** states outsource their services to businesses and border control is no exception. This has become a lucrative business for a host of corporations specializing in security, incarceration, and surveillance (Andersson 2014). For example, European

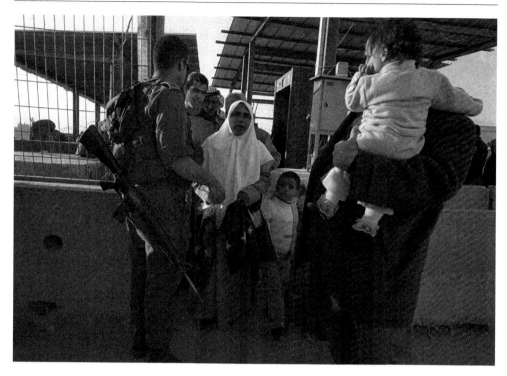

Figure 13.5 Palestinian crossing through the Qalandia Checkpoint in the Israeli-occupied West Bank. (Courtesy of Rula Halawani and Rema Hammami)

governments contract private companies as well as African governments to deter Africans from trying to migrate to Europe and to run centres for the screening of asylum seekers, a practice that the United States is also implementing on its border with Mexico. They have fuelled an 'illegality industry', businesses profiting from the plight of migrants who are reimagined as criminals.

The fortification of borders and the proliferation of walls around the world could be understood as a consolidation of the state's authority over its territory and its boundaries. But for political scientist Wendy Brown (2014), on the contrary, it demonstrates the diminished power of the state relative to global forces. While efforts by the states to regulate migration flows are legitimate, the strategies they have put in place not only fail to achieve their objectives, but they also cause untold suffering to migrants. And for those who do make it to a country where they can seek asylum, the struggle is far from over.

Cosmopolitans, expatriates, and third culture kids

Cosmopolitanism is a perspective on the world that recognizes that all human beings, regardless of their race, nationality, religious, or political orientation share a common humanity and find value in human diversity and commonality. The articulation of cosmopolitanism goes back to the ancient Greeks and others in antiquity. When asked where he came from, Greek philosopher Diogenes (4th century BCE) replied, 'I am a *kosmopolitês*', namely a citizen of the world. But the globalization that the world has experienced since the late twentieth century has made it possible for an increasing number of people to affiliate with this way of being in the world. What philosopher Martha Nussbaum (2019) calls 'world citizens' are people who see themselves as inhabiting a heterogeneous world, feel comfortable in different cultural contexts, cultivate social relations with people of different origins, and are self-critical about their own assumptions.

Cosmopolitans can base their outlooks on life on different criteria, as Swedish anthropologist Ulf Hannerz (1996) has argued. Consumption, for example, can be the basis of cosmopolitanism, as people are keen to experience different cuisines, travels, and experiences. This kind of cosmopolitanism is primarily associated with those who can afford to welcome diversity, but also who want to do so on their own terms. Thus they may appreciate difference, but they are likely to object if their neighbours keep a sheep on the balcony in anticipation of a religious feast. Alternatively, cosmopolitanism can be based on a political engagement with the problems of the world, including climate change, conflict, and the rise of new forms of nationalism (Figure 13.6).

Cosmopolitanism is also found among people who are not privileged: migrants who find themselves surrounded by people of different origins, speaking a multitude of languages, and engaging in diverse cultural practices, often develop a sense of solidarity with those who are struggling like them to make a living in a country that is not their own. Places can also be cosmopolitan: the huge building complex in Kowloon, Hong Kong, that goes by the name

Figure 13.6 The commodification of cosmopolitanism: the Villaggio shopping mall in Doha, Qatar, in 2019, juxtaposing a replica of a Venetian gondola with high-end American and European luxury brand shops in an oil-rich desert nation-state. (Courtesy of Susan Brownell)

Figure 13.7 Chungking Mansions is a huge building in Kowloon, Hong Kong, that houses a large number of retail businesses, guest houses, restaurants, and residences, which cater to traders and visitors from all over the world. (Courtesy of Gordon Mathews)

Chungking Mansions is a labyrinth of small shops, low-cost hotels, restaurants, bars, and other businesses run by and catering to people from a multitude of countries (Mathews 2011). It is estimated that 70% of all mobile phones in Africa have passed through the building (Figure 13.7).

In contrast, **expatriates**, a term that literally means those who live outside their native country, travel the world for employment and new experiences but remain within enclaves of people of similar backgrounds and outlooks as themselves. Unlike immigrants who move to a different country to live permanently, expatriates often move from country to country, spending a few years in each. They generally do not learn local languages, they have limited experience of the host countries, and they avoid developing sustained social relations with the local inhabitants. A subcategory are people who practise **flexible citizenship** (Ong 1999), which enables them to reap the benefits of residency or citizenship in multiple countries while minimizing the responsibilities of citizenship. Typical of this privileged class are finance workers, entrepreneurs, managers, and technocrats, who have resources (e.g., qualifications, wealth, networks) that they can market in different contexts. These resources enable them to choose where to live, where to exercise their profession, and where to locate their spouses and children. The citizenship strategies of these flexible citizens are not based on political participation but on the logic of flexible accumulation, namely the strategic manipulation of technologies and other resources to maximize the acquisition of capital. Some countries raise much needed funds by offering citizenship to anyone able to pay a fee or invest in the country. These schemes often attract wealthy tax dodgers, money launderers, and other shady types, and they have the potential effect of down-grading the value of the country's citizenship because other countries become suspicious of all bearers of the country's passport. In host countries, the stereotype of the wealthy Chinese busi-nessmen who 'commute' between Hong Kong and Sydney, Vancouver, or Silicon Valley, where their 'astronaut families' live and attend school, has been the object of populist resentment.

One group of people for whom the idea of home is a complex idea are the children of cos-mopolitans, expatriates, diplomats, and other mobile parents who grow up as **third culture kids** (TCKs), spending developmental years outside their parents' countries of origin, which may already be diverse (Benjamin and Dervin 2015). TCKs recognize a 'home culture' but may be equally or more familiar with the cultures of the countries where they grow up. Drawing on two or more cultures, TCKs adapt to new places and cultures with ease, finding themselves 'at home' just about anywhere but sometimes also feeling that they really have no home. They often speak several languages, have **hybrid** identities, and are at ease in the different cultures they have integrated into. The capacity to see the world from multiple perspectives, or to **code-switch** between behaviours and languages, enables TCKs to develop skills from childhood that adult cosmopolitans have to work hard to learn. Many TCKs are predisposed to become anthro-pologists as they already have the ability to view the world from several positions simultaneously. TCKs may belong everywhere and nowhere, but consider this an asset because of their class position, rights to citizenship, international education, and cosmopolitan networks.

Tourism: temporary and contingent mobility

Tourism is another type of mobility: tourists move temporarily to a new place to seek experi-ences that are not part of their regular existence, including sunbathing, sightseeing, partying, attending events, meeting new people, taking part in sport activities, or helping the poor. In the seventeenth and eighteenth centuries, young British men from wealthy families would go on a 'grand tour' to places like Italy and Egypt to visit antiquities, have a few adventures, and experi-ence a bit of exoticism. But tourism on a large scale as we know it today emerged at the con-vergence of several developments in the second part of the twentieth century: increasingly convenient and affordable transportation, a specialized infrastructure (hotels, restaurants, tours, etc.), increasing prosperity in the Global North in the three decades following World War II, and the idea that non-work time should be filled with activities, rather than an occasion to rest or socialize. This is often referred to as the 'culture of leisure'.

Tourism today is supported by an enormous industry, estimated to employ globally almost ten per cent of those in work in 2015. But local people generally benefit only marginally from tourism, as the bulk of the wealth it generates goes into the pockets of the large corporations in the Global North that own the hotels, cruise ships, and travel agencies. At the same time, tour-ism is particularly vulnerable to unexpected turns of events, as its collapse as a consequence of the 2020 Covid-19 pandemic illustrates. Tourism comes in many forms, which nevertheless share certain characteristics: tourists seek to escape from work and market-driven life, yet tour-ism is deeply embedded in the market and ends up confirming tourists' expectations and impos-ing their needs (comfort, food, entertainment, schedule) onto local contexts (Stasch 2017).

One kind of tourism, 'primitivist tourism', consists of people visiting remote areas of the world such as the Amazon or Papua New Guinea to see how people there lead a different kind of life from the visitors'. The Korowai, who live in the lowland forest of Papua, are one such destination (Stasch 2019): until recent decades, the Korowai wore no clothing, occasionally practised cannibalism and, most dramatically, built houses at the top of trees, three to ten metres above the ground, all of which conform to tourists' ideas of primitive exoticism. These houses have been the object of considerable public attention and are reproduced in photographs and films that circulate widely. To emphasize the Korowai's exoticism and difference, the houses are presented as their regular homes, even though few families actually occupy them. Today, Korowai build tree houses mainly for tourists and camera crews. Tours to visit the Korowai, guided by Indonesian guides, are offered to well-to-do urbanites in search of a unique experience that few of their compatriots have (thus giving them what Bourdieu called 'distinction'). These tours are carefully staged: Korovai people are asked to build tree houses, stage feasts, and put away the tokens of 'civilization' from their lives. This staging, which tourists are largely oblivious to, enables the tourists to project their own ideas about the 'primitive' and the 'civilized', interpreting what they see in terms that echo nineteenth-century evolutionism.

Another kind of tourism is illustrated by Chinese Tahitians 'returning' to the village that their ancestors left when they migrated to French Polynesia during the second half of the nineteenth century and the early part of the twentieth century to work on plantations, as part of the large wave of labour migrants that left impoverished regions of China for all four corners of the world (Trémon 2020). These 'heritage tourists' are full of romanticized expectations about finding their long-lost relatives and the homes of their grandparents but, like diasporic Circassians who visit the ancestral homeland described in this chapter's opening vignette, find instead a disappointing reality: the ancestral village has now been absorbed into an enormous urban sprawl, the streets are dusty and rubbish-strewn, and the traffic jams unbearable. Those who descend from more recent migrants are able to find relatives, but those whose families have been implanted in Tahiti for a century or more have to content themselves with a generalized experience that is not very different from that of ordinary tourists. Starting as spiritual and intellectual journeys in quest of kinship histories and connections, their trip ends up stressing their otherness and **alienation** from the land of their ancestors: they speak the local dialect of Chinese haltingly at best and cannot write it, they find the food strange and have difficulties handling chopsticks, and they ultimately long to return to Tahiti, where they belong. These experiences are common occurrences among descendants of migrants who 'return' to the homeland of their forebears.

Diametrically opposed to tourism in search of origins is that which began in the 1960s as part of the counterculture 'hippie' movement. In the 1960s, hippies travelled from Europe through the Middle East to India on buses or hitchhiking to escape the strictures of bourgeois capitalist life and find religious enlightenment, abundant drugs, cheap lifestyles, or all of these at once. The movement survives but in different forms. Some turn transnational mobility into a life project, at least as long as they have the vitality and means to travel. 'Global nomads' in the late 1990s and early 2000s were people who left behind comfortable lives in the Global North, rejected any tie to a homeland, and embraced a certain kind of cosmopolitanism (D'Andrea 2007). They spend their time travelling between well-known sites like Ibiza in the Balearic Islands, known then and now for its hedonistic party atmosphere, Goa, a former Portuguese colony on the west coast of India that became a countercultural destination for Westerners in the 1960s, and Pune, the site of the ashram founded by Indian guru Rajneesh, who late in life (when he was known as Osho) became embroiled in legal troubles. In these places, where they often stayed for extended periods of time, they survived by taking on odd jobs as traders, DJs, party promoters, tour guides, yoga teachers, therapists, and spiritual counselors. While they regarded ordinary tourists with disdain, in fact they shared many characteristics with them, including a lack of significant engagement with the locations to which they sojourned and their inhabitants, other than through the lens of their romantic and utopian visions. Global nomadism still exists, although people in locations like Goa have since grown impatient with the city's countercultural image, and Indian tourists have replaced visitors from the Global North, which locals do not necessarily see as an improvement.

Mobility and transnationalism as heterogeneous concepts

Throughout their 100,000-year history, humans have always journeyed from place to place, although mobility has greatly intensified since the beginning of the twentieth century. Since the middle of the century, as a sequel to colonialism, migration has become an integral part of the experience of an increasing number of people. Mobility can take on many different forms, depending on who is involved, the time frame, and the routes that people take. Transnational people today often maintain multiple allegiances and have a complex understanding of home and belonging. In the last half century, migration has also emerged as a topic of intense political debate in many parts of the world, often tied to issues of global security and a redefinition of the concept of border. Increasingly, migrating legally is the prerogative of the privileged, while poor people, many from the formerly colonized world, who seek a better life for themselves and their children are criminalized and vilified by national authorities on the one hand and left vulnerable to abuse and exploitation by human traffickers on the other.

Key thinkers mentioned in this chapter:

Wendy Brown; Ulf Hannerz; Martha Nussbaum

Key terms mentioned in this chapter (see Glossary):

Anthropocene; Asylum; Code-switch; Cosmopolitanism; Diaspora; Expatriate; Flexible citizenship; Genocide; Gift economy; Governmentality; Integration; Islamophobia; Migration; Mobility; Multiculturalism; Nationalism; Redistribution; Reciprocity; Refugee; Remittance; Third culture kid; Tourism; Transnational; Transnationalism

Questions for discussion/review:

1   What similarities and differences are there between transnationals and migrants?
2   Why are people forced to seek new countries to live in because of economic hardship not classed as refugees?
3   Discuss what is meant by the term governmentality.
4   In what ways are borders 'multilayered and found in multiple locations'?
5   What is cosmopolitanism?

Media and the technological transformation of social relations

Since the early 1990s, Japan has experienced a protracted social and economic crisis that has affected many aspects of people's lives. One manifestation of the social malaise that has resulted is the emergence of a new social type, the *hikikomori* ('socially withdrawn'): youth, mostly male, who isolate themselves from family, friends, school, and work, and spend all their time online, surviving on junk food and wrestling with addiction of various kinds (Allison 2013). They typically lock themselves up in their bedrooms, sometimes for years, sneaking out when no one else is around to grab food from the household fridge or use the bathroom. Estimates suggest that there are a million *hikikomori*. Most start to withdraw in their mid-teens because of school pressure, bullying, or anxiety about the future, in a cultural context where the stigma of social failure and worry about reputation (*sekentei*) are major concerns. Rather than being the result of the personal failings of an entire generation, as it is often depicted in the media, the situation of the *hikikomori* is a symptom of the general economic and social problems that Japanese society faces today, although a particularly dramatic one.

In the United States, Internet addiction rehabilitation programmes work with young men who have similarly locked themselves away from social interaction and spend 15 hours or more a day playing video games. Some start playing at age four but by age nine have developed what psychologists call a dependence. Some commentators estimate that between 1% and 13% of the general population, and as many as 20% of the young, have some form of Internet addiction.

Fears about the potential dangers of the online world and new technologies, for young men in particular, have some basis in fact, but how such dangers manifest themselves, why they emerge, and how they vary across societies are largely unknown questions. It may be that young men harmed by online addictions today would, in a time before the Internet, have found other ways to withdraw from society. Becoming *hikikomori* may be how **alienated** middle-class Japanese young men today express their concerns about the lack of employment opportunities, their distrust of institutions, and the meaninglessness of life in a society driven by consumerism and conformism. Yet, despite the isolating potential of online communications and games, most people are able to balance their online and offline interactions so that their online experiences enhance and extend their offline lives. And, of course, the Internet and online games are just the latest in a long history of developments in communication media which offer individuals new ways of defining themselves and expressing their interests, and concerns (Figure 14.1).

For many centuries, in the Global North as well as elsewhere, writing and print were the main technologies of communication. By comparison, post-print communication technologies, such the telegraph, the telephone, radio, photography, film, video, and computers, have developed and proliferated since the nineteenth century on a scale and with a speed unprecedented in history. Many technologies, such as the telegraph and the telephone, were initially expensive to use and for most people limited to special occasions and emergencies. When they were first

DOI: 10.4324/9781315737805-14

Figure 14.1 Young people playing video games in an Internet café in the disadvantaged Rocinha favelas, Rio de Janeiro, Brazil, 2012. (Courtesy of Susan Brownell)

developed, tape recorders and video recorders were only used by professionals in television production or for medical purposes, with domestic video recorders for middle-class households being marketed only from the 1970s. Other technologies such as television did not become widespread in the Global North until the middle of the twentieth century and restricted viewers to programmes made by state agencies or entertainment corporations. Personal entertainment and communication platforms, including Facebook, Instagram, YouTube, Twitter, Snapchat, and TikTok, which have changed how people communicate, organize their lives, and relate to themselves and others, are new media made possible by the relatively recent development of the Internet and computer technologies.

Starting in the late 1980s, the Global North experienced a telecommunication revolution as mobile phone technology developed, initially producing telephones that were the size of shoeboxes and that only the wealthy could afford, then increasingly portable units that could be used to send and receive calls and basic texts. After 2004, smartphones that could access the Internet became more sophisticated, enabling transnational corporations that manufacture telephones to make huge profits by rolling out new models and luring customers with promises of new levels of capability, sophistication, and glamour.

These developments also revolutionized communication in the Global South, where landline telephones were only available to the middle and upper classes because they required customers to have fixed dwellings and to be financially recognizable (by having bank accounts, credit histories, etc.). Mobile telephones, in contrast, presented no such requirements and could be prepaid in cash. Thus, in many parts of the Global South, people 'leapfrogged' from face-to-face communication to mobile telephone communication without going through the century of landline usage that characterized the history of communication in the Global North. However,

Box 14.1 Media ethnography and rapidly changing technology

One salient characteristic of media technology in the contemporary era is how quickly it changes, turning what was the cutting-edge technology of one moment into the dust of oblivion and quaintness of another moment. These changes are driven as much by technological advances as by the corporate drive to sell new products to consumers, since capitalism can only survive by constantly stimulating consumption and expanding into new markets.

One of us, Niko Besnier, was a relatively early user of computer technology. I began using bulky mainframe computers as a Ph.D. student in 1982 (starting on an IBM 370, a mainframe computer that dominated the market from 1970 to 1990) for a variety of purposes and for a while I supported myself as a programmer working with a computer language (EDL) that has long been forgotten. At the time, email messages consisted of one line that appeared at the top or bottom of the screen, somewhat like today's instant messaging. Messages gradually became longer but they rapidly scrolled on the screen and one had to interrupt the scroll to read messages longer than one screen. I first used the Internet in 1995, which at that time only offered information but did not allow the user to contribute anything. By the end of the 1980s, Ethernet connections were common, although many home computer users still had to depend on ordinary telephone lines to access electronic communication, and WiFi became commercially available in 1997.

Around 2000, Web 2.0 emerged, giving Internet users an interactive role: adding comments, writing blogs, and buying online. It also gave rise to social media. The names of the early social media platforms (Friendster, MySpace, Bebo) now barely ring a bell. I remember seeing in 2004 a group of students at a cafeteria on the UCLA campus, where I was teaching, huddled around a laptop excitedly using a new website called Facebook. However, not everyone around the world uses the same digital tools: for many reasons, including technological property interests and nationalism, corporations in China and Russia have developed their own Internet platforms. In China, the social media platform is Weibo, e-commerce takes place on Alibaba, and for heterosexual dating one turns to Tantan and Momo. Sooner or later, all will become outdated, which in some cases may already have happened by the time this book is published.

How does one conduct ethnographic research on such a moving target? It is important to remember that all ethnography is grounded in a particular time and place. So studying how people use communicative technology is no different from trying to understand how people conduct other aspects of their lives, except that the technology they use is replaced more rapidly than, say, the bicycles they ride to work or the food they eat for lunch. We learn about the human condition from people's relationship to the world around them (objects, other people, infrastructures, institutions, etc.) no matter where and when these relationships take place. Studying how people learned to take the train or shop in department stores in the late nineteenth and early twentieth century can be as instructive about how humans organize their lives today as how they interact with the newest features of the latest smartphone (Figure 14.2).

Figure 14.2 Mobile telephone advertisements plastered on a trade store in Suva, the capital of Fiji. In countries of the Global South, mobile telephone technology has revolutionized many aspects of people's lives. (Courtesy of Domenica Gisella Calabrò)

using a mobile phone is predicated on a number of factors: access to electricity to recharge the phone; access to a telecommunication signal; and money to pay for usage charges. For many people in the Global South, none of these requirements is a given.

Few people today live completely beyond the reach of information technology. But while some can access the Internet at any time, others are less likely to be able to use online resources; women, the poor, the elderly, the disabled, and minorities generally have more limited access to technology than men, the wealthy, and the mainstream. Technological advancements may thus exacerbate pre-existing forms of social inequality, referred to as the **digital divide**. They have also given rise to an extraordinary explosion of conspiracy theories, counterfactual information, and other types of content designed to manipulate and misinform that began circulating on the Internet in the 2010s, aggravating knowledge gaps and political divides.

Photographs, weddings, and consumption

People around the world today are used to taking digital photographs on phones and sharing them instantly with friends and family. The world is saturated with visual images as people capture every moment of their daily lives in the ephemeral snaps they take. While they may appear to be superficial, photographs are meaningful objects, a form of material culture indexing social relationships preserved in visual form.

Yet for much of the time since its invention in Europe in the late 1830s, photography was expensive and required the skills of professional photographers. In Taiwan, an island state about

80 miles off the southeast coast of China, photography was the preserve of the wealthy well into the twentieth century. In the 1920s, only the rich could afford wedding photographs and, until the 1960s, if families had any photos at all, they were likely to be prized possessions kept on display in their homes. These photographs depicted newlyweds in stiff unsmiling poses and served as proof of marriage. By the 1980s, Taiwan had gone from widespread poverty to become one of the world's richest nations, and photography had become cheap enough to be accessible to the majority of the population.

In a country where city streets are filled with mass-produced images of airbrushed, beautiful women selling every conceivable commodity, it is surprising that almost all couples about to be married are willing to pay for large wedding portraits that look like commercial advertisements (Adrian 2003). In these portraits, the couple is depicted in romantic, individualistic, and emotionally intimate poses against backdrops symbolizing cosmopolitanism and upward mobility, and the bride looks nothing like the actual woman, as she is dressed and made up to look like a Western bride. While this suggests that the portraits are the result of images of beauty imported from the West, they in fact represent a more complicated social phenomenon.

Before marriage, young people enjoy relative freedom and spend their income on fashion and entertainment. After marriage, women are expected to prioritize having children, caring for older relatives, and attending to ancestral altars. Women know this work will limit their freedom and take a toll on their looks. The reality of married life is one of duty rather than desire. The wedding portraits are thus fantasy depictions of a life the bride will never lead. On the day of the daylong photoshoot, she is treated like a celebrity by the photographer, make-up artists, and wardrobe assistants. It is a **rite of passage** that transforms a single woman into a married woman, producing inauthentic images that are nevertheless invested with social value and meaning by the bride, her friends, and the family.

Displayed at the wedding banquet and then hung above the newlyweds' bed, the portraits are more meaningful for the bride than the wedding ceremonies, over which she has no control because these are organized by the elders in the family. The portraits are also meaningful in that they are used as status markers: the larger the portraits, the greater the number purchased, the more fashionable the designs and layout, the greater the prestige that accrues to the bride. This is a form of competitive consumption in which couples try to outdo friends and relatives with the scale, scope, and sheer excess of their wedding portraits.

The artificiality of the photographs in which ordinary looking women can be transformed, with time, money, and skill, into generically beautiful brides allows women to recognize that the mass media is an artificial construct. The consumerism that the photographs appear to rejoice in is rather a visual representation of the emptiness of a world built on consumption.

Indigenous media, visual politics

Before it was possible to share information on the Internet, the Kayapó, an Indigenous people who live in the tropical rainforest of the Brazilian Amazon, used the media technology that was available to them to protect their territories and culture in innovative ways. The Kayapó have a long history of contacts with outsiders that were not of their choosing or to their benefit. Outsiders, such as gold miners and loggers, have brought diseases and caused environmental destruction, and politicians have authorized the development of enormous hydroelectric dams on their land, threatening ecosystems, habitats, and livelihoods.

The Kayapó first obtained video cameras in 1985, which they initially used to record culturally significant activities (T. Turner 1992). But control over the equipment and recordings was not equally distributed: ambitious young men became cameramen and video editors, gaining new technological knowledge that elders did not have, and which they transformed into bids for powerful political positions within the group. The Kayapó also made recordings of their interactions with politicians, engineers, and power brokers such as representatives of the World Bank, which they showed not only to fellow villagers but also to foreign environmentalists to garner support for their causes (Conklin 1997). Politicians quickly realized that recordings of their statements could be used to hold them to account if they reneged on their promises. Additionally, the Kayapó noticed that when they appeared in videos dressed as they often were, in t-shirts and shorts, no one paid them much attention, but when they wore traditional headdresses and decorated themselves in body paint, international journalists filmed not only the protests but also the Indigenous cameramen recording the protests. The juxtaposition of the Amazonian Indian in body paint and feathers handling the latest technology produced such striking visual images that it guaranteed that the Kayapó's campaigns to protect the rainforest would become international news. What they could not express verbally to national and international audiences because of language barriers, they managed to communicate through strategic media representations. Through their innovative use of technology, the Kayapó reconfigured their interventions in national and international politics.

Whereas the Kayapó had to get the attention of dominant national and international media to communicate their protests, the Zapatistas in Mexico were able to transmit their own messages independently of mainstream media (Khasnabish 2008). The Zapatistas, a militant movement, represent the interests of four impoverished Indigenous groups in Chiapas, Mexico's southernmost state. During the twentieth century, these groups suffered greatly as they had only limited access to healthcare, education, and employment, and their land was expropriated. Literacy levels were low and few spoke Spanish, Mexico's national language.

The economic situation of Indigenous groups in Mexico was already difficult when, on 1 January 1994, the North American Free Trade Act (NAFTA) came into force. NAFTA was an economic trade agreement between Canada, the United States, and Mexico that further undermined Indigenous people's already fragile peasant economy (Stephen 2002). Armed women and men protested by taking control of municipal buildings in six townships on the day NAFTA came into effect and Mexican troops responded by killing hundreds of them. The national and international reaction against this violence was so indignant that it put pressure on the government of Mexico to negotiate with the Zapatistas (Figure 14.3).

Despite various setbacks, the information posted on Internet bulletin boards by supporters outside Mexico transformed the Zapatista protests from a regional movement about local rights into an Indigenous **social movement** that attracted the support of national and international agents. Individuals with technological expertise spread awareness of social and political events taking place thousands of miles from where they were located. The cyber age of computer-mediated communication run by grassroots individuals and organizations, working independently of and often in opposition to mainstream media or authorities, had arrived. The individuals and groups recording and disseminating Zapatista news, articulating their demands and chronicling their activities, demonstrated the potential of new technologies to reach global audiences while bypassing traditional news media. In effect, the Zapatistas paved the way for future social movements across the globe such as the Occupy Movement, the Arab Spring, and the Indignados movement in Spain, all of which made effective use of new technologies (Postill 2018).

As in the case of the Kayapó, the Zapatistas overcame language barriers by attracting attention to their message in visual form. During their protests, they wore black ski masks, and the sight

Figure 14.3 Masked Zapatista dolls for sale, Chiapas, Mexico, 2014. (Courtesy of Adam Jones/ Wikimedia)

of thousands of Indians with identically covered faces became a globally recognizable image. This image dramatized the stereotype of 'faceless' Indians who, for 500 years, had been invisible and denied a voice. Yet one group in the Indigenous population continued to be silenced, albeit unintentionally, namely women. While their rights were frequently championed online, such as the right to choose their own spouse, access education, and hold political office, few were in a position to speak and write for themselves, and their voices were represented by others (Belausteguigoitia 2006). Despite good intentions, these others put forward perspectives and demands believing them to be those of the Zapatista women but which, inevitably, were shaped by their own, usually Euro-American and feminist, worldviews.

This led to a paradoxical situation. Zapatista women were visible online as Indigenous women, yet as they came to be seen as representatives of universal and global 'women's issues', their specific needs receded from view. For example, one of these needs was the 'right to rest'. With heavy workloads, women did not have the time to become literate, learn computer skills, or speak for themselves online. And as long as their voices are mediated by others, no matter how well-intentioned, Indigenous women remain disadvantaged. The examples of the Kayapó and the Zapatistas demonstrate that new media technologies can serve the needs of Indigenous groups, make protests efficacious, and at the same time introduce new forms of inequality and social differentiation.

Yet new media technologies have also facilitated the democratization of knowledge, with ready access to information for larger numbers of both producers and consumers. This democratization is not limited to political information. For example, religious knowledge, which in the past was limited to specialized groups, also became accessible to new audiences. In Egypt, recordings distributed on cassettes from the 1970s onwards made it possible for working-class individuals to listen to recitations of the Qur'an and the sermons of popular Islamic preachers, at times and in places of their own choosing (Hirschkind 2006, 110). These cassette recordings also enabled women, who often do not go to mosques to hear sermons, to listen to them at home. To illustrate how access to media democratized religious knowledge, Charles Hirschkind described a conversation he witnessed while riding in a shared taxi in Cairo between the taxi driver, a boy, and a veiled woman. The discussion was sparked by a religious sermon the driver was playing and the boy's request that he play music instead. Each party reaffirmed a Muslim identity and belief in the Qur'an. At one point during the discussion, the boy sought to prove that music was not *haram* (forbidden) in Islam by arguing that the *hadith* (account of the prophet's sayings or deeds) used by the taxi driver to justify his position against music was not authoritative.

What is particularly interesting about this exchange was that all the parties involved, a child, a woman, and a taxi driver, felt confident enough to discuss theological matters in a public setting. In the past, this kind of discussion would have been limited to religious scholars. None was theologically trained yet all expressed reasoned points of view. This is one example of how the mass production of cassette sermons in Egypt has resulted in a community in which informed ethical debate on faith can take place in a shared space shaping public practice and perceptions of what it means to be Muslim today.

Media, nation building, and political transformations

New media technologies can also facilitate the engagement of ordinary citizens in processes of nation building. After three decades of an independence war against Ethiopia, Eritrea became an independent nation in 1993, but by this time about a third of Eritreans were living outside the country. Many Eritreans led precarious lives in low paid and insecure employment, and they were dispersed across many different countries, forming a **diaspora**. One way in which they remained in contact with their homeland was through listservs, online discussions about how Eritrea should be governed (Bernal 2014). For them, nationhood was produced in the act of online collective community building, and crucial to this was Dehai, a computer-mediated network that began in 1992, predating the Internet. Dehai means both 'voice' and 'news' in Tigrinya, the dominant language of Eritrea. When the Internet took off, www.dehai.org became the primary **cyberspace** location and virtual space for sharing information about Eritrea. Dehai was set up by ordinary Eritreans without the support of political, military, or other organizations.

Participants in Dehai compared it to a surrogate homeland, a space for socializing with fellow Eritreans as one might do in local tea shops or the homes of friends in Eritrea. Yet discussions on Dehai were not the same as those one might have in person because people engaged with others who would otherwise not be part of their social network, because they came from different regions of the country or were not of the same ethnicity. One similarity, however, was that the Dehai virtual **public sphere** was primarily a male one. Dehai became one of the spaces in which participants 'lived' while in the diaspora, while considering their 'real life' still to be back home in Eritrea. In cyberspace, diasporic Eritreans had created a virtual nation in which they had a meaningful place.

One particularly interesting feature of Dehai involved the development of Eritrea's constitution. During three years of debate about the Eritrean constitution, members of the constitutional commission were openly active on Dehai, and so Eritreans in cyberspace were able to participate in important political and social developments taking place in Eritrea, and help to shape the constitution of the country. Eritrean politicians joined the Dehai online community established by ordinary people and used this forum to help guide their political decisions about the future constitution of the state.

In contrast, in Iceland, where 94% of the small and homogeneous population has access to the Internet, it was the government that called on its citizens to revise the constitution following the global financial crash of 2008 brought about by the speculation of bankers and weak controls on the financial sector. While other governments such as Greece, Spain and the United Kingdom responded by imposing austerity measures on their populations, Iceland arrested the bankers responsible for the collapse of the economy and continued to fund public services. Icelanders thought part of the problem leading to the financial collapse was the constitution of the country, which favoured the political class and conservative interests. In 2009, the newly elected government appointed a committee to put together a national assembly of 950 randomly selected citizens (Postill 2018). The assembly concluded that a new constitution was needed, and parliament organized a popular election for 25 seats on the Constitutional Assembly Council (CAC) to draft the constitution. All citizens were entitled to stand for election and the 25 CAC members invited citizens to participate in drafting the constitution via Facebook, Twitter, YouTube, and Flickr. Suggestions, revisions, and debates were discussed across social networks and, even though the new constitution was, for various reasons, never adopted, it was nonetheless an original and inclusive process of democratic participation in reforming the state that utilized new technologies.

In Eritrea and Iceland, two different nations in different circumstances, far reaching and inclusive forms of popular debate and intervention that would not have been possible without social media have changed how citizens interact with and shape the state. In both cases, social media were essential to involve individuals in discussions about the kind of social and political world they wanted for their nation. In the case of Eritrea, it was politicians who joined an already constituted online group, while in Iceland it was the government that took the initiative of setting up the online forum.

New technologies, however, can also provide a space for those who seek to limit the ideas and political positions of others and may exacerbate social exclusion. Women and members of minority ethnic groups, for example, are more likely to find themselves on the receiving end of hostile trolls in cyberspace than white men. In 2016, one national British broadsheet newspaper found that, of the ten most attacked writers it had published, eight were women and two were black men. These writers were attacked as much for their gender and ethnicity as for what they said.

Governments around the world increasingly use surveillance techniques on their own citizens to monitor or suppress dissent. It has also been alleged that some governments engage in cyber espionage to interfere with elections taking place in other nations. In October 2016, the United States Office of the Director of National Intelligence and Department of Homeland Security accused Russia of interfering in the U.S. presidential elections (Hemment 2017). There is also clear evidence that the algorithms used by Internet search engines such as Google and Yahoo to track and predict user behaviour have been purposefully manipulated in equally troubling ways. One consequence is that extremist views, revisionist history, and conspiracy theories appear as featured results when users seek information. This might change how some people view the world, and so could be considered social engineering by unelected individuals acting without a social mandate (Johnson 2018). However, anthropologists considering these developments in cyber technologies do not simply assume that people who go online and find themselves directed to unwholesome sites would just accept what they read. Rather, they ask why most people do not take patently biased web pages seriously. This is not simply a matter of preaching to the converted, but of understanding enough about what is happening offline in people's social lives to make sense of what they take from what they find online.

New communication technologies have created a new social type, that of the online blogger. Anyone with access to the right technology and with something to say can blog. Most bloggers deal with relatively inconsequential matters like entertainment or fashion, while others have toppled governments. The Arab Spring, which reshaped the political landscape in many Muslim countries for a number of years, began in Tunisia on 17 December 2010 with the self-immolation of a young street vendor, Mohamed Bouazizi. That day, the police had confiscated the fruit and vegetables that he was selling, demanding a bribe in return for his goods. In desperate protest against this routine form of corruption, Bouazizi set himself on fire in front of a government building, which his cousin recorded and uploaded to the Internet. Soon protests spread across the country as leaderless crowds took to public spaces to debate politics. Within weeks, the dictatorship running the country fell. Elections were held in 2011, a new constitution came into effect the following year, more women than before have seats in parliament, and Internet freedom has significantly improved.

Other uprisings took place across North Africa and the Middle East, demanding an end to corrupt governments, to restricted political freedoms, and to social oppression, and they existed simultaneously online and offline. But these movements did not just happen because the technology existed to give the protestors a platform. Rather, they were made possible because bloggers and activists had been working for years before the Arab Spring to bring about social justice in their respective countries.

Since the early 2000s, long before the Arab Spring, bloggers in Egypt had engaged with each other to end human rights abuses, political torture, and corruption. They were located across the political spectrum, from secular-liberal activists to members of the conservative Muslim Brotherhood (Hirschkind 2011). The widespread use of mobile phones enabled individuals to film acts of harassment or violence by state forces against citizens. For example, in May 2005, during a demonstration against the Egyptian president that had been organized via social media, riot police and thugs attacked a small group of protestors, which bloggers filmed and posted on their websites. Egyptian journalists opposed to the political regime were able to use material provided by the bloggers in their articles without risking state persecution, as they were simply citing sources. In fact, opposition journalists sometimes found that it was possible to get stories they could not print into the newspapers by first giving the story to a blogger and then using the blog as the source for the story they went on to publish.

While the events in Tunisia began the wave of protests that swept across North Africa and the Middle East, networks of bloggers from across the political spectrum were already in place. Bloggers did not advocate for any one political or religious perspective, and the networks they had developed were non-hierarchical and open to anyone who had something to contribute. A new form of sociality had emerged through online posts, creating a shared and transformational experience among people aspiring for a better future, what Émile Durkheim (1915) had described as **effervescence**, when anything seems possible.

Unfortunately, the effervescence did not last and the social and political freedoms that protesters had hoped for have largely failed to materialize. In Tunisia, while democracy has returned, the economic situation has not improved and the standard of living has fallen. In Egypt, the protests toppled the government of President Hosni Mubarak and elections were held but the new president, Mohamed Mursi, was deposed in 2013 by the military and the situation in the country has since worsened on many fronts: Internet freedoms have declined, journalists are

Figure 14.4 Crowds gathered in protest on 27 November 2012 at Tahrir Square in Cairo, Egypt. (Courtesy of Gigi Ibrahim/Wikimedia, licensed under a Creative Commons Attribution 2.0 Generic license)

more likely to be imprisoned and the economic situation of many remains grim. In Libya, Syria, and Yemen, calls for political reform have led to protracted wars as various factions vie for power, displacing millions and causing catastrophic famines. New communicative technologies make it possible to share knowledge widely and to organize in innovative ways, but they alone are not sufficient to bring about positive social and political change (Figure 14.4).

Mediated relationships: friendship, love, and influence

While communicative technologies on their own do not have an effect on the people who use them (put differently, they do not have **agency**), the interaction between users and technologies can encourage particular ways of communicating. For example, when Ilana Gershon (2010) conducted research in the 2000s on undergraduates' communicative practices at the university where she teaches in the U.S. Midwest, she found that the medium the students chose to communicate with one another carried considerable weight. They initiated romantic relationships by switching from a less intimate medium, such as Facebook, to a more exclusive one, such as texting, and this switch had an effect on how people saw their evolving relationships. But relationships were also ended using a variety of communicative devices, which ranged from a Facebook 'defriending' to an old-fashioned letter on cream-coloured paper, and the choice of medium to break up was often as much the object of grievance as the breakup itself. Thus students understood that the choice of medium affects the nature of the message that it communicates, and different media constitute a repertoire of communicative possibilities in people's lives, each with its possibilities, constraints, and norms of appropriateness, all subject to negotiation. Of course, relationships before Facebook were also started and ended using the media and technologies available to people at the time, so perhaps all that can be said of new communication technologies is that they offer an expanded range of media for people to use, incorporate, and evaluate their everyday relationships with others.

Social media platforms like Facebook encourage users to present themselves to others as particular kinds of persons, namely collections of skills, assets, and consumption practices (such as the films and singers they like), which they employ to form alliances and networks with others. The self that emerges from social media is one that **neoliberalism** favours, one that is similar to a business that offers particular products to customers or other businesses. For instance, the number of friends or followers one has becomes important to one's presentation of self. Even though a Facebook 'friend' is qualitatively different from a friend in non-mediated life, their quantity and who they are can become a significant measure of who the Facebook page owner is. This is not lost on potential employers, who use Facebook pages to assess a job applicant's desirability and appropriateness. Facebook pages offer an abundance of information about a person, but at the same time this information remains ambiguous: when one views someone's photograph taken at a party, one does not know what went on at the party, who was there, and what kind of relationship the person had with other participants. Social media are thus both potentially useful and potentially risky.

With its wide reach, the Internet has broadened considerably the opportunities for people to forge new relationships. Dating apps, marriage sites, Facebook, and other platforms enable people to connect with one another for friendship, sex, romance, or marriage. They enable people who have lost touch with one another to reconnect, in ways that were impossible or unlikely in pre-Internet days, when personals published in a newspaper or magazine were the closest equivalent. The Internet also offers novel opportunities for fraud and crime, as trustworthiness and sincerity are particularly difficult to assess in computer-mediated communication. The notorious '419' scams, named after the section in the Nigerian legal code of the law they break, consist in people (usually men) in countries of the Global South conning people in wealthy countries into sending them money, often through circuitous means, with promises of romance or financial deals, or by pretending to be in need because of misfortune. Investigative reporters have documented how the lives of people duped by these endeavours are affected, sometimes ending in suicide or murder.

Women in countries like China and the Philippines and men in the United States and Europe can meet on dating sites, allowing each to fulfil desires that range from the need for love, the gendered idealization of foreign partners, and the wish to escape economic precarity (Constable 2003). In seeking what is often referred to by the somewhat condescending term 'mail-order marriages', Western men sometimes idealize the **orientalized** femininity, modesty, and old-fashioned gender ideals of Asian women, while Asian women covet the possibility of not having to work to support themselves and their families. However, these relationships often have qualities that go beyond the stereotypes and their critique by those who find that they perpetrate both gender and global inequalities. In many cases, the women in these marriages are in fact professionals in their own countries, often better qualified than their Western prospective husbands, and perfectly aware of the broader context of structural inequality.

Yet such marriages are not entirely risk free. While there is no evidence to show that the women involved are more at risk of domestic violence than any other group of women, those who do find themselves subjected to violence may find it hard to seek the support they may need because of language and cultural barriers, as well as legal restrictions on spousal visas. While for women and men seeking a marriage partner the Internet was the medium that enabled them to find what they sought, for anthropologist Nicole Constable, who researched

Internet-based relationships, it worked as a research tool as she participated in online discussions, corresponded with Internet introduction agencies, and spent time in the cybercafés where prospective marriage partners surfed Internet sites.

For people who do not have access to computers, other forms of communication technology can serve as instruments to forge desired social engagements. In Papua New Guinea, the increasing availability of mobile phones in the early 2010s gave rise to a new type of social relation, the 'phone friend', namely a person one meets and knows only over one's mobile phone. To find phone friends, Papua New Guineans in the hinterlands of the country dial numbers at random with the intent of forming friendships or, in some cases, long-distance romantic relationships (Wardlow 2018). Many random calls fail as the recipient does not pick up or refuses the advance, but when they do work, participants view the phone friendship as superior to face-to-face relationships because they are free of the demands, expectations, and negative feelings that characterize face-to-face social relations, even though they often involve inventing identities, sometimes at both ends. Women living with HIV in the highlands of the country, who are often the target of stigma and violence in their home environment, call their regular phone friends at moments of emotional despair and economic uncertainty. These relationships fulfil a much-needed therapeutic need in the women's lives. As the example of the phone friends in Papua New Guinea shows, relationships mediated by technology are not limited to socially meaningful relations between couples or between groups of friends who also meet offline; in some instances, significant relationships can be built between individuals who will never meet in person.

The Internet has enabled new kinds of social identities to emerge, as people try to capitalize on the popularity made possible by digital media technologies, such as video platforms and blogs. Some have been successful in developing the status of 'microcelebrity' or 'influencer', namely people who derive status or profit or both from their media performances, juggling between different platforms such as Facebook, Instagram, TikTok, Twitter, YouTube, and blogs. In Singapore, for example, influencers, who emerged in the mid-2000s, are primarily women aged 15 to 35 who amass large numbers of online followers thanks to their good looks and astute self-branding strategies (Abidin 2017). They develop a particular kind of strategic intimacy with their followers that is not unlike the intimacy that regular celebrities foster with their followers through the media, persuading them to identify with them, whether they are located in Singapore or elsewhere in the world. Some organize face-to-face meetings with fans in cafés and other venues, thus adding non-digital encounters to their repertoire of communicative strategies with fans.

The influencers incorporate products and services in their media posts, which earn them the paid endorsement of the corporations that supply them, principally fashion, beauty products, food and beverage, travel, and electronics, persuading their followers to become consumers of these products. Management agencies have emerged to groom influencers and pitch them to potential corporate sponsors for a share of the profits that their commercial endorsement generates. Whether in Singapore or elsewhere, influencers thus engage in a form of labour, one that capitalizes on the particular kind of self encouraged by neoliberal capitalism, dependent on self-branding, flexibility, and entrepreneurialism, endlessly adapting to opportunities and feedback. At the same time, these strategies are highly dependent on the fickleness of markets and audiences, and leave little room for long-term planning.

Individuals are not the only entities that have found ways to appropriate the potential of new media. Entire countries can use media technologies to exert their political influence on the global scene, a strategy that political scientists call 'soft power'. Soft power contrasts with other means that states have taken to exert power, such as military force or economic pressure. But, in most countries, media are created by agents other than the state, and this is where anthropologists come in. The classic example of soft power is the international presence that the United States claimed throughout the twentieth century and still today by exporting 'Hollywood films' (which today are often not produced in Hollywood but in global locations). Since the late twentieth century, Japan is the country that has emerged as a major source of soft power through the global popularity of manga, *anime*, and figures like Pokemon and Hello Kitty. Ian Condry (2013) conducted fieldwork in *anime* studios in Tokyo, participating in editorial meetings, brainstorming retreats, and conventions, interviewing executives, artists, fans, and a host of other agents, even being called upon as a voice actor for an anxiety-provoking two-line part.

The *anime* industry is full of contradictions. On the one hand, *anime* is a profoundly innovative genre of popular culture, both in terms of the technologies it mobilizes and the ideas it conveys, but it is also the product of very traditional work-intensive collaborative manufacturing methods. It is a genre of unparalleled global reach that has re-configured Japan as a producer of 'cool', but it is also associated with its obsessive geeks and misfits (whom Japanese people call *otaku*, a word that has entered the English language), and as an industry it barely survives financially. As a product that many commentators have read as a 'Japanese essence', *anime* is in large part the product of exploited labour in China and Vietnam.

Mediated *anime* objects move in several ways. Most simply, they move across national boundaries, as *otaku* fans in Europe and North America invest long hours of unremunerated time subtitling and translating *anime*, flirting dangerously with copyright infringement. *Anime* also moves across media, configurations, and audiences, from television to games, merchandise, trading cards, illegally subtitled versions on YouTube, all the way to Japanese *otaku* who apply (unsuccessfully) to the government for the right to legally marry *anime* characters. As most fans of *anime* globally are unaware, *anime* is produced during countless sleepless hours by junior employees driven by a passion for the genre and its importance to the global image of Japan, in its protracted state of economic and existential crisis, as a giant producer of global popular culture. But the work takes a toll on their lives.

Development through entertainment

For seventy years before the advent of the Internet, it was left to radio and television to provide mass entertainment for large segments of the population of the world. This ability to reach large numbers of people in their own homes has, at certain times and in particular places, encouraged governments to utilize such media for social engineering projects. For example, the British radio soap opera *The Archers*, set in the fictional village of Ambridge, was originally conceived in the early 50s as a way to educate farmers about new farming techniques and increase food production. Most listeners today are neither farmers nor rural residents, and the series, which still runs, now addresses a wide range of social issues while continuing to incorporate story lines on farming matters.

Soap operas are generally domestic in form, are set in the present, deal with intimate family matters, and foreground women characters. Popular soaps attract loyal audiences who become involved with the life histories of the characters, which they often know in great detail. Anthropologists ask questions about what kind of cultural object a soap opera is, who watches, and what impact it has on everyday life.

One Indian soap opera dealing with women's issues, *Main Kuch Bhi Kar Sakti Hoon* ('I, a woman, can achieve anything'), was launched in 2014 and quickly became immensely popular. It was the most watched television series in the world, with over 400 million viewers across 50

Box 14.2   Media and language

The widespread availability of mobile phones throughout the world starting in the late 1990s gave rise to new forms of communication, particularly SMS (an acronym for 'short message service') texting. SMS messages were initially limited to 160 characters and spaces, so to pack in as much information as possible, people around the world devised new ways of abbreviating words, such as 'tmrw' and 'OMG'. (When smartphones with full keyboards and predictive text came into use these practices became less necessary.)

Among the Giriama of Kenya, one of the poorest and most marginal groups in the country, by the mid-2000s, young people had latched onto mobile phones and text messaging even when they had trouble making ends meet (McIntosh 2010). Young Giriama texted in English, the language of modernity and education; Swahili, Kenya's national lingua franca; and Giriama, the local language, which is associated with family life, tradition, and 'backwardness'. But the choice of language for texting was associated with different purposes and practices. Texts in English were the only ones in which they abbreviated and manipulated spelling (e.g., *O dia wats up ... Tomorw hav pa-t* 'oh dear, what's up ... tomorrow [we're] having a party'), and these messages were about trendy, modern, and cosmopolitan topics. Young Giriama explained that they used abbreviations because they were in a hurry, but being in a hurry was part of what it means to be trendy. In contrast, they texted in Swahili for serious matters, such as conducting business or communicating with elders, which required deference. Lastly, even though they asserted that they 'never' texted in Kigiriama, they in fact did when they needed to communicate about obligations and matters relating to close social relations, the opposite of the playfulness of English.

Not everyone was enthusiastic about SMS. Some thought it undermined education and intelligence, a classic reaction with echoes throughout the world. Some elderly Giriama thought that mobile phones and texting were instruments of witchcraft (how else could messages be sent through the air?) and the spelling manipulations of SMS as evidence. The witchcraft was manipulated by white people, who travel extensively and have stolen the power of African spirits to appropriate them for their own purposes, undermining traditional life in Africa. In this view, young people used the secret language of SMS to hide things from their elders, preferring to be modern and hip rather than acting as dutiful daughters and sons. Technology thus enables new communicative practices, but it is also given local meanings that reflect ongoing anxieties and tensions.

countries. The series focuses on a woman doctor who gives up a high paid career in the city to work in a village. It was devised to tackle India's pressing social issues, including teenage sexuality, contraception, and violence against women. Storylines explored, for example, acid attacks against women and sex-selective abortions.

With partial funding from U.K. foreign aid, the programme was developed by an NGO, Population Foundation of India, which was surprised by the level of interest it generated. The organization's viewer feedback hotline was overwhelmed by callers and collapsed within hours of the screening of the first show. Follow-up surveys suggested that the series changed attitudes towards education and early marriage for rural girls in some of the poorer Indian states. Such programmes work not only because they convey their message in an entertainment format, but also because viewers do not need to be literate to understand them. Where people have little education, television and radio are important sources of easily consumable information that enters directly into homes, making the consumption of the media feel effortless.

However, it would be naïve to imagine that soap opera audiences passively assimilate the messages producers intend them to receive. Viewers take from programmes what makes sense to them, and they can also reject or re-interpret the content depending on their own social circumstances. And, of course, most soap operas are produced not by development organizations but by entertainment corporations to attract audiences and advertisers. In fact, the earliest soaps, on the radio in 1930s North America, were invented to fit around the advertising of cleaning products (hence the term 'soaps') and were broadcast in the afternoon, when women had finished their household chores and had time to relax.

In rural Egypt, poor women who watched television soaps in the 1980s were not simply passive recipients of the values promoted by the programme writers, but rather made up their own minds about what messages to take from the soaps and spoke, for example, with relish about the glamorous but flawed woman characters in the series *Hilmiya Nights* (Abu-Lughod 1995). Even though it was not the writers' intention, poor women viewers took pleasure in seeing how the actresses played defiant and strong characters, or how they went from one failed marriage to another. While the women characters were made to suffer for their transgressive behaviours, what the women viewers focused on was how beautifully dressed and assertive the characters were. The women's marginal social position and poverty required them to veil and dress respectably as a form of moral protection, while watching television soaps allowed them to vicariously enjoy the bold actions of fictitious women living lives they could never lead themselves.

The rise in popularity of television in rural Egypt has had other consequences. Families stayed at home more often in the evenings watching television rather than visiting neighbours, and so social interactions beyond the immediate family declined. Before streaming and on-demand viewing, watching television programmes at set times required that women plan household chores around the television schedule. On a positive note, gathering around the television can bring families together across the generations and potentially open discussions about social issues that may not have arisen otherwise, even when viewing soaps made purely for entertainment and profit.

Soap operas make up a global market. Korean soap operas are routinely screened in the Arabian Gulf and series filmed in the Philippines and Turkey are popular in many other parts of the world. Yet, when a series produced in Brazil, a major exporter of soap operas, is aired in Senegal, viewers may share in some of the emotions experienced by characters but at the same time draw moral lessons that differ from those that the producers intended (Werner 2006). Women are critical of some of the goings-on they view on the screen as 'not what we do here', yet they also find in them resources to express and confirm their identities as women.

Because soap operas privilege kinship, they offer a space in which women viewers can imaginatively play out family scenarios as they themselves try to make sense of living in their own societies undergoing rapid social change. When a soap opera character behaves badly, a member of the family may proclaim that she or he is 'crazy' and so everyone present hears that her or his behaviour is inappropriate. Such evaluations articulate cultural values with social norms, and children and young people who watch the show with their mothers and grandmothers are socialized about morality. Beyond the family, women may talk about soap operas with friends, neighbours, or co-workers. A community develops based on shared knowledge of a media product, which allows for personal reflection and opinion but without, at the same time, risking much: the programmes are not real life and one can withdraw from viewing at any time.

Television as a medium has transformed how families gather, how they learn about the world, and how individuals develop a sense of self in relation to the lives they watch unfold on screen.

Box 14.3   Fieldwork in and of cyberspace

Anthropologists have developed methods for researching media that both draw on the discipline's traditional methodological strengths and innovate new approaches. They seek to go beyond general information about who has access to media in different locations, asking instead how people access them, for what purpose, and with what consequences. Thus, when they are interested in what television programmes mean to people, they watch television with them, listen to their comments and interpretations, note how the television set itself figures among other household items or other contexts, and watch how people negotiate television viewing with other activities, such as cooking or taking care of children. Because media can create new structures of inequality and new ways of questioning existing inequalities, anthropologists analyze how access to media changes power relations among people.

To study the role that social media plays in people's lives, some anthropologists have conducted 'digital ethnography' (or cyber-ethnography), observing how people integrate media into particular aspects of their lives and who they communicate with through social media (relatives, friends, romantic interests, complete strangers, etc.). Alternatively, they may adapt ethnographic methods, with their concerns with identities, power relations, economic activities, and cultural creativity, to the online worlds that people create. This is what Tom Boellstorff (2015) did in his ethnography of Second Life, an online virtual world that was popular in the late 2000s and early 2010s, asserting that the alternative worlds that users of the platform created were just as 'real' as the real world in which they lived their offline lives. Like all ethnographers, digital ethnographers centralize participant observation and long-term engagement, and make use of the tools that online platforms offer, such as the ability to save activities and to communicate with other users using chat or voice.

Viewers are not naïve and do not necessarily interpret what they view in the ways the television producers intend. What they make of the programmes they view depends on where they are located, socially as well as geographically. Today, as fewer young people in the Global North watch television, and as the proliferation of computers, tablets, and smart phones enables family members to view different programmes simultaneously, interactions between the generations, the sharing of knowledge, and the transmission of cultural values have all been affected in ways that remain to be understood.

Our mediated world

People shape new media technologies to their own ends and give them meanings that may differ from one cultural context to another. So a soap opera produced in one location may mean one thing to those who produced it and something quite different to those who watch it in different locations. New technologies provide some people, like the *hikikomori*, with the means to isolate themselves from family and society as a form of individual protest about the state of the social world. But media technologies also offer some people opportunities to make new contacts, revive or maintain already existing ones, find love across national boundaries, or share information to achieve political goals. While all these things were obviously possible before the invention of media technologies, these have changed the social world by enabling us to engage with ideas, movements, and other people both more broadly and faster than ever before.

New media technologies have also democratized knowledge in domains such as religion, allowing groups such as women and the poor to gain religious expertise and to do so in places and times of their own choosing. But in other contexts, the democratizing potential that many thought the Internet would make possible proved illusory; instead, it has enabled the proliferation of information designed to manipulate people's perceptions of the world. Media technologies may furnish new market opportunities to those who are positioned to exploit them, but they can also result in new forms of precarious labour and exploitation. Anthropologists insist that no technology is ever neutral. How technology is used, who gets to use it, and to what ends tell us a great deal about the social and cultural environment in which it is used, as well as about the values and desires of the people who use it. In all cases, however, these technologies mediate social relations and this is why anthropology has so much to say about them.

Key terms mentioned in this chapter (see Glossary):

Agency; Development; Diaspora; Digital divide; Nation building; Neoliberalism; Social media; Social movement

Questions for discussion/review:

1   Why is it important for anthropologists to study people's offline world to understand their online world?
2   What new social identities have digital media technologies made possible and what kinds of social relations do they foster?
3   To what extent have new media democratized access to knowledge and with what effect?
4   How do new media alter relations between people and between people and the state?

Chapter 15

The environment

In November 2013, one of the strongest tropical cyclones ever recorded, Typhoon Haiyan, killed over 6,300 people in the Philippines, caused massive destruction, and displaced hundreds of thousands of people who lost their homes and livelihoods. The Philippines has also had to deal with heatwaves and severe floods which, along with the increasing frequency and severity of cyclones, are most likely the effect of global warming resulting from human-produced carbon emissions (Figure 15.1).

In September 2015, disaster survivors, community organizations, and **non-governmental organizations** (NGOs) submitted a petition to the Commission on Human Rights of the Philippines requesting an investigation into the responsibility of petrochemical companies such as Shell and BP, alleging that the climate change to which their products contribute constituted a violation of human rights. The following year, the Commission wrote to 47 companies, accusing them of breaching people's fundamental rights to life, food, water, sanitation, adequate housing, and to self-determination (Greenpeace Philippines 2015, 5). This case was the first of its kind, a legal landmark that many hoped would result in recommendations to other governments on how to hold large corporations accountable for the damage they cause to the environment. Since then, similar climate liability cases have been brought against corporations and governments in other countries.

In late 2019, the Commission produced its final report, which concluded that companies that pollute the environment have the legal and moral responsibility to respect human rights and invest in clean energy. The Commission also stated that major fossil fuel firms may be held legally responsible for the damage caused by carbon emissions.

The planet's climate has always fluctuated. There have been ice ages alternating with periods of intense heat and, in between, periods during which the climate was temperate and relatively constant. These shifts, which spanned thousands of years, have been caused by a multitude of factors, such as variations in the sun's radiation, changes in the earth's orbit, and natural phenomena like volcanic eruptions and large meteors crashing on earth. What is radically new about today's climate fluctuations is that they are in significant measure a consequence of human activity and, in contrast to climate fluctuations in the past, they are taking place at an extraordinarily rapid pace. This is so significant that some scientists have made a case for declaring that we have entered a new geological epoch, the **Anthropocene**, a term that combines the Greek words for 'human' (*anthropos*) and 'recent' (*kainos*), the last being used to designate a period of time or epoch. It captures the fact that, for the first time ever, humans are the most significant agents of change on the planet. This may be humanity's last epoch.

DOI: 10.4324/9781315737805-15

Figure 15.1 Destruction caused by Typhoon Haiyan, Philippines, 2013. (Courtesy of Henry Donati/Department for International Development, licensed under a Creative Commons Attribution 2.0 Generic license)

Anthropology of the environment

Wherever human beings have lived on earth, they have altered the environment to meet their subsistence needs and have sometimes done so in environmentally destructive ways. For example, humans in both prehistoric and historical times have hunted to extinction animal species like the Tasmanian tiger, the largest carnivorous marsupial that humans encountered, and the giant moa in New Zealand. In other cases, humans have rendered their own environment uninhabitable. For example, Easter Islanders in the southeast Pacific erected their famous religious stone statues, known as *moai*, but to transport the stone from quarries they used wooden logs, cutting down the island's forests until there was no longer enough wood to build homes or canoes (Milton 2002). Without trees, the soil lost its nutrients. Even though the islanders understood this, they nonetheless continued to erect statues, depriving the island of valuable resources and causing a major population breakdown, which slavery and colonialism further exacerbated.

Just as humans have altered the environment in which they live, the environment has also shaped people's social and political organizations, relations with neighbours, and many other aspects of their lives. For example, the Maring-speaking Tsembaga people in the Highlands of New Guinea numbered about 200 in the early 1960s, when Roy Rappaport conducted **fieldwork** among them. He published his work as *Pigs for the Ancestors* (1968), which became a classic study of human interactions with the environment. The Tsembaga cultivated root crops such as taro and yams and raised pigs, but did not eat pork on a regular basis. However, the pigs, which were considered men's wealth but were primarily cared for by women, played an important role in their social, political, and ritual life.

Taking care of pigs is labour intensive and pigs can wreak havoc on gardens, so when the pig population grew too large, which happened about every 12 to 15 years, the Tsembaga staged a

Figure 15.2 Decorated Tsembaga men on dance grounds during a pig sacrifice festival, some displaying wealth items for exchange, November 1963. (Courtesy of Roy A. Rappaport Photograph Collection, University of California San Diego Libraries)

ritual slaughter of part of their pig herd and held a huge feast, to which neighbouring villages were invited. These feasts had social, political, and religious meanings, in that they strengthened the bonds with allied clans who were invited to the feast, and the Tsembaga also saw them as an offering to the spirits of their ancestors, hence the title of Rappaport's ethnography. At the same time, the feasts signalled the beginning of a period of war with neighbouring groups that the Tsembaga defined as their enemies. Hostilities were highly ritualized, but they killed about 12% of the male population (Figure 15.2).

For Rappaport, the Tsembaga organized their lives in order to maintain the ecosystem in a state of equilibrium, and he suggested that this was the case for other societies, although in different forms. But by presenting the Tsembaga as a small bounded community, he did not consider the fact that ecosystems could be affected by many different factors, including changes in people's beliefs and practices and social and political changes arising from beyond the society.

Other anthropologists have shown that human beings interact with the environment in which they live in other ways, such as drawing on features of the natural landscape as a moral space. For example, as anthropologist Keith Basso showed, for the Western Apache of Arizona in the western United States, the environment is full of stories (Basso 1984). The names the Western Apache give to places, such as 'Water flows inward underneath a cottonwood tree' (which in the Apache language is a single word), are typically descriptive, and many of these names are associated with myths or historical events that took place in these locations. The stories often contain a moral lesson, and Apache people can pass moral judgement on others by merely mentioning a place name. The target of the criticism feels it 'like an arrow'. For example, the place name that translates as 'men stand above here and there' alludes to an Apache policeman who, some time in the past, forgot his Apache identity by behaving too much like a white man. Basso tells the story of a scene he witnessed in the late 70s, when a 17-year-old Apache girl who had just returned from boarding school attended a ceremony with fashionable pink curlers in her hair, instead of the free-flowing hairstyle that was required of young women taking part in the event. Two weeks later, out of the blue, her grandmother told the story of the policeman who had behaved like a white man at the place called 'men stand above here and there'. Knowing that her grandmother was criticizing her, the girl left and threw the curlers away, later telling Basso, 'I know that place, it stalks me every day' (1984, 57). In such ways, Apaches incorporate the environment into their moral universe through stories associated with places.

These two very different ethnographic examples are instances of environmental anthropology, namely the study of how members of a society shape its environment, either by design or without intentionally meaning to. Interactions with the environment in turn shape the cultural, social, economic, and political life of the society. As a species that differs from other animals in degree rather than in kind, human beings are firmly located in the environment in which they live.

Having moved away from earlier studies of human groups as discrete and autonomous entities, environmental anthropologists today are concerned with the global consequences of local human-environment interactions, recognizing that human groupings are always embedded in large-scale political and ecological systems. Some anthropologists approach human engagement with the environment as activists and advocates, in addition to being researchers. Increasingly, anthropologists concerned with environmental issues work in interdisciplinary groups and engage with scientists, policy makers, and others to understand the complex historical and contemporary dynamics that have made our planet what it is today. This applied anthropological work contributes to culturally sensitive local-level environment conservation projects and to a global understanding of the environmental problems that humans face.

Ethnoecology

Everywhere, people classify the plants, animals, landforms, and other features of the environment in which they live. Understanding conceptual models of the environment is the work of ethnoecologists, who have documented Indigenous people's often sophisticated knowledge of medicinal plants, natural insecticides, animal behaviour, and soil responses. But in many parts of the world, this knowledge is threatened by the destruction of Indigenous lands and cultural extinction. One estimate by Brazilian anthropologist Darcy Ribeiro suggests that 87 Indigenous groups in Brazil became extinct during the first half of the twentieth century, and other groups have experienced such rapid culture changes that the knowledge that would, in the past, have passed down from elders to youth has vanished (D. Ribeiro 1970, 250). While not all Indigenous people interact with their environments in sustainable fashion, requiring us to be wary of the problematic romantic image of a **noble savage** in harmony with nature, it is clear that many such groups have a profound knowledge of their environments and how to maintain them.

Pharmaceutical companies take Indigenous knowledge seriously because it can potentially translate into significant economic benefits for them. By the 1990s, one estimate of the global value of products identified as having medicinal properties thanks to Indigenous people's knowledge ran into tens of billions of U.S. dollars (Posey 1990). However, Indigenous peoples who shared their knowledge with pharmaceutical companies earned less than 0.001% of the

Box 15.1   Subfields in environmental anthropology

The term environmental anthropology came into use in the 1990s as anthropologists took an interest in the environment following events such as the 1992 United Nations conference on the environment in Rio de Janeiro. The term was originally used to refer to applied anthropologists whose work concerned environmental issues and for those who studied environmental groups and organizations. However, anthropologists had long worked in subfields such as cultural ecology. Today, environmental anthropology is generally considered an umbrella term that includes any anthropological approach to the environment from a socio-cultural, biological, applied, or other perspective. Anthropologists approach the environment from different perspectives, ranging from the scientific to the humanistic.

Cultural ecology, a term coined by Julian Steward in 1937, is the study of culture and environment from a materialist perspective. A key assumption was that cultures evolve within their local environments. Steward focused on subsistence strategies and the economic organization of cultures, particularly the technologies that people deployed to live from the environment. For example, the organization of hunters and the tools they used when hunting varied depending on the environment they lived in and the kinds of animals they hunted. He reasoned that societies that hunted similar game would develop similar social institutions even if environmental conditions were different. However, this approach also risked **environmental determinism**, namely the problematic notion that the environment produced culture.

In the 1960s, **ecological anthropology** developed as a reaction against cultural ecology. Ecological anthropologists recognized that people did not engage with the environment in its totality but rather with selected aspects of it. While retaining the focus on materiality of cultural ecology, ecological anthropology recognized that local groups were not isolated but were part of a complex global system.

Idealist approaches to the environment include **ethnoecology**, which studies how people understand the environment by classifying it and acting on it through a cultural lens. In this approach, it is culture that determines and organizes the environment. This approach often draws heavily on linguistic analyses of things found in nature.

Human ecology, a multi-disciplinary approach to understanding human-environment interactions, combines the study of human ecological activities with how groups make sense of their environments and seeks to understand the relationship between them. Human ecologists focus on human impacts on the environment and this is what distinguishes their field from non-human ecology. **Political ecology** added to this a dimension of power and incorporates the wider political-economic context. There are other subfields in anthropology that study the environment, but in all approaches – scientific or humanist, materialist or idealist – what anthropologists bring to the study of the environment is an understanding of the role of culture in human-environment relations.

profits from the manufacture of the drugs that resulted from their generosity. Other businesses interested in 'natural' products for the body, such as foods and cosmetics, are keen to benefit from Indigenous people's knowledge. These situations have led to calls for international agreements, ethical codes of practice, and education for Indigenous populations to protect them from exploitation and from the possible destruction of the environments that attracted the

Box 15.2   Environmental pollution and global health

Today, the complexity and intersecting nature of the environmental, health, and socio-political issues that bring the very survival of human and other animal life on the planet into question can no longer be ignored. It is self-evident that people need clean water and air to survive and that pollution can cause ill-health. Often, the illnesses caused by environmental degradation and pollution, from rising temperatures to dirty air and the use of harmful pesticides in agriculture or chemical processes in industry, do not result in immediate sickness but become evident over time. Chronic illnesses like kidney and cardiovascular disease, diabetes, and cancer are now recognized as connected to planetary health, encompassing climate change and the diminishing diversity of our ecosystems. Not everyone is at equal risk: the young, the old, and those who are marginalized in racial, class, or caste terms suffer disproportionately as a consequence of environmental pollution.

Flint, in the United States, a small city with a majority black population, switched its water supply in 2014 from a relatively clean source to the cheaper Flint River to save money (McKenna 2018). The Flint River water tasted bad, and was discoloured and contaminated with lead from industry, but residents were assured it was safe to drink. Yet people began to suffer from rashes and hair loss, women miscarried in higher than expected numbers, and children had dangerous levels of lead in their blood. This was not a natural disaster but the result of ignoring both environmental laws and the majority black population for some 18 months as it lobbied for action to remedy the situation. The people of Flint were harmed not only physically by tainted water but also racially as politicians ignored the health concerns of people who were already reeling from deindustrialization, high unemployment, and urban decay.

In India's capital, Delhi, the ever-dwindling water supply is a persistent cause of anxiety but it is the quality of the air that today sparks most concern, with the *Times of India* declaring in 2016 that the air was so polluted it was tantamount to genocide (Ghertner 2020). In November each year, a combination of stagnant winds, crop burning in neighbouring states, and heavy metals released by fireworks during religious celebrations add to already high levels of industrial and car exhaust fumes (Figure 15.3). On the religious holiday Diwali in 2016, levels of dangerous particulate matter in the air were over 50 times the World Health Organization's guideline. Schools and construction sites were closed as people with asthma and other cardiovascular and respiratory diseases packed the hospitals. This was an environmental emergency but one that has been long in the making: Indians today have the smallest lungs in the world and the highest rate of death from respiratory disease. But air pollution not only affects the lungs and heart, it can also be linked to growth retardation and lowered IQs.

The Indian Supreme Court has been petitioned to tackle air pollution and in 2000 declared 'any disturbance of the basic environmental elements, namely, air, water and soil, which are necessary for "life", would be hazardous to "life" within the meaning of Article 21 of the Constitution' (Ghertner 2020, 139). Here the quality of the environment is understood in terms of citizenship rights. However, not all citizens deprived of clean air are equal. Those who have no choice but to go to work even when officials advise inhabitants to remain indoors because of dangerously high levels of air pollution, those who live on the streets, or those who cannot afford home air purifiers are overwhelmingly poor and of lower **caste**. Additionally, air pollution is metaphorically associated with colonial era notions of the 'polluting poor', whose slums are cleared and jobs lost when polluting industries are closed to protect the health of those who live in middle-class neighbourhoods. Such 'bourgeois environmentalism' continues the caste system's division between the pure and the impure, with the Dalits considered the most polluted of all. Those who can afford to live in 'clean bubbles' may use techno-logical means to protect themselves and leave the poor to suffer from environmentally produced ill health.

In both Flint and Delhi, environmental pollution, which is the outcome of human industry, urbanization, and political decision making, causes most harm to those least able to protect themselves because of race, social class, and caste marginalization. The environment is thus not simply a matter of nature but also one of citizenship, human rights, and environmental justice.

pharmaceutical, food, and beauty industries to them. However, some have argued that setting up ethical guidelines without the full participation of Indigenous people fails to take their interests into account. While debates continue on how to approach these complex issues, environments and cultures continue to be threatened. If they are destroyed, the discussions about ethical recompense for the intellectual knowledge and property rights of Indigenous people risk becoming meaningless.

Multispecies ethnography

Another aspect of the environment where anthropologists have made important contributions is the relationship between humans and non-human animals. In the circumpolar region of Finland, the lives of the Saami reindeer herders and hunters have dramatically changed since the

Figure 15.3 Air pollution in Delhi, India, 2019. (Courtesy of Prami.ap90/Wikimedia, licensed under a Creative Commons Attribution-Share Alike 4.0 International license)

end of World War II (Ingold 1977). They no longer walk on foot or use wooden skis to follow their herds to the best grazing land, but instead use snowmobiles and have mechanized reindeer herding. As a result, they have become increasingly dependent on money to pay for the new technology and the number of people involved in reindeer herding has decreased. Over time, as work patterns changed, so did how Saami cooperated with each other and so did relations between people and animals. While studying these changes, Tim Ingold rethought human-animal relations, formulating an approach that drew on the philosophical tradition of **phenomenology**. Rather than first constructing a classification system to explain the world and then approaching the environment through it, he argued that human knowledge of the environment was derived from the experience of people who inhabit it and who come to know it through their activities. This approach sees the intellectual understanding of the environment and the experience of it through the senses as constituting a single phenomenon. Non-human animals also constitute the environment and this insight leads to the possibility that non-human animals can exert **agency**. The interaction of human and non-human animals in experiencing and constructing the environment and each other is what multispecies ethnography focuses on.

In the twenty-first century, multispecies ethnographers have sought to move to centre stage the animals, fungi, and microbes that previously were peripheral to ethnography. By rejecting the idea of human exceptionalism, that is to say the idea that human beings are always at the centre of things and the drivers of change, anthropologists can reconsider contacts between humans and animals or other lifeforms and how they co-produce the environments in which they live. When we accept that we have always lived with non-human beings and have been shaped by them, nature and culture become part of the same system.

In fact, early versions of these ideas were already present in the works of nineteenth-century anthropologists like Lewis Henry Morgan. In the 1860s, when anthropology and natural history were not yet separate disciplines, Morgan studied how beavers transmitted knowledge to their young about how to build lodges, dams, and canals, and compared it to how human beings learn engineering. Over a century later, in the 1970s, Gregory Bateson explored the possibility that humans and dolphins could communicate, through play for example. His work opened up the possibility that the minds of humans and some non-humans were more similar to one another than previously thought.

In Bali, Indonesia, people and monkeys co-create environmental niches around Hindu temples that they inhabit together, forging cross-species bonds of an economic, social, and moral nature (Fuentes 2010). In the forest temples of the inland village of Padangtegal, long-tailed macaques and humans have shared space for centuries. Nowadays, tourists visit both the temples and the monkeys. Balinese tour guides and monkeys can often be found sitting in the shade, just a few metres apart, waiting for the tourists to arrive so that they can start work. Humans and monkeys are in the same social and economic position of dependence on the tourists (Figure 15.4).

The monkeys are an important tourist attraction, so villagers near the temples reinvest revenues from tourism in reforestation and in the care of the monkeys. As a result, forested areas have expanded and the monkey population has risen. The primatologists working on the site originally feared that a rapidly growing monkey population would lead to conflict with humans, and suggested cutting down the monkey population through sterilization and culling. The Balinese villagers, however, minimized possible conflicts with the monkeys differently, by feeding them and thus preventing them from raiding their crops. Villagers also teach the tourists not to antagonize the monkeys out of ignorance. Different groups, the scientists, the villagers, the tourist

Figure 15.4 Long-tailed macaques, Balinese villager, and a Labrador sharing a resting space in Uluwatu (Bali), a temple village popular with tourists, in 2017; the village woman's job is to mediate between tourists and the monkeys who steal from them, for example, a monkey who has stolen a pair of sunglasses will wait for her to trade it back for food. (Courtesy of Jeffrey V. Peterson)

guides, and the tourists, have responded differently to the same potential risks because they operated from different understandings of the relationships among species.

Monkeys are allowed to take the ritual food offerings at the temples as the Balinese believe that they help take the offerings to the spirit world, but only once the ritual is over. The Balinese associate the monkeys with the Hindu god Hanuman, an avatar of the god Shiva, who fought with his army of monkeys against the demon king Ravana. Like others during the temple rituals, the monkeys wait to play their part in the religious ceremony, and conflicts only arise if the monkeys break the rules by grabbing the food too early. Informed by social, economic, and religious practices and knowledge, the Balinese have found ways for people and monkeys to interact to the benefit of both.

Human-animal interactions demonstrate that nature and culture form a continuum rather than being in opposition to one another. Relations between species are fluid and may change over time. Cross-species relations depend not only on the biological, ecological, and geographical contexts, but also on the social, economic, and religious perspectives that shape them. Thinking of animals as **agents** with their own needs and social relations, which may cross the boundaries between species, challenges anthropocentric views of the world.

Entangled, interconnected, and multi-sited: the anthropology of the environment today

Local events with global consequences, such as the Chernobyl nuclear disaster in 1986, have demonstrated the extent to which people and the planet are interconnected, and have encouraged some anthropologists to become involved in formulating environmental policy. Some do so by working with international organizations like the World Bank, researching the effects of development projects such as the construction of dams. Other anthropologists work against such organizations and support activist groups who oppose large-scale development projects. For example, the Narmada Valley dam project in west India, which began in 1978 with funds from the World Bank, consists of plans for 30 major dams, 135 medium-sized ones, and 3,000 small ones. While everyone agrees that clean drinking water, reliable electricity supplies, and improved irrigation for crops are needed, the enormous project has caused considerable environmental destruction and the displacement of many thousands of people who have received little compensation.

Many local and international NGOs, environmental activists, scientists, and anthropologists opposed the project. Protestors marched, fasted, and conducted a 'noncooperation movement' by refusing to pay taxes. The police beat, arrested, and jailed many of them. This **social movement** was based on the mass mobilization of large numbers of people and gained considerable local, national, and international support. It eventually forced the World Bank to commission a report, which concluded that the Bank should withdraw its funding because it could not guarantee that the human rights of people who lived in the affected areas would be respected. It showed that the number of people who would be displaced was much higher than the Indian government had stated and that the dam would not provide as much water or generate as much electricity as promised. The project was also environmentally destructive, as many plants and animals would not survive, and the dams would increase the likelihood of earthquakes.

Because of the Narmada Valley dam controversy, development banks have revised their funding policies for major projects around the world. For example, the World Bank now requires information on the environmental consequences of projects and on the terms of resettlement of displaced populations before it approves funding. People affected by World Bank–funded projects can submit their concerns to an Inspection Panel, and a World Commission on Large Dams has been set up to negotiate international standards for the environment and human rights.

These developments have given visibility to the plight of disempowered local populations who bear the brunt of development projects, but they have not always achieved all the outcomes protestors seek. In the Narmada case, as a consequence of the World Bank withdrawing from the project, international oversight was reduced, leaving the Indian government greater power to push through its plans despite local protests. As the Indian government is no longer held to international standards for development projects, the success of the protestors in getting the World Bank to withdraw funding turned out to have been a victory that came at great cost.

Social movements throughout India and elsewhere in the world resist environmentally destructive and inhumane models of development that destroy the livelihoods of the poor while providing lucrative opportunities for political and business elites. These latter profit from international and state-funded projects and then move on to the next project when the first is completed or has failed, leaving behind devastated landscapes and destitute populations. While some development projects make positive contributions to local populations and are environmentally sustainable, others become 'sacrifice zones', places where corporations set up resource-extraction wherever they decide a profit can be made, often aided by state deregulation, with little regard for the people who live there.

The study of sacrifice zones allows anthropologists to make sense of the global environmental damage by human beings on the planet. Often this anthropology is made up of several local studies, producing **multi-sited ethnographies.** This approach demonstrates how humans, animals and the environment in one location are connected to those located elsewhere. This kind of work produces a new appreciation for the potential for regeneration of the environment and for how some species have found ways to survive human depredations. It also shows that even if we, as a human species, do not survive the environmental and climatic changes we have caused, then other forms of life will survive us.

One example is the aromatic wild matsutake mushroom that grows in the ruins of forests in China, Finland, Sweden, and the North American Northwest, on the roots of pine trees that have been cut down by the logging industry (Tsing 2015). The mushrooms acquire a distinctive smell from the trees on which they grow, from which they absorb the carbohydrates they need to survive. In turn, their uncontrolled growth helps reforestation by providing the tree with various life-giving minerals, in a symbiotic relationship that biologists call mycorrhizae. Their smell attracts some forest-dwelling species, like bears and deer, and repels others, like slugs and bacteria. No one has managed to cultivate matsutake mushrooms despite multiple experiments, so the only way to obtain them is by foraging, an endeavour that rests crucially on pickers being able to identify the mushroom by its smell. In the North American Northwest, this back-breaking work is done by refugees from Laos, Cambodia, and Vietnam, veterans of the Vietnam War (the same that brought the refugees to the United States), undocumented Latinx immigrants, and Native Americans. These people all belong to disenfranchised minorities who lead **precarious** lives in the United States, juggling life and work to try to cope with insecure employment, irregular income, and unstable conditions.

At the other end of the chain are gourmet restaurants in Japan and Korea, where the matsutake is considered a prized delicacy, making it the most expensive mushroom in the world and a favourite gift exchanged between business partners and family members, the pleasure of which surpasses the enjoyment of eating the gift. Matsutake used to grow in Japan's forests, but deforestation associated with the increased urbanization of the country caused its disappearance in the 1970s, and thus Japanese suppliers must import it from overseas, a delicate procedure because the mushroom quickly loses its prized aroma, and the dried version has little appeal. The trade is enabled by the time-space compression that has come to characterize **globalization**, which brings together unlike sets of fungi, plants, people, industries, and locations. In Japan, what started as mushrooms picked by disenfranchised foragers has become a prized food item sold at auctions.

The team of anthropologists who followed the paths of matsutake mushrooms conducted fieldwork in many different locations, among foragers, wholesalers, auctioneers, restaurant chefs, consumers, and the scientists who study plants and ecologies. As each member was able to spend considerable time at each location along the matsutake mushrooms' journey and to draw on their own previous acquaintance with the context, their collaboration enabled them to avoid a common pitfall of multi-sited ethnography, namely fieldwork that is too brief and superficial to tap into the subtleties of life (Choy, Faier, Hathaway, Inoue, Satsuka, and Tsing 2009).

They describe their ethnographic project as a work of 'third nature'. Here, 'first nature' refers to the ecological relations among animals, plants, and people, while 'second nature' is understood as the changes made to the environment because of capitalist incursions. Today's 'third nature' is what survives and may even thrive in spite of capitalism. Third nature is not an example of never-ending human progress and mastery over nature, but rather an assortment of entangled ways and forms of life that are brought together in sometimes unexpected fashion, transcending national boundaries.

This does not, however, reduce the ecological to the economic or vice versa, rather both are as intertwined and entangled as the matsutake mushroom that lives in the ruins of capitalist resource extraction. In an uncertain world, the matsutake mushroom and the imaginative possibilities it suggests offer ways of making sense of what our planet has become. The mushroom suggests collaborations that may be open to us, and how such multi-species, transnational, and global connections may make survival possible in these precarious times.

In northwest Argentina, where towns and whole cities have fallen into ruin as colonialist advances gave way to alternating waves of capitalist expansion and retreat, the environment has also been shaped by destruction. Here Gastón Gordillo (2014) studied the relationships people in the Gran Chaco region of Argentina have with the environment. In particular, he was interested in how people engage with, use, and understand the ruined material remnants of Spanish colonization. He was also interested in how contemporary forest clearing to make space for agribusiness farms growing soy on a large scale for sale to China has altered the environment and the lives of local inhabitants.

In the Gran Chaco, places such as the La Manga church, abandoned by Jesuits in the early nineteenth century, may have looked like ruins to the anthropologist but were not considered as such by the people who lived near it. The church was a place where people in their hundreds gathered to celebrate and where images of the Virgin Mary and Saint Roche were carried in procession as people danced, sang, and drank through the night. As long as it attracted people from nearby ranches and towns, the church was a node in space that connected different places and drew together people who otherwise might have no reason to meet. For local people who went there year after year, it was a place of ritual, celebration, and shared memory. When it ceased to be used as a church, the place had an afterlife that remained meaningful well into the 1970s, when the logging camps around it were dismantled and workers lost their jobs. In other words, material objects, like the church, have social lives and their ruins have afterlives determined by history.

People too embody the past and its afterlife. Some of the inhabitants of the Chaco are the descendants of Indigenous people who experienced violent contact with the colonizers. The cowboys the anthropologist met acknowledged this mixed heritage. But today, it is their way of life that is at risk as bulldozers tear down forests and destroy livelihoods to make place for vast soy farms. Older waves of destruction in the name of progress have given way to new waves of destruction, and the cowboys who drove out the Indigenous populations in the past are now at risk of disappearing themselves.

Climate change, rising sea levels, and low-lying islands

As we mentioned in the introduction, change in the earth's climate in our contemporary era has two salient characteristics that distinguish it from climate variations that the earth has experienced since its creation: it is caused by human activity and it is extremely rapid. Most human activity that causes climate change is related to industry: resource extraction, manufacture, transportation, and food production all generate enormous amounts of greenhouse gases that are released into the atmosphere and reduce the ozone layer, which no longer can block sunrays effectively, causing global warming (Figure 15.5).

Sometimes the problem comes from surprising quarters. For example, New Zealand has always taken pride in its 'green' and 'pure' image, which it has been successful in using as a branding strategy in the tourism industry that is central to its economy, along with agriculture (Shore 2017). However, since the 1990s and particularly between 2008 and 2017, successive governments have promoted deregulated pro-business **neoliberal** policies and have encouraged

Figure 15.5 The landscape around Mount Kronos, which held mythical meaning for the ancient Greeks, was devastated by massive fires that raged in the Peloponnese (Greece) in 2007; such fires have become increasingly frequent throughout the world, enabled by unprecedented heat waves and droughts. (Courtesy of Susan Brownell)

farmers to switch from small-scale agricultural operations to industrial-scale farming. Large farms now own thousands of cows that produce milk for the manufacture of milk powder for export to China, the Middle East, and other destinations. The problem is that cows' digestive system produces large amounts of methane, a greenhouse gas that, released into the atmosphere, contributes to global warming. In addition, the large amount of manure produced by intensive farming has polluted many rivers and fields and has contributed to cases of tap water becoming unsafe to drink, while cow urine has increased the salt content of water tables.

Globally, some pro-business politicians, industrialists, and a small minority of scientists claim that the earth's climate has always varied and that there is no evidence that contemporary changes are the result of industrial waste, the consumption of fossil fuel (e.g., by cars, airplanes, factories), or the industrialization of food production. As anthropologists, we are bound to listen to all perspectives and understand where these perspectives are grounded. Yet the pattern is clear. Climate-change deniers are invariably exposed as being in the service of industrial interests and benefit materially from the lack of oversight on the effects that industries have on the environment, while the vast majority of scientists around the world have presented incontrovertible evidence that contemporary climate change is radically different from previous climate patterns.

In the next few decades, climate change will have many consequences for the lives of humans, animals, and plants on the planet, including unlivable temperatures in areas like the Arabian Peninsula, the increased frequency, intensity, and geographical distribution of severe weather events, the elimination of life forms unable to adapt to rapidly changing conditions, and food and water shortages. One of the most dramatic consequences is the rising sea levels. Scientists estimate that, by the end of the twenty-first century, sea levels worldwide may rise by between 18 and 59cms above the levels recorded in 1990. The rise in sea level means that many coastal areas, some inhabited by large populations, may become uninhabitable. For example, cities such as New York, Tokyo, Amsterdam, and London, and entire countries such as Bangladesh will need to take new precautions in order to prevent flooding and anticipate storms. Particularly vulnerable are small island nation-states with little or no elevation above sea level. Countries like Tuvalu, Tokelau, and the Marshall Islands in the Pacific and the Maldives in the Indian Ocean are composed entirely of coral atolls and low-lying coral islands, many of which do not rise more than two metres above sea level. Other countries like Kiribati in the Pacific and the Bahamas in the Caribbean are largely made up of low-lying islands. These island nation-states are generally impoverished and lack the infrastructure that wealthier low-lying countries like the Netherlands are able to deploy to prevent damage from rising sea levels.

This damage is already well underway. When Niko Besnier conducted fieldwork on Nukulaelae, a small atoll of Tuvalu, starting in 1980, before 'global warming' was even a term, the 350 inhabitants of the atoll were noticing that seawater was seeping into the gardens, threatening the food plants on which the inhabitants depended, and no one knew why (Besnier 2009). Food gardens are especially vulnerable on these atolls because they are located at the bottom of large pits that generations of islanders have dug up in order to access fertile soil and freshwater, as the surface of the land is just coral sand. Islanders reorganized the village's **division of labour** so that all able-bodied young men could spend their working days building sea walls with coral rocks to try to protect the gardens. This tedious work turned out to be largely ineffective, and additionally it created intergenerational tensions, as the young men felt that they were being underpaid and underappreciated. It also hastened the commoditization of labour and the decreased importance of gift exchange as people now expected to be paid. This example demonstrates that world problems operate on different scales. Global warming is a large-scale event because it is caused by industrial and domestic emissions everywhere in the world and emissions do not stop at national boundaries. Yet global warming radically threatens the organization of local lives, creating new conflicts and problems.

This example also shows that, even before global warming became the pressing global problem that it is today, people in areas of the world that were most affected by its consequences were already taking things into their own hands. But for Tuvaluans and other people in similar situations, local conditions have little to offer to help them limit the damaging effects of global warming: only a narrow range of food plant species can grow in ecologically impoverished environments, raising houses above ground would represent a large investment that people cannot afford, and effective sea barriers require engineering skills and material resources that are simply beyond reach. One solution is to emigrate. In fact, many people from the smaller islands of Tuvalu have moved to the main atoll and capital of the country, Funafuti. But land is scarce on over-crowded Funafuti and many migrants from the outer islands are obliged to build homes on land that Funafuti Islanders have long deemed uninhabitable because it is prone to flooding during exceptionally high tides, which are occurring more and more frequently. An alternative is to move to industrial countries such as Australia and New Zealand, as many of the more fortunate have done by finding ways to circumvent these countries' stringent immigration regulations, which do not welcome poor and unskilled immigrants. Climate change is affecting people differently in such countries, with the more destitute being the most vulnerable.

The world press and documentaries often depict Tuvaluans and members of nations facing similar predicaments as 'climate refugees'. While emotionally evocative, this concept has problems (Farbotko, Stratford, and Lazrus 2015). First, it suggests that people in this situation are passive victims, which they clearly are not. Second, the status of climate refugee has no internationally recognized legal standing and countries are under no obligation to accept people who leave their homes because of environmental pressures, as they are (theoretically at least) in the case of refugees fleeing violence. Third, the concept of climate refugee obscures the fact that the desire to migrate because of rising sea levels is compounded by the desire to migrate for many other reasons, including employment, education, and health services. In fact, throughout the twentieth century, many Tuvaluans were labour migrants, moving to work in phosphate fields in such places as Ocean Island and Nauru, where many spent decades of their lives. Thousands of young men today have found employment as seamen on cargo ships owned by transnational corporations. Moving away from one's home because it has become uninhabitable may be different from moving with the intention of returning, which has consequences for people's sense of national and cultural identity, but the extent to which the two kinds of migrations differ from one another remains an open question. Climate change migrations must thus be understood in this larger historical and ethnographic context rather than in the over-simplified terms in which they are frequently couched in the media.

In some places, economic survival depends on the very activities that contribute to climate change. For example, in the Solomon Islands and Papua New Guinea, economic development has led to widespread deforestation and large-scale intensive agriculture. The consumers who benefit from these ventures are located in distant and larger economies, and thus are removed from the immediate damage to the environment and livelihood they cause. In Trinidad and Tobago, the wealthiest country in the Caribbean, oil extraction has contributed to the economic prosperity of the nation-state while the global consumption of the same commodity simultaneously makes it vulnerable to the effects of rising sea levels (Hughes 2013). The argument is sometimes made that countries like Trinidad and Tobago may be extracting fossil fuels, but on the global scale they are marginal consumers of these environmentally harmful forms of energy.

Human action contributing to global warming can only be tackled by international agreements on policy and practice enforced by the countries that produce the greenhouse gases and emissions in large quantities. Expecting those most directly affected by rising sea levels to adapt to the environmental damage caused by global warming means that those who cause most global warming are not themselves taking responsibility for its consequences. While the first to suffer from climate change are the poor, the powerless, and the inhabitants of marginal areas, in time it will affect everyone on earth. The destruction caused by typhoon Haiyan that the chapter started with has become, along with other severe weather events, increasingly frequent and widespread.

The environment as an anthropological concern

Human beings have always had a complex relationship with the environment, taking from it what they needed to survive and transforming it as they invented new technologies such as agriculture. Human groups have used many kinds of social, environmental, and political measures to allow resources to replenish or to avoid problematic over-abundance. But in some cases, humans have also recklessly damaged their local environments to meet what they considered to be their social, political, economic, or religious needs. However, since the late eighteenth century, industrialization and capitalist expansion have caused environmental depredation that in the twentieth century reached a larger scale than ever before because it is no longer confined to local contexts. The increasing production and consumption of fossil fuel have produced

---

Box 15.3   Climate disasters as social and cultural events

Human beings have often blamed unusual natural events, such as diseases and disasters, on each other. For example, John Wesley, the founder of the Christian revival movement that would come to be known as Methodism, famously attributed the earthquake that devastated Lisbon, Portugal, in 1755 to God's wrath for the inhabitants' sins, an explanation that sparked a heated debate among Enlightenment philosophers of the day. The Christian scriptures, with their scenes of natural calamities meted out by God to punish erring populations, offer copious examples that can be compared to the effects of global warming. Thus, when Fiji, in the southwestern Pacific, was hit in 2016 by Tropical Cyclone Winston, one of the most powerful storms ever recorded, considerable debate ensued among Fijians over who or what was responsible (Cox, Finau, Kant, Tarai, and Titifanue 2018).

Since they were Christianized in the nineteenth century, Indigenous Fijians, who constitute over 50% of the country's population of just under one million (the remainder being Indo-Fijians, most of whom are Hindu or Muslim), have incorporated various Christian denominations into their culture, social structure, and forms of nationalism. Following the cyclone, the government launched the slogan and hashtag #StrongerThanWinston to encourage relief efforts to the affected regions and to foster a sense of national resilience. Pentecostal Christians, who constitute a small but vocal minority, took exception to this slogan, arguing that God had caused the storm as punishment for the nation's sins and that humans could not be stronger than God. Methodists, who constitute a majority, were mostly circumspect in their causal explanations, although many blamed the storm on the government of the prime minister Frank Bainimarama, who took power in a coup in 2007 and has since promoted race- and religion-blind politics that grate against Methodist Fijians' desires to promote Christianity as a nationalist project. What these positions fail to do is contextualize climate change in a political economic context, and this is what Bainimarama's government does by framing the storm as evidence of the reckless policies of industrial countries that are causing climate change, particularly the Australian government's controversial promotion of the coal-mining industry, despite ample evidence that coal is a major threat to the earth's climate.

Thus people in Fiji, and everywhere in the world, try to make sense of increasingly frequent climate events in terms of their local belief systems and ideologies, but these can be diverse, contested, and even contradictory in practice. Yet when confronted with human suffering, Fijian beliefs that the storm was divine punishment gave way to all-out efforts to help those whose homes and livelihoods had been destroyed.

---

carbon-gas emissions that have created climate change of an unprecedented scale and speed. The colonial and postcolonial periods have witnessed numerous conflicts between groups of people over environmental exploitation, yet in some places industrial exploitation is the only way that people have to escape poverty. Because of global warming, entire countries, entire populations, and with them distinct cultures and ways of life are under threat, compounding pressing problems like poverty and political disenfranchisement. Few issues cause as much anxiety in the world in which we live as the damage that humans have done to the environment, and anthropologists have important contributions to make to understanding and helping to alleviate these world problems.

Key thinkers mentioned in this chapter:

Keith Basso; Gregory Bateson; Tim Ingold; Lewis Henry Morgan; Roy Rappaport; Julian Steward

Key terms mentioned in this chapter (see Glossary):

Anthropocene; Cultural Ecology; Ecological anthropology; Environmental anthropology; Ethnoecology; Globalization; Human ecology; Multi-sited ethnographies; Multispecies ethnography; Non-governmental organizations; Social movement

Questions for discussion/review:

1 Explain how human groups shape and are shaped by their environments.
2 What can multispecies ethnography add to our knowledge of the environment?
3 Why is climate change migration a more complicated phenomenon than it might at first appear to be?
4 Discuss how climate and environment are understood in cultural terms.

Glossary

achieved status   social status that derives from a person's achievements.

activist anthropology or **engaged anthropology**   collaborative research between anthropologists and groups that are generally marginalized or disempowered to achieve a social or political outcome for the benefit of the groups.

affective labour   work designed to take care of other people and make them feel good about themselves and the situation in which they find themselves.

affiliation   the creation and maintenance of a kin relation by marriage.

affine   relative by marriage.

age   measure of how long a person has lived, often reckoned in years but always in tacit comparison with other people.

agency   the ability of an individual to take decisions and act upon them, contrasted with structure; *see also* structure.

agent   a person who is able to take decisions and act upon them; the term is often used as a synonym of 'individual' or 'person'.

agnate   a person descended from the same male ancestor as oneself.

alienable   quality of an object that enables the identity of its owner or previous owner to be eliminated, characteristic of a commodity; *see also* inalienable.

alienation   the condition of estrangement from others or society, or the estrangement of a worker from the product of their labour in a capitalist system in which they exchange their labour for wages and have no control over what they produce.

allochthony   the state of not being considered an original inhabitant of a region; *see also* autochthony.

animism   a belief that all inanimate and animate forms of life contain a living soul or power.

Anthropocene   the current geological age in which human activity has a dominant effect on the environment and climate.

anthropometry   the pseudo-scientific study of the measurements of the human body developed in the nineteenth century and used by early anthropologists to measure human variation.

applied anthropology   the use of anthropological perspectives to identify and solve social problems, also known as practising anthropology.

arranged marriage   a marriage system in which who one marries is the primary responsibility of senior members of one's family; *see also* companionate marriage, elective marriage.

ascribed status   social status inherited from the context in which a person is born.

assimilation   a process in which ethnic groups, particularly immigrants, adapt to and are absorbed into the dominant culture.

assisted reproductive technology (ART)   the use of technology, such as in vitro fertilization, or other people, through surrogacy, to conceive a child.

asylum   protection offered by a state to a person seeking refugee status.

audit culture   the increasingly demanding bureaucratic accountability procedures placed by academic managers on researchers and teachers.

austerity   economic situation that the state declares to be in crisis, justifying funding cuts in social welfare.

autochthony   the state of being considered an original inhabitant of a region; *see also* allochthony.

avoidance   the requirement in some societies that some people who are in a specific kin relationship refrain from being together or interacting.

balanced reciprocity   *see* reciprocity.

barter   the exchange of objects of a different nature and comparable value that does not establish a social relationship between the parties.

big man (or *bigman*)   a type of leader who must rely on his ability to persuade and on the support of his kin networks in order to exert authority, particularly associated with male leadership in the egalitarian societies of Melanesia.

bilateral descent   a system of kinship in which people are considered to be equally related to others on both their mother's and their father's side; *see also* matrilineal descent, patrilineal descent, unilineal descent.

biopower   a form of institutional power that structural entities (e.g., the state, the medical world, the market) exert on agents through non-coercive actions (e.g., counselling, encouraging, enumeration) that agents come to incorporate into their own designs for self-improvement.

bourgeoisie   in Marxism, the class of people who own the means of production; *see also* petty bourgeoisie, proletariat.

bride service   labour carried out by the groom for the family of his spouse, which usually begins before the marriage and may extend for a considerable period of time after marriage.

bridewealth   money, property, or goods that a man or his family gives to his wife's family in order to legitimate conjugal rights; *see also* dowry.

capital   resources available to agents, which can be economic (wealth, income), symbolic (honour, prestige), cultural (skills, qualifications), or social (networks, relationships).

care chain   a system of care whereby one person is employed to take care of other people's dependents (children, elderly relatives) while leaving her or his own dependents in the care of relatives.

caste   a system of social stratification in which people belong to groups based on occupation (or the occupation of their ancestors) and only marry people who belong to the same group (endogamy); the canonical example is that of India, where the caste system is culturally structured in terms of relative ritual purity.

chain migration   migration in which migrants facilitate the subsequent migration of people of the same family, village, or region.

chosen family   a family-like structure composed of people who are not related by blood but nurture relations of mutual support akin to those of a traditional family, despite the lack of legal recognition.

cisgender   gender that corresponds to the sexual identity of the person at birth; *see also* transgender.

citizenship   the act of participating in the activities of a nation-state as a claim to belonging, or status conferred on persons who meet the legal requirements of a state to share in the rights and duties of citizens.

civil union   a legally recognized union between two people of the same or different gender that grants similar rights to those of a married couple.

clan   a group of people who all descend from an actual or assumed common ancestor.

classificatory kin   a system of organizing relatives in which certain categories of distinct relatives (e.g., sibling, cousin) are referred to by the same terms; *see also* descriptive kin.

code-switching   the alternation of two or more languages within or across interactions.

colonialism   the political and economic control of one nation over another involving settlement and often exploitation of both people and natural resources.

commodification or **commoditization**   the process of transforming goods, services, relationships, people, objects, and ideas into entities that have a quantifiable economic value.

commodity   an object or entity that is transacted between people in a capitalist system and that is assigned a quantifiable economic value; *see also* gift.

commons   resources, such as land, institutions, and services, to which all citizens have the right of use.

communitas   the shared feelings of togetherness, equality, and solidarity experienced by people coming together in a ritual context.

community   a social group bound together by mechanical solidarity; by extension, any structured social group brought together by a sense to belonging together; *see also* society.

companionate marriage   a marriage system in which the person one marries is determined by the bonds of mutual affection of the concerned individuals; *see also* arranged marriage, elective marriage.

comparison   the act of finding similarities and differences between social and cultural entities and elaborating generalizations from the process.

complex marriage   an uncommon marriage system in which many men are married to many women at the same time.

consanguineal kin   relative by blood.

consumption   the acquisition and use of material objects or experiences to produce social meaning and identity.

cosmopolitanism   a perspective on the world that embraces social and cultural diversity.

cross-cousin   the child of one's father's sister or mother's brother; *see also* parallel cousin.

cultural ecology   the study of humans' cultural adaptation to the environment from a materialist perspective.

cultural evolutionism   an anthropological theory of the nineteenth century that maintained that human societies could be ordered and progressed along a continuum from primitive to civilized.

cultural relativism   the recognition that all aspects of human society and culture have a logic determined by the local context.

culturalization of citizenship   the redefinition of citizenship from a legal concept to being a matter of culture.

culture   the totality of symbols, beliefs, and representations that members of a human group recognize and that guide their actions.

culture and personality   a mid-twentieth-century anthropological theory that maintained that a normative personality type characterized each society, which helped determine how well integrated individuals are.

cyberspace   the digital field site where anthropologists study socio-cultural phenomena such as digital communities in interactive online spaces.

decolonizing anthropology   a critical process responding to the realization that anthropological knowledge is constructed by diverse voices that include those that have not traditionally been recognized, rather than by members of dominant groups and nations.

descent   the assignation of one's social identity on the basis of one's ancestry.

descriptive kin   a system of organizing relatives in which all categories of distinct relatives are referred to by different terms; *see also* classificatory kin.

deterritorialization   the state of being disconnected socially and culturally from a particular location.

diaspora   a group of people who have dispersed to two or more locations from a location they consider to be their traditional homeland.

digital divide   the inequality created by relative access to digital resources, in particular the internet.

disease   the pathological condition of one's body that is considered objectively measurable; *see also* illness.

disenchantment   the loss of a sense of wonder and mystery as people increasingly lead their life according to rational principles.

distinction   status measured in terms of a person's access to various forms of social and cultural resources.

diversity   the variability of practices and beliefs across the world's societies, the recognition of which is fundamental to anthropology.

dividuality   a cultural way of conceptualizing the person that emphasizes adaptability to context and attentiveness to social relations.

division of labour   the distribution of work according to social dimensions such as social class or gender to meet the needs of society.

dowry   money, property, or goods that a woman or her family brings with her when she marries in order to legitimate conjugal rights; *see also* bridewealth.

Dreaming   among Australian Aboriginal peoples, the world of spirits that interact with humans.

duty   the expectation that society places on an individual; *see also* right.

ecological anthropology   the study of how people engage with aspects of the environment in the context of global dynamics.

effervescence   emotion felt by members of a group when they come together and are unified and transformed by the experience of a shared ecstatic moment.

egalitarianism   a social system that prioritizes the equal status of all or some of its members and showcases the value of sharing and consensus.

elective marriage   a marriage system in which who one marries is the primary responsibility of the concerned individuals; *see also* arranged marriage, companionate marriage.

empathy   the capacity to experience the world from the perspective of another person or group, to understand and share in their feelings, which is essential to the success of ethnography.

enclosure   the transformation of public land to private property.

endangered language   language that is not being transmitted to younger generations and thus risks disappearing.

endocannibalism   the consumption of the flesh of a member of one's family or group, usually as part of a mortuary ritual; *see also* exocannibalism.

endogamy   a marriage system that prescribes that individuals marry within their group; *see also* exogamy.

engaged anthropology   *see* activist anthropology.

environmental determinism   the assumption that the physical environment shapes the social and cultural system of a group.

equality of opportunity   the notion that everyone in society should be given the same chances in life, with no one being disadvantaged because of who they are or what they have.

equality of outcome   the notion that everyone in society should have the same resources.

ethics   system of values that vary across societies and over time; in anthropological research, ethics requires that anthropologists abide by the explicit intention to do no harm.

ethnicity   a form of identification based on the ideology of a common history and common social and cultural practices, defined in contrast to a larger whole or to neighbouring groups.

ethnocentrism   more or less conscious bias that privileges one's own culture as superior to others as the standard of values.

ethnoecology   the study of how groups understand the ecosystems in which they live and classify what they find in them.

ethnographic fieldwork   the methods used by ethnographers to gather data in the context of participant observation.

ethnography   the study of society and cultures from an anthropological perspective, which privileges participant observation during fieldwork.

ethnoscience   the study of the knowledge systems of different societies, particularly relating to the natural world.

exocannibalism   the consumption of the flesh of someone outside one's family or group; *see also* endocannibalism.

exogamy   a marriage system that prescribes that individuals marry outside their group; *see also* endogamy.

expatriate   person who chooses to live outside of her or his native country for employment or other reasons and largely remains within enclaves of people in the same situation.

family   a group of people who consider themselves related to one another.

feminist anthropology   an approach to anthropology that prioritizes the study of difference and inequality on the basis of gender and its interaction with other forms of difference.

fictive or **voluntary kin**   person to whom one is not related by blood or marriage with whom one forms a kinship bond characterized by feelings and obligations similar to those of one's kin.

fieldnotes   texts that ethnographers compile to record their observations of the social practices of the people among whom they conduct fieldwork.

fieldwork   the methods used by ethnographers to gather data in the context of participant observation.

food desert   area where the only source of groceries are small 'express' shops that sell low-quality processed food because grocery shops have been put out of business by large chains reachable only by car.

fostering   the rearing of a child by someone who is not the child's natural or adoptive parent.

four-field anthropology   an approach to anthropology associated with the practice of the discipline in North America that encompassed physical anthropology, archaeology, socio-cultural anthropology, and linguistic anthropology.

fraternal polyandry   a marriage system in which one woman marries a set of brothers.

gender   the social and cultural features attributed to people on the basis of their perceived female or male identity.

gender hierarchy or **stratification**   a social ordering in which the gender groups are ranked in terms of dominance and power.

gender role   social norms of appropriate and acceptable ways to behave according to one's gender, generally shaped by conceptions of femininity and masculinity.

gender stereotype   generalizations about the characteristics and attributes a person should have, or roles a person should perform, based on gender.

gender stratification   structures of inequality designed to maintain a power differential between the genders.

genealogical method   the analysis of kinship through the collection of people's genealogies.

generalized reciprocity   *see* reciprocity.

generation   a category of people who share similar life experiences; more specifically, a generation set (sometimes age set) is a category of people, part of a hierarchy, whose members are thought to belong together according to certain criteria, such as having passed together through rites of passage.

genetrix   biological mother; *see also* mater.

genitor   biological father; *see also* pater.

genocide   the systematic attempt to kill an ethnic or religious group by a group in power.

gift   an object or other entity that is exchanged from one person to another with the purpose of establishing and maintaining social relations over time, particularly in a non-capitalist system; *see also* commodity.

gift economy   an economic system based on the exchange and circulation of gifts.

globalization   the contemporary state of the world in which technology has decreased the importance of distance, time, and boundaries, and has enabled the unprecedented mobility of people, capital, resources, and information around the world.

governmentality   ways in which populations are controlled through non-coercive means that include biopower.

griot   person who specialized in making music and delivering oratorical performances in praise of higher-ranking persons.

habitus   ways of thinking, feeling, and acting that constitute human beings' everyday lives shaped by social structures and in turn acting upon social structures through agency.

heteronormativity   the privileging of traditionally normative gender and sexual roles.

holistic   an approach to the study of the social world that emphasizes that all aspects of this social world should be understood in relation to one another.

homosociality   positive social relations between people of the same gender.

household   a group of people who share a residence and engage in common practices of production and consumption; the term is also applied to the location where such people reside.

human ecology   the study of how humans interact with the environment with special attention to human impact on the environment.

hunter-gatherer   member of a society that meets its dietary needs by hunting for meat and gathering vegetable food.

hybridity   the mixing of distinct elements to produce something new.

hypergamy   a marriage practice in which a woman marries someone of a higher social status; *see also* hypogamy.

hypogamy   a marriage practice in which a woman marries someone of a lower social status; *see also* hypergamy.

ideational   of symbols, beliefs, and representations that make up culture; *see also* material.

ideology   a systematic set of beliefs often relating to ideas involving politics, economics, and religion.

illness   the pathological condition of one's body that is given social and cultural meaning.

imagined community   a large group of people who recognize themselves as a nation through mutual affinity and shared symbols and histories.

inalienable   quality of an object that attaches the identity of its owner or previous owner to the object, characteristic of a gift; *see also* alienable.

incest   sexual relation between specified kin that are prohibited by cultural norms or law.

incorporation   *see* rite of passage.

Indigenous   a social group who are recognized as being the original inhabitants of a region, in contrast to settlers who arrived later and have become dominant; *see also* settler colonialism.

inequality   the result of differential access to material, cultural, and political resources resulting in some people consistently having access to more than others.

informed consent   permission given by research participants to take part in ethnographic research after the ethnographer has explained to them the nature of the research.

initiation ritual   rite of passage in the form of a ceremony or test that marks the admission of a person into a specific social group, such as a generation set or an organization.

integration   policies designed to encourage migrants to conform to the norms of the majority.

intersectionality   the recognition that structures of inequality based on one social criterion (e.g., race, sexuality, religion) aggravates or alleviates inequality based on other social criteria.

intersex   one of a range of medical conditions that stem from the non-standard alignment of genetic information, hormonal functions, and external and internal sexual organs.

interview   a form of interaction, governed by local norms, in which one person poses questions to another to elicit information about society and culture.

invented tradition   a tradition viewed as grounded in the distant past by its practitioners while in fact it is usually the product of recent historical social or political processes.

in-vitro fertilization   a form of technologically assisted reproduction in which an ovum is fertilized by sperm outside the body.

Islamophobia   the fear and denigration of Islam or Muslims, often resulting in prejudice and discrimination.

jus domicilii, jus sanguinis, jus soli   bases upon which people can claim a right to legal citizenship, through residence, descent, and place of birth, respectively.

karyotype   an individual's collection of chromosomes.

kin   a person one is related to through the principles of kinship.

kinship   the system that members of a society use to determine the structure of families.

language acquisition   the process through which children develop a first language or language in infancy.

language revitalization   efforts to revive the use of an endangered language.

language socialization   the process through which children develop into social beings through their verbal interactions with others.

life cycle   the sum total of the changes that humans go through from birth until death.

life stage   category that subdivides the life cycle.

lineage   a descent group from a common ancestor through either the mother's or the father's side.

lingua franca   a language employed by people who do not share a native language but nevertheless need to communicate with one another.

linguistic ideology   the set of socially and politically charged ideas that people attribute to language but are in fact about the speakers of the language.

lumpenproletariat   in Marxism, the class of people who fall outside of the structures of economic production because they lack the resources to be part of them.

marriage   a legally, religiously, or socially recognized formal union of two or more people who usually live together and usually form an economic unit.

mater   socially recognized mother; *see also* genetrix.

material   of concrete aspects of society, including economic elements, social relations, and structures of power; *see also* ideational.

matrifocality   a household structure headed by a woman.

matriline   a descent group whose members are related through female members; *see also* patriline.

matrilineal descent   a system of kinship in which people trace descent through women only; *see also* bilateral descent, patrilineal descent, unilineal descent.

matrilocal residence   a practice that prescribes that a man reside in or near the household of his wife's family; *see also* neolocal residence, patrilocal residence.

means of production   the resources and instruments used to produce goods that then generate wealth.

mechanical solidarity   *see* solidarity.

medicalization   the transformation of a physiological event into a medical problem that requires specialized attention.

meritocracy   a system in which a person's status is determined by her or his achievements.

migration   the geographical movement of people of a more or less permanent nature.

mobility   the temporary or permanent geographical movement of people.

moiety   a division of society into two groups for the purpose of marriage selection and ritual life.

monogamy   a marriage practice in which each person is married to a single spouse; *see also* polygamy.

monotheism   the belief in a single deity; *see also* polytheism.

moral economy   an economic system based on principles of equality and justice, which are not necessarily institutionalized.

multiculturalism   a political system that recognizes and values the ethnic and cultural diversity of the nation.

multi-sited ethnography   a research perspective that seeks to study people, objects, and ideas as they emerge in multiple locations.

nation   a large group of people who share symbols of belonging, histories, and a mutual affinity of belonging to the same political entity.

nationalism   feelings of loyalty to one's own nation.

nation-state   the combined entity formed by the state and the nation when these coincide.

necropolitics   political or economic decision making that turns a particular group of people into a dispensable population.

negative reciprocity   *see* reciprocity.

neoliberalism   economic and political system that favours free market values, deregulation, and individual autonomy.

neolocal residence   a practice that prescribes that a married couple reside in a household that differs from that of the families of the spouses; *see also* matrilocal residence, patrilocal residence.

noble savage   Westerners' representation of non-Western people, associated in particular with the Romantic era, as lacking civilization but being innocent and purer than civilized people.

non-governmental organization   not-for-profit organization focused on tackling social issues, particularly to promote humanitarian efforts and international development.

organic solidarity   *see* solidarity.

orientalism   a mode of representation of the other that assumes fundamental differences between Western and other societies, with the former being superior to the other, which has historically legitimized the West's colonial domination of other societies.

orthodoxy   approach to religion that claims to be the only correct interpretation of doctrines.

parallel cousin   the child of a one's father's brother or mother's sister; *see also* cross-cousin.

participant observation   a qualitative ethnographic research method that involves the researchers immersing themselves in the researched group and participating as fully as possible in its activities to understand their social organization.

pater   socially recognized father; *see also* genitor.

patriarchy   a social system in which men claim dominance over political, economic, and social life.

patriline   a descent group whose members are related through male members; *see also* matriline.

patrilineal descent   a system of kinship in which people trace descent through men only; *see also* bilateral descent, matrilineal descent, unilineal descent.

patrilocal residence   a practice that prescribes that a woman reside in or near the household of her husband's family; *see also* matrilocal residence, neolocal residence.

petty bourgeoisie   in Marxism, the class of people who do not own the means of production but do not have to sell their labour to survive; *see also* bourgeoisie, proletariat.

phenomenology   a philosophical approach that centralizes people's consciousness of their experiences and objects in the world and their actions based on these experiences.

political ecology   the study of how humans interact with the environment in a political-economic context.

pollution   quality ascribed to a person of a certain social category that is viewed as culturally and religiously harmful to others.

polyandry   a marriage system in which one woman is married to more than one man.

polygamy   a marriage system in which one man is married to more than one woman or one woman is married to more than one man; *see also* monogamy, polygyny, polyandry.

polygyny   a marriage system in which one man is married to more than one woman.

polytheism   the belief in many deities; *see also* monotheism.

postcolonial studies   an interdisciplinary research perspective that studies the legacies of colonialism on contemporary societies.

postmodernism   a research perspective grounded in the suspicion of the faith in science inherited from the Enlightenment, insisting on the fact that knowledge is always contingent on the context in which it is produced.

potlatch   a competitive exchange ritual, formerly common among American Indians of the American Northwest, in which one village invited in turn the inhabitants of allied villages for feasting and often extravagant gift giving.

practice theory   an anthropological and sociological theory that seeks to understand the social and cultural world through analysis of people's embodied actions and knowledge in relation to social structures, particularly those that have political significance.

practicing anthropology   *see* applied anthropology.

precarity   the state of living without security and predictability and with limited access to essential resources to sustain one's life.

preferential marriage   marriage practice that is viewed as better than others, but is not prescribed.

prescriptive marriage rules   marriage practices that are required; *see also* proscriptive marriage rules.

primary sexual characteristics   aspects of human anatomy that are involved in potential reproduction and that distinguish the sexes; *see also* secondary sexual characteristics.

proletariat   in Marxism, the class of people who have to sell their labour in order to survive; *see also* bourgeoisie.

proscriptive marriage rules   marriage practices that are forbidden; *see also* prescriptive marriage rules.

public anthropology   the use of anthropological knowledge in the public sphere, such as the media, with the intent of engaging with public affairs.

public sphere   the realm of society in which different opinions can be expressed on matters of general social and political concern.

queer   a person or perspective that embraces a diversity of gender and sexual expressions with the aim of questioning traditional norms.

race   the social classification of human beings according to subjective evaluations of their phenotype.

racism   the ideology and practice of imputing inherent differences between 'races' and ranking some as superior to others to uphold structures of inequality and discrimination.

rank   system of social stratification according to birth right, or the social status of a person according to such a social system.

reciprocity   non-market exchange practices over extended periods of time practised in gift-based economies; reciprocity is generalized when parties give without keeping accounts; reciprocity is balanced when parties exchange objects of similar value; reciprocity is negative when one party gains at the expense of another party.

redistribution   the transfer of resources between people so as to achieve relative wealth equality.

reflexivity   a critical and analytic perspective on one's own assumptions and to claims of objectivity; reflexive anthropology is anthropological work that foregrounds the intersubjective nature of anthropological knowledge.

refugee   legal status granted to a person who has left her or his country of origin because of persecution.

relativism   *see* cultural relativism.

religious pluralism   the coexistence of well-differentiated religious traditions in the same place at the same time.

religious syncretism   the simultaneous belief in the precepts of different religions and the concurrent practice of their rituals; the blending and incorporation of beliefs and ritual practices from different traditions.

remittance   transfer of money or other resources from people working away from their home to support people who have remained in the country of origin.

reproduction (social)   mechanisms that ensure the continuity of the structure of social groups over time.

resistance   a form of agency that seeks to undermine the power exerted by structural entities or powerful agents.

right   the claim that an individual can place on society; *see also* duty.

rite of passage   ritual marking the transition of a person from one social status, often a stage in the life cycle, to another; it typically consists of three stages, separation, the removal of the person undergoing the rite from society; liminality, the state of being in transition from one social status to another; and incorporation, the return of the person undergoing the rite to society.

ritual　purposive and scripted action imbued with social and cultural meaning.

ritualized homosexuality　initiation ritual that involves same-sex sexual contact between a person undergoing initiation and a person who is already initiated.

salvage anthropology　the nineteenth- and early-twentieth-century study of social groups thought to be at risk of extinction.

secondary sexual characteristics　aspects of human anatomy that distinguish the sexes but are not involved in potential reproduction; *see also* primary sexual characteristics.

secularism　a political ideology that affirms that political and social institutions should be independent of religion.

separation　*see* rite of passage.

settler colonialism　a form of colonialism in which people from the colonizing country have moved to the colonized area permanently and have become dominant; *see also* Indigenous.

sex　the division of beings into groups grounded in biological characteristics that are involved in potential reproduction but are most frequently associated with other forms of human activity.

sex-reassignment surgery　the surgical procedure by which a person's sexual anatomy is altered to conform to the person's gender identity.

sexuality　capacity to experience sexual attraction to another person, an object, or a context.

sexual orientation　sexual and emotional attraction to a specific gender or genders.

shaman　ritual specialist capable of mediating between humans and spirits and curing illnesses.

situated knowledge　the recognition that all knowledge is produced in a given historical and political context and is determined by the social identity of the researcher.

social class　a form of social stratification traditionally determined by income, education, and occupation, but also by access to other kinds of resources such as social networks and personal taste.

social movement　individuals, groups, or organizations that come together to act in support of a particular political or social cause, frequently by protesting.

social relation　cluster of actions that shape the relationship between people (as well as, in some circumstances, deities, animals, etc.) in a socially recognizable way.

social reproduction　the maintenance of people's lives through acts of care, support, and nurturance, which are often overlooked in traditional socio-economic models.

society　the structure of human relations of people in systems of relationships that endure over time; members of a society typically share a common culture.

solidarity　feelings of social cohesion and actions based on them designed to ensure the reproduction of society; mechanical solidarity is based on people all sharing the same values and lifeways; organic solidarity is based on people's dependence on one another because of work specialization.

state　the institutions and processes that constitute the political structure of a country.

stratification　the organization of a social entity in which different groups have unequal and ranked positions with respect to access to resources.

status　position in society, measured in terms of wealth, power, and prestige.

status group　in Weberian analysis, groups of people who fall in the same social class because they respond in similar ways to specific situations.

structural adjustment programme　reorganization of the functions of the state to reduce state spending, imposed primarily on countries of the Global South as a condition for being granted a loan by the World Bank, the International Monetary Fund, or wealthy countries.

structural functionalism   an anthropological theory of the first part of the twentieth century that asserted that all aspects of society are designed to maintain the structure of society over time as a discrete, bounded, and unchanging entity.

structuralism   an anthropological theory of the mid-twentieth century that focused on the meaning-producing relations of elements within a social or cultural system.

structural violence   systemic oppression to which dominant social institutions or structures subject people that prevents them from meeting their basic needs.

structure   an entity, commonly an institution like the state or the law, that constrains and regulates the actions of agents; *see also* agency.

sumptuary law   a law that restricts who can display particular signs of consumption, such as clothing, on the basis of social status.

surrogacy   arrangement in which a woman agrees to carry and give birth to a child on behalf of another person or other persons, who will become the child's parents.

survey work   the collection of a large amount of empirical data about society and culture in a relatively short period of time, associated in particular with late-nineteenth-century anthropological methods.

symbol   an entity that stands for another entity.

symbolic anthropology   an anthropological theory of the late twentieth century that focused on the structure of symbols that make up culture.

synaesthesia   a neurological condition which produces a sense impression on one part of the body when a stimulus is applied to another, for instance when hearing a certain sound may be perceived as a colour or taste.

third-culture kid   child raised in a country or countries that differ from that of the parents and who develops an affinity with the cultures of those countries.

totem   animal or other natural object used as a spiritual or symbolic representation of a clan or family.

tradition   practice that is passed on from generation to generation, often considered to have cultural meaning.

transactionalism   an anthropological theory that seeks to understand society and culture as arising from people's day-to-day interactions with one another.

transgender   a person who takes on the attributes of the opposite gender from the sex assigned at birth or who chooses an ambiguous gender identity.

transition   a term used to describe the change from one sex to another, i.e. from female to male or vice versa.

transnational   operating across the boundaries of nation-states.

undocumented migrant   a person who moves to a country, usually to seek a better life, where she or he is not recognized as having the legal right to reside.

unilineal descent   a system of kinship in which descent is traced through either their mother's or their father's ancestors, but not both; *see also* bilateral descent, matrilineal descent, patrilineal descent.

universal basic income   regular and unconditional payment by the state to every person in a country regardless of wealth and income, designed to ensure that everyone has enough to live on and to alleviate poverty.

voluntary kin   *see* fictive kin.

References

Abarca, Gray Albert, and Susan Bibler Coutin. 2018. 'Sovereign Intimacies: The Lives of Documents within U.S. State–Noncitizen Relationships'. *American Ethnologist* 45, no. 1: 7–19.

Abidin, Crystal. 2017. 'Influencer Extravaganza: Commercial "Lifestyle" Microcelebrities in Singapore'. In *The Routledge Companion to Digital Ethnography*, edited by Larissa Hjorth, Heather Horst, Anne Galloway, and Genevieve Bell, 158–168. New York: Routledge.

Abu El-Haj, Nadia. 2007. 'The Genetic Reinscription of Race'. *Annual Review of Anthropology* 36:283–300.

Abu-Lughod, Lila. 1995. 'The Objects of Soap Opera: Egyptian Television and the Cultural Politics of Modernity'. In *Worlds Apart: Modernity through the Prism of the Local*, edited by Daniel Miller, 190–210. London: Routledge.

Açıksöz, Salih Can. 2020. *Sacrificial Limbs: Masculinity, Disability, and Political Violence in Turkey*. Oakland: University of California Press.

Adrian, Bonnie. 2003. *Framing the Bride: Globalizing Beauty and Romance in Taiwan's Bridal Industry*. Berkeley: University of California Press.

Al-Gazali, Lihadh, and Bassam R. Ali. 2010. 'Genetic Disorders in the United Arab Emirates'. In *Genetic Disorders Among Arab Populations*, edited by Ahmad S. Teebi, 639–676. Heidelberg: Springer.

Allison, Anne. 1994. *Nightwork: Sexuality, Pleasure, and Corporate Masculinity in a Tokyo Hostess Club*. Chicago: University of Chicago Press.

Allison, Anne. 2013. *Precarious Japan*. Durham, NC: Duke University Press.

Alonso Bejarano, Carolina, Lucia López Juárez, Mirian A. Mijangos García, and Daniel M. Goldstein. 2019. *Decolonizing Ethnography: Undocumented Immigrants and New Directions in Social Science*. Durham, NC: Duke University Press.

American Anthropological Association. 1998. 'AAA Statement on Race'. *American Anthropologist* 100, no. 3: 712–713.

American Anthropological Association. 2007. *American Anthropological Association's Executive Board Statement on the Human Terrain System Project*. http://s3.amazonaws.com/rdcms-aaa/files/production/public/FileDownloads/pdfs/pdf/EB_Resolution_110807.pdf.

Anderson, Benedict. 2016a. *Imagined Communities: Reflections on the Origin and Spread of Nationalism*. London: Verso. (First published 1983.)

Anderson, Benedict. 2016b. *A Life beyond the Boundaries*. London: Verso.

Andersson, Ruben. 2014. *Illegality, Inc.: Clandestine Migration and the Business of Bordering Europe*. Berkeley: University of California Press.

Andrikopoulos, Apostolos. 2013. 'Migration, Class and Symbolic Status: Nigerians in the Netherlands and Greece'. In *Long Journeys: African Migrants on the Road*, edited by Alessandro Triulzi and Robert Lawrence McKenzie, 165–185. Leiden: Brill.

Appadurai, Arjun. 1996. *Modernity at Large: Cultural Dimensions of Globalization*. Minneapolis: University of Minnesota Press.

Ardener, Edwin. 1971. 'Introductory Essay: Social Anthropology and Language'. In *Social Anthropology and Language*, edited by Edwin Ardener, ix–cii. London: Tavistock.

Arens, William. 1979. *The Man-Eating Myth: Anthropology and Anthropophagy*. Oxford: Oxford University Press.

Ariès, Philippe. 1962. *Centuries of Childhood: A Social History of Family Life*. Translated by Robert Baldick. London: Jonathan Cape. (First published 1960.)

Asad, Talal. 1993. *Genealogies of Religion: Discipline and Reasons of Power in Christianity and Islam*. Baltimore, MD: Johns Hopkins University Press.

Asad, Talal. 2003. *Formations of the Secular: Christianity, Islam, Modernity*. Stanford, CA: Stanford University Press.

Aulino, Felicity. 2016. 'Rituals of Care for the Elderly in Northern Thailand: Merit, Morality, and the Everyday of Long-Term Care'. *American Ethnologist* 43, no. 1: 91–102.

Awondo, Patrick, Peter Geschiere, and Graeme Reid. 2012. 'Homophobic Africa? Toward A More Nuanced View'. *African Studies Review* 55, no. 3: 145–168.

Balzani, Marzia. 2003. *Modern Indian Kingship: Changing Traditions and Rituals of Legitimation in Jodhpur*. Oxford: James Currey; Santa Fe, NM: School of American Research Press.

Balzani, Marzia. 2011. 'Constructing Culture and Credibility in Asylum and Immigration Tribunals: The Case of Forced Marriage'. In *Forced Marriage: Introducing a Social Justice and Human Rights Perspective*, edited by Aisha K. Gill and Anitha Sundari, 200–220. London: Zed.

Balzani, Marzia. 2020. *Ahmadiyya Islam and the Muslim Diaspora: Living at the End of Days*. London: Routledge.

Barth, Fredrik. 1998. 'Introduction'. In *Ethnic Groups and Boundaries: The Social Organisation of Cultural Difference*, edited by Fredrik Barth, 9–38. Long Grove, IL: Waveland. (First published 1969.)

Basch, Linda Green, Nina Glick Schiller, and Cristina Szanton Blanc. 1994. *Nations Unbound: Transnational Projects, Postcolonial Predicaments, and Deterritorialized Nation-states*. London: Routledge.

Basso, Keith H. 1984. *Wisdom Sits in Places: Landscape and Language among the Western Apache*. Albuquerque: University of New Mexico Press.

Bayly, C. A. 2004. *The Birth of the Modern World 1780–1914: Global Connections and Comparisons*. Oxford: Blackwell.

Belausteguigoitia, Marisa. 2006. 'On Line, off Line and in Line: The Zapatista Rebellion and the Uses of Technology by Indian Women'. In *Native on the Net: Indigenous and Diasporic Peoples in the Virtual Age*, edited by Kyra Landzelius, 97–111. London: Routledge.

Benedict, Ruth. 1934. 'Anthropology and the Abnormal'. *Journal of General Psychiatry* 10, no. 1: 59–80.

Benjamin, Saija, and Fred Dervin. 2015. *Migration, Diversity, and Education: Beyond Third Culture Kids*. New York: Palgrave Macmillan.

Benton, Adia. 2015. *HIV Exceptionalism: Development through Disease in Sierra Leone*. Minneapolis: University of Minnesota Press.

Bernal, Victoria. 2014. *Nation as Network: Diaspora, Cyberspace, and Citizenship*. Chicago: University of Chicago Press.

Bernstein, Anya. 2019. *The Future of Immortality: Remaking Life and Death in Contemporary Russia*. Princeton, NJ: Princeton University Press.

Besnier, Niko. 2009. *Gossip and the Everyday Production of Politics*. Honolulu: University of Hawai'i Press.

Besnier, Niko. 2011. *On the Edge of the Global: Modern Anxieties in a Pacific Island Nation*. Stanford, CA: Stanford University Press.

Besnier, Niko, and Kalissa Alexeyeff, eds. 2014. *Gender on the Edge: Transgender, Gay, and Other Pacific Islanders*. Honolulu: University of Hawai'i Press.

Besnier, Niko, Susan Brownell, and Thomas F. Carter. 2018. *The Anthropology of Sport: Bodies, Borders, Biopolitics*. Oakland: University of California Press.

Besnier, Niko, Daniel Guinness, Mark Hann, and Uroš Kovač. 2018. 'Rethinking Masculinity in the Neoliberal Age: Cameroonian Footballers, Fijian Rugby Players, and Senegalese Wrestlers'. *Comparative Studies in Society and History* 60, no. 4: 839–872.

Bianchi, Robert R. 2017. 'Reimagining the Hajj'. *Social Sciences* 6, no. 2, article 36, https://www.mdpi.com/2076-0760/6/2/36.

Biehl, João. 2005. *Vita: Life in a Zone of Social Abandonment*. Berkeley: University of California Press.

Billig, Michael. 1995. *Banal Nationalism*. London: Sage.

Bloch, Maurice. 1987. 'The Ritual of the Royal Bath in Madagascar: The Dissolution of Death, Birth and Fertility into Authority'. In *Rituals of Royalty: Power and Ceremonial in Traditional Societies*, edited by David Cannadine and Simon Price, 271–297. Cambridge: Cambridge University Press.

Boellstorff, Tom. 2015. *Coming of Age in Second Life: An Anthropologist Explores the Virtually Human*. Princeton, NJ: Princeton University Press.

Bohannan, Paul. 1959. 'The Impact of Money on an African Subsistence Economy'. *Journal of Economic History* 19, no. 4: 491–503.

Bonetti, Roberta. 2012. 'Coffins for Wear and Consumption: *Abebuu Adekai* as Memory Makers among the Ga of Ghana'. *Res* 61–62: 262–278.

Bonilla, Yarimar, and Jonathan Rosa. 2015. '#Ferguson: Digital Protest, Hashtag Ethnography, and the Racial Politics of Social Media in the United States'. *American Ethnologist* 42, no. 1: 4–17.

Bourdieu, Pierre. 1977. *Outline of the Theory of Practice*, translated by Richard Nice. Cambridge: Cambridge University Press. (First published 1972.)

Bourdieu, Pierre. 1991. *Language and Symbolic Power*, translated by Gino Raymond and Matthew Adamson. Cambridge, MA: Harvard University Press.

Bourdieu, Pierre. 2010. *Distinction: A Social Critique of the Judgement of Taste*, translated by Richard Nice. Abingdon, UK: Routledge. (First published 1979.)

Bourgois, Philippe, and Jeffrey Schonberg. 2009. *Righteous Dopefiend*. Berkeley: University of California Press.

Brettell, Caroline B. 1993. 'Fieldwork, Text, and Audience'. In *When They Read What We Write: The Politics of Ethnography*, edited by Caroline B. Brettell, 1–24. Westport, CT: Bergin & Garvey.

Briggs, Charles L. 1986. *Learning How to Ask: A Sociolinguistic Appraisal of the Role of the Interview in Social Science Research*. Cambridge: Cambridge University Press.

Brightman, Robert. 1993. *Grateful Prey: Rock Cree Human-Animal Relationships*. Berkeley: University of California Press.

Brodkin, Karen. 1998. *How Jews Became White Folks and What That Says About Race in America*. New Brunswick, NJ: Rutgers University Press.

Brown, Peter J. 1991. 'Culture and the Evolution of Obesity'. *Human Nature* 2, no. 1: 31–57.

Brown, Wendy. 2014. *Walled States, Waning Sovereignty*. New York: Zone.

Brownell, Susan E. 1993. 'Qing Dynasty Grand Sacrifice and Communist National Sports Games: Rituals of the Chinese State?' *Journal of Ritual Studies* 7, no. 1: 45–63.

Caplan, Pat. 2016. 'Big Society or Broken Society? Food Banks in the UK'. *Anthropology Today* 32, no. 1: 5–9.

Caplan, Pat, ed. 2003. *The Ethics of Anthropology: Debates and Dilemmas*. London: Routledge.

Carrier, James. 1995. *Gifts and Commodities: Exchange in Western Capitalism since 1700*. New York: Routledge.

Cassell, Joan, and Sue-Ellen Jacobs, eds. n.d. 'Handbook of Ethical Issues in Anthropology'. https://www.americananthro.org/ParticipateAndAdvocate/Content.aspx?ItemNumber=1944.

Cattelino, Jessica. 2008. *High Stakes: Florida Seminole Gaming and Sovereignty*. Durham, NC: Duke University Press.

Chase, Cheryl. 1998. 'Hermaphrodites with Attitude: Mapping the Emergence of Intersex Political Activism'. *GLQ* 4, no. 2: 189–211.

Cerwonka, Allaine, and Liisa Malkki. 2007. *Improvising Theory: Process and Temporality in Ethnographic Fieldwork*. Chicago: University of Chicago Press.

Choy, Timothy K., Lieba Faier, Michael J. Hathaway, Miyako Inoue, Shiho Satsuka, and Anna Tsing. 2009. 'A New Form of Collaboration in Cultural Anthropology: Matsutake Worlds'. *American Ethnologist* 36, no. 2: 380–403.

Clarke, Morgan. 2007. 'The Modernity of Milk Kinship'. *Social Anthropology* 15, no. 3: 287–304.

Classen, Constance. 1990. 'Sweet Colours, Fragrant Songs'. *American Ethnologist* 17, no. 4: 722–735.

Classen, Constance. 1997. 'Foundations for an Anthropology of the Senses'. *International Social Science Journal* 49, no. 153: 401–412.

Classen, Constance, David Howes, and Anthony Synnott. 1994. *Aroma: The Cultural History of Smell*. London: Routledge.

Cole, Jennifer. 2014. 'Producing Value among Malagasy Marriage Migrants in France: Managing Horizons of Expectation'. *Current Anthropology* 55, no. S9: S85–S94.

Comaroff, Jean. 1996. 'The Empire's Old Clothes: Fashioning the Colonial Subject'. In *Cross-Cultural Consumption: Global Markets, Local Realities*, edited by David Howes, 19–38. London: Routledge.

Condry, Ian. 2013. *The Soul of Anime: Collaborative Creativity and Japan's Media Success Story*. Durham, NC: Duke University Press.

Conklin, Beth A. 1997. 'Body Paint, Feathers, and VCRs: Aesthetics and Authenticity in Amazonian Activism'. *American Anthropologist* 24, no. 4: 711–737.

Conklin, Beth A. 2001. *Consuming Grief: Compassionate Cannibalism in an Amazonian Society*. Austin: University of Texas Press.

Constable, Nicole. 2003. *Romance on a Global Stage: Pen Pals, Virtual Ethnography, and 'Mail-Order' Marriages*. Berkeley: University of California Press.

Constable, Nicole. 2007. *Maid to Order in Hong Kong: Stories of Migrant Workers*. Ithaca, NY: Cornell University Press. (First published 1997.)

Constable, Nicole. 2009. 'The Commodification of Intimacy: Marriage, Sex, and Reproductive Labor'. *Annual Review of Anthropology* 38: 49–64.

Cook, Emma. 2016. *Reconstructing Adult Masculinities: Part-time Work in Contemporary Japan*. London: Routledge.

Coontz, Stephanie. 2016. *The Way We Never Were: American Families and the Nostalgia Trap*. 2nd edition. New York: Basic Books. (First published 1993.)

Cox, John, Glen Finau, Romitesh Kant, Jope Tarai, and Jason Titifanue. 2018. 'Disaster, Divine Judgment, and Original Sin: Christian Interpretations of Tropical Cyclone Winston and Climate Change in Fiji'. *The Contemporary Pacific* 30, no. 2: 380–411.

Crapanzano, Vincent. 1980. *Tuhami: Portrait of a Moroccan*. Chicago: University of Chicago Press.

Danely, Jason. 2014. *Aging and Loss: Mourning and Maturity in Contemporary Japan*. New Brunswick, NJ: Rutgers University Press.

Daughtry, Martin. 2015. *Listening to War: Sound, Music, Trauma, and Survival in Wartime Iraq*. Oxford: Oxford University Press.

Degani, Michael. 2017. 'Modal Reasoning in Dar es Salaam's Power Network'. *American Ethnologist* 44, no. 2: 300–314.

De León, Jason. 2015. *The Land of Open Graves: Living and Dying on the Migrant Trail*. Berkeley: University of California Press.

De Silva, Cara, ed. 1996. *In Memory's Kitchen: A Legacy from the Women of Terezín*, translated by Biance Steiner Brown. Northvale, NJ: Jason Aronson.

Denisen, Isak (Karen Blixen). 2015. *Babette's Feast and Other Stories*. London: Penguin. (First published 1958.)

Deomampo, Daisy. 2016. *Transnational Reproduction: Race, Kinship, and Commercial Surrogacy in India*. New York: NYU Press.

Derrida, Jacques. 1992. 'Given Time: The Time of the Kings', translated by Peggy Kamuf. *Critical Inquiry* 18, no. 2: 161–187.

Devlieger, Clara. 2018. 'Contractual Dependencies: Disability and the Bureaucracy of Begging in Kinshasa, Democratic Republic of Congo'. *American Ethnologist* 45, no. 4: 455–469.

Dirks, Nicholas B. 2001. *Castes of Mind: Colonialism and the Making of Modern India*. Princeton, NJ: Princeton University Press.

Doostdar, Alireza. 2019. 'Impossible Occultists: Practice and Participation in an Islamic Tradition'. *American Ethnologist* 46, no. 2: 176–189.

Douglas, Mary. 2002. *Purity and Danger: An Analysis of Concepts of Pollution and Taboo*. London: Routledge. (First published 1966.)

Dumont, Louis. 1980. *Homo Hierarchicus: The Caste System and its Implications*. Chicago: University of Chicago Press. (First published 1966.)

Durkheim, Émile. 1915. *The Elementary Forms of the Religious Life*, translated by Joseph Ward Swain. London: George Allen & Unwin. (First published 1912.)

D'Andrea, Anthony. 2007. *Global Nomads: Techno and New Age as Transnational Countercultures in Ibiza and Goa*. London: Routledge.

Edmonds, Alexander. 2010. *Pretty Modern: Beauty, Sex, and Plastic Surgery in Brazil*. Durham, NC: Duke University Press.

Edwards, Jeanette. 2000. *Born and Bred: Idioms of Kinship and New Reproductive Technologies in England*. Oxford: Oxford University Press.

Elliot, Alice. 2016. 'The Makeup of Destiny: Predestination and the Labor of Hope in a Moroccan Emigrant Town'. *American Ethnologist* 43, no. 3: 488–499.

Eriksen, Annelin. 2016. 'Pentecostalism and Egalitarianism in Melanesia: A Reconsideration of the Pentecostal Gender Paradox'. *Religion and Society* 7, no. 1: 37–50.

Evans, Nicholas, and Stephen C. Levinson, 2009. 'The Myth of Language Universals: Language Diversity and its Importance for Cognitive Science'. *Behavioral and Brain Sciences* 32, no. 5: 429–492.

Evans-Pritchard, E. E. 1976. *Witchcraft, Oracles and Magic among the Azande*. Oxford: Oxford University Press. (First published 1937.)

Fader, Ayala. 2009. *Mitzvah Girls: Bringing Up the Next Generation of Hasidic Jews in Brooklyn*. Princeton, NJ: Princeton University Press.

Faier, Lieba. 2009. *Intimate Encounters: Filipina Women and the Remaking of Rural Japan*. Berkeley: University of California Press.

Fanon, Frantz. 2008. *Black Skin, White Masks*, translated by Richard Philcox. New York: Grove Press. (First published 1952.)

Farbotko, Carol, Elaine Stratford, and Heather Lazrus. 2015. 'Climate Migrants and New Identities? The Geopolitics of Embracing or Rejecting Mobility'. *Social & Cultural Geography* 17, no. 4: 533–552.

Farmer, Paul. 2001. *Infections and Inequalities: The Modern Plagues*. Berkeley: University of California Press (First published 1999.)

Farmer, Paul. 2005. *Pathologies of Power: Health, Human Rights, and the New War on the Poor*. Berkeley: University of California Press.

Federici, Silvia. 2018. *Re-enchanting the World: Feminism and the Politics of the Commons*. Oakland: PM Press.

Feld, Steven. 1996. 'Waterfalls of Song: An Acoustemology of Place Resounding in Bosavi, Papua New Guinea'. In *Senses of Place*, edited by Steven Feld and Keith H. Basso, 91–135. Santa Fe, NM: School of American Research Press.

Feld, Steven. 2012. *Sound and Sentiment: Birds, Weeping, Poetics, and Song in Kaluli Expression*. Durham, NC: Duke University Press. (First published 1982.)

Firmin, Anténor. 2002. *The Equality of the Human Races*, translated by Asselin Charles. Urbana: University of Illinois Press. (First published 1885.)

Foucault, Michel. 2008. *The Birth of Biopolitics: Lectures at the Collège de France, 1978–1979*, translated by Graham Burchell. New York: Picador. (First published 2004.)

Freeman, Carla. 2000. *High Tech and High Heels in the Global Economy: Women, Work, and Pink-Collar Identities in the Caribbean*. Durham, NC: Duke University Press.

Freeman, Derek. 1983. *Margaret Mead and Samoa: The Making and Unmaking of an Anthropological Myth*. Cambridge, MA: Harvard University Press.

Fuentes, Agustín. 2010. 'Naturalcultural Encounters in Bali: Monkeys, Temples, Tourists and Ethnoprimatology'. *Cultural Anthropology* 25, no. 4: 600–624.

Gans, Herbert J. 1979. 'Symbolic Ethnicity: The Future of Ethnic Groups and Cultures in America'. *Ethnic and Racial Studies* 2, no. 1: 1–20.

Geertz, Clifford. 1966. 'Religion as a Cultural System'. In *Anthropological Approaches to the Study of Religion*, edited by Michael Banton, 1–46. London: Tavistock.

Geertz, Clifford. 1974. '"From the Native's Point of View": On the Nature of Anthropological Understanding'. *Bulletin of the American Academy of Arts and Sciences* 28, no. 1: 26–45.

Geertz, Clifford. 1998. 'Deep Hanging Out'. *New York Review of Books* 45, no. 16: 69–72.

Gell, Alfred. 1995. 'The Language of the Forest: Landscape and Phonological Iconism in Umeda'. In *The Anthropology of Landscape: Perspectives on Place and Space*, edited by Eric Hirsch and Michael O'Hanlon, 232–254. Oxford: Clarendon Press.

Gellner, Ernest. 2006. *Nations and Nationalism*. Ithaca, NY: Cornell University Press. (First published 1983.)

Gershon, Ilana. 2010. *The Break-Up 2.0: Disconnecting over New Media*. Ithaca, NY: Cornell University Press.

Gershon, Ilana. 2017. *Down and Out in the New Economy: How People Find (or Don't Find) Work Today*. Chicago: University of Chicago Press.

Geschiere, Peter. 1997. *The Modernity of Witchcraft: Politics and the Occult in Postcolonial Africa*. Charlottesville: University of Virginia Press.

Geschiere, Peter. 2009. *The Perils of Belonging: Autochthony, Citizenship, and Exclusion in Africa and Europe*. Chicago: University of Chicago Press.

Gewertz, Deborah, and Frederick Errington. 1991. *Twisted Histories, Altered Contexts: Representing the Chambri in the World System*. Cambridge: Cambridge University Press.

Gewertz, Deborah, and Frederick Errington. 1999. *Emerging Class in Papua New Guinea: The Telling of Difference*. Cambridge: Cambridge University Press.

Gewertz, Deborah, and Frederick Errington. 2002. 'Margaret Mead and the Death of Alexis Gewertz Shepard'. *Amherst Magazine* (Spring): 10–15, http://www3.amherst.edu/magazine/issues/02spring/features/gewertz.html, consulted 24 October 2019.

Gewertz, Deborah, and Frederick Errington. 2010. *Cheap Meat: Flap Food Nations in the Pacific Islands*. Berkeley: University of California Press.

Ghertner, Asher D. 2020. 'Airpocalypse: Distributions of Life amidst Delhi's Polluted Airs'. *Public Culture* 32, no. 1: 133–162.

Gilmore, Lee. 2010. *Theater in a Crowded Fire: Ritual and Spirituality at Burning Man*. Berkeley: University of California Press.

Gingrich, Andre. 2012. 'Comparative Methods in Socio-Cultural Anthropology Today'. In *The SAGE Handbook of Social Anthropology*, edited by Richard Fardon, Olivia Harris, Trevor H. J. Marchand, Mark Nuttall, Cris Shore, Veronica Strang, and Richard A. Wilson, 211–222. Los Angeles: Sage.

Ginsburg, Faye, and Rayna Rapp. 2020. 'Disability/Anthropology: Rethinking the Parameters of the Human'. *Current Anthropology* 61, no. S21: S4–S15.

Glennie, Evelyn, Sander L. Gilman, and Youn Kim. 2018. 'Is There Disabled Music? Music and the Body from Dame Evelyn Glennie's Perspective'. In *The Oxford Handbook of Music and the Body*, edited by Youn Kim and Sander L. Gilman, 318–330. Oxford: Oxford University Press.

Gluckman, Max. 1956. *Custom and Conflict in Africa*. Oxford: Blackwell.

Godelier, Maurice. 1986. *The Making of Great Men: Male Domination and Power among the New Guinea Baruya*. Cambridge: Cambridge University Press. (First published 1982.)

Godelier, Maurice. 1992. 'Some Things You Give, Some Things You Sell, but Some Things You Must Keep for Yourselves: What Mauss Did Not Say about Sacred Objects'. In *The Enigma of Gift and Sacrifice*, edited by Edith Wyschogrod, 19–37. New York: Fordham University Press.

González, Roberto G. 2008. '"Human Terrain": Past, Present and Future Applications'. *Anthropology Today* 24, no. 1: 21–26.

González, Roberto G., and Nando Sigona. 2017. 'Mapping the Soft Borders of Citizenship'. In *Within and Beyond Citizenship: Borders, Membership and Belonging*, edited by Roberto G. González and Nando Sigona, 1–16. Abingdon, UK: Routledge.

Goody, Jack. 2002. 'The Anthropology of the Senses and Sensations'. *La Ricerca Folklorica* 45:17–28.

Gordillo, Gastón. 2002. 'The Breath of the Devils: Memories and Places of an Experience of Terror'. *American Ethnologist* 2, no. 1: 33–57.

Gordillo, Gastón. 2014. *Rubble: The Afterlife of Destruction*. Durham, NC: Duke University Press.

Gottlieb, Alma. 2004. *The Afterlife Is Where We Come From: The Culture of Infancy in West Africa*. Chicago: University of Chicago Press.

Gough, Kathleen. 1959. 'The Nayars and the Definition of Marriage'. *Journal of the Royal Anthropological Institute* 89, no. 1: 23–34.

Graeber, David. 2013. *The Democracy Project: A History, a Crisis, a Movement*. New York: Penguin Random House.

Green, Sarah. 2005. *Notes from the Balkans: Locating Marginality and Ambiguity on the Greek-Albanian Border*. Princeton, NJ: Princeton University Press.

Greenpeace Philippines. 2015. *Petition to the Commission on Human Rights of the Philippines Requesting for Investigation of the Responsibility of the Carbon Majors for Human Rights Violations or Threats of Violations Resulting from the Impacts of Climate Change* (22 September), www.greenpeace.org/seasia/ph/PageFiles/105904/Climate-Change-and-Human-Rights-Complaint.pdf.

Gregory, Chris. 1982. *Gifts and Commodities.* London: Academic Press.

Gross, Toomas. 2012. 'Changing Faith: The Social Costs of Protestant Conversion in Rural Oaxaca'. *Ethnos* 77, no. 3: 344–371.

Gruber, Thibaut, Klaus Zuberbühler, Fabrice Clément, and Carel van Schaik. 2015. 'Apes Have Culture but May Not Know that They Do'. *Frontiers in Psychology* 6:91.

Guinness, Daniel, and Niko Besnier. 2016. 'Nation, Nationalism, and Sport: Fijian Rugby in the Local–Global Nexus'. *Anthropological Quarterly* 89, no. 4: 1109–1142.

Guinness, Daniel, and Sebastián Fuentes. 2018. '"Good Players" and "Good People": Masculinities, Mobilities, and Class in Argentinian Rugby'. *Journal of Latin American and Caribbean Anthropology* 24, no. 2: 443–460.

Gupta, Akhil. 1995. 'Blurred Boundaries: The Discourse of Corruption, the Culture of Politics, and the Imagined State'. *American Ethnologist* 22, no. 2: 375–402.

Guyer, Jane. 1991. 'Female Farming in Anthropology and African History'. In *Gender at the Crossroads of Knowledge: Feminist Anthropology in the Postmodern Era,* edited by Micaela di Leonardo, 257–277. Berkeley: University of California Press.

Guyer, Jane. 2004. *Marginal Gains: Monetary Transactions in Atlantic Africa.* Chicago: University of Chicago Press.

Hage, Ghassan. 2003. *Against Paranoid Nationalism: Searching for Hope in a Shrinking Society.* Annandale, NSW: Pluto.

Hammami, Rema. 2019. 'Destabilizing Mastery and the Machine: Palestinian Agency and Gendered Embodiment at Israeli Military Checkpoints'. *Current Anthropology* 60, no. S19: S87–S97.

Han, Clara. 2003. *Life in Debt: Times of Care and Violence in Neoliberal Chile.* Berkeley: University of California Press.

Hannerz, Ulf. 1996. *Transnational Connections: Culture, People, Places.* London: Routledge.

Hansen, Karen Tranberg. 2000. *Salaula: The World of Secondhand Clothing and Zambia.* Chicago: University of Chicago Press.

Hardin, Rebecca. 2019. *Faith and the Pursuit of Health: Cardiometabolic Disorders in Samoa.* New Brunswick, NJ: Rutgers University Press.

Härkönen, Heidi. 2014. *Kinship, Love, and Life Cycle in Contemporary Havana, Cuba: To Not Die Alone.* New York: Palgrave Macmillan.

Hartblay, Cassandra. 2017. 'Good Ramps, Bad Ramps: Centralized Design Standards and Disability Access in Urban Russian Infrastructure'. *American Ethnologist* 44, no. 1: 9–22.

Haviland, John B. 1979. 'How to Talk to your Brother-in-law in Guugu Yimidhirr'. In *Languages and their Speakers,* edited by Timothy Shopen, 160–239. Cambridge, MA: Winthrop.

Hemment, Julie. 2017. 'Red Scares and Orange Mobilizations: A Critical Anthropological Perspective on the Russian Hacking Scandal'. *Slavic Review,* 76, no. S1: S66–S80.

Henderson, Frances B., and Bertin M. Louis. 2017. 'Black Rural Lives Matters: Ethnographic Research about an Anti-Racist Interfaith Organization in the U.S. South'. *Transforming Anthropology* 25, no. 1: 50–67.

Herdt, Gilbert, ed. 1982. *Rituals of Manhood: Male Initiation in Papua New Guinea.* Berkeley: University of California Press.

Herdt, Gilbert. 2005. *The Sambia: Ritual, Sexuality, and Change in Papua New Guinea.* Belmont, CA: Wadsworth. (First published 1987.)

Herzfeld, Michael. 1992. *The Social Production of Indifference: Exploring the Symbolic Roots of Western Bureaucracy.* Chicago: University of Chicago Press.

High, Casey. 2012. 'Shamans, Animals and Enemies: Human and non-Human Agency in an Amazonian Cosmos of Alterity'. In *Animism in Rainforest and Tundra: Personhood, Animals, Plants and Things in Contemporary Amazonia and Siberia,* edited by Marc Brightman, Vanessa Elisa Grotti, and Olga Ulturgasheva, 130–145. New York: Berghahn.

Hirschkind, Charles. 2006. *The Ethical Soundscape: Cassette Sermons and Islamic Counterpublics*. New York: Columbia University Press.

Hirschkind, Charles. 2011. 'From the Blogosphere to the Street: Social Media and Egyptian Revolution'. *Oriente Moderno* 9, no. 1: 61–74.

Ho, Karen. 2009. *Liquidated: An Ethnography of Wall Street*. Durham, NC: Duke University Press.

Hobsbawn, Eric, and Terrence Ranger, eds. 1983. *The Invention of Tradition*. Cambridge: Cambridge University Press.

Hogle, Linda F. 2005. 'Enhancement Technologies and the Body'. *Annual Review of Anthropology* 34: 695–716.

Hopkins, Keith. 1980. 'Brother-Sister Marriage in Roman Egypt'. *Comparative Studies in History and Society* 22, no. 3: 303–354.

Howell, Signe. 2006. *The Kinning of Foreigners: Transnational Adoption in a Global Perspective*. Oxford: Berghahn.

Howes, David. 2014. 'Introduction to Sensory Museology'. *The Senses and Society* 9, no. 3: 259–267.

Hsu, Elizabeth. 2011. 'The Biological in the Cultural: The Five Agents and the Body Ecologic in Chinese Medicine'. In *Holistic Anthropology: Emergence and Convergence*, edited by David Parkin and Stanley Ulijaszek, 91–126. Oxford: Berghahn.

Hughes, David M. 2013. 'Climate Change and the Victim Slot: From Oil to Innocence'. *American Anthropologist* 115, no. 4: 570–581.

Hurston, Zora Neale. 2018. *Barracoon: The Story of the Last 'Black Cargo'*. New York: Harper Collins.

Ingold, Tim. 1977. *The Skolt Lapps Today*. London: Cambridge University Press.

Ingold, Tim. 1996. *Key Debates in Anthropology*. London: Routledge.

Inhorn, Marcia. 2006. 'Making Muslim Babies: IVF and Gamete Donation in Sunni versus Shi'a Islam'. *Culture, Medicine and Psychiatry* 30, no. 4: 427–450.

Irvine, Judith T. 1989. 'When Talk Isn't Cheap: Language and Political Economy'. *American Ethnologist* 16, no. 2: 248–267.

Ivakhiv, Adrian. 2001. *Claiming Sacred Ground: Pilgrims and Politics at Glastonbury and Sedona*. Bloomington: Indiana University Press.

Jacobsen, Kristina. 2020. 'When Coronavirus Emptied the Streets, Music Filled It'. *SAPIENS*, 26 March, https://www.sapiens.org/culture/coronavirus-sardinia-music/.

Jeffrey, Craig. 2010. *Timepass: Youth, Class, and the Politics of Waiting in India*. Stanford, CA: Stanford University Press.

Johnson, Jessica. 2018. 'The Self-Radicalization of White Men: "Fake News" and the Affective Networking of Paranoia'. *Communication, Culture & Critique* 11, no. 1: 100–115.

Kaell, Hillary. 2016. 'Can Pilgrimage Fail? Intent, Efficacy, and Evangelical Trips to the Holy Land'. *Journal of Contemporary Religion* 31, no. 3: 393–408.

Kahn, Susan. 2004. 'Eggs and Wombs: The Origins of Jewishness'. In *Kinship and Family: An Anthropological Reader*, edited by David Parkin and Linda Stone, 369–377. Oxford: Wiley Blackwell.

Kallius, Annastiina, Daniel Monterescu, and Prem Kumar Rajaram. 2016. 'Immobilizing Mobility: Border Ethnography, Illiberal Democracy, and the Politics of the "Refugee Crisis" in Hungary'. *American Ethnologist* 43, no. 1: 25–37.

Kanafani, Aida Sami. 1983. *Aesthetics and Ritual in the United Arab Emirates: The Anthropology of Food and Personal Adornment among Arabian Women*. Syracuse, NY: Syracuse University Press.

Karakasidou, Anastasia, 1997. *Fields of Wheat, Hills of Blood: Passages to Nationhood in Greek Macedonia, 1870–1990*. Chicago: University of Chicago Press.

Kessler, Suzanne. 1990. 'The Medical Construction of Gender: Case Management of Intersexed Infants'. *Signs* 16, no. 1: 3–26.

Khasnabish, Alex. 2008. *Zapatismo Beyond Borders: New Imaginations of Political Possibility*. Toronto: University of Toronto Press.

King, Charles. 2019. *Gods of the Upper Air: How a Circle of Renegade Anthropologists Reinvented Race, Sex, and Gender in the Twentieth Century*. New York: Doubleday.

Kirksey, S. Eben, and Stefan Helmreich. 2010. 'The Emergence of Multispecies Ethnography'. *Cultural Anthropology* 25, no. 4: 545–576.

Kirsch, Stuart. 2018. *Engaged Anthropology: Politics beyond the Text*. Oakland: University of California Press.

Kisch, Shifra. 2004. 'Negotiating (Genetic) Deafness in a Bedouin Community'. In *Genetics, Disability, Deafness*, edited by John Vickrey Van Cleve, 195–227. Washington, DC: Gallaudet University Press.

Kloos, David. 2019. 'Experts beyond Discourse: Women, Islamic Authority, and the Performance of Professionalism in Malaysia'. *American Ethnologist* 46, no. 2: 162–175.

Kohrman, Matthew. 2018. 'Introduction'. In *Poisonous Pandas: Chinese Cigarette Manufacturing in Critical Historical Perspectives*, edited by Matthew Kohrman, Gan Quan, Liu Wennan, and Robert N. Proctor, 1–33. Stanford, CA: Stanford University Press.

Kopnina, Helen, and Eleanor Shoreman-Ouimet. 2011. *Environmental Anthropology Today*. New York: Routledge.

Laidlaw, James. 2000. 'A Free Gift Makes No Friends'. *Journal of the Royal Anthropological Institute* 6, no. 4: 617–634.

Lamb, Sarah. 2019. 'On Being (Not) Old: Agency, Self-care, and Life-course Aspirations in the United States'. *Medical Anthropology Quarterly* 33, no. 2: 263–281.

Larkin, Brian. 2014. 'Techniques of Inattention: The Mediality of Loudspeakers in Nigeria'. *Anthropological Quarterly* 87, no. 4: 989–1015.

Law, Lisa. 2005. 'Home Cooking: Filipino Women and Geographies of the Senses in Hong Kong'. *Cultural Geographies* 8, no. 3: 264–283.

Leach, Edmund R. 1961. 'Asymmetric Marriage Rules, Status Difference, and Direct Reciprocity: Comments on an Alleged Fallacy'. *Southwestern Journal of Anthropology* 17, no. 4: 343–351.

Leacock, Eleanor Burke. 1981. *Myths of Male Dominance: Collected Articles on Women Cross-Culturally*. New York: Monthly Review Press.

Lepani, Katherine. 2012. *Islands of Love, Islands of Risk: Culture and HIV in the Trobriands*. Nashville, TN: Vanderbilt University Press.

Lepani, Katherine. 2017. 'Doba and Ephemeral Durability: The Enduring Material Value of Women's Work in the Trobriand Regenerative Economy'. In *Sinuous Objects: Revaluing Women's Wealth in the Contemporary Pacific*, edited by Anna-Karina Hermkens and Katherine Lepani, 37–60. Canberra: ANU Press.

Lepowsky, Maria. 2019. 'Malinowski and the White Traders: Kula and Colonial Cultures'. Unpublished manuscript.

Levine, Lawrence W. 1984. 'William Shakespeare and the American People: A Study in Cultural Transformation'. *American Historical Review* 89, no. 1: 34–66.

Levine, Nancy. 1988. *The Dynamics of Polyandry: Kinship, Domesticity, and Population on the Tibetan Border*. Chicago: University of Chicago Press.

LeVine, Robert. 2004. 'Challenging Expert Knowledge: Findings from an African Study of Infant Care and Development', In *Childhood and Adolescence: Cross-Cultural Perspectives and Applications*, edited by Uwe P. Gielen and Jaipaul Roopnarine, 149–165. Westport, CT: Praeger.

Lévi-Strauss, Claude. 1963. 'The Bear and the Barber'. *Journal of the Royal Anthropological Institute* 93, no. 1: 1–11.

Lindley, Anna. 2010. *The Early Morning Phone Call: Somali Refugees' Remittances*. New York: Berghahn.

Lock, Margaret. 2001. *Twice Dead: Organ Transplants and the Reinvention of Death*. Berkeley: University of California Press.

Loftsdóttir, Kristín. 2010. 'The Loss of Innocence: The Icelandic Financial Crisis and Colonial Past'. *Anthropology Today* 26, no. 6: 9–13.

Lucia, Amanda J. 2020. *White Utopias: The Religious Exoticism of Transformational Festivals*. Oakland: University of California Press.

Luhrmann, T. M. 1989. *Persuasions of the Witch's Craft: Ritual Magic in Contemporary England*. Cambridge: Cambridge University Press.

Macdonald, Judith. 2000. 'The Tikopia and "What Raymond Said"'. In *Ethnographic Artifacts: Challenges to a Reflexive Anthropology*, edited by Sjoerd R. Jaarsma and Marta A. Rohatynskyj, 107–124. Honolulu: University of Hawai'i Press.

Machin, Rosana. 2014. 'Sharing Motherhood in Lesbian Reproductive Practices'. *BioSocieties* 9: 42–59.

Macpherson, Hannah. 2009. 'Articulating Blind Touch: Thinking Through the Feet'. *The Senses and Society* 4, no. 2: 179–193.

Maeckelbergh, Marianne. 2009. *The Will of the Many: How the Alterglobalisation Movement Is Changing the Face of Democracy*. London: Pluto.

Mahmood, Saba. 2005. *Politics of Piety: The Islamic Revival and the Feminist Subject*. Princeton, NJ: Princeton University Press.

Mains, Daniel. 2012. *Hope is Cut: Youth, Unemployment, and the Future in Urban Ethiopia*. Philadelphia: Temple University Press.

Malinowski, Bronislaw. 1922. *Argonauts of the Western Pacific: An Account of Native Enterprise and Adventure in the Archipelagoes of Melanesian New Guinea*. London: George Routledge & Sons.

Malinowski, Bronislaw. 1929. *The Sexual Life of Savages in North-Western Melanesia: An Ethnographic Account of Courtship, Marriage, and Family Life among the Natives of the Trobriand Islands, British New Guinea*. London: George Routledge & Sons.

Malinowski, Bronislaw. 1948. *Magic, Science, and Religion, and Other Essays*, edited by Robert Redfield. Boston: Beacon Press. (First published 1925.)

Malinowski, Bronislaw. 1967. *A Diary in the Strict Sense of the Term*. London: Routledge & Kegan Paul.

Mallon, Sean, and Sébastien Galliot. 2018. *Tatau: A History of Sāmoan Tattooing*. Wellington, New Zealand: Te Papa Press.

Mani, Lata. 1998. *Contentious Traditions: The Debate on Sati in Colonial India*. Berkeley: University of California Press.

Mankekar, Purnima, and Akhil Gupta. 2019. *Future Tense: Affective Labor and Disjunctive Temporalities*. Durham, NC: Duke University Press.

Marks, Jonathan. 1992. *What It Means to be 98% Chimpanzee: Apes, People, and their Genes*. Berkeley: University of California Press.

Martínez, Pedro Santiago, Claudia Muñoz, Mariela Nuñez-Janes, Stephen Pavey, Fidel Castro Rodríguez, and Marco Saavedra. 2020. *Eclipse of Dreams: The Undocumented-Led Struggle for Freedom*. Chico, CA: AK Press.

Masquelier, Adeline, ed. 2005. *Dirt, Undress, and Difference: Critical Perspectives on the Body's Surface*. Bloomington: Indiana University Press.

Mathews, Gordon. 2011. *Ghetto at the Center of the World: Chungking Mansions, Hong Kong*. Chicago: University of Chicago Press.

Mauss, Marcel. 1973. 'Techniques of the Body', translated by Ben Brewster. *Economy and Society* 2, no. 1: 70–88. (First published 1923.)

Mauss, Marcel. 2016. *The Gift*, translated by Jane Guyer. Chicago: HAU books. (First published 1923–24.)

Mbembe, Achille. 2003. *Necropolitics*. Durham, NC: Duke University Press.

McElhinny, Bonnie. 2005. '"Kissing a Baby Is Not at All Good for Him": Infant Mortality, Medicine, and Colonial Modernity in the U.S.-Occupied Philippines'. *American Anthropologist* 107, no. 2: 183–194.

McIntosh, Janet. 2010. 'Mobile Phones and Mipoho's Prophecy: The Powers and Dangers of Flying Language'. *American Ethnologist* 37, no. 2: 337–353.

McKenna, Brian. 2018. 'The Agony of Flint: Poisoned Water, Racism and the Specter of Neoliberal Fascism'. *Anthropology Now* 10, no. 3: 45-58.

McNevin, Anne. 2006. 'Political Belonging in a Neoliberal Era: The Struggle of the Sans-Papiers'. *Citizenship Studies* 10, no. 2: 135–151.

Mead, Margaret. 1928. *Coming of Age in Samoa: A Psychological Study of Primitive Youth for Western Civilization*. New York: William Morrow.

Meiu, George Paul. 2017. *Ethno-erotic Economies: Sexuality, Money, and Belonging in Kenya*. Chicago: University of Chicago Press.

Merlan, Francesca. 2020. 'Ghost Twitter in Indigenous Australia: Sentience, Agency, and Ontological Difference'. *HAU* 10, no. 1: 209–235.

Merry, Sally Engle. 2003. 'Human Rights Law and the Demonization of Culture (and Anthropology Along the Way)'. *Political and Legal Anthropology Review* 26, no. 1: 55–77.

Middleton, Townsend, and Jason Cons. 2014. 'Coming to Terms: Reinserting Research Assistants into Ethnography's Past and Present'. *Ethnography* 15, no. 3: 279–290.

Miller, Laura. 2006. *Beauty Up: Exploring Contemporary Japanese Body Aesthetics*. Chicago: University of Chicago Press.

Mills, David. 2003. '"Like a Horse in Blinkers"? A Political History of Anthropology's Research Ethics'. In *Ethics of Anthropology: Debates and Dilemmas*, edited by Pat Caplan, 37–54. New York: Routledge.

Milton, Kay. 2002. *Environmentalism and Cultural Theory: Exploring the Role of Anthropology in Environmental Discourse*. London: Routledge.

Mintz, Sidney. 1985. *Sweetness and Power: The Place of Sugar in Modern History*. New York: Penguin.

Mookherjee, Nayanika. 2010. 'Friendships and Encounters on the Political Left in Bangladesh'. In *Taking Sides: Ethics, Politics and Fieldwork in Anthropology*, edited by Heidi Armbruster and Anna Lærke, 65–87. New York: Berghahn.

Morton, Helen. 1996. *Becoming Tongan: An Ethnography of Childhood*. Honolulu: University of Hawai'i Press.

Mosse, David. 2005. *Cultivating Development: An Ethnography of Aid Policy and Practice*. London: Polity.

Mosse, George L. 1985. *Nationalism and Sexuality: Respectability and Abnormal Sexuality in Modern Europe*. New York: Howard Fertig.

M'Charek, Amade. 2020. 'Tentacular Faces: Race and the Return of the Phenotype in Forensic Identification'. *American Anthropologist* 122, no. 2: 369–380.

Nanda, Serena. 1998. *Neither Man nor Woman: The Hijras of India*. Belmont, CA: Wadsworth. (First published 1989.)

Nanda, Serena. 2000. 'Arranging a Marriage in India'. In *Stumbling Toward Truth: Anthropologists at Work*, edited by Philip R. Devita, 196–204. Prospect Heights, IL: Waveland Press.

Narayan, Kirin. 1993. 'How Native Is a "Native" Anthropologist?' *American Anthropologist* 95, no. 3: 671–686.

Narotzky, Susana. 2016. 'Between Inequality and Injustice: Dignity as a Motive for Mobilization during the Crisis'. *History and Anthropology* 27, no. 1: 74–92.

Narotzky, Susana, and Paz Moreno. 2002. 'Reciprocity's Dark Side: Negative Reciprocity, Morality and Social Reproduction'. *Anthropological Theory* 2, no. 3: 281–305.

Narotzky, Susana, and Antonio Maria Pusceddu. 2020. 'Social Reproduction in Times of Crisis: Inter-generational Tensions in Southern Europe'. In *Grassroots Economies: Living with Austerity in Southern Europe*, edited by Susana Narotzky, 143–170. London: Pluto.

Nettle, Daniel, and Suzanne Romaine. 2000. *Vanishing Voices: The Extinction of the World's Languages*. Oxford: Oxford University Press.

Newell, Sasha. 2012. *The Modernity Bluff: Crime, Consumption, and Citizenship in Côte d'Ivoire*. Chicago: University of Chicago Press.

Newman, Alyssa. 2019. 'Mixing and Matching: Sperm Donor Selection for Interracial Lesbian Couples'. *Medical Anthropology* 38, no. 8: 710–724.

Nguyen, Minh T.N. 2016. 'Trading in Broken Things: Gendered Performances and Spatial Practices in a Northern Vietnamese Rural–Urban Waste Economy'. *American Ethnologist* 43, no. 1: 116–129.

Niehaus, Isak. 2002. 'Renegotiating Masculinity in the South African Lowveld: Narratives of Male–Male Sex in Labour Compounds and in Prisons'. *African Studies* 61, no. 1: 77–97.

Nugent, David. 1982. 'Closed Systems and Contradiction: The Kachin In and Out of History'. *Man* 17, no. 3: 508–527.

Nussbaum, Martha. 2019. *The Cosmopolitan Tradition: A Noble but Flawed Ideal*. Cambridge, MA: Harvard University Press.

Obeyesekere, Gananath. 1966. 'Methodological and Philosophical Relativism'. *Man* 1, no. 3: 368–374.

Oboler, Regine Smith. 1980. 'Is the Female Husband a Man? Woman/Woman Marriage among the Nandi of Kenya'. *Ethnology* 19, no. 1: 69–88.

Ochs [Keenan], Elinor. 1974. 'Norm-Makers, Norm-Breakers: Uses of Speech by Men and Women in a Malagasy Community'. In *Explorations in the Ethnography of Speaking*, edited by Richard Bauman and Joel Sherzer, 125–137. Cambridge: Cambridge University Press.

Ochs, Elinor. 1988. *Culture and Language Development: Language Acquisition and Language Socialization in a Samoan Village*. Cambridge: Cambridge University Press.

Ochs, Elinor, and Carolina Izquierdo. 2009. 'Responsibility in Childhood: Three Developmental Trajectories'. *Ethos* 37, no. 4: 391–413.

Ochs, Juliana. 2011. *Security and Suspicion: An Ethnography of Everyday Life in Israel*. Philadelphia: University of Pennsylvania Press.

O'Hanlon, Michael 1989. *Reading the Skin: Adornment, Display and Society among the Wahgi*. London: British Museum Press.

Okely, Judith. 1983. *The Traveller Gypsies*. Cambridge: Cambridge University Press.

Ong, Aihwa. 1999. *Flexible Citizenship: The Cultural Logics of Transnationality*. Durham, NC: Duke University Press.

Organisation for Economic Cooperation and Development. 2017. *Interrelations between Public Policies, Migration and Development in the Philippines*. Paris: Organization for Economic Cooperation and Development and Scalabrini Migration Center. http://dx.doi.org/10.1787/9789264272286-en.

Ortner, Sherry. 1974. 'Is Female to Male as Nature Is to Culture?' In *Woman, Culture, and Society*, edited by Michelle Z. Rosaldo and Louise Lamphere, 68–87. Stanford, CA: Stanford University Press.

Parish, Jane. 2000. 'From the Body to the Wallet: Conceptualizing Akan Witchcraft at Home and Abroad'. *Journal of the Royal Anthropological Institute* 6, no. 3: 487–500.

Parkes, Peter. 2004. 'Milk Kinship in Southeast Europe: Alternative Social Structures and Foster Relations in the Caucasus and the Balkans'. *Social Anthropology* 12, no. 3: 341–358.

Parry, Jonathan. 1989. 'On the Moral Perils of Exchange'. In *Money and the Morality of Exchange*, edited by Jonathan Parry and Maurice Bloch, 64–93. Cambridge: Cambridge University Press.

Parry, Jonathan, and Maurice Bloch, eds. 1989. *Money and the Morality of Exchange*. Cambridge: Cambridge University Press.

Peers, Laura. 2013. '"Ceremonies of Renewal": Visits, Relationships, and Healing in Museum Space'. *Museum Worlds* 1, no. 1: 136–152.

Piot, Charles. 2010. *Nostalgia for the Future: West Africa after the Cold War*. Chicago: University of Chicago Press.

Posey, Darrell. 1990. 'Intellectual Property Rights: And Just Compensation for Indigenous Knowledge'. *Anthropology Today* 6, no. 1: 13–16.

Postill, John. 2018. *The Rise of Nerd Politics: Digital Activism and Political Change*. London: Pluto.

Price, David. 2002. 'Lessons from Second World War Anthropology: Peripheral, Persuasive and Ignored Contributions'. *Anthropology Today* 18, no. 3: 14–20.

Pritzker, Sonya E. 2014. *Living Translation: Language and the Search for Resonance in U.S. Chinese Medicine*. Oxford: Berghahn.

Pun, Ngai. 2005. *Made in China: Women Factory Workers in a Global Workplace*. Durham, NC: Duke University Press.

Rachiotis, George, David Stuckler, Martin McKeeand, and Christos Hadjichristodoulou. 2015. 'What Has Happened to Suicides during the Greek Economic Crisis? Findings from an Ecological Study of Suicides and their Determinants (2003–2012)'. *BMJ Open* 2015, no. 5: e007295. https://bmjopen.bmj.com/content/5/3/e007295.responses.

Radice, Martha. 2020 'Doing/Undoing/Redoing Carnival in New Orleans in the Time of COVID-19'. *Canadian Anthropology Society Culture Blog*, 20 April, https://cascacultureblog.wordpress.com/2020/04/20/doing-undoing-redoing-carnival-in-new-orleans-in-the-time-of-covid-19/.

Rajadesingan, Ashwin, Ramaswami Mahalingam, and David Jurgens. 2019. '*Smart, Responsible, and Upper Caste Only: Measuring Caste Attitudes through Large-Scale Analysis of Matrimonial Profiles*'. In *Proceedings of the Thirteenth International AAAI Conference on Web and Social Media*, 393–404. https://arxiv.org/pdf/1904.04176.pdf.

Ramakrishnan, Srilaksmi. 2012. '"Wheatish" Grooms and "Innocent" Divorcées: Commodifying Attributes in the Discourse of Indian Matrimonials'. *Discourse and Society* 23, no. 4: 432–449.

Rappaport, Roy. 1968. *Pigs for the Ancestors: Ritual in the Ecology of a New Guinea People*. New Haven, CT: Yale University Press.

Rebhun, L.A. 2004. 'Sexuality, Color, and Stigma among Northeast Brazilian Women'. *Medical Anthropology Quarterly* 18, no. 2: 183–199.

Ribeiro, Darcy. 1970. *Os Índios e a Civilização*. Rio de Janeiro: Civilização Brasileira.

Ribeiro, Gustavo Lins. 2014. 'World Anthropologies: Anthropological Cosmopolitanisms and Cosmopolitics'. *Annual Review of Anthropology* 43:483–498.

Rice, Tom. 2003. 'Soundselves: An Accoustemology of Sound and Self in the Edinburgh Royal Infirmary'. *Anthropology Today* 19, no. 4: 4–9.

Robbins, Joel. 2004. 'The Globalization of Pentecostal and Charismatic Christianity'. *Annual Review of Anthropology* 33:117–143.

Robbins, Joel. 2013. 'Beyond the Suffering Subject: Toward an Anthropology of the Good'. *Journal of the Royal Anthropological Institute* 19, no. 3: 447–462.

Rosaldo, Michelle Z. 1974. 'Women, Culture, and Society: A Theoretical Overview'. In *Women, Culture, and Society*, edited by Michelle Z. Rosaldo and Louise Lamphere, 14–42. Stanford, CA: Stanford University Press.

Rosenblatt, Daniel. 1997. 'The Antisocial Skin: Structure, Resistance, and "Modern Primitive" Adornment in the United States'. *Cultural Anthropology* 12, no. 3: 287–334.

Roth-Gordon, Jennifer. 2017. *Race and the Brazilian Body: Blackness, Whiteness, and Everyday Language in Rio de Janeiro*. Oakland: University of California Press.

Rubin, Gayle. 1975. 'The Traffic in Women: Notes on the "Political Economy" of Sex'. In *Toward an Anthropology of Women*, edited by Rayna R. Reiter, 157–210. New York: Monthly Review Press.

Sabaté, Irene. 2016. 'The Spanish Mortgage Crisis and the Re-emergence of Moral Economies in Uncertain Times'. *History and Anthropology* 27, no. 1: 107–120.

Sabatello, Maya. 2014. 'Posthumously Conceived Children: An International and Human Rights Perspective'. *Journal of Law and Health* 27, no. 1: 29–67.

Saerberg, Siegfried. 2010. 'Just Go Straight Ahead'. *The Senses and Society* 5, no. 3: 364–381.

Sahlins, Marshall. 1972. *Stone Age Economics*. Chicago: Aldine-Atherton.

Sahlins, Marshall. 2004. 'On the Sociology of Primitive Exchange'. In *The Relevance of Models for Social Anthropology*, edited by Michael Banton, 139–236. London: Tavistock. (First published 1965.)

Said, Edward. 1978. *Orientalism*. New York: Pantheon.

Salama, Rasha Aziz Attia, and Abeer Kamal Saleh. 2016. 'Effectiveness of Premarital Screening Program for Thalassemia and Sickle Cell Disorders in Ras Al Khaimah, United Arab Emirates'. *Journal of Genetic Medicine* 13, no. 1: 26–30.

Saller, Richard. 1984. '"Familia, Domus", and the Roman Conception of the Family'. *Phoenix* 38, no. 4: 336–355.

Sams, Kelley, Alice Desclaux, Julienne Anoko, Francis Akindès, Marc Egrot, Khoudia Sow, Bernard Taverne, Blandine Bila, Michèle Cros, Moustapha Keïta-Diop, Mathieu Fribault, and Annie Wilkinson. 2017. 'From Ebola to Plague and Beyond: How Can Anthropologists Best Engage Past Experience to Prepare for New Epidemics?' *Fieldsights, Cultural Anthropology* website, 7 December, https://culanth.org/fieldsights/from-ebola-to-plague-and-beyond-how-cananthropologists-best-engage-past-experience-to-prepare-for-new-epidemics.

Savigliano, Marta E. 1995. *Tango and the Political Economy of Passion*. Boulder, CO: Westview.

Scheld, Suzanne. 2007. 'Youth Cosmopolitanism: Clothing, the City and Globalization in Dakar, Senegal'. *City and Society* 19, no. 2: 232–253.

Scheper-Hughes, Nancy. 2000. 'The Global Traffic in Human Organs'. *Current Anthropology* 41, no. 2: 191–224.

Schlosser, Eric. 2001. *Fast Food Nation: The Dark Side of the All-American Meal*. New York: Houghton Mifflin.

Schultz, Dorothea E. 2001. 'Music Videos and the Effeminate Vices of Urban Culture in Mali'. *Africa* 71, no. 3: 345–372.

Scott, James C. 1998. *Seeing Like a State: How Certain Schemes to Improve the Human Condition Have Failed*. New Haven, CT: Yale University Press.

Selka, Stephen. 2010. 'Morality in the Religious Marketplace: Evangelical Christianity, Candomblé, and the Struggle for Moral Distinction in Brazil'. *American Ethnologist* 37, no. 2: 291–307.

Seremetakis, Nadia. 1996. *The Senses Still: Perception and Memory as Material Culture in Modernity*. Chicago: Chicago University Press.

Seymour, Susan C. 2015. *Cora Du Bois: Anthropologist, Diplomat, Agent*. Lincoln: University of Nebraska Press.

Shahrani, Nazif M. 2002. 'War, Factionalism, and the State in Afghanistan'. *American Anthropologist* 104, no. 3: 715–722.

Shami, Seteney. 2000. 'Prehistories of Globalization: Circassian Identity in Motion'. *Public Culture* 12, no. 1: 177–204.

Shankman, Paul. 2009. *The Trashing of Margaret Mead: Anatomy of an Anthropological Controversy*. Madison: University of Wisconsin Press.

Sharp, Lesley A. 2006. *Strange Harvest: Organ Transplants, Denatured Bodies, and the Transformed Self*. Berkeley: University of California Press.

Shaw, Alison. 2001. 'Kinship, Cultural Preference and Immigration: Consanguineous Marriage among British Pakistanis'. *Journal of the Royal Anthropological Institute* 7, no. 2: 315–334.

Shaw, Rosalind. 1997. 'The Production of Witchcraft/Witchcraft as Production: Memory, Modernity, and the Slave Trade in Sierra Leone'. *American Ethnologist* 24, no. 4: 856–876.

Shih, Chuan-kang. 2010. *Quest for Harmony: The Moso Traditions of Sexual Union and Family Life*. Stanford, CA: Stanford University Press.

Shore, Cris. 2017. '"100 Percent Pure New Zealand": National Branding and the Paradoxes of Scale'. In *Small Countries: Structures and Sensibilities*, edited by Ulf Hannerz and Andre Gingrich, 47–66. Philadelphia: University of Pennsylvania Press.

Shostak, Marjorie. 2000. *Nisa: The Life and Words of a !Kung Woman*. Cambridge, MA: Harvard University Press. (First published 1981).

Simpson, Audra. 2014. *Mohawk Interruptus: Political Life across the Borders of Settler States*. Durham, NC: Duke University Press.

Simpson, Bob. 1994. 'Bringing the "Unclear" Family into Focus: Divorce and Remarriage in Contemporary Britain'. *Man* 29, no. 4: 831–852.

Simpson, Bob. 1997. 'On Gifts, Payments and Disputes: Divorce and Changing Family Structures in Contemporary Britain'. *Journal of the Royal Anthropological Institute* 3. no. 4: 731–746.

Simpson, Bob. 2001. 'Making "Bad" Deaths "Good": The Kinship Consequences of Posthumous Conception'. *Journal of the Royal Anthropological Institute* 7, no. 1: 1–18.

Solway, Jacqueline S. 1990. 'Affines and Spouses, Friends and Lovers: The Passing of Polygyny in Botswana'. *Journal of Anthropological Research* 46, no. 1: 41–66.

Spooner, Brian. 1988. 'Weavers and Dealers: The Authenticity of an Oriental Carpet'. In *The Social Life of Things: Commodities in Cultural Perspective*, edited by Arjun Appadurai, 195–235. Cambridge: Cambridge University Press.

Stasch, Rupert. 2017. 'Tourism'. *Cambridge Encyclopedia of Anthropology*. http://doi.org/10.29164/17tourism.

Stasch, Rupert. 2019. 'Primitivist Tourism and Anthropological Research: Awkward Relations'. *Journal of the Royal Anthropological Institute* 25, no. 3: 526–545.

Stephen, Lynn. 2002. *Zapata Lives! Histories and Cultural Politics in Southern Mexico*. Berkeley: University of California Press.

Steward, Julian. 1955. *Theory of Culture Change: The Methodology of Multilinear Evolution*. Urbana: University of Illinois Press.

Stocking, George. 1987. *Victorian Anthropology*. New York: The Free Press.

Stoler, Ann Laura. 1995. *Race and the Education of Desire: Foucault's History of Sexuality and the Colonial Order of Things*. Durham, NC: Duke University Press.

Stoller, Paul, and Cheryl Olkes. 1986. 'Bad Sauce, Good Ethnography'. *Cultural Anthropology* 1, no. 3: 336–352.

Stout, Noelle. 2015. 'When a *Yuma* Meets Mama: Commodified Kin and the Affective Economies of Queer Tourism in Cuba'. *Anthropological Quarterly* 88, no. 3: 665–692.

Stout, Noelle. 2016. 'Petitioning a Giant: Debt, Reciprocity, and Mortgage Modification in the Sacramento Valley'. *American Ethnologist* 43, no. 1: 158–171.

Strathern, Andrew. 2008. *The Rope of Moka: Big-men and Ceremonial Exchange in Mount Hagen New Guinea.* Cambridge: Cambridge University Press. (First published 1971.)

Strathern, Marilyn. 1987. 'An Awkward Relationship: The Case of Feminism and Anthropology'. *Signs* 12, no. 2: 276–292.

Strathern, Marilyn. 1988. *The Gender of the Gift: Problems with Women and Problems with Society in Melanesia.* Berkeley: University of California Press.

Strathern, Marilyn, ed. 2000. *Audit Cultures: Anthropological Studies in Accountability, Ethics, and the Academy.* London: Routledge.

Stringer, Chris. 2012. 'What Makes a Modern Human'. *Nature* 485, no. 3 May: 33–35.

Takemaru, Naoko. 2010. *Women in the Language and Society of Japan: The Linguistic Roots of Bias.* Jefferson, NC: McFarland.

Tcherkézoff, Serge. 2000. *Le mythe occidental de la sexualité polynésienne, 1928–1999.* Paris: Presses universitaires de France.

Tett, Gillian. 2010. *Fool's Gold: The Inside Story of J.P. Morgan and How Wall St. Greed Corrupted Its Bold Dream and Created a Financial Catastrophe.* New York: Free Press.

Thompson, Charis. 2006. 'Strategic Naturalizing: Kinship in an Infertility Clinic'. In *Feminist Anthropology: A Reader,* edited by Ellen Lewis, 271–288. Oxford: Blackwell.

Ticktin, Miriam. 2011. *Casualties of Care. Immigration and the Politics of Humanitarianism in France.* Berkeley: University of California Press.

Tidey, Sylvia. 2016. 'Between the Ethical and the Right Thing: How (Not) to Be Corrupt in Indonesian Bureaucracy in an Age of Good Governance'. *American Ethnologist* 43, no. 4: 663–676.

Torpey, John. 2000. *The Invention of the Passport: Surveillance, Citizenship, and the State.* Cambridge: Cambridge University Press.

Towle, Evan B., and Lynn M. Morgan. 2002. 'Romancing the Transgender Native: Rethinking the Use of the "Third Gender" Concept'. *GLQ* 8, no. 4: 469–497.

Trémon, Anne-Christine. 2020. *Pour la cause de l'ancêtre: Relation diasporique et transformations d'un village globalisé, Shenzhen, Chine.* Nanterre, France: Publications de la Société d'ethnologie.

Trouillot, Michel-Rolph. 1991. 'Anthropology and the Savage Slot: The Poetics and Politics of Otherness'. In *Recapturing Anthropology: Working in the Present,* edited by Richard G. Fox, 17–44. Santa Fe, NM: School of American Research Press.

Tsing, Anna. 2015. *The Mushroom at the End of the World: On the Possibility of Life in Capitalist Ruins.* Princeton, NJ: Princeton University Press.

Turner, Terrence. 1992. 'Defiant Images: The Kayapo Appropriation of Video'. *Anthropology Today* 8, no. 6: 5–16.

Turner, Victor. 1974. 'Pilgrimages as Social Processes'. In *Dramas, Fields, and Metaphors: Symbolic Action in Human Society,* 166–230. Ithaca, NY: Cornell University Press.

Turner, Victor. 1979. *The Ritual Process: Structure and Anti-Structure.* Chicago: University of Chicago Press. (First published 1969.)

Turton, David. 2004. 'Lip-Plates and the "People who Take Photographs": Uneasy Encounters between Mursi and Tourists in Southern Ethiopia'. *Anthropology Today* 20, no. 3: 3–8.

Twilley, Nicola. 2015. 'Accounting for Taste: How Packaging Can Make Food More Flavorful'. *New Yorker,* 2 November.

Tylor, Edward Burnett. 1871. *Primitive Culture: Researches into the Development of Mythology, Philosophy, Religion, Art, and Custom.* Vol. 1. London: John Murray.

Van Gennep, Arnold. 1960. *The Rites of Passage,* translated by Monika B. Vizedom and Gabrielle L. Caffee. Chicago: University of Chicago Press. (First published 1909.)

Vogt, Evon Z. 1994. *Fieldwork among the Maya: Reflections on the Harvard Chiapas Project.* Albuquerque: University of New Mexico Press.

Walley, Christine. 2013. *Exit Zero: Family and Class in Post-Industrial Chicago*. Chicago: University of Chicago Press. (Also http://www.exitzeroproject.org, consulted March 2018.)

Walsh, Eileen Rose. 2005. 'From Nü Guo to Nü'er Guo: Negotiating Desire in the Land of the Mosuo'. *Modern China* 31, no. 4: 448–486.

Wardlow, Holly. 2006. *Wayward Women: Sexuality and Agency in a New Guinea Society*. Berkeley: University of California Press.

Wardlow, Holly. 2018. 'HIV, Phone Friends and Affective Technology in Papua New Guinea'. In *The Moral Economy of Mobile Phones: Pacific Perspectives*, edited by Robert J. Foster and Heather A. Horst, 39–52. Canberra: Australian National University Press.

Watson, James. 1982. 'Of Flesh and Bones: The Management of Death Pollution in Cantonese Society'. In *Death and the Regeneration of Life*, edited by Maurice Bloch and Jonathan Parry, 155–186. Cambridge: Cambridge University Press.

Weber, Max. 1978. *Economy and Society: An Outline of Interpretive Sociology*, edited by Guenther Roth and Claus Wittich. Berkeley: University of California Press. (First published 1922.)

Weber, Max. 1992. *The Protestant Ethic and the Spirit of Capitalism*, translated by Talcott Parsons. London: Routledge. (First published 1905.)

Weiner, Annette. 1996. *Women of Value, Men of Renown: New Perspectives in Trobriand Exchange*. Austin: University of Texas Press.

Werner, Jean-François. 2006. 'How Women Are Using Television to Domesticate Globalization: A Case Study on the Reception and Consumption of Telenovelas in Senegal'. *Visual Anthropology* 19, no. 5: 443–472.

Weston, Kath. 1997. *Families We Choose: Lesbians, Gays, Kinship*. New York: Columbia University Press. (First published 1991.)

Willerslev, Rane. 2007. *Soul Hunters: Hunting, Animism, and Personhood among the Siberian Yukhagir*. Berkeley: University of California Press.

Wilson, Alice. 2017. 'Ambivalences of Mobility: Rival State Authorities and Mobile Strategies in a Saharan Conflict'. *American Ethnologist* 44, no. 1: 77–90.

Winegar, Jessica. 2016. 'A Civilized Revolution: Aesthetics and Political Action in Egypt'. *American Ethnologist* 43, no. 4: 609–622.

Wnuk, Ewelina, and Asifa Majid. 2014. 'Revisiting the Limits of Language: The Odor Lexicon of Maniq'. *Cognition* 131: 125–138.

Wolf, Eric. 1982. *Europe and the People without History*. Berkeley: University of California Press.

World Health Organization. 2019. *World Health Statistics Overview 2019: Monitoring Health for Sustainable Development Goals*. Geneva: World Health Organization. https://apps.who.int/iris/bitstream/handle/10665/311696/WHO-DAD-2019.1-eng.pdf, consulted 24 October 2019.

Wynn, L.L., and Mark Israel. 2018. 'The Fetishes of Consent: Signatures, Paper, and Writing in Research Ethics Review'. *American Anthropologist* 120, no. 4: 795–806.

Xiang, Biao. 2005. *Transcending Boundaries: Zhejiangcun, the Story of a Migrant Village in Beijing*, translated by Jim Weldon. Leiden: Brill. (First published 2000.)

Yan, Yunxiang. 1996. *The Flow of Gifts: Reciprocity and Social Networks in a Chinese Village*. Stanford, CA: Stanford University Press.

Yanagisako, Sylvia. 2015. 'Households in Anthropology'. In *International Encyclopedia of the Social and Behavioral Sciences*, edited by James D. Wright, vol. 11, 228–232. Amsterdam: Elsevier.

Yang, Mayfair, ed. 2008. *Chinese Religiosities: Afflictions of Modernity and State Formation*. Berkeley: University of California Press.

Zelizer, Viviana A. 2007. *The Purchase of Intimacy*. Princeton, NJ: Princeton University Press.

Zhang, Li. 2010. *In Search of Paradise: Middle Class Living in a Chinese Metropolis*. Ithaca, NY: Cornell University Press.

Zheng, Tiantian. 2009. *Red Lights: The Lives of Sex Workers in Postsocialist China*. Minneapolis: University of Minnesota Press.

Zhemukhov, Sufian. 2012. 'The Birth of Modern Circassian Nationalism'. *Nationalities Papers*, 40, no. 4: 503–524.

Index